Roberta Aitcheson

Forever He will be, the
Lamb upon the tree
I'll gladly bow my
knee, and Worship Him
alone

MAKING MELODY
HYMN BOOK

MAKING MELODY
HYMN BOOK

"Be filled with the Spirit; speaking to yourselves in psalms and hymns and spiritual songs, singing and making melody in your heart to the Lord"
Ephesians 5. 18, 19

ASSEMBLIES OF GOD PUBLISHING HOUSE,
106-114 Talbot Street, Nottingham NG1 5GH

First Published 1983
Reprinted 1993

ISBN 0 946586 01 2

Produced in England by
NUPRINT LIMITED
Station Road, Harpenden, Herts AL5 4SE

PREFACE

Singing has always been prominent in the worship and witness of the Christian Church, and the development of its music has expressed the progress and response of Christians throughout generations.

Many of the older hymns, although having little theological influence, still remain like rocks which have resisted the eddying currents of change. Likewise, the rich doctrines of Wesleyan hymnology and the fervour of the Revival hymns of the last century have found a permanent place in the hearts of Christians all over the world. We believe, however, that new hymns are necessary to meet the needs of a new generation, thus enlarging our Treasury with hymns old and new.

The Hymnbook Committee believe that this collection will be invaluable to Spirit-filled believers in both personal and congregational devotions and worship.

These are days when the Wind of the Spirit is blowing through the Churches and 'Making Melody' reflects this glorious movement by providing a combination of doctrinal, evangelical and devotional hymns, all conveying great Biblical truth and experience.

A very necessary innovation in the music edition is the inclusion of guitar chords.

The Committee are grateful to the authors and copyright owners for their kind permission, in some cases freely given, to include their hymns in this book. Exhaustive search has been made to trace copyright owners, but should there have been any inadvertent infringement, the Committee tender their apology and will remedy the omission in future editions.

'LET US SING UNTO THE LORD!'
(Psalm 95:1)

Eric Dando
A. Hughes
P. Lowe
A. F. Missen
K. W. Munday
H. D. Palmer
MAKING MELODY
HYMNBOOK COMMITTEE

CONTENTS

Section I

1 We worship and adore Thee
Before the mercy seat,
We give Thee praise and glory,
Dear Lord, it is so sweet.

2 We worship and adore Thee
Who once for us was slain,
Thou liv'st and reign'st in glory,
Thou soon wilt come again.

3 We worship and adore Thee,
For Thy redeeming grace,
Thou set Thy love upon us,
To Thee be all the praise.

4 We worship and adore Thee,
A tribute, Lord, we bring,
Of praise and glad thanksgiving,
And crown Thee King of kings.

2 All hail the power of Jesu's name!
Let angels prostrate fall;
Bring forth the royal diadem,
And crown Him Lord of all.

2 Crown Him, ye martyrs of our God,
Who from His altar call;
Extol the stem of Jesse's rod,
And crown Him Lord of all.

3 Ye chosen seed of Israel's race,
A remnant weak and small,
Hail Him who saves you by His
grace,
And crown Him Lord of all.

4 Ye Gentile sinners, ne'er forget
The wormwood and the gall;
Go, spread your trophies at His feet,
And crown Him Lord of all.

5 Let every kindred, every tribe,
On this terrestrial ball,
To Him all majesty ascribe,
And crown Him Lord of all.

6 O that with yonder sacred throng
We at His feet may fall,
Join in the everlasting song,
And crown Him Lord of all.
Edward Perronet.

3 Come, let us join our cheerful
songs
With angels round the throne;
Ten thousand thousand are their
tongues,
But all their joys are one.

2 'Worthy the Lamb that died,' they
cry,
'To be exalted thus';
'Worthy the Lamb', our lips reply,
'For He was slain for us.'

3 Jesus is worthy to receive
Honour and power divine:
And blessings more than we can give
Be, Lord, for ever Thine.

4 Let all that dwell above the sky,
And air, and earth, and seas,
Conspire to lift Thy glories high,
And speak Thine endless praise.

5 The whole creation join in one,
To bless the sacred name
Of Him that sits upon the throne,
And to adore the Lamb.
Isaac Watts.

4 'Great is Thy faithfulness,' O God
my Father,
There is no shadow of turning with
Thee;
Thou changest not, Thy compassions
they fail not;
As Thou hast been Thou forever wilt
be.

Worship and Praise

'Great is Thy faithfulness! Great is Thy faithful-
ness!'
Morning by morning new mercies I see;
All I have needed Thy hand hath provided,
'Great is Thy faithfulness,' Lord, unto me!

2 Summer and winter and springtime
and harvest,
Sun, moon and stars in their courses
above,
Join with all nature in manifold
witness
To Thy great faithfulness, mercy and
love.

3 Pardon for sin and a peace that
endureth,
Thy own dear presence to cheer and
to guide;
Strength for today and bright hope
for tomorrow,
Blessings all mine, with ten thousand
beside!

T. O. Chisholm.

5   My God, how wonderful Thou
art,
Thy majesty how bright!
How beautiful Thy mercy seat,
In depths of burning light!

2 How dread are Thine eternal years,
O everlasting Lord,
By prostrate spirits day and night
Incessantly adored!

3 How beautiful, how beautiful,
The sight of Thee must be,
Thine endless wisdom, boundless
power
And awful purity!

4 O how I fear Thee, living God,
With deepest, tenderest fears,
And worship Thee with trembling
hope,
And penitential tears!

5 Yet I may love Thee too, O Lord,
Almighty as Thou art,
For Thou hast stooped to ask of me
The love of my poor heart.

6 No earthly father loves like Thee;
No mother, e'er so mild,
Bears and forbears as Thou hast done
With me, Thy sinful child.

7 Father of Jesus, love's reward,
What rapture will it be
Prostrate before Thy throne to lie,
And gaze, and gaze on Thee!

6   I'll praise my Maker while I've
breath,
And when my voice is lost in death,
Praise shall employ my nobler powers;
My days of praise shall ne'er be past,
While life and thought and being
last,
Or immortality endures.

2 Happy the man whose hopes rely
On Israel's God; He made the sky
And earth and seas, with all their
train;
His truth for ever stands secure;
He saves the oppressed, He feeds
the poor,
And none shall find His promise
vain.

3 The Lord gives eyesight to the blind;
The Lord supports the fainting mind;
He sends the labouring conscience
peace;
He helps the stranger in distress,
The widow and the fatherless,
And grants the prisoner sweet
release.

4 I'll praise Him while He lends me
breath;
And when my voice is lost in death,
Praise shall employ my nobler powers;
My days of praise shall ne'er be past,
While life and thought and being
last.
Or immortality endures.

I. Watts.

7   Now in a song of grateful praise,
To Thee, O Lord, my voice I'll
raise:
With all Thy saints I'll join to tell,
My Jesus hath done all things well.

2 How sovereign, wonderful, and free
Has been Thy love to sinful me!
Thou savedst me from the jaws of hell;
My Jesus hath done all things well.

3 Since e'er my soul has known His love,
What mercies He has made me prove!
Mercies which do all praise excel!
My Jesus hath done all things well.

4 And when to that bright world I rise,
And join the anthems of the skies,
Above the rest this note shall swell,
My Jesus hath done all things well.

Samuel Medley.

8 Immortal, invisible, God only wise,
In light inaccessible hid from our eyes,
Most blessèd, most glorious, the Ancient of Days,
Almighty, victorious, Thy great name we praise.

2 Unresting, unhasting, and silent as light,
Nor wanting, nor wasting, Thou rulest in might!
Thy justice like mountains high soaring above,
Thy clouds which are fountains of goodness and love.

3 To all life Thou givest—to both great and small;
In all life Thou livest, the true life of all;
We blossom and flourish as leaves on the tree,
And wither and perish—but nought changeth Thee.

4 Great Father of Glory, pure Father of Light,
Thine angels adore Thee, all veiling their sight;
All laud we would render; O help us to see:
'Tis only the splendour of light hideth Thee.

5 Immortal, invisible, God only wise,
In light inaccessible hid from our eyes,
Most blessèd, most glorious, the Ancient of Days,
Almighty, victorious, Thy great name we praise.

Walter Chalmers Smith.

9 My God, I have found
The thrice blessèd ground,
Where life and where joy and true comfort abound.

Hallelujah! Thine the glory,
Hallelujah! Amen.
Hallelujah! Thine the glory,
Revive us again!

2 'Tis found in the blood
Of Him who once stood
My refuge and safety,
my surety with God.

3 He bore on the tree
The sentence for me,
And now both the surety
and sinner are free.

4 And though here below
'Mid sorrow and woe,
My place is in heaven
with Jesus I know.

5 And this I shall find
For such is His mind
'He'll not be in glory
and leave me behind.'

John Gambold.

10 Let all the world in every corner sing:
"My God and King!"
The heavens are not too high,
His praise may thither fly:
The earth is not too low,
His praises there may grow.
Let all the world in every corner sing:
"My God and King!"

2 Let all the world in every corner sing:
"My God and King!"
The church with psalms must shout,
No door can keep them out:
But, more than all, the heart
Must bear the largest part.
Let all the world in every corner sing:
My God and King!

George Herbert.

11   Lord of all being, throned afar,
Thy glory flames from sun and
star;
Centre and soul of every sphere,
Yet to each loving heart how near.

2 Sun of our life, Thy quickening ray
Sheds on our path the glow of day;
Star of our hope, Thy softened light
Cheers the long watches of the night.

3 Our midnight is Thy smile withdrawn;
Our noontide is Thy gracious dawn;
Our rainbow arch, Thy mercy's sign;
All, save the clouds of sin, are Thine.

4 Lord of all life, below, above,
Whose light is truth, whose warmth is
love,
Before Thy ever-blazing throne
We ask no lustre of our own.

5 Grant us Thy truth to make us free
And kindling hearts that burn for
Thee,
Till all Thy living altars claim
One holy light, one heavenly flame.

O. W. Holmes.

12   Jesus has loved me—
wonderful Saviour!
Jesus has loved me, I cannot tell why:
Came He to rescue sinners all
worthless,
My heart He conquered for Him I
would die.

Glory to Jesus, wonderful Saviour!
Glory to Jesus, the One I adore.
Glory to Jesus, wonderful Saviour!
Glory to Jesus, and praise evermore.

2 Jesus has saved me—wonderful
Saviour!
Jesus has saved me, I cannot tell
how;
All that I know is He was my ransom,
Dying on Calvary with thorns on His
brow.

3 Jesus will lead me—wonderful
Saviour!
Jesus will lead me, I cannot tell
where;
But I will follow through joy or
sorrow,
Sunshine or tempest sweet peace or
despair.

4 Jesus will crown me—wonderful
Saviour!
Jesus will crown me, I cannot tell
when;
White throne of splendour hail I with
gladness,
Crowned with the plaudits of angels
and men.

J. W. Macgill.

13   O Lord of heav'n and earth and
sea,
To Thee all praise and glory be;
How shall we show our love to Thee,
Who givest all?

2 Thou didst not spare Thine only Son,
But gav'st Him for a world undone;
And freely with the blessèd One
Thou givest all.

3 We lose what on ourselves we spend,
We have as treasure without end
Whatever, Lord, to Thee we lend,
Who givest all.

4 To Thee, from whom we all derive
Our life, our gifts, our power to give!
O may we ever with Thee live,
Who givest all.

5 Thou giv'st the Spirit's blessèd
dower,
Spirit of life, and love, and power,
And dost His sevenfold graces
shower,
Upon us all.

6 For souls redeemed, for sins forgiven,
For means of grace and hopes of
heaven,
Father, all praise to Thee be given,
Who givest all.
C. Wordsworth.

14   Come, every thankful heart
That loves the Saviour's name,
Your noblest powers exert
To celebrate His fame!
Tell all above and all below
The debt of love to Him you owe.

2 He left His starry crown,
He laid His robes aside,
On wings of love came down,
And wept, and bled, and died:
What He endured, O who can tell,
To save our souls from death and hell!

3 From the dark grave He rose,
The mansion of the dead;
And thence His mighty foes
In glorious triumph led:
Up through the sky the Conqueror
rode,
And reigns on high the Saviour God.

4 From thence He'll quickly come,
His chariot will not stay,
And bear our spirits home
To realms of endless day;
Then shall we see His lovely face
And ever be in His embrace.

5 Jesus, we ne'er can pay
The debt we owe Thy love;
Yet tell us how we may
Our gratitude approve:
Our hearts, our all, to Thee we give,
The gift, though small, do Thou
receive.
Samuel Stennett.

15   Oh, for a thousand tongues to
sing
My great Redeemer's praise,
The glories of my God and King,
The triumphs of His grace!

2 My gracious Master and my God,
Assist me to proclaim,
To spread through all the earth abroad
The honours of Thy name.

3 Jesus! the name that charms our
fears,
That bids our sorrows cease;
'Tis music in the sinner's ears,
'Tis life, and health, and peace.

4 He breaks the power of cancelled sin,
He sets the prisoner free;
His blood can make the foulest clean,
His blood availed for me.

5 Hear Him, ye deaf; His praise, ye
dumb,
Your loosened tongues employ;
Ye blind, behold your Saviour come;
And leap, ye lame, for joy!
Charles Wesley.

16   Lord, enthroned in Heavenly
splendour,
First begotten from the dead,
Thou alone, our strong Defender,
Liftest up Thy people's head.
Alleluia. Alleluia.
Jesu, True and Living Bread!

2 Here our humblest homage pay we;
Here in loving reverence bow;
Here, for faith's discernment pray we,
Lest we fail to know Thee now.
Alleluia.
Thou art here, we ask not how.

3 Though the lowliest form doth veil
Thee
As of old in Bethlehem,
Here as there Thine angels hail Thee,
Branch and Flower of Jesse's stem.
Alleluia.
We in worship join with them.

4 Paschal Lamb, Thine Offering,
finished
Once for all when Thou wast slain,
In its fulness undiminished
Shall for evermore remain,
Alleluia.
Cleansing souls from every stain.

5 Life-imparting Heavenly Manna,
  Stricken Rock with streaming Side,
  Heaven and earth with loud Hosanna,
  Worship Thee, the Lamb who died.
  Alleluia.
  Risen, ascended, glorified!

Unknown.

17 Praise to the Holiest in the height,
  And in the depth be praise:
  In all His words most wonderful,
  Most sure in all His ways.

2 O loving wisdom of our God!
  When all was sin and shame,
  A second Adam to the fight,
  And to the rescue came.

3 O wisest love! that flesh and blood
  Which did in Adam fail,
  Should strive afresh against the foe,
  Should strive, and should prevail.

4 And that a higher gift than grace
  Should flesh and blood refine,
  God's presence, and His very self
  And essence all-divine.

5 O generous love! that He, who smote
  In man for man the foe,
  The double agony in man
  For man should undergo.

6 And in the garden secretly,
  And on the Cross on high,
  Should teach His brethren, and
    inspire
  To suffer and to die.

7 Praise to the Holiest in the height,
  And in the depth be praise:
  In all His words most wonderful,
  Most sure in all His ways.

J. H. Newman

18 Praise the Lord, sing hallelujah!
  Children of God's gracious choice;
  Let His praises rise as thunder,
  Let the whole earth hear his voice;
  Till the song of His salvation
  Makes his broken world rejoice!

2 Man's imprisoning night is shattered
  As the impact of His Word;
  Light and life spring forth eternal
  Where that mighty voice is heard;
  Let the powers of death and darkness
  Own the triumph of their Lord!

3 Praise the Lord until His glory
  Floods the farthest realms of earth,
  'Till from every tribe and nation
  Souls rise up in glad rebirth;
  Haste the day of His appearing
  When all creatures own His worth.

4 Praise the Lord, sing hallelujah!
  Sound His sovereign grace abroad,
  'Till His Word is loved and honoured
  Everywhere man's feet have trod;
  'Till His ransomed family gathers
  Safely round the throne of God!

Margaret Clarkson.

19 My heart and voice I raise,
  To spread Messiah's praise;
  Messiah's praise let all repeat;
  The universal Lord,
  By whose almighty word
  Creation rose in form complete.

2 A servant's form He wore,
  And in His body bore
  Our dreadful curse on Calvary:
  He like a victim stood,
  And poured His sacred blood,
  To set the guilty captives free.

3 But soon the Victor rose
  Triumphant o'er His foes,
  And led the vanquished host in
    chains:
  He threw their empire down,
  His foes compelled to own,
  O'er all the great Messiah reigns.

4 With mercy's mildest grace,
  He governs all our race
  In wisdom, righteousness, and love;
  Who to Messiah fly
  Shall find redemption nigh,
  And all His great salvation prove.

5 Hail, Saviour, Prince of Peace!
  Thy kingdom shall increase,
  Till all the world Thy glory see,
  And righteousness abound,
  As the great deep profound,
  And fill the earth with purity!

B. Rhodes.

20 O magnify the Lord with me,
     Ye people of His choice!
  Let all to whom He lendeth breath
  Now in His name rejoice;
  For love's blest revelation,
  For rest from condemnation,
  For uttermost salvation,
  To Him give thanks.

> Let all the people praise Thee,
> Let all the people praise Thee!
> Let all the people praise
> Thy name for ever and for evermore, for evermore,
> O Lord! Let all the people praise Thee,
> Let all the people praise Thee,
> Let all the people praise
> Thy name for ever and for evermore

2 O praise Him for His holiness,
  His wisdom and His grace;
  Sing praises for the precious blood
  Which ransom'd all our race;
  In tenderness He sought us,
  From depths of sin He brought us,
  The way of life then taught us,
  To Him give thanks.

3 Had I a thousand tongues to sing,
  The half could ne'er be told
  Of love so rich, so full and free,
  Of blessings manifold;
  Of grace that faileth never,
  Peace flowing as a river
  From God the glorious Giver,
  To Him give thanks.

Mrs C. H. Morris.

21 Let earth and heaven combine,
     Angels and men agree,
  To praise in songs divine
  The incarnate Deity;
  Our God contracted to a span,
  Incomprehensibly made man.

2 He laid His glory by,
  He wrapped Him in our clay;
  Unmarked by human eye,
  The latent Godhead lay;
  Infant of days He here became,
  And bore the mild Immanuel's name.

3 Unsearchable the love
  That hath the Saviour brought;
  The grace is far above
  Mankind's or angel's thought:
  Suffice for us that God, we know,
  Our God is manifest below.

4 He deigns in flesh to appear,
  Widest extremes to join;
  To bring our vileness near,
  And make us all divine:
  And we the life of God shall know,
  For God is manifest below.

5 Made perfect first in love,
  And sanctified by grace,
  We shall from earth remove,
  And see His glorious face:
  Then shall His love be fully showed,
  And man shall then be lost in God.

Charles Wesley.

22 Joy to the world; the Lord is come!
  Let earth receive her King;
  Let every heart prepare Him room,
  And Heaven and nature sing.

2 Joy to the world; the Saviour reigns!
  Let men their songs employ;
  While fields and floods, rocks, hills and plains,
  Repeat the sounding joy.

3 He rules the world with truth and grace;
  And makes the nations prove
  The glories of His righteousness,
  And wonders of His love.

Isaac Watts.

23 O worship the King,
    All glorious above,
O gratefully sing
His power and His love;
Our Shield and Defender,
The Ancient of Days,
Pavilioned in splendour,
And girded with praise.

2 O tell of His might,
    O sing of His grace,
Whose robe is the light,
Whose canopy space.
His chariots of wrath
The deep thunder-clouds form,
And dark is His path
On the wings of the storm.

3 Thy bountiful care,
    What tongue can recite?
It breathes in the air,
It shines in the light,
It streams from the hills,
It descends to the plain,
And sweetly distils
In the dew and the rain.

4 Frail children of dust,
    And feeble as frail;
In Thee do we trust,
Nor find Thee to fail;
Thy mercies, how tender,
How firm to the end,
Our Maker, Defender,
Redeemer, and Friend!

5 O measureless Might!
    Ineffable Love!
While angels delight
To hymn Thee above,
The humbler creation,
Though feeble their lays,
With true adoration
Shall lisp to Thy praise.
R. Grant.

24 Hail, Thou once despised Jesus!
    Hail, Thou Galilean King!
Thou didst suffer to release us,
Thou didst free salvation bring:
Hail, Thou agonizing Saviour,
Bearer of our sin and shame;
By Thy merits we find favour;
Life is given through Thy name!

2 Paschal Lamb, by God appointed,
    All our sins were on Thee laid;
By Almighty love anointed,
Thou hast full atonement made:
All Thy people are forgiven
Through the virtue of Thy blood;
Opened is the gate of heaven:
Peace is made 'twixt man and God.

3 Jesus, hail! enthroned in glory,
    There for ever to abide;
All the heavenly host adore Thee,
Seated at Thy Father's side.
There for sinners Thou art pleading,
There Thou dost our place prepare,
Ever for us interceding,
Till in glory we appear.

4 Worship, honour, power and blessing,
    Thou art worthy to receive;
Loudest praises, without ceasing.
Meet it is for us to give.
Help, ye bright angelic spirits,
Bring your sweetest, noblest lays;
Help to sing our Saviour's merits,
Help to chant Immanuel's praise!
J. Bakewell.

25 Praise the Saviour, ye who know
    Him;
Who can tell how much we owe Him?
Gladly let us render to Him
All we have and are.

2 'Jesus' is the name that charms us;
He for conflicts fits and arms us;
Nothing moves and nothing harms
    us,
When we trust in Him.

3 Trust in Him, ye saints for ever;
He is faithful, changing never;
Neither force nor guile can sever
Those He loves from Him.

4 Keep us, Lord, oh, keep us cleaving
To Thyself and still believing,
Till the hour of our receiving
Promised joys in Heaven.

5 Then we shall be where we would be;
Then we shall be what we should be;
Things which are not now, nor could be,
Then shall be our own.
T. Kelly.

26 O the deep, deep love of Jesus,
Vast, unmeasured, boundless, free!
Rolling as a mighty ocean
In its fulness over me.
Underneath me, all around me,
Is the current of Thy love;
Leading onward, leading homeward,
To my glorious rest above.

2 O the deep, deep love of Jesus,
Spread His praise from shore to shore;
How He loveth, ever loveth,
Changeth never, nevermore;
How He watches o'er His loved ones,
Died to call them all His own;
How for them He intercedeth,
Watcheth o'er them from the throne.

3 O the deep, deep love of Jesus,
Love of every love the best:
'Tis an ocean vast of blessing,
'Tis a haven sweet of rest.
O the deep, deep love of Jesus,
'Tis a heaven of heavens to me;
And it lifts me up to glory,
For it lifts me up to Thee.
S. Trevor Francis.

27 Praise, my soul, the King of heaven;
To His feet thy tribute bring;
Ransomed, healed, restored, forgiven,
Who like thee His praise should sing?
Praise Him! praise Him!
Praise the everlasting King.

2 Praise Him for His grace and favour
To our fathers in distress;
Praise Him, still the same for ever,
Slow to chide and swift to bless:
Praise Him! praise Him!
Glorious in His faithfulness.

3 Father-like He tends and spares us;
Well our feeble frame He knows;
In His hands He gently bears us,
Rescues us from all our foes:
Praise Him! praise Him!
Widely as His mercy flows.

4 Angels, help us to adore Him!
Ye behold Him face to face;
Sun and moon, bow down before Him;
Dwellers all in time and space,
Praise Him! praise Him!
Praise with us the God of grace.
H. F. Lyte.

28 Let me sing—for the glory of Heaven
Like a sunbeam has swept o'er my heart;
I would praise Thee for sins all forgiven,
For Thy love, which shall never depart.

2 If Thy works praise Thee, Giver of good,
If the sun shines his praise unto Thee,
If the wind, as it sighs through the wood,
Makes a murmur of song from each tree—

3 Then these lips, sure, a tribute shall bring,
Though unworthy the praises must be;
Shall all nature be vocal and sing,
And no psalm of rejoicing from me?

4 O wonderful, glorious Redeemer!
I would worship Thee, Saviour Divine;
And rejoice, though surrounded with praises,
Thou wilt still hear a song such as mine:

5 A song of a sinner forgiven,
And a song that is music to Thee;
A song of a pilgrim to Heaven,
Yes, a song from a sinner like me!
S. Trevor Francis.

29 Praise the Lord with heart and
voice,
Joyfully serving your King,
Come and worship at His throne,
Lovingly, gratefully sing;
Happy every hour, trusting in His
power,
Unto the Giver of our salvation praises
bring.

Praise Him! sing with melody,
Heart and voice,
Praise Him everlastingly,
Come, rejoice;
Hail Him, Lord, most glorious,
Mighty One victorious,
Praise His holy name.
Praise Him, Heavenly company.
Angels bright,
Crown Him now and evermore,
Lord of light;
Praise Him, all creation.
God of our salvation,
Boundless in majesty,
King eternal;
Praise His name.

2 Praise the dear Redeemer's name,
Crown Him with beauty and light,
Just and true are all His ways,
Wonderful, boundless, His might;
Glad hosannas swelling, loud His
goodness telling,
Fountain of blessing our joy eternal
day and night.

3 Praise the Lord with heart and voice,
Ever adoringly raise
Hallelujahs sweet and strong,
Unto the 'Ancient of Days';
Shout with acclamation, hail Him all
creation,
Worship Jehovah, O come rejoicing,
sound His praise.

Lizzie De Armond.

30 O Saviour, precious Saviour,
Whom yet unseen we love,
O name of might and favour,
All other names above!
We worship Thee, we bless Thee,
To Thee alone we sing;
We praise Thee, and confess Thee
Our holy Lord and King.

2 O Bringer of salvation,
Who wondrously has wrought,
Thyself the revelation
Of love beyond our thought;
We worship Thee, we bless Thee,
To Thee alone we sing;
We praise Thee, and confess Thee
Our gracious Lord and King.

3 In Thee all fulness dwelleth,
All grace and power divine;
The glory that excelleth,
O Son of God, is Thine;
We worship Thee, we bless Thee,
To Thee alone we sing;
We praise Thee, and confess Thee
Our glorious Lord and King.

4 O grant the consummation
Of this our song above
In endless adoration,
And everlasting love!
Then shall we praise and bless Thee
Where perfect praises ring,
And evermore confess Thee
Our Saviour and our King.

Frances Ridley Havergal.

31 Fill Thou my life, O Lord my God,
In every part with praise,
That my whole being may proclaim
Thy being and Thy ways.

2 Not for the lip of praise alone,
Not e'en the praising heart,
I ask, but for a life made up
Of praise in every part.

3 Praise in the common things of life,
Its goings out and in;
Praise in each duty and each deed,
However small and mean.

4 Fill every part of me with praise;
Let all my being speak
Of Thee and of Thy love, O Lord,
Poor though I be and weak.

5 So shalt Thou, Lord, from me, e'en
me,
Receive the glory due;
And so shall I begin on earth
The song for ever new.

6 So shall no part of day or night
From sacredness be free;
But all my life, in every step,
Be fellowship with Thee.

H. Bonar.

32   Hark, hark, my soul! angelic songs
are swelling,
O'er earth's green fields and ocean's
wave-beat shore:
How sweet the truth those blessèd
strains are telling
Of that new life when sin shall be no
more:
Angels of Jesus, angels of light,
Singing to welcome the pilgrims of
the night.

2 Onward we go, for still we hear them
singing,
'Come, weary souls, for Jesus bids
you come';
And through the dark, its echoes
sweetly ringing,
The music of the Gospel leads us
home:
Angels of Jesus, angels of light,
Singing to welcome the pilgrims of
the night.

3 Far, far away, like bells at evening
pealing,
The voice of Jesus sounds o'er land
and sea,
And laden souls, by thousands
meekly stealing,
Kind Shepherd turn their weary steps
to Thee:
Angels of Jesus, angels of light,
Singing to welcome the pilgrims of
the night.

4 Angels, sing on, your faithful watches
keeping;
Sing us sweet fragments of the songs
above:
Till morning's joy shall end the night
of weeping,
And life's long shadows break in
cloudless love:
Angels of Jesus, angels of light,
Singing to welcome the pilgrims of
the night.

F. W. Faber.

33   Let me come closer to Thee, Lord
Jesus,
Oh, closer day by day;
Let me lean harder on Thee, Lord
Jesus,
Yes, harder all the way.

2 Let me show forth Thy beauty, Lord
Jesus,
Like sunshine on the hills;
Oh, let my lips pour forth Thy
sweetness
In joyous sparkling rills!

3 Yes, like a fountain, precious Lord
Jesus,
Make me and let me be;
Keep me and use me daily, Lord
Jesus,
For Thee, for only Thee.

4 In all my heart and will, Lord Jesus,
Be altogether King;
Make me a loyal subject, Lord Jesus,
To Thee in everything.

5 Thirsting and hung'ring for Thee,
Lord Jesus,
With blessèd hunger here,
Longing for home on Zion's moun-
tain —
No thirst, no hunger there.

J. L. Lyne.

34   Our eyes have seen the glory of
our Saviour, Christ the Lord;
He's seated at His Father's side in love
and full accord;
From there upon the sons of men His
Spirit is out-poured,
All hail, ascended King!

Glory, glory, Hallelujah,
Glory, glory, Hallelujah,
Glory, glory, Hallelujah,
All hail, ascended King!

2 He came to earth at Christmas and
was made a man like us;
He taught, He healed, He suffered —
and they nailed Him to a cross;
He rose again on Easter Day — our
Lord victorious,
All hail, ascended King!

3 The good news of His Kingdom must
    be preached to every shore,
The news of peace and pardon, and
    the end of strife and war;
The secret of His Kingdom is to serve
    Him evermore,
All hail, ascended King!

4 His Kingdom is a family of men of
    every race,
They live their lives in harmony,
    enabled by His grace;
They follow His example till they see
    Him face to face,
All hail, ascended King!

5 We thank Him for the blessings which
    are yours and which are mine,
We thank Him for the lives and loves
    which in the darkness shine,
We thank Him in our fellowship and
    share the bread and wine,
All hail, ascended King!

6 To Jesus be the glory and the
    vict'ry and the crown;
When He'd ascended up to heaven,
    He sent His Spirit down;
We ask that He may guide and guard
    our country and our town,
All hail, ascended King!

7 And now we bring ourselves to Him,
    because we love Him most;
We join our hymns and shouts of
    praise with all the heavenly host;
To God the Father, God the Son and
    God the Holy Ghost,
All hail, ascended King!

Roland Meredith.

35   Dwelling in the secret place,
        Overshadowed by His grace,
Looking up into His face,
Seeing only Jesus.

2 Hidden there from all alarm,
    Safe from danger, fear and harm;
Holden up by His strong arm,
Seeing only Jesus.

3 Dwelling there, how truly blest!
Leaving all, how sweet to rest,
Head upon my Saviour's breast,
Seeing only Jesus.

4 Resting there, no more to roam,
Drawing near to Heaven and home,
Waiting there until He come,
Seeing only Jesus.

Grace Clement.

36   Praise Him! Praise Him! Jesus,
        our blessèd Redeemer!
Sing, O earth, His wonderful love
    proclaim!
Hail Him! Hail Him! highest
    archangels in glory;
Strength and honour give to His holy
    name!
Like a shepherd, Jesus will guard His
    children,
In His arms He carries them all day
    long.
O ye saints that dwell on the mountain
    of Zion,
Praise Him! praise Him! ever in joyful
    song.

2 Praise Him! Praise Him! Jesus our
    blessèd Redeemer,
For our sins, He suffered and bled and
    died;
He, our rock, our hope of eternal
    salvation,
Hail Him! hail Him! Jesus the Crucified.
Loving Saviour, meekly enduring
    sorrow,
Crowned with thorns that cruelly
    pierced His brow;
Once for us rejected, despised and
    forsaken,
Prince of Glory, ever triumphant now.

3 Praise Him! Praise Him! Jesus our
    blessèd Redeemer,
Heavenly portals, loud with
    hosannahs ring;
Jesus, Saviour, reigneth for ever and
    ever,
Crown Him, crown Him, Prophet and
    Priest and King!
Death is vanquished! Tell it with joy,
    ye faithful,

Where is now thy victory, boasting grave?
Jesus lives! no longer thy portals are cheerless,
Jesus lives, the mighty and strong to save.

Fanny J. Crosby.

37 Lord Jesus Christ, we seek Thy face;
Within the veil we bow the knee;
Oh, let Thy glory fill the place,
And bless us while we wait on Thee.

2 We thank Thee for the precious blood
That purged our sins and brought us nigh;
All cleansed and sanctified to God,
Thy holy Name to magnify.

3 Shut in with Thee, far, far above
The restless world that wars below:
We seek to learn and prove Thy love,
Thy wisdom and Thy grace to know.

4 The brow that once with thorns was bound,
Thy hands, Thy side, we fain would see;
Draw near, Lord Jesus, glory crowned,
And bless us while we wait on Thee.

Alex Stewart.

38 Praise to the Lord, the Almighty, the King of creation;
O my soul, praise Him, for He is thy health and salvation;
All ye who hear,
Brothers and sisters draw near,
Praise Him in glad adoration.

2 Praise to the Lord, who doth prosper thy work and defend thee;
Surely His goodness and mercy here daily attend thee;
Ponder anew
What the Almighty can do,
If with His love He befriend thee.

3 Praise to the Lord, who, when tempests their warfare are waging,
Who, when the elements madly around thee are raging,
Biddeth them cease,
Turneth their fury to peace,
Whirlwinds and waters assuaging.

4 Praise to the Lord, who when darkness and sin is abounding,
Who, when the godless do triumph, all virtue confounding,
Sheddeth His light,
Chaseth the horrors of night,
Saints with His mercy surrounding.

5 Praise to the Lord! O let all that is in me adore Him!
All that hath life and breath, come now with praises before Him!
Let the Amen
Sound from His people again:
Gladly for aye we adore Him.

6 Praise to the Lord, who, when sickness with terror uniting,
Deaf to entreaties of mortals, its victims is smiting,
Pestilence quells,
Sickness and fever dispels,
Grateful thanksgiving inviting.

Joachim Neander.

39 When morning gilds the skies,
My heart awaking cries,
'May Jesus Christ be praised!'
Alike at work and prayer
To Jesus I repair:
'May Jesus Christ be praised!'

2 When sleep her balm denies,
My silent spirit sighs,
'May Jesus Christ be praised!'
When evil thoughts molest,
With this I shield my breast—
'May Jesus Christ be praised!'

3 Does sadness fill my mind,
A solace here I find,
'May Jesus Christ be praised!'
Or fades my earthly bliss,
My comfort still is this,
'May Jesus Christ be praised!'

4 To God, the Word, on high,
The hosts of angels cry,
'May Jesus Christ be praised!'
Let mortals, too, upraise
Their voice in hymns of praise:
'May Jesus Christ be praised!'

5 Let earth's wide circle round,
In joyful notes resound,
'May Jesus Christ be praised!'
Let air, and sea, and sky,
From depth to height, reply,
'May Jesus Christ be praised!'

6 Be this, while life is mine
My canticle divine,
'May Jesus Christ be praised!'
Be this the eternal song
Through all the ages on,
May Jesus Christ be praised!'

trs. E. Caswall.

40 With gladness we worship, rejoice
as we sing,
Free hearts and free voices how
blessèd to bring,
The old, thankful story shall scale
Thine abode,
Thou King of all glory, most bountiful
God.

2 Thy right would we give Thee—true
homage Thy due,
And honour eternal, the universe
through,
With all Thy creation, earth, Heaven
and sea,
In one acclamation we celebrate
Thee.

3 Renewed by Thy Spirit, redeemed by
Thy Son,
Thy children revere Thee for all Thou
hast done.
O Father! returning to love and to
light,
Thy children are yearning to praise
Thee aright.

4 We join with the angels, and so there
is given
From earth Hallelujah, in answer to
Heaven.

Amen! Be Thou glorious below and
above,
Redeeming, victorious, and infinite
love!

G. Rawson.

41 Rejoice and be glad!
The Redeemer has come!
Go, look on His cradle,
His Cross, and His tomb.

Sound His praises, tell the story
Of Him who was slain!
Sound His praises, tell with gladness,
He liveth again!

2 Rejoice and be glad!
It is sunshine at last!
The clouds have departed,
The shadows are past.

3 Rejoice and be glad!
For the blood hath been shed;
Redemption is finished,
The price hath been paid.

4 Rejoice and be glad!
Now the pardon is free!
The Just for the unjust
Has died on the tree.

5 Rejoice and be glad!
For the Lamb that was slain
O'er death is triumphant,
And liveth again.

6 Rejoice and be glad!
For our King is on high;
He pleadeth for us on
His throne in the sky.

7 Rejoice and be glad!
For He cometh again;
He cometh in glory
The Lamb that was slain.

Sound His praises, tell the story
Of Him who was slain!
Sound His praises, tell with gladness,
He cometh again!

H. Bonar.

42 O worship the Lord in the beauty
of holiness!
Bow down before Him, His glory
proclaim;

With gold of obedience and incense
 of lowliness,
Kneel and adore Him, the Lord is His
 name.

2 Low at His feet lay thy burden of
 carefulness,
 High on His heart He will bear it for
 thee,
 Comfort thy sorrows, and answer thy
 prayerfulness,
 Guiding thy steps as may best for thee
 be.

3 Fear not to enter His courts in the
 slenderness
 Of the poor wealth thou wouldst
 reckon as thine:
 Truth in its beauty and love in its
 tenderness:
 These are the offerings to lay on His
 shrine.

4 These, though we bring them in
 trembling and fearfulness,
 He will accept for the name that is
 dear;
 Mornings of joy give for evenings of
 tearfulness,
 Trust for our trembling, and hope for
 our fear.

5 O worship the Lord in the beauty of
 holiness!
 Bow down before Him, His glory
 proclaim;
 With gold of obedience and incense
 of lowliness,
 Kneel and adore Him, the Lord is His
 name.
                              J. S. B. Monsell.

43 If I but knew Thee as Thou art,
    O Loveliness unknown,
 With what desire, O Lord, my heart
 Would claim Thee for its own.

2 But I am dull and blind, O Lord,
 Unapt of Thee to learn;
 Thee I but dimly in Thy word,
 As in a glass, discern.

3 With faith's warm finger, through the
 veil,
 I seek to touch Thy hand;
 I feel the imprint of the nail
 And partly understand.

4 At Thy spread table as I kneel
 I own Thy presence dear,
 Partaking of the simple meal
 I sense that Thou art near.

5 But, ah, my lonely spirit tires
 Of knowing Thee in part.
 O Jesus, how my soul desires
 To see Thee as Thou art!
                              I. MacPherson.

44 Thou art worthy, Thou art
    worthy,
    Thou art worthy, O Lord.
 Thou art worthy, to receive glory,
 Glory and honour and power.
 For Thou hast created, hast all things
 created,
 For Thou hast created all things.
 And for Thy pleasure they are
 created;
 Thou art worthy, O Lord.

2 Thou art worthy, Thou art worthy,
 Thou art worthy, O Lamb.
 Thou art worthy, to receive glory,
 And power at the Father's right hand.
 For Thou hast redeemed us, hast
 ransomed and cleaned us
 By Thy blood setting us free.
 In white robes arrayed us, kings and
 priests made us,
 And we are reigning in Thee.
                              Tom Smail

45 The God of Abraham praise,
    Who reigns enthroned above,
 Ancient of everlasting days,
 And God of love!
 Jehovah! Great I AM!
 By earth and Heaven confest,
 I bow, and bless the sacred Name for
 ever blest.

2 The God of Abraham praise,
At whose supreme command
From earth I rise, and seek the joys
At His right hand.
I all on earth forsake,
Its wisdom, fame, and power;
And Him my only portion make,
My shield and tower.

3 He by Himself hath sworn;
I on His oath depend:
I shall, on eagles' wings upborne,
To Heaven ascend.
I shall behold His face,
I shall His power adore,
And sing the wonders of His grace
For evermore.

4 The whole triumphant host
Give thanks to God on high;
'Hail, Father, Son, and Holy Ghost!'
They ever cry.
Hail, Abraham's God and mine!
I join the Heavenly lays;
All might and majesty are Thine,
And endless praise.

Thomas Olivers.

46 Ye servants of God,
Your Master proclaim,
And publish abroad
His wonderful name;
The name all victorious
Of Jesus extol;
His Kingdom is glorious,
And rules over all.

2 God ruleth on high,
Almighty to save;
And still He is nigh,
His presence we have!
The great congregation
His triumph shall sing,
Ascribing salvation
To Jesus our King.

3 Salvation to God,
Who sits on the throne;
Let all cry aloud,
And honour the Son:
The praises of Jesus
All angels proclaim,
Fall down on their faces,
And worship the Lamb.

4 Then let us adore
And give Him His right;
All glory and power,
All wisdom and might;
All honour and blessing,
With angels above;
And thanks never-ceasing,
And infinite love.

Charles Wesley.

47 Be glad in the Lord and rejoice,
All ye that are upright in heart;
And ye that have made Him your
choice,
Bid sadness and sorrow depart.

Rejoice! . . . rejoice! . . .
Be glad in the Lord and rejoice!
Rejoice! . . . rejoice! . . .
Be glad in the Lord and rejoice!

2 Be joyful, for He is the Lord,
On earth and in Heaven supreme;
He fashions and rules by His word;
The 'Mighty' and 'Strong' to redeem.

3 What though in the conflict for right
Your enemies almost prevail!
God's armies, just hid from your
sight,
Are more than the foes which assail.

4 Though darkness surround you by
day.
Your sky by the night be o'er-cast,
Let nothing your spirit dismay,
But trust till the danger is past.

5 Be glad in the Lord, and rejoice,
His praises proclaiming in song;
With harp, and with organ, and voice,
The loud hallelujahs prolong!

M. E. Servoss.

48 Down from His splendour in glory
He came,
Into a world of woe;
Took on Himself all my guilt and my
shame,
Why should He love me so?

How can I help but love Him,
When He loved me so?
How can I help but love Him,
When He loved me so?

2 I am unworthy to take of His grace,
Wonderful grace so free;
Yet Jesus suffered and died in my
place,
E'en for a soul like me.

3 He is the fairest of thousands to me,
His love is sweet and true;
Wonderful beauty in Him I now see,
More than I ever knew.

Elton M. Roth.

49   Now thank we all our God,
With hearts, and hands, and
voices;
Who wondrous things hath done,
In whom His world rejoices;
Who, from our mother's arms,
Hath blessed us on our way
With countless gifts of love,
And still is ours today.

2 O may this bounteous God
Through all our life be near us,
With ever-joyful hearts
And blessèd peace to cheer us,
And keep us in His grace,
And guide us when perplexed,
And free us from all ills
In this world and the next.

3 All praise and thanks to God
The Father now be given,
The Son, and Him who reigns
With Them in highest Heaven—
The one, eternal God,
Whom earth and Heaven adore;
For thus it was, is now,
And shall be evermore.

Martin Rinkart.
trs. Catherine Winkworth.

50   With harps and with vials there
stand a great throng
In the presence of Jesus, and sing
this new song.

Unto Him who hath loved us and washed
us from sin,
Unto Him be the glory for ever! Amen!

2 All these once were sinners, defiled in
His sight,
Now arrayed in pure garments in
praise they unite.

3 He maketh the rebel a priest and a
king,
He hath bought us and taught us this
new song to sing.

4 How helpless and hopeless we sinners
had been,
If He never had loved us 'till cleansed
from our sin.

5 Aloud in His praises our voices shall
ring,
So that others, believing, this new
song shall sing.

A. T. Pierson.

51   Dear Lord and Father of mankind,
Forgive our foolish ways!
Re-clothe us in our rightful mind,
In purer lives Thy service find,
In deeper reverence, praise.

2 In simple trust like theirs who heard,
Beside the Syrian sea,
The gracious calling of the Lord,
Let us, like them, without a word
Rise up and follow Thee.

3 O Sabbath rest by Galilee!
O calm of hills above,
Where Jesus knelt to share with Thee
The silence of eternity,
Interpreted by love.

4 With that deep hush subduing all
Our words and works that drown
The tender whisper of Thy call,
As noiseless let Thy blessing fall
As fell Thy manna down.

5 Drop Thy still dews of quietness,
Till all our strivings cease;
Take from our souls the strain and
stress,
And let our ordered lives confess
The beauty of Thy peace.

Worship and Praise

6 Breathe through the heats of our
   desire
Thy coolness and Thy balm;
Let sense be dumb, let flesh retire;
Speak through the earthquake, wind,
   and fire,
O still, small voice of calm!

J. G. Whittier.

52   For all the Lord has done for me
    I never will cease to praise Him;
And for His grace so rich and free
I never will cease to praise Him.

> I never will cease to praise Him,
> My Saviour! My Saviour!
> I never will cease to praise Him,
> He's done so much for me.

2 He gives me strength for every day,
   I never will cease to praise Him;
He leads and guides me all the way,
I never will cease to praise Him.

3 Although the world His love neglect,
   I never will cease to praise Him;
I could not such a Friend reject,
I never will cease to praise Him.

4 He saves me every day and hour,
   I never will cease to praise Him;
Just now I feel His cleansing power,
I never will cease to praise Him.

5 While on my journey here below
   I never will cease to praise Him;
And when to that bright world I go,
I never will cease to praise Him.

Charles H. Gabriel.

53   Lord, for the years Your love has
    kept and guided,
Urged and inspired us, cheered us on
   our way;
Sought us and saved us, pardoned
   and provided,
Lord of the years, we bring our thanks
   today.

2 Lord, for that Word, the Word of life
   which fires us,
Speaks to our hearts and sets our soul
   ablaze;

Teaches and trains, rebukes us and
   inspires us,
Lord of the Word, receive Your
   people's praise.

3 Lord, for our land, in this our
   generation,
Spirits oppressed by pleasure, wealth
   and care;
For young and old, for common-
   wealth and nation,
Lord of our land, be pleased to hear
   our prayer.

4 Lord, for our world, when men
   disown and doubt Him,
Loveless in strength and comfortless
   in pain;
Hungry and helpless, lost indeed
   without Him,
Lord of the world, we pray that Christ
   may reign.

5 Lord for ourselves; in living power
   remake us—
Self on the cross and Christ upon the
   throne—
Past put behind us, for the future take
   us,
Lord of our lives, to live for Christ
   alone.

Timothy Dudley-Smith.

54   Jesus, Jesus, Jesus,
    Sweetest name on earth;
How can I, a sinner,
Come to know its worth?

2 Oh! the sinful sorrow,
Oh! the strangest shame,
That I saw no beauty
In that sacred Name.

3 Never felt the sweetness,
Never knew the grace,
Never saw the love-pain
In that wounded face!

4 Never found the mystery
In that simple word
Jesus, Jesus, Jesus,
Saviour, Lover—Lord.

5 Now 'tis past and over,
  Gone my sin and shame,
  Jesus, Jesus did it,
  Glory to His Name!

6 I have seen the glory
  Of His tender face.
  I have felt with wonder
  Thrills of holy grace.

7 Wonderful compassion
  Reaching even me,
  Bows my humbled spirit
  In captivity.

8 Jesus! Jesus! Jesus!
  Loved me in my shame,
  Oh! the joy and rapture
  Of that sacred Name.

  A. Paget Wilkes.

55 What a wonderful Saviour is
      Jesus,
  What a wonderful Friend is He,
  For He left all the glory of Heaven,
  Came to earth to die on Calvary:

  Sing Hosanna! Sing Hosanna!
  Sing Hosanna to the King of kings!
  Sing Hosanna! Sing Hosanna!
  Sing Hosanna to the King.

2 He arose from the grave, Hallelujah,
  And He lives never more to die,
  At the Father's right hand interceding
  He will hear and heed our faintest cry.

3 He is coming some day to receive us,
  We'll be caught up to Heaven above,
  What a joy it will be to behold Him,
  Sing forever of His grace and love.

56 I cannot breathe enough of Thee,
      O gentle breeze of love,
  More fragrant than the myrtle tree
  The Rose of Sharon is to me,
  The balm of Heav'n above,
  The balm of Heav'n above.

2 I cannot gaze enough on Thee,
  Thou Fairest of the fair;
  My heart is filled with ecstasy,

As in Thy face of radiancy
I see such beauty there,
I see such beauty there.

3 I cannot work enough for Thee,
  My Saviour, Master, Friend;
  I do not wish to go out free,
  But ever, always, willingly,
  To serve Thee to the end,
  To serve Thee to the end.

4 I cannot sing enough of Thee,
  The sweetest name on earth,
  A note so full of melody
  Comes from my heart so joyously,
  And fills my soul with mirth,
  And fills my soul with mirth.

5 I cannot speak enough of Thee,
  I have so much to tell:
  Thy heart it beats so tenderly
  As Thou dost draw me close to Thee,
  And whisper 'All is well',
  And whisper 'All is well'.

  W. Spencer Walton.

57 Praise the King of Glory, He is
      God alone;
  Praise Him for the wonders He to us
      hath shown;
  For His promised presence all the
      pilgrim way,
  For the flaming pillar, and the cloud
      by day.

  Praise . . . Him, shining angels, strike . . .
      your harps of gold;
  All . . . His hosts adore Him, who . . . His face
      behold . . .
  Through . . . His great dominion, while . . . the
      ages roll,
  All His works shall praise Him; bless the Lord,
      my soul!

2 Praise Him for redemption, free to
      every soul;
  Praise Him for the Fountain that can
      make us whole;
  For His gifts of kindness and His
      loving care,
  For the blest assurance that He
      answers prayer.

3 Praise Him for the trials sent as cords
   of love,
   Binding us more closely to the things
   above;
   For the faith that conquers, hope that
   naught can dim,
   For the land where loved ones gather
   unto Him.

E. E. Hewitt.

58 It passeth knowledge, that dear
   love of Thine,
   My Jesus Saviour; yet this soul of
   mine
   Would of Thy love, in all its breadth
   and length,
   Its height and depth, its everlasting
   strength,
   Know more and more.

2 It passeth telling, that dear love of
   Thine,
   My Jesus, Saviour; yet these lips of
   mine
   Would fain proclaim to sinners far and
   near,
   A love which can remove all guilty
   fear,
   And love beget.

3 It passeth praises, that dear love of
   Thine,
   My Jesus, Saviour; yet this heart of
   mine
   Would sing that love, so rich, so full,
   so free,
   Which brings a rebel sinner, such as
   me,
   Nigh unto God.

4 But though I cannot sing, or tell, or
   know
   The fulness of Thy love, while here
   below,
   My empty vessel I may freely bring:
   O Thou, Who art of love the living
   spring,
   My vessel fill.

5 I am an empty vessel—not one
   thought
   Or look of love, I ever to Thee
   brought;

Yet I may come, and come again to
   Thee,
   With this, the empty sinner's only
   plea—
   Thou lovest me.

6 Oh, fill me, Jesus Saviour, with Thy
   love!
   Lead, lead me to the living fount
   above;
   Thither may I, in simple faith, draw
   nigh,
   And never to another fountain fly,
   But unto Thee.

7 And when my Jesus face to face I
   see,
   When at His lofty throne I bow the
   knee,
   Then of His love, in all its breadth and
   length,
   Its height and depth, its everlasting
   strength,
   My soul shall sing.

Mary Shekleton.

59 O Love Divine, how sweet Thou
   art!
   When shall I find my willing heart
   All taken up by Thee?
   I thirst, I faint, I die to prove
   The greatness of redeeming love,
   The love of Christ to me.

2 Stronger His love than death or hell!
   Its riches are unsearchable;
   The first-born sons of light
   Desire in vain its depths to see;
   They cannot reach the mystery,
   The length, and breadth, and height.

3 God only knows the love of God:
   Oh, that it now were shed abroad
   In this poor stony heart!
   For love I sigh, for love I pine:
   This only portion, Lord, be mine—
   Be mine this better part!

Charles Wesley.

60 Thou Shepherd of Israel, and
   mine,
   The joy and desire of my heart,

For closer communion I pine,
I long to reside where Thou art.

2 The pasture I languish to find,
Where all who their Shepherd obey,
Are fed on His bosom reclined,
And screened from the heat of the
day.

3 Ah, show me that happiest place,
That place of Thy people's abode,
Where saints in an ecstasy gaze,
And hang on a crucified God.

4 Thy love for a sinner declare,
Thy passion and death on the tree,
My spirit to Calvary bear,
To suffer and triumph with Thee.

5 'Tis there, with the lambs of Thy flock
There only I covet to rest;
To lie at the foot of the Rock,
Or rise to be hid in Thy breast.

6 'Tis there I would always abide,
And never a moment depart,
Concealed in the cleft of Thy side,
Eternally hid in Thy heart.

7 How good is the God we adore,
Our faithful, unchangeable Friend:
Whose love is as great as His power,
And knows neither measure nor end.

8 'Tis Jesus, the First and the Last,
Whose Spirit shall guide us safe
home;
We'll praise Him for all that is past,
And trust Him for all that's to come.
C. Wesley (first 6 verses).

61 I lift my heart to Thee,
Saviour divine;
For Thou art all to me,
And I am Thine.
Is there on earth a closer bond than
this
That my Belovèd's mine, and I am
His?

2 Thine am I by all ties;
But chiefly Thine,
That through Thy sacrifice

Thou, Lord, art mine.
By Thine own cords of love, so
sweetly wound
Around me, I to Thee am closely
bound.

3 To Thee, Thou dying Lamb,
I all things owe;
All that I have, and am,
And all I know.
All that I have is now no longer mine,
And I am not my own; Lord, I am
Thine.

4 How can I, Lord, withhold
Life's brightest hour
From Thee; or gathered gold,
Or any power?
Why should I keep one precious thing
from Thee,
When Thou hast given Thine own
dear self to me?

5 I pray Thee, Saviour, keep
Me in Thy love,
Until death's holy sleep
Shall me remove
To that fair realm where, sin and
sorrow o'er,
Thou and Thine own are one for ever-
more.
C. E. Mudie.

62 I need Thee, precious Saviour,
Oh, Thou art all to me;
Before the Throne for ever,
I stand complete in Thee.
Though Satan loud accuses,
Yet I can ever see,
The blood of Christ most precious,
The sinner's perfect plea.

2 I need Thee, precious Saviour,
I need a friend like Thee:
A friend to sooth and comfort,
A friend to care for me;
I need Thy heart, Lord Jesus,
To feel each anxious care;
To bear my every burden,
And all my sorrow share.

3 I need Thee, precious Saviour,
  I need Thee day by day,
  To fill me with Thy fulness,
  To lead me on my way:
  I need Thy Holy Spirit
  To teach me what I am—
  To show me more of Jesus,
  To point me to the Lamb.

4 I need Thee, precious Saviour,
  And hope·to see Thee soon,
  Encircled with the rainbow,
  And seated on Thy Throne;
  There, with Thy blood-bought
    people,
  My joy shall ever be,
  To sing Thy praise, Lord Jesus,
  And ever gaze on Thee.

                            F. Whitfield.

63 Here from the world we turn,
      Jesus to seek;
  Here may His loving voice
  Graciously speak!
  Jesus, our dearest Friend,
  While at Thy feet we bend,
  Oh, let Thy smile descend!
  'Tis Thee we seek.

2 Come, Holy Comforter,
  Presence divine,
  Now in our longing hearts
  Graciously shine!
  Oh, for Thy mighty power!
  Oh, for a blessèd shower,
  Filling this hallowed hour
  With joy divine.

3 Saviour, Thy work revive!
  Here may we see
  Those who are dead in sin
  Quickened by Thee!
  Come to our hearts tonight,
  Make every burden light,
  Cheer Thou our waiting sight;
  We long for Thee.

                        Fanny J. Crosby.

64 This is the day when light was first
      created,
  Symbol and gift of order and design.

In light is God's intention clearly
  stated;
The break of day reveals His loving
  mind.

2 This is the day of man's complete
  surprising,
  Repeat of Easter: Christ has come to
  life!
  Now is the feast of love's revolt and
  rising
  Against the rule of hell and death and
  grief.

3 We join to praise, with every race and
  nation,
  The God who with mankind His Spirit
  shares;
  Strong wind of change and earth's
  illumination,
  Dispelling static thoughts and darkest
  fears.

4 This is the day of worship and of
  vision,
  Great birthday of the Church in every
  land.
  Let Christian men confess their sad
  division,
  And seek the strength again as one to
  stand.

5 We pray that this, the day of re-
  creation,
  May hallow all the week that is to
  come.
  Help us, O Lord, to lay a good
  foundation
  For all we do at work, at school, at
  home.

                            F. Kaan.

65 Eternal Light! Eternal Light!
      How pure the soul must be,
  When, placed within Thy searching
  sight,
  It shrinks not, but, with calm delight,
  Can live, and look on Thee!

2 The spirits that surround Thy throne
  May bear the burning bliss;
  But that is surely theirs alone,
  Since they have never, never known
  A fallen world like this.

3 Oh, how shall I, whose native sphere
   Is dark, whose mind is dim,
   Before the Ineffable appear,
   And on my naked spirit bear
   The uncreated beam?

4 There is a way for man to rise
   To that sublime abode:
   An offering and a sacrifice,
   A Holy Spirit's energies,
   An advocate with God, —

5 These, these prepare us for the sight
   Of Holiness above:
   The sons of ignorance and night
   May dwell in the Eternal Light,
   Through the Eternal Love!
                    T. Binney.

66   Speak, Lord, in Thy stillness,
     While I wait on Thee;
   Hushed my heart to listen
   In expectancy.

2 Speak, O blessèd Master,
   In this quiet hour;
   Let me see Thy face, Lord,
   Feel Thy touch of power.

3 For the words Thou speakest,
   They are life indeed;
   Living bread from Heaven,
   Now my spirit feed!

4 Satiate my being,
   With Thy fulness fill;
   As the dew descending,
   Let Thy speech distil.

5 All to Thee is yielded,
   I am not mine own;
   Blissful, glad surrender,
   I am Thine alone.

6 Speak, Thy servant heareth;
   Be not silent, Lord!
   Waits my soul upon Thee
   For the quickening word.

7 Fill me with the knowledge
   Of Thy glorious will;
   All Thine own good pleasure
   In Thy child fulfil.

8 Like a watered garden,
   Full of fragrance rare,
   Lingering in Thy presence,
   Let my life appear.
                    E. May Grimes.

67   My soul shouts glory to the Son
     of God,
   For the work free grace hath done;
   My faith looks upward with a stead-
     fast eye
   That is clear as the noonday sun.

   Hallelujah! Hallelujah!
   Hallelujah to the Saviour I adore;
   I will praise Him, I will praise Him,
   Hallelujah! I will praise Him evermore.

2 My soul shouts glory to the Son of
   God,
   Not a cloud nor a care I see;
   My hope is clinging with a perfect
   trust
   To the cross He has borne for me.

3 My soul shouts glory to the Son of
   God,
   In His secret place I dwell;
   His constant presence overshades me
   there,
   And my joy there is none can tell.

4 My soul shouts glory to the Son of
   God,
   And I know it will not be long;
   Till o'er the river, where the saints
   have gone,
   I shall join their eternal song.
                    Fanny J. Crosby.

68   Nearer, still nearer, close to Thy
     heart,
   Draw me, my Saviour, so precious
   Thou art;
   Fold me, O fold me close to Thy
   breast,
   Shelter me safe in that 'Haven of
   Rest',
   Shelter me safe in that 'Haven of
   Rest'.

2 Nearer, still nearer, nothing I bring,
Naught as an offering to Jesus my
King;
Only my sinful, now contrite heart,
Grant me the cleansing Thy blood
doth impart,
Grant me the cleansing Thy blood
doth impart.

3 Nearer, still nearer, Lord, to be Thine,
Sin, with its follies, I gladly resign;
All of its pleasures, pomp and its
pride,
Give me but Jesus my Lord crucified,
Give me but Jesus my Lord crucified.

4 Nearer, still nearer, while life shall
last,
Till all its struggles and trials are past;
Then through eternity, ever I'll be
Nearer, my Saviour, still nearer to
Thee,
Nearer, my Saviour, still nearer to
Thee.

Mrs. C. H. Morris.

69   Nothing between, Lord, nothing
between;
Let me Thy glory see,
Draw my soul close to Thee,
Then speak in love to me —
Nothing between, Nothing between.

2 Nothing between, Lord, nothing
between;
Let not earth's din and noise
Stifle Thy still small voice;
In it let me rejoice —
Nothing between.

3 Nothing between, Lord, nothing
between;
Nothing of earthly care,
Nothing of tear or prayer,
No robe that self may wear —
Nothing between.

4 Nothing between, Lord, nothing
between;
Unbelief disappear,
Vanish each doubt and fear,
Fading when Thou art near —
Nothing between.

5 Nothing between, Lord, nothing
between;
Till Thine eternal light,
Rising on earth's dark night,
Bursts on my open sight —
Nothing between.

E.H.H.

70   There is a place of quiet rest,
Near to the heart of God;
A place where sin cannot molest,
Near to the heart of God.

O Jesus, blest Redeemer,
Sent from the heart of God;
Hold us, who wait before Thee,
Near to the heart of God.

2 There is a place of comfort sweet,
Near to the heart of God;
A place where we our Saviour meet,
Near to the heart of God.

3 There is a place of full release,
Near to the heart of God;
A place where all is joy and peace,
Near to the heart of God.

71   O for a closer walk with God,
A calm and heavenly frame,
A light to shine upon the road
That leads me to the Lamb.

2 Where is the blessedness I knew
When first I saw the Lord?
Where is that soul-refreshing view
Of Jesus and His word?

3 What peaceful hours I once enjoyed!
How sweet their memory still!
But they have left an aching void
The world can never fill.

4 Return, O holy Dove! return,
Sweet messenger of rest!
I hate the sins that made Thee mourn,
And drove Thee from my breast.

5 The dearest idol I have known,
Whate'er that idol be,
Help me to tear it from Thy Throne,
And worship only Thee.

6 So shall my walk be close with God,
Calm and serene my frame;
So purer light shall mark the road
That leads me to the Lamb.
W. Cowper.

72 Love divine, all loves excelling,
Joy of Heaven, to earth come
down!
Fix in us Thy humble dwelling,
All Thy faithful mercies crown.
Jesus, Thou art all compassion,
Pure, unbounded love Thou art;
Visit us with Thy salvation,
Enter every trembling heart.

2 Breathe, oh, breathe Thy loving Spirit
Into every troubled breast!
Let us all in Thee inherit,
Let us find the promised rest;
Take away the love of sinning;
Alpha and Omega be;
End of faith, as its beginning,
Set our hearts at liberty.

3 Come, almighty to deliver,
Let us all Thy grace receive!
Suddenly return, and never,
Never more Thy temples leave;
Thee we would be always blessing,
Serve Thee as Thy hosts above,
Pray, and praise Thee without ceasing,
Glory in Thy perfect love.

4 Finish then Thy new creation,
Pure and spotless may we be;
Let us see our whole salvation
Perfectly secured by Thee!
Changed from glory into glory,
Till in Heaven we take our place;
Till we cast our crowns before Thee,
Lost in wonder, love, and praise.
Charles Wesley.

73 Listen to my prayer, Lord,
Hear my humble cry;
When my heart is fainting,
To your throne I fly.

2 In earth's farthest corner
You will hear my voice;
Set me on Your rock, Lord,
Then I shall rejoice.

3 You have been my shelter
When the foe was near,
As a tower of refuge
Shielding me from fear.

4 I will rest for ever
In your care and love,
Guarded and protected
As by wings above.

5 All that I have promised,
Help me to fulfil;
And in all who love You
Work Your perfect will.

6 May Your truth and mercy
Keep me all my days;
Let my words and actions
Be my songs of praise.
J. E. Seddon.

74 Here is love, vast as the ocean,
Loving kindness as the flood;
When the Prince of Life my ransom,
Shed for me His precious blood.
Who His love will not remember?
Who can cease to sing His praise?
He shall never be forgotten,
Through Heaven's everlasting days.

2 On the mount of crucifixion,
Fountains opened deep and wide,
Through the flood gates of God's
mercy
Flowed the vast and gracious tide;
Grace and love like mighty rivers
Poured incessant from above,
And Heaven's peace and perfect
justice
Kissed a guilty world in love.

3 Let me all Thy love accepting,
Love Thee, ever all my days;
Let me seek Thy Kingdom only
And my life be to Thy praise;
Thou alone shalt be my glory,
Nothing in the world I see:
Thou hast cleansed and sanctified
me,
Thou Thyself hast set me free.

4 In Thy truth Thou dost direct me
By Thy Spirit through Thy Word;
And Thy grace my need is meeting,
As I trust in Thee, my Lord.
All Thy fulness Thou art pouring
In Thy love and power in me,
Without measure, full and boundless,
As I yield myself to Thee.

75 Sweet is the work, my God, my
King,
To praise Thy Name, give thanks and
sing;
To show Thy love by morning light,
And talk of all Thy truth at night.

2 Sweet is the day of sacred rest,
No mortal cares disturb my breast,
O may my heart in tune be found,
Like David's harp of solemn sound!

3 My heart shall triumph in the Lord,
And bless His works and bless His
word:
Thy works of grace, how bright they
shine!
How deep Thy counsels, how divine!

4 And I shall share a glorious part,
When grace has well refined my
heart,
And fresh supplies of joy are shed,
Like holy oil, to cheer my head.

5 Then shall I see, and hear, and know,
All I desired or wished below;
And every power find sweet employ
In that eternal world of joy.
Isaac Watts.

76 I come to the garden alone,
While the dew is still on the roses,
And the voice I hear,
Falling on my ear,
The Son of God discloses.

And He walks with me, and He talks with me,
And He tells me I am His own;
And the joy we share as we tarry there,
None other has ever known.

2 He speaks, and the sound of His voice
Is so sweet the birds hush their
singing,
And the melody that He gave to me,
Within my heart is ringing.

3 I'd stay in the garden with Him
Though the night around me be
falling,
But He bids me go; Through the voice
of woe
His voice to me is calling.
C. Austin Miles.

77 The God of love my Shepherd is,
And He that doth me feed;
While He is mine and I am His,
What can I want or need?

2 He leads me to the tender grass,
Where I both feed and rest;
Then to the streams that gently pass:
In both I have the best.

3 Or if I stray, He doth convert,
And bring my mind in frame;
And all this not for my desert,
But for His holy Name.

4 Yea, in death's shady black abode
Well may I walk, not fear;
For Thou art with me, and Thy rod
To guide, Thy staff to bear.

5 Surely Thy sweet and wondrous love
Shall measure all my days;
And, as it never shall remove,
So neither shall my praise.
G. Herbert.

78 No more veil! God bids me enter
By the new and living way—
Not in trembling hope I venture,
Boldly I His call obey:
There, with Him, my God I meet,
God upon the mercy seat!

2 In the robes of spotless whiteness,
With the blood of priceless worth,
He has gone into that brightness,
Christ rejected from the earth—

Christ accepted there on high,
And in Him do I draw nigh.

3 Oh, the welcome I have found there,
God in all His love made known!
Oh, the glories that surround there,
Those accepted in His Son!
Who can tell the depths of bliss
Spoken by the Father's kiss?

4 One with Him, O Lord, before Thee,
There I live, and yet not I;
Christ it is Who there adores Thee;
Who more dear, or Who more nigh?
All the Father's heart mine own—
Mine—and yet His Son's alone.

5 All the worth I have before Him
Is the value of the Blood;
I present when I adore Him,
Christ the first-fruits unto God;
Him with joy doth God behold,
Thus is my acceptance told.

Frances Bevan.

79 Jesus, the very thought of Thee
With sweetness fills my breast;
But sweeter far Thy face to see,
And in Thy presence rest.

2 Nor voice can sing, nor heart can frame,
Nor can the memory find
A sweeter sound than Thy blest name,
O Saviour of mankind.

3 O Hope of every contrite heart,
O Joy of all the meek,
To those who fall, how kind Thou art!
How good to those who seek!

4 But what to those who find? Ah, this
Nor tongue nor pen can show;
The love of Jesus, what it is,
None but His loved ones know.

5 Jesus, our only joy be Thou,
As Thou our prize wilt be;
Jesus, be Thou our glory now,
And through eternity.

St. Bernard of Clairvaux.

80 'Within the Veil': Be this beloved, thy portion,
Within the secret of thy Lord to dwell;
Beholding Him, until thy face His glory,
Thy life His love, thy lips His praise shall tell.

2 'Within the Veil', for only as thou gazest
Upon the matchless beauty of His face,
Canst thou become a living revelation
Of His great heart of love, His untold grace.

3 'Within the Veil', His fragrance poured upon thee,
Without the Veil, that fragrance shed abroad;
'Within the Veil', His hand shall tune the music
Which sounds on earth the praises of thy Lord.

4 'Within the Veil', thy spirit deeply anchored,
Thou walkest calm above a world of strife;
'Within the Veil' thy soul with Him united,
Shall live on earth His resurrection life.

Freda Hanbury Allen.

81 God is our strength and refuge,
Our present help in trouble;
And we therefore will not fear,
Though the earth should change!
Though mountains shake and tremble,
Though swirling waters are raging,
God the Lord of Hosts is with us evermore!

2 There is a flowing river,
Within God's holy city;
God is in the midst of her,
She shall not be moved!
God's help is swiftly given,
Thrones vanish at His presence;
God the Lord of Hosts is with us evermore!

3 Come, see the works of our Maker,
Learn of His deeds all powerful;
Wars will cease across the world
When He shatters the spear!
Be still and know your Creator,
Uplift Him in the nations;
God the Lord of Hosts is with us ever-
more!

Richard Bewes.

82 Jesus, I am resting, resting
In the joy of what Thou art;
I am finding out the greatness
Of Thy loving heart.
Thou hast bid me gaze upon Thee,
And Thy beauty fills my soul,
For, by Thy transforming power,
Thou hast made me whole.

Jesus, I am resting, resting
In the joy of what Thou art;
I am finding out the greatness
Of Thy loving heart.

2 Oh, how great Thy loving kindness,
Vaster, broader than the sea!
Oh, how marvellous Thy goodness,
Lavished all on me!
Yes, I rest in Thee, Belovèd,
Know what wealth of grace is Thine,
Know Thy certainty of promise,
And have made it mine.

3 Simply trusting Thee, Lord Jesus,
I behold Thee as Thou art;
And Thy love so pure, so changeless,
Satisfies my heart.
Satisfies its deepest longings,
Meets, supplies its every need,
Compasseth me round with blessings;
Thine is love indeed!

4 Ever lift Thy face upon me,
As I work and wait for Thee;
Resting 'neath Thy smile, Lord Jesus,
Earth's dark shadows flee.
Brightness of my Father's glory,
Sunshine of my Father's face,
Keep me ever trusting, resting,
Fill me with Thy grace.

Jean Sophia Pigott.

83 Pleasant are Thy courts above,
In the land of light and love;
Pleasant are Thy courts below,
In this land of sin and woe.
O! my spirit longs and faints
For the converse of Thy saints,
For the brightness of Thy face,
For Thy fulness, God of grace!

2 Happy birds that sing and fly
Round Thy altars, O Most High!
Happier souls that find a rest
In a Heavenly Father's breast!
Like the wandering dove that found
No repose on earth around,
They can to their ark repair,
And enjoy it ever there.

3 Happy souls! their praises flow
Even in this vale of woe;
Waters in the desert rise,
Manna feeds them from the skies.
On they go from strength to strength,
Till they reach Thy throne at length;
At Thy feet adoring fall,
Who hast led them safe through all.

4 Lord, be mine this prize to win:
Guide me through a world of sin;
Keep me by Thy saving grace;
Give me at Thy side a place.
Sun and shield alike Thou art;
Guide and guard my erring heart:
Grace and glory flow from Thee;
Shower, O shower them, Lord, on
me!

H. F. Lyte.

84 The Lord is my Shepherd, I shall
not want,
He maketh me down to lie
In pastures green, He leadeth me
The quiet waters by.

His yoke is easy, His burden is light,
I've found it so, I've found it so;
He leadeth me by day and by night
Where living waters flow.

2 My soul crieth out, 'Restore me again,
And give me the strength to take
The narrow path of righteousness,
E'en for His own Name's sake.'

3 Yea, though I should walk in the
  valley of death,
E'en, yet will I fear no ill!
For Thou art with me, and Thy rod
And staff they comfort still.

85   All people that on earth do dwell,
     Sing to the Lord with cheerful
       voice;
Him serve with mirth, His praise forth
  tell;
Come ye before Him and rejoice.

2 Know that the Lord is God indeed;
Without our aid He did us make;
We are His flock, He doth us feed,
And for His sheep He doth us take.

3 O enter then His gates with praise,
Approach with joy His courts unto;
Praise, laud, and bless His name
  always,
For it is seemly so to do.

4 For why? the Lord our God is good;
His mercy is for ever sure;
His truth at all times firmly stood,
And shall from age to age endure.
William Kethe.

86   The sands of time are sinking,
     The dawn of Heaven breaks;
The summer morn I've sighed for,
The fair sweet morn awakes;
Dark, dark hath been the midnight,
But day-spring is at hand,
And glory, glory dwelleth
In Immanuel's land.

2 O Christ, He is the fountain,
The deep, sweet well of love;
The streams of earth I've tasted,
More deep I'll drink above;
There to an ocean fulness
His mercy doth expand,
And glory, glory dwelleth
In Immanuel's land.

3 With mercy and with judgment,
My web of time He wove,
And aye the dews of sorrow
Were lustred by His love:
I'll bless the hand that guided,
I'll bless the heart that planned,
When throned where glory dwelleth
In Immanuel's land.

4 Oh, I am my Belovèd's,
And my Beloved is mine!
He brings a poor vile sinner
Into His 'House of wine;'
I stand upon His merit,
I know no other stand,
Not e'en where glory dwelleth
In Immanuel's land.

5 The bride eyes not her garment,
But her dear bridegroom's face;
I will not gaze at glory,
But on my King of grace;
Not at the crown He gifteth,
But on His piercèd hand;
The Lamb is all the glory
Of Immanuel's land.

6 I've wrestled on towards Heaven,
'Gainst storm, and wind, and tide;
Now like a weary trav'ller
That leaneth on His guide;
Amid the shades of evening,
While sinks life's lingering sand,
I hail the glory dawning
In Immanuel's land.
A. R. Cousin.

87   Thou, the Rose of Sharon,
     Let Thy praises roll;
Lily of the valley,
Flower of my soul;
Chiefest of ten thousand,
Round my heart entwine;
I am my Belovèd's,
My Beloved is mine.

Thou, the Rose of Sharon,
Let Thy praises roll!
Lily of the valley,
Flower of my soul.

2 Lead me by still waters,
  Hold me by the hand;
  And upon the mountains
  Give me grace to stand;
  Wind and storm and fire
  Raging, but my choice
  Ever is to listen
  For Thy still, small voice.

3 Jesus, Lord and Master,
  Glorious Nazarene:
  Close behind Thy reapers
  I would humbly glean:
  But Thy grace hath brought me
  To Thy house above,
  And Thy banner o'er me,
  Ever more is Love.

4 Water cannot quench it,
  Floods can never drown;
  Substance cannot buy it,
  Love's a priceless crown:
  Oh, the wondrous story,
  Mystery divine;
  I am my Belovèd's,
  My beloved is mine.

R. Kelso Carter.

88   The Lord's my Shepherd, I'll not
      want;
  He makes me down to lie
  In pastures green; He leadeth me
  The quiet waters by.

2 My soul He doth restore again;
  And me to walk doth make
  Within the paths of righteousness,
  E'en for His own Name's sake.

3 Yea, though I walk in death's dark
      vale,
  Yet will I fear none ill;
  For Thou art with me; and Thy rod
  And staff me comfort still.

4 My table Thou hast furnishèd
  In presence of my foes;
  My head Thou dost with oil anoint
  And my cup overflows.

5 Goodness and mercy all my life
  Shall surely follow me,
  And in God's house for evermore
  My dwelling place shall be.

Whittingham and Rous.

89   O God, our help in ages past,
      Our hope for years to come,
  Our shelter from the stormy blast,
  And our eternal home.

2 Under the shadow of Thy throne
  Thy saints have dwelt secure:
  Sufficient is Thine arm alone,
  And our defence is sure.

3 Before the hills in order stood,
  Or earth received her frame,
  From everlasting Thou art God,
  To endless years the same.

4 A thousand ages in Thy sight
  Are like an evening gone,
  Short as the watch that ends the
      night
  Before the rising sun.

5 Time like an ever-rolling stream,
  Bears all its sons away;
  They fly forgotten, as a dream
  Dies at the opening day.

6 O God, our help in ages past,
  Our hope for years to come,
  Be Thou our guard while troubles
      last,
  And our eternal home.

Isaac Watts.

90   This earth belongs to God,
      The world, its wealth, and all its
          people:
  He formed the waters wide
  And fashioned every sea and shore.
  Who may go up the hill of the Lord
  And stand in the place of holiness?
  Only the one whose heart is pure,
  Whose hands and lips are clean.

2 Lift high your heads, you gates,
Rise up, you everlasting doors, as
Here now the King of glory
Enters into full command.
Who is the King, this King of glory,
Where is the throne He comes to
claim?
Christ is the King, the Lord of glory,
Fresh from His victory.

3 Lift high your heads, you gates,
And fling wide open the ancient
doors, for
Here comes the King of glory
Taking universal power.
Who is the King, this King of glory,
What is the power by which He
reigns?
Christ is the King, His cross His glory,
And by love He rules.

4 All glory be to God
The Father, Son, and Holy Spirit;
From ages past it was,
Is now, and evermore shall be.
C. Idle.

91 Thank You for every new good
morning,
Thank You for every fresh new day,
Thank You that I may cast my
burdens
Wholly on to You.

2 Thank You for every friend I have,
Lord,
Thank You for every one I know,
Thank You when I can feel forgive-
ness
To my greatest foe.

3 Thank You for leisure and employ-
ment,
Thank you for every heartfelt joy,
Thank you for all that makes me
happy,
And for melody.

4 Thank You for every shade and
sorrow,
Thank You for comfort in Your Word,
Thank You that I am guided by You
Everywhere I go.

5 Thank You for grace to know Your
Gospel,
Thank You for all Your Spirit's power,
Thank You for Your unfailing love
Which reaches far and near.

6 Thank You for free and full salvation,
Thank You for grace to hold it fast.
Thank You, O Lord I want to thank
You
That I'm free to thank!
M. G. Schneider.

92 To God be the glory, great things
He hath done,
So loved He the world that He gave us
His Son,
Who yielded His life an atonement for
sin,
And opened the Life Gate that all may
go in.

Praise the Lord, praise the Lord,
Let the earth hear His voice,
Praise the Lord, praise the Lord,
Let the people rejoice!
O come to the Father through Jesus the Son,
And give Him the glory, great things He hath
done.

2 O perfect redemption, the purchase of
blood,
To every believer the promise of God;
The vilest offender who truly believes,
That moment from Jesus a pardon
receives.

3 Great things He hath taught us, great
things He hath done,
And great our rejoicing through Jesus
the Son;
But purer, and higher, and greater will
be
Our wonder, our transport when
Jesus we see.
Fanny J. Crosby.

93 The King of love my Shepherd is,
Whose goodness faileth never;
I nothing lack if I am His,
And He is mine for ever.

2 Where streams of living water flow
  My ransomed soul He leadeth,
  And where the verdant pastures
    grow,
  With food celestial feedeth.

3 Perverse and foolish oft I strayed,
  But yet in love He sought me,
  And on His shoulder gently laid,
  And home rejoicing brought me.

4 In death's dark vale I fear no ill
  With Thee, dear Lord, beside me;
  Thy rod and staff my comfort still,
  Thy cross before to guide me.

5 And so through all the length of days
  Thy goodness faileth never;
  Good Shepherd, may I sing Thy praise
  Within Thy house for ever.

Sir Henry W. Baker.

94   Bless the Lord, O my soul,
       And all within me, honour His
         Name!
     Bless the Lord, O my soul,
     And never forget all His blessings.

     He forgives all your sin
     And He heals all your ills,
     He redeems your life from the pit,
     He shows mercy upon you
     And steadfast love,
     He renews your youth by good
       things.

2 Bless the Lord, O my soul,
  And all within me, honour His Name!
  Bless the Lord, O my soul,
  And never forget all His blessings.

  Justice for the oppressed
  With compassion and grace,
  Slow to anger, abounding in love—
  He is not always chiding
  But in His love
  He does not remember our sins.

3 As the heavens are high
  To those who fear Him, His love is
    great.
  As the East from the West
  So far He removes our sins from us.

Days of man are like grass
Or a flower of the field;
As the wind passes over, it goes.
But on those who obey Him
With steadfast love
He bestows His love evermore.

4 Bless the Lord, King of all!
  All you His angels doing His word!
  Bless the Lord, all His hosts,
  And all of His works in creation.
  Bless the Lord, O my soul!

Michael Baughen.

95   Let us sing to the God of salvation,
       Let us sing to the Lord our rock!
     Let us come to His house with
       thanksgiving!
     Let us come before the Lord and
       sing!

     Praise our Maker,
     Praise our Saviour,
     Praise the Lord our everlasting King.
     Every throne must bow before Him,
     God is Lord of everything!

2 In His hand are the earth's deep
    places
  And the strength of the hills is His!
  All the sea is the Lord's, for HE made
    it,
  By His hands the dry land was
    formed.

3 Let us worship the Lord our Maker,
  Let us kneel to the Lord our God;
  For we all are the sheep of His
    pasture,
  He will guide us by His powerful
    hand.

4 Let today be the time when you hear
    Him!
  May our hearts not be hard or cold,
  Lest we stray from the Lord in rebel-
    lion,
  As His people did in time of old.

Richard Bewes.

96   Let us with a gladsome mind
       Praise the Lord for He is kind;

For His mercies shall endure,
Ever faithful, ever sure.

2 Let us sound His Name abroad,
For of gods He is the God;

3 He, with all-commanding might,
Filled the new-made world with light;

4 All things living He doth feed,
His full hand supplies their need;

5 He His chosen race did bless
In the wasteful wilderness;

6 He hath with a piteous eye
Looked upon our misery;

7 Let us then with gladsome mind
Praise the Lord, for He is kind.

John Milton.

Section II

THE GODHEAD

THE TRINITY

97 Praise the Father, God of justice;
Sinners tremble at His voice,
Crowns and creatures fall before Him,
Saints triumphantly rejoice.

2 Praise the Son, Who comes with
burning,
Purging sin and healing pain,
By Whose Cross and resurrection
We may die to rise again.

3 Praise the Spirit; power and wisdom,
Peace that like a river flows,
Word of Christ and consolation,
Life by whom His body grows.

4 Praise the Father, Son and Spirit,
One in three and three in one,
God our Judge and God our Saviour,
God our heaven on earth begun!

M. Perry.

98 Holy, holy, holy, Lord God
Almighty!
Early in the morning our song shall
rise to Thee;
Holy, holy, holy, merciful and mighty,
God our Heaven on earth begun!

2 Holy, holy, holy! all the saints adore
Thee,
Casting down their golden crowns
around the glassy sea;

Cherubim and seraphim falling down
before Thee,
Which wert and art, and evermore
shalt be.

3 Holy, holy, holy! though the darkness
hide Thee,
Though the eye of sinful man Thy
glory may not see,
Only Thou art holy; there is none
beside Thee,
Perfect in power, in love, and purity.

4 Holy, holy, holy, Lord God Almighty!
All Thy works shall praise Thy name in
earth and sky and sea;
Holy, holy, holy, merciful and mighty,
God in Three Persons, blessed Trinity!

Reginald Heber.

99 We give immortal praise
To God the Father's love,
For all our comforts here,
And better hopes above.
He sent His own eternal Son
To die for sins that man had done.

2 To God the Son belongs
Immortal glory too,
Who bought us with His blood
From everlasting woe;
And now He lives, and now He reigns,
And sees the fruit of all His pains.

The Godhead

3 To God the Spirit's Name
Immortal worship give,
Whose new creating power
Makes the dead sinner live.
His work completes the great design,
And fills the soul with joy divine.

4 Almighty God, to Thee
Be endless honours done,
The undivided Three,
And the mysterious One.
Where reason fails, with all her
powers,
There faith prevails and love adores.

Isaac Watts.

100 Holy, Holy, Holy, Holy,
Holy, Holy, Lord God Almighty;
And we lift our hearts before You as a
token of our love,
Holy, Holy, Holy, Holy.

2 Gracious Father, gracious Father,
We're so glad to be Your children,
gracious Father;
And we lift our heads before You as a
token of our love,
Gracious Father, gracious Father.

3 Precious Jesus, precious Jesus,
We're so glad that You've redeemed
us, precious Jesus,
And we lift our hands before You as a
token of our love,
Precious Jesus, precious Jesus.

4 Holy Spirit, Holy Spirit,
Come and fill our hearts anew, Holy
Spirit,
And we lift our voice before You as a
token of our love,
Holy Spirit, Holy Spirit.

5 Holy, Holy, Holy, Holy,
Holy, Holy, Lord God Almighty;
And we lift our hearts before You as
a token of our love,
Holy, Holy, Holy, Holy.

6 Hallelujah, hallelujah, hallelujah,
hallelujah,

And we lift our hearts before You as a
token of our love,
Hallelujah, hallelujah.

Jimmy Owens.

101 Lead us Heavenly Father, lead us
O'er the world's tempestuous sea;
Guard us, guide us, keep us, feed us,
For we have no help but Thee;
Yet possessing every blessing
If our God our Father be.

2 Saviour, breathe forgiveness o'er us;
All our weakness Thou dost know:
Thou didst tread this earth before us,
Thou didst feel its keenest woe;
Lone and dreary, faint and weary,
Through the desert Thou didst go.

3 Spirit of our God descending,
Fill our hearts with Heavenly joy,
Love with ev'ry passion blending,
Pleasure that can never cloy:
Thus provided, pardoned, guided,
Nothing can our peace destroy.

James Edmeston.

102 Thou whose almighty word
Chaos and darkness heard,
And took their flight,
Hear us, we humbly pray,
And where the gospel day
Sheds not its glorious ray,
Let there be light!

2 Thou who didst come to bring
On Thy redeeming wing
Healing and sight,
Health to the sick in mind,
Sight to the inly blind,
O now to all mankind
Let there be light!

3 Spirit of truth and love,
Life-giving, holy Dove,
Speed forth Thy flight:
Move on the water's face,
Spreading the beams of grace,
And in earth's darkest place
Let there be light!

4 Blessèd and holy Three,
  Glorious Trinity,
  Wisdom, love, might;
  Boundless as ocean's tide
  Rolling in fullest pride,
  Through the earth far and wide,
  Let there be light!
J. Marriott.

CREATION AND PROVIDENCE

103 Come, ye thankful people, come,
    Raise the song of harvest home:
All is safely gathered in,
Ere the winter storms begin;
God our Maker doth provide
For our wants to be supplied;
Come to God's own temple, come,
Raise the song of harvest home!

2 All the world is God's own field,
  Fruit unto His praise to yield;
  Wheat and tares together sown,
  Unto joy or sorrow grown;
  First the blade, and then the ear,
  Then the full corn shall appear;
  Lord of harvest, grant that we
  Wholesome grain and pure may be.

3 For the Lord our God shall come,
  And shall take His harvest home;
  From His field shall in that day
  All offences purge away;
  Give His angels charge at last
  In the fire the tares to cast;
  But the fruitful ears to store
  In His garner evermore.

4 Even so, Lord, quickly come
  To Thy final Harvest-home,
  Gather Thou Thy people in,
  Free from sorrow, free from sin;
  There for ever purified,
  In Thy presence to abide:
  Come, with all Thine angels, come,
  Raise the glorious Harvest-home.
H. Alford.

104 Fairest Lord Jesus! Ruler of all
    nature!
O Thou of God and man the Son!
Thee will I cherish, Thee will I honour,
Thou, my soul's glory, joy and crown!

2 Fair are the meadows, fairer still the
  woodlands,
  Robed in the blooming garb of spring,
  Jesus is fairer, Jesus is purer,
  Who makes the woeful heart to sing!

3 Fair is the sunshine, fairer still the
  moonlight,
  And all the twinkling, starry host,
  Jesus shines brighter, Jesus shines
  purer,
  Than all the angels Heaven can boast!
'Munster Gesangbuck'.

105 O Love of God, how strong and
    true;
Eternal, and yet ever new;
Uncomprehended and unbought,
Beyond all knowledge and all
thought!

2 O Heavenly Love, how precious still,
  In days of weariness and ill,
  In nights of pain and helplessness,
  To heal, to comfort, and to bless.

3 O wide embracing, wondrous Love;
  We read Thee in the sky above,
  We read Thee in the earth below,
  In seas that swell and streams that
  flow.

4 We read Thee best in Him, who came
  To bear for us the Cross of shame,
  Sent by the Father from on high,
  Our life to live, our death to die.

5 We read Thy power to bless and save
  E'en in the darkness of the grave;
  Still more in resurrection light
  We read the fulness of Thy might.

6 O Love of God, our shield and stay
  Through all the perils of our way;
  Eternal Love, in Thee we rest,
  For ever safe, for ever blest.
Horatius Bonar.

The Godhead

106 For the fruits of His creation
    Thanks be to God;
For His gifts to every nation,
Thanks be to God;
For the ploughing, sowing, reaping,
Silent growth while men are sleeping,
Future needs in earth's safe keeping,
Thanks be to God.

2 In the just reward of labour,
God's will is done;
In the help we give our neighbour,
God's will is done;
In our world-wide task of caring
For the hungry and despairing,
In the harvests men are sharing,
God's will is done.

3 For the harvests of His Spirit,
Thanks be to God;
For the good all men inherit,
Thanks be to God;
For the wonders that astound us,
For the truths that still confound us,
Most of all, that love has found us,
Thanks be to God.
F. Pratt Green.

107 Standing at the portal
    Of the opening year,
Words of comfort meet us,
Hushing every fear;
Spoken through the silence
By our Father's voice,
Tender, strong, and faithful,
Making us rejoice.

Onward then, and fear not,
Children of the day!
For His Word shall never,
Never pass away!

2 I, the Lord, am with thee,
Be thou not afraid,
I will help and strengthen,
Be thou not dismayed!
Yea, I will uphold thee
With My own right hand,
Thou art called and chosen
In My sight to stand.

3 For the year before us,
O what rich supplies!
For the poor and needy
Living streams shall rise;

For the sad and sinful
Shall His grace abound;
For the faint and feeble
Perfect strength be found.

4 He will never fail us,
He will not forsake;
His eternal covenant
He will never break.
Resting on His promise,
What have we to fear?
God is all-sufficient
For the coming year.
Frances Ridley Havergal.

108 We plough the fields and scatter
    The good seed on the land,
But it is fed and watered
By God's almighty hand;
He sends the snow in winter,
The warmth to swell the grain,
The breezes and the sunshine,
And soft refreshing rain.

All good gifts around us,
Are sent from Heav'n above;
Then thank the Lord, O thank the Lord
For all His love!

2 He only is the Maker
Of all things near and far,
He paints the wayside flower,
He lights the evening star;
The winds and waves obey Him,
By Him the birds are fed;
Much more to us His children
He gives our daily bread.

3 We thank Thee then, O Father,
For all things bright and good,
The seed-time and the harvest,
Our life, our health, our food;
Accept the gifts we offer
For all Thy love imparts,
And, what Thou most desirest,
Our humble, thankful hearts.
Matthias Claudius.
trs. Miss Jane M. Campbell.

109 You can't stop rain from falling
    down,
Prevent the sun from shining,
You can't stop spring from coming in,

Or winter from resigning,
Or still the waves or stay the winds,
Or keep the day from dawning;
You can't stop God from loving you,
His love is new each morning.

2 You can't stop ice from being cold,
You can't stop fire from burning,
Or hold the tide that's going out,
Delay its sure returning,
Or halt the progress of the years,
The flight of fame and fashion;
You can't stop God from loving you,
His nature is compassion.

3 You can't stop God from loving you,
Though you may disobey Him,
You can't stop God from loving you,
However you betray Him;
From love like this no power on earth
The human heart can sever,
You can't stop God from loving you,
Not God, not now, nor ever.

J. Gowans.

110 God moves in a mysterious way
His wonders to perform;
He plants His footsteps in the sea,
And rides upon the storm.

2 Deep in unfathomable mines
Of never-failing skill,
He treasures up His bright designs,
And works His sovereign will.

3 Ye fearful saints, fresh courage take!
The clouds ye so much dread
Are big with mercy; and shall break
In blessings on your head.

4 Judge not the Lord by feeble sense,
But trust Him for His grace;
Behind a frowning providence
He hides a smiling face.

5 His purposes will ripen fast,
Unfolding every hour;
The bud may have a bitter taste,
But sweet will be the flower.

6 Blind unbelief is sure to err,
And scan His work in vain;
God is His own interpreter,
And He will make it plain.

W. Cowper.

111 O Lord my God, when I in awe-
some wonder
Consider all the works Thy hand hath
made,
I see the stars, I hear the mighty
thunder,
Thy power throughout the universe
displayed.

Then sings my soul, my Saviour God, to Thee:
How great Thou art, how great Thou art!
Then sings my soul, my Saviour God, to Thee;
How great Thou art, how great Thou art.

2 When through the woods and forest
glades I wander
And hear the birds sing sweetly in the
trees;
When I look down from lofty
mountain grandeur,
And hear the brook and feel the gentle
breeze.

3 And when I think that God, His Son
not sparing,
Sent Him to die, I scarce can take it in,
That on the Cross, my burden gladly
bearing,
He bled and died to take away my sin.

4 When Christ shall come with shout of
acclamation
And take me home, what joy shall fill
my heart!
Then shall I bow in humble adoration,
And there proclaim, my God, how
great Thou art.

Stuart K. Hine.

112 For Thy mercy and Thy grace,
Faithful through another year,
Hear our song of thankfulness,
Father and Redeemer, hear.

2 Lo, our sins on Thee we cast,
Lo, to Thee we now arise,
And, forgetting all the past,
Press towards our glorious prize.

3 Dark the future: let Thy light
Guide us bright and morning Star;
Fierce our foes, and hard the fight:
Arm us, Saviour, for the war.

4 In our weakness and distress,
Rock of strength, be Thou our stay;
In the pathless wilderness
Be our true and living way.

5 Keep us faithful, keep us pure,
Keep us evermore Thine own:
Help, O help us to endure;
Fit us for the promised crown.

H. Downton.

Section III

THE LORD JESUS CHRIST

HIS BIRTH

113 Angels from the realms of glory,
Wing your flight o'er all the earth;
You who sang creation's story
Now proclaim Messiah's birth.

Come and worship!
Christ the new-born King.
Come and worship!
Worship Christ, the new-born King.

2 Shepherds in the fields abiding,
Watching o'er your flocks by night;
God with man is now residing,
Yonder shines the Infant light.

3 Sages, leave your contemplations,
Brighter visions beam afar!
Seek the great 'Desire of nations'.
You have seen His natal star.

114 As with gladness men of old
Did the guiding star behold,
As with joy they hailed its light,
Leading onward, beaming bright:
So, most gracious Lord, may we
Evermore be led to Thee.

2 As with joyful steps they sped,
Saviour, to Thy lowly bed,
There to bend the knee before
Thee whom Heaven and earth adore:
So may we with willing feet
Ever seek Thy mercy seat.

3 As they offered gifts most rare
At Thy cradle rude and bare;
So may we with holy joy,
Pure, and free from sin's alloy,
All our costliest treasures bring,
Christ, to Thee, our Heavenly King.

4 Holy Jesus, every day
Keep us in the narrow way;
And when earthly things are past,
Bring our ransomed souls at last
Where they need no star to guide,
Where no clouds Thy glory hide.

W. C. Dix.

115 Brightest and best of the sons of
the morning,
Dawn on our darkness, and lend us
thine aid;
Star of the East, the horizon
adorning,
Guide where our infant Redeemer is
laid.

2 Cold on His cradle the dew-drops are
shining;
Low lies His head with the beasts of
the stall;
Angels adore Him in slumber
reclining,
Maker, and Monarch, and Saviour of
all.

3 Say, shall we yield Him, in costly
devotion,
Odours of Edom, and offerings divine,
Gems of the mountain and pearls of
the ocean,
Myrrh from the forest or gold from the
mine?

4 Vainly we offer each ample oblation;
Vainly with gifts would His favour
secure;
Richer by far is the heart's adoration;
Dearer to God are the prayers of the
poor.

5 Brightest and best of the sons of the
  morning,
Dawn on our darkness, and lend us
  Thine aid;
Star of the East, the horizon
  adorning,
Guide where our infant Redeemer is
  laid.

R. Heber.

116 Infant holy,
    Infant lowly,
For His bed a cattle stall;
Oxen lowing,
Little knowing
Christ the Babe is Lord of all.
Swift are winging
Angels singing,
Nowells ringing,
Tidings bringing,
Christ the Babe is Lord of all.
Christ the Babe is Lord of all.

2 Flocks were sleeping,
  Shepherds keeping
Vigil till the morning new.
Saw the glory,
Heard the story,
Tidings of a gospel true.
Thus rejoicing,
Free from sorrow,
Praises voicing,
Greet the morrow,
Christ the Babe was born for you!
Christ the Babe was born for you!

trs. E. M. G. Reed.

117 No room for the Baby at
    Bethlehem's inn,
Only a cattle shed.
No home on this earth for the dear
  Son of God,
Nowhere to lay His head,
Only a Cross did they give to our
  Lord,
Only a borrowed tomb.
Today He is seeking a place in your
  heart,
Will you still say to Him 'No room'?

2 O Lord, in my heart there's a welcome
  for Thee.
Gladly I now would say,

Come in, blessèd Saviour, my heart
  and my life
Henceforth would own Thy sway.
Long hast Thou waited and long
  knocked in vain
Outside my heart's closed door;
Oh, cleanse me from sin, then, dear
  Lord, enter in
And dwell there for evermore.

118 Hark! the herald angels sing
    Glory to the new-born King,
Peace on earth, and mercy mild,
God and sinners reconciled.
Joyful, all ye nations rise,
Join the triumph of the skies;
With the angelic host proclaim,
Christ is born in Bethlehem.

  Hark! the herald angels sing
  Glory to the new-born King.

2 Christ, by Highest Heaven adored,
  Christ, the everlasting Lord,
Late in time behold Him come,
Offspring of a virgin's womb!
Veiled in flesh the Godhead see;
Hail the incarnate Deity!
Pleased as man with men to dwell,
Jesus, our Immanuel.

3 Mild He lays His glory by,
  Born that man no more may die,
Born to raise the sons of earth,
Born to give them second birth.
Hail the Heaven-born Prince of Peace!
Hail the Sun of Righteousness!
Light and life to all He brings,
Risen with healing in His wings.

Charles Wesley.

119 O come, all ye faithful,
    Joyful and triumphant,
To Bethlehem hasten now with glad
  accord;
Lo! in a manger
Lies the King of angels;

  O come, let us adore Him,
  O come, let us adore Him,
  O come, let us adore Him, Christ the Lord!

The Lord Jesus Christ

2 Raise, raise, choirs of angels,
  Songs of loudest triumph;
  Through Heaven's high arches be
    your praises poured;
  Now to our God be
  Glory in the highest;

3 Amen! Lord, we bless Thee,
  Born for our salvation,
  O Jesus! for ever be Thy name
    adored;
  Word of the Father,
  Now in flesh appearing;

18th Century.

120 O little town of Bethlehem,
    How still we see thee lie!
  Above thy deep and dreamless sleep
  The silent stars go by;
  Yet in thy dark streets shineth
  The everlasting Light;
  The hopes and fears of all the years
  Are met in thee tonight.

2 O morning stars, together
  Proclaim the holy birth
  And praises sing to God the King,
  And peace to men on earth;
  For Christ is born of Mary,
  And gathered all above,
  While mortals sleep, the angels keep
  Their watch of wondering love.

3 How silently, how silently,
  The wondrous gift is given!
  So God imparts to human hearts
  The blessings of His Heaven.
  No ear may hear His coming;
  But in this world of sin,
  Where meek souls will receive Him,
    still
  The dear Christ enters in.

P. Brooks.

121 Once in royal David's city,
    Stood a lowly cattle shed,
  Where a mother laid her Baby
  In a manger for His bed.
  Mary was that mother mild,
  Jesus Christ her little Child.

2 He came down to earth from Heaven,
  Who is God and Lord of all,
  And His shelter was a stable,
  And His cradle was a stall:
  With the poor and mean and lowly
  Lived on earth our Saviour holy.

3 And through all His wondrous child-
    hood
  He would honour and obey,
  Love and watch the lowly mother,
  In whose gentle arms He lay.
  Christian children all must be
  Mild, obedient, good as He.

4 For He is our childhood's pattern:
  Day by day like us He grew;
  He was little, weak and helpless;
  Tears and smiles like us He knew:
  And He feeleth for our sadness,
  And He shareth in our gladness.

5 And our eyes at last shall see Him,
  Through His own redeeming love;
  For that Child, so dear and gentle,
  Is our Lord in Heaven above;
  And He leads His children on
  To the place where He is gone.

6 Not in that poor, lowly stable,
  With the oxen standing by,
  We shall see Him—but in Heaven,
  Set at God's right hand on high;
  When like stars His children crowned,
  All in white shall wait around.

C. F. Alexander.

122 Come and join the celebration,
    It's a very special day;
    Come and share our jubilation,
    There's a new King born today!

1 See the shepherds hurry down to
    Bethlehem;
  Gaze in wonder at the Son of God
    who lay before them.

2 Wise men journey, led to worship by a
    star,
  Kneel in homage, bringing gifts from
    lands afar, so,

3 'God is with us,' round the world the
    message bring,

He is with us, 'Welcome', all the bells on earth are pealing.

V. Collison.

123 The first Nowell the angel did say
Was to certain poor shepherds in fields as they lay;
In fields where they lay keeping their sheep,
On a cold winter's night that was so deep.

Nowell, Nowell, Nowell, Nowell,
Born is the King of Israel.

2 They lookèd up and saw a star
Shining in the east, beyond them far,
And to the earth it gave great light,
And so it continued both day and night.

3 And by the light of that same star,
Three wise men came from country far;
To seek for a King was their intent,
And to follow the star wherever it went.

4 This star drew nigh to the north-west;
Over Bethlehem it took its rest,
And there it did both stop and stay
Right over the place where Jesus lay.

5 Then entered in those wise men three
Full reverently upon their knee,
And offered there in His presence
Their gold, and myrrh, and frankincense.

6 Then let us all with one accord
Sing praises to our Heavenly Lord,
That hath made Heaven and earth of nought,
And with His blood mankind hath bought.

Traditional.

124 What child is this, Who laid to rest,
On Mary's lap is sleeping?
Whom angels greet with anthems sweet,
While shepherds watch are keeping?

This, this is Christ the King,
Whom shepherds guard and angels sing:
Haste, haste to bring Him laud,
The Babe, the Son of Mary.

2 Why lies He in such mean estate
Where ox and ass are feeding?
Good Christian fear: for sinners here
The silent Word is pleading.

3 So bring Him incense, gold, and myrrh,
Come, peasant, king, to own Him.
The King of kings salvation brings,
Let loving hearts enthrone Him.

W. C. Dix.

125 Silent night, holy night!
Sleeps the world; hid from sight,
Mary and Joseph in stable bare
Watch o'er the Child beloved and fair
Sleeping in Heavenly rest,
Sleeping in Heavenly rest.

2 Silent night, holy night!
Shepherds first saw the light;
Heard resounding clear and long,
Far and near, the angel song:
'Christ the Redeemer is here',
'Christ the Redeemer is here'.

3 Silent night, holy night!
Son of God, O how bright
Love is smiling from Thy face!
Strikes for us now the hour of grace,
Saviour, since Thou art born,
Saviour, since Thou art born.

J. Mohr.
trs. S. A. Brooke.

126 See Him a-lying on a bed of straw;
A draughty stable with an open door;
Mary cradling the Babe she bore;
The Prince of Glory is His name.

O now carry me to Bethlehem
To see the Lord appear to men:
Just as poor as was the stable then,
The Prince of Glory when He came.

2 Star of silver sweep across the skies,
Show where Jesus in the manger lies,
Shepherds swiftly from your stupor rise
To see the Saviour of the world.

3 Angels, sing again the song you sang,
   Bring God's glory to the heart of man:
   Sing that Bethlehem's little Baby can
   Be salvation to the soul.

4 Mine are riches—from Your poverty:
   From Your innocence, eternity;
   Mine, forgiveness by Your death for
   me,
   Child of sorrow for my joy.

M. Perry.

127 Away in a manger, no crib for a
   bed,
   The little Lord Jesus laid down His
   sweet head.
   The stars in the bright sky looked
   down where He lay,
   The little Lord Jesus asleep in the hay.

2 The cattle are lowing, the Baby
   awakes,
   But little Lord Jesus, no crying He
   makes.
   I love You Lord Jesus! Look down
   from the sky,
   And stay by my side until morning is
   nigh.

3 Be near me, Lord Jesus; I ask You to
   stay
   Close by me for ever and love me, I
   pray.
   Bless all the dear children in Your
   tender care,
   And fit us for Heaven to live with You
   there.

Anon.

128 It came upon the midnight clear,
   That glorious song of old,
   From angels bending near the earth
   To touch their harps of gold:
   Peace on the earth, goodwill to men
   From Heav'n's all gracious King—
   The world in solemn stillness lay
   To hear the angels sing.

2 Still through the cloven skies they
   come
   With peaceful wings unfurled:
   And still their Heavenly music floats
   O'er all the weary world:
   Above its sad and lowly plains
   They bend on hovering wing,
   And ever, o'er its Babel sounds,
   The blessèd angels sing.

3 O ye, beneath life's crushing load
   Whose forms are bending low,
   Who toil along the climbing way
   With painful steps and slow;
   Look up! for glad and golden hours
   Come swiftly on the wing;
   Oh, rest beside the weary road,
   And hear the angels sing!

4 For lo! the days are hastening on,
   By prophet-bards foretold,
   When, with the ever-circling years,
   Comes round the age of gold;
   When peace shall over all the earth
   Its ancient splendours fling,
   And the whole world send back the
   song
   Which now the angels sing!

E. H. Sears.

129 While shepherds watched their
   flocks by night,
   All seated on the ground,
   The angel of the Lord came down,
   And glory shone around.

2 Fear not! said he; for mighty dread
   Had seized their troubled mind:
   Glad tidings of great joy I bring
   To you and all mankind.

3 To you, in David's town, this day
   Is born, of David's line,
   A Saviour, who is Christ the Lord;
   And this shall be the sign.

4 The Heavenly Babe you there shall
   find
   To human view displayed,
   All meanly wrapped in swaddling
   bands
   And in a manger laid.

5 Thus spake the seraph; and forthwith
Appeared a shining throng
Of angels praising God, who thus
Addressed their joyful song.

6 All glory be to God on high,
And to the earth be peace:
Goodwill henceforth from Heaven to men
Begin and never cease!

Nahum Tate.

130 Christians, awake, salute the happy morn,
Whereon the Saviour of mankind was born:
Rise to adore the mystery of love,
Which hosts of angels chanted from above;
With them the joyful tidings first begun
Of God incarnate and the Virgin's Son.

2 Then to the watchful shepherds it was told,
Who heard the angelic herald's voice: Behold,
I bring good tidings of a Saviour's birth
To you and all the nations upon earth:
This day hath God fulfilled His promised word,
This day is born a Saviour, Christ the Lord.

3 He spake; and straightway the celestial choir
In hymns of joy, unknown before, conspire,
The praises of redeeming love they sang,
And Heaven's whole orb with hallelujah's rang;
God's highest glory was their anthem still,
Peace upon earth, and unto men goodwill.

4 To Bethlehem straight the enlightened shepherds ran,
To see the wonder God had wrought for man:
Then to their flocks, still praising God, return,
And their glad hearts with holy rapture burn;
Amazed, the wondrous tidings they proclaim,
The first apostles of His infant fame.

5 O may we keep and ponder in our mind
God's wondrous love in saving lost mankind;
Trace we the Babe, who hath retrieved our loss,
From the poor manger to the bitter Cross;
Tread in His steps, assisted by His grace,
Till man's first Heavenly state again takes place.

6 Then may we hope, the angelic hosts among,
To sing, redeemed, a glad triumphal song;
He that was born upon this joyful day
Around us all His glory shall display;
Saved by His love, incessant we shall sing
Eternal praise to Heaven's almighty King.

John Byrom.

131 O Son of God we too would gather round You
Like those who gathered round Your manger bed,
Summoned by choirs of angel hosts from Heaven
Like kings who came, who were by starlight led.
Like them we gaze in awe and adoration
To see the baby born in Bethlehem.
He took our flesh, He shared our human sorrows,
His birth reveals God's love, God's peace to sinful men.

2 O Lamb of God we too would kneel
   before You
   As shepherds knelt on that first
   Christmas morn
   Hearing the songs of angel choirs
   in Heaven
   Who bring their praise, for Christ the
   King is born.
   Like them we come to bring our
   praise and worship,
   For God is here, we greet Him face to
   face.
   Behold His love within a lowly
   manger
   Much more than we deserve, here lies
   His wondrous grace.

3 O Son of man, we too would seek
   Your presence
   As long ago men thronged Your
   earthly days
   Seeking Your help, Your miracles of
   healing
   By quiet lake in busy city ways.
   Like them we come our varied
   burdens bearing
   Knowing that You and You alone can
   heal,
   Needing Your healing touch, Your
   words of comfort
   To every seeking heart Yourself dear
   Lord reveal.

C. Porteous.

132 See, amid the winter's snow,
   Born for us on earth below,
See, the Lamb of God appears,
Promised from eternal years.

   Hail, thou ever blessèd morn!
   Hail, redemption's happy dawn!
   Sing through all Jerusalem:
   Christ is born in Bethlehem!

2 Lo, within a manger lies
   He who built the starry skies,
   He who, throned in height sublime,
   Sits amid the cherubim.

3 Say, ye holy shepherds say,
   What your joyful news today;
   Wherefore have ye left your sheep
   On the lonely mountain steep?

4 As we watched at dead of night,
   Lo, we saw a wondrous light:
   Angels, singing peace on earth,
   Told us of the Saviour's birth.

5 Sacred Infant, all divine,
   What a tender love was Thine,
   Thus to come from highest bliss
   Down to such a world as this!

6 Teach, O teach us, holy Child,
   By Thy face so meek and mild,
   Teach us to resemble Thee
   In Thy sweet humility.

E. Caswall.

HIS LIFE AND WORK

133 Jesus, good above all other,
   Gentle child of gentle mother.
In a stable born our brother,
Give us grace to persevere.

2 Jesus, cradled in a manger,
   For us facing every danger,
   Living as a homeless stranger,
   Make we Thee our King most dear.

3 Jesus, for Thy people dying,
   Risen Master, death defying,
   Lord in Heaven, Thy grace supplying,
   Keep us to Thy presence near.

4 Jesus, who our sorrows bearest,
   All our thoughts and hopes Thou
   sharest;
   Thou to man the truth declarest;
   Help us all Thy truth to hear.

5 Lord, in all our doings guide us;
   Pride and hate shall ne'er divide us;
   We'll go on with Thee beside us,
   And with joy we'll persevere.

P. Dearmer.

134 Come and praise the Lord our King,
   Hallelujah!
Come and praise the Lord our King,
Hallelujah.

1 Christ was born in Bethlehem,
   Hallelujah,
   Son of God and Son of Man,
   Hallelujah:

2 He grew up an earthly child,
   Hallelujah,
   Of the world, but undefiled,
   Hallelujah:

3 Jesus died at Calvary, Hallelujah,
   Rose again triumphantly, Hallelujah:

4 He will cleanse us from our sin,
   Hallelujah,
   If we live by faith in Him, Hallelujah:

5 We will live with Him one day,
   Hallelujah,
   And for ever with Him stay, Hallelujah:
   Anon.

135 Oh, how sweet the glorious
   message,
   Simple faith may claim;
   Yesterday, today, for ever,
   Jesus is the same.
   Still He loves to save the sinful,
   Heal the sick and lame;
   Cheer the mourner, still the tempest,
   Glory to His name!

   Yesterday, today, for ever,
   Jesus is the same,
   All may change, but Jesus never!
   Glory to His name,
   Glory to His name,
   Glory to His name,
   All may change, but Jesus never!
   Glory to His name.

2 Him who pardoned erring Peter,
   Never need'st thou fear;
   He that came to faithless Thomas,
   All thy doubt will clear.
   He who let the loved disciple
   On His bosom rest,
   Bids thee still, with love as tender,
   Lean upon His breast.

3 He who 'mid the raging billows,
   Walked upon the sea;
   Still can hush our wildest tempest,
   As on Galilee.
   He who wept and prayed in anguish,
   In Gethsemane,
   Drinks with us each cup of trembling,
   In our agony.

4 As of old He walked to Emmaus,
   With them to abide;
   So through all life's way He walketh,
   Ever near our side.

Soon again shall we behold Him,
Hasten, Lord, the day!
But 'twill still be 'this same Jesus',
As He went away.
   A. B. Simpson.

136 One day when Heaven was filled
   with His praises,
   One day when sin was as black as
   could be,
   Jesus came forth to be born of a
   virgin,
   Dwelt amongst men, my example is
   He!

   Living, He loved me; dying, He saved me;
   Buried, He carried my sins far away,
   Rising, He justified freely for ever:
   One day He's coming — O glorious day.

2 One day they led Him up Calvary's
   mountain,
   One day they nailed Him to die on the
   Tree;
   Suffering anguish, despised and
   rejected;
   Bearing our sins, my Redeemer is He!

3 One day they left Him alone in the
   garden,
   One day He rested, from suffering
   free;
   Angels came down o'er His tomb to
   keep vigil;
   Hope of the hopeless, my Saviour is
   He!

4 One day the grave could conceal Him
   no longer,
   One day the stone rolled away from
   the door;
   Then He arose, over death He had
   conquered;
   Now is ascended, my Lord evermore!

5 One day the trumpet will sound for
   His coming,
   One day the skies with His glory will
   shine;
   Wonderful day my belovèd ones
   bringing;
   Glorious Saviour, this Jesus is mine!
   J. Wilbur Chapman.

137 There was a Saviour came
seeking His sheep,
He is mine!
Fording the torrent so rushing and
deep,
He is mine!
I was the sheep that had wandered
away,
He is mine!
Me on His shoulder He gently did lay,
He is mine!

He is mine!
He is mine!
Loving me, seeking me, finding me, keeping
me,
He is mine!

2 Steep was the mountain and dark was
the night,
He is mine!
He came a-seeking, He pitied my
plight,
He is mine!
I could not hope for a happy return,
He is mine!
But over me His kind spirit did yearn,
He is mine!

3 Great was the gladness when He
brought me home,
He is mine!
Never a murmur and never a frown,
He is mine!
Showered upon me His pardoning
love,
He is mine!
Told my homecoming to Heaven
above,
He is mine!

4 Say, do you wonder why always I
sing,
He is mine!
Call Him my Saviour, my glorious
King,
He is mine!
Would you not like to be able to say
He is mine?
O He is waiting to be this today,
Yours and mine!

Edward H. Joy.

138 O I love to read of Jesus and His
love; and His love!

How He left His Father's mansion far
above, far above;
How He came on earth to live,
How He came His life to give:
O I love to read of Jesus and His love,
and His love!

It's just like Him to take my sins away,
To make me glad and free,
To keep me day by day
It's just like Him to give His life for me,
That I might go to Heaven, and ever with Him
be.

2 O I love to read of Jesus as He went,
as He went
Everywhere to do His Father's will
intent, will intent;
How He gave the blind their sight,
How He gave the wronged ones right,
How He swift deliverance to the
captive sent, captive sent.

3 O I love to read of Jesus on the tree!
on the tree!
For it shows how great the love that
died for me, died for me;
And the blood that from His side
Flowed, when on the Cross He died,
Paid my debt and evermore doth
make me free, make me free.

4 O my dear and precious Saviour, at
Thy feet! at Thy feet!
Here I give myself, and all I have
complete, have complete;
I will serve Thee all my days
With a heart all filled with praise,
And I'll thank Thee face to face when
we shall meet, we shall meet.

W. L. Stone.

139 When Christ drew near to dwell
with men
And bear with man his earthly lot,
He brought the knowledge of the
Lord
To sinful hearts which knew Him not.

2 When Christ drew near with pardon-
ing love
And freed men from remorse and
tears,
His triumph over death assured
Their victory over sins and fears.

3 When Christ draws near His own -
today,
The fulness of His power to give,
The Holy Spirit makes Him known,
And by His life we all may live.

4 Draw near, O Christ, unveil Thy face,
The God of glory and of grace;
My heart reveal, with pardon seal,
And bring me to Thy holy place.
Miriam M. Richards.

140 Who is He in yonder stall,
At Whose feet the shepherds fall?

'Tis the Lord! oh, wondrous story!
'Tis the Lord, the King of Glory!
At His feet we humbly fall—
Crown Him! crown Him, Lord of all!

2 Who is He in deep distress
Fasting in the wilderness?

3 Who is He the people bless
For His words of gentleness?

4 Who is He to whom they bring
All the sick and sorrowing?

5 Who is He that stands and weeps
At the grave where Lazarus sleeps?

6 Who is He the gathering throng
Greet with loud triumphant song?

7 Lo! at midnight, who is He
Prays in dark Gethsemane?

8 Who is He on yonder tree
Dies in grief and agony?

9 Who is He who from the grave
Comes to succour, help, and save?

10 Who is He who from His throne
Rules through all the worlds alone?
B. R. Hanby.

141 What a wonderful, wonderful
love,
Brought our Saviour to earth below.
And our sins, which were scarlet are
cleansed,
For His blood washes whiter than
snow.

Isn't He wonderful, wonderful, wonderful,
Isn't He wonderful, wonderful?
Eyes not seen, ears not heard,
What's recorded in God's Word,
Isn't He wonderful, wonderful?

2 There was wonderful power in His
Word,
For He spoke, and the sea was still.
All the halt and the blind were made
whole,
Evil spirits obeyed His great will.

3 When He left He the comforter gave,
Every promise He made is true.
And the power that was His may be
ours,
'Greater works than all these shall ye
do.'

4 'That they all may be one,' was His
prayer,
O what wisdom and love sublime.
That we all may be one, let us pray,
One in spirit redeeming the time.
Verses H. Buffum, Jr.
Chorus Anon.

142 Wonderful birth, to a manger He
came,
Made in the likeness of man, to proclaim
God's boundless love for a world sick
with sin,
Pleading with sinners to let Him come
in.

Wonderful Name He bears,
Wonderful crown He wears,
Wonderful blessings His triumphs afford;
Wonderful Calvary,
Wonderful grace for me,
Wonderful love of my wonderful Lord!

2 Wonderful life, full of service so free,
Friend to the poor and the needy was
He;
Unfailing goodness on all He
bestowed,
Undying faith in the vilest He showed.

3 Wonderful death, for it meant not
defeat,
Calvary made His great mission
complete,
Wrought our redemption, and when
He arose,
Banished for ever the last of our foes.

4 Wonderful hope, He is coming again,
Coming as King o'er the nations to reign;
Glorious promise, His word cannot fail,
His righteous Kingdom at last must prevail!

A. H. Ackley.

143 Thou didst leave Thy throne
And Thy kingly crown,
When Thou camest to earth for me;
But in Bethlehem's home
Was there found no room
For Thy holy nativity:
O come to my heart, Lord Jesus;
There is room in my heart for Thee.

2 Heaven's arches rang
When the angels sang,
Proclaiming Thy royal degree;
But of lowly birth
Cam'st Thou, Lord, on earth,
And in great humility:
O come to my heart, Lord Jesus;
There is room in my heart for Thee.

3 The foxes found rest,
And the birds their nest,
In the shade of the cedar tree;
But Thy couch was the sod,
O Thou Son of God,
In the deserts of Galilee:
O come to my heart, Lord Jesus;
There is room in my heart for Thee.

4 Thou camest, O Lord,
With the living word
That should set Thy people free;
But, with mocking scorn,
And with crown of thorn,
They bore Thee to Calvary:
O come to my heart, Lord Jesus;
Thy Cross is my only plea.

5 When Heaven's arches ring,
And her choirs shall sing,
At Thy coming to victory,
Let Thy voice call me home,
Saying, Yet there is room,

There is room at My side for thee!
And my heart shall rejoice, Lord Jesus,
When Thou comest and callest for me.

E. E. S. Elliott.

144 Tell me the story of Jesus,
Write on my heart every word!
Tell me the story most precious,
Sweetest that ever was heard.
Tell how the angels in chorus
Sang, as they welcomed His birth,
'Glory to God in the highest,
Peace and good tidings to earth'.

Tell me the story of Jesus,
Write on my heart every word,
Tell me the story most precious,
Sweetest that ever was heard.

2 Fasting alone in the desert,
Tell of the days that He passed;
How He was tried and was tempted,
Yet was triumphant at last.
Tell of the years of His labours,
Tell of the sorrows He bore;
He was despised and afflicted,
Homeless, rejected, and poor.

3 Tell of the Cross where they nailed Him,
Dying in anguish and pain;
Tell of the grave where they laid Him;
Tell how He liveth again.
Love, in that story so tender,
Clearer than ever I see;
Stay, let me weep while you whisper
Love paid the ransom for me.

Fanny J. Crosby.

145 Jesus my Saviour to Bethlehem came,
Born in a manger to sorrow and shame;
Oh, it was wonderful blest be His Name!
Seeking for me, for me!

Seeking for me! Seeking for me!
Seeking for me! Seeking for me!
Oh, it was wonderful—blest be His name!
Seeking for me, for me!

2 Jesus my Saviour, on Calvary's tree,
Paid the great debt, and my soul He
set free;
Oh, it was wonderful—how could it
be?
Dying for me, for me!

Dying for me, Dying for me!
Dying for me, Dying for me!
Oh, it was wonderful—how could it be?
Dying for me, for me!

3 Jesus my Saviour, the same as of old,
While I was wandering afar from the
fold,
Gently and long did He plead with my
soul,
Calling for me, for me!

Calling for me! Calling for me!
Calling for me! Calling for me!
Gently and long did He plead with my soul,
Calling for me, for me!

4 Jesus my Saviour shall come from on
high
Sweet is the promise as weary years
fly;
Oh, I shall see Him descending the
sky,
Coming for me, for me!

Coming for me! Coming for me!
Coming for me! Coming for me!
Oh, I shall see Him descending the sky,
Coming for me, for me!

A.N.

146 My Lord has garments so
wondrous fine,
And myrrh their texture fills;
Its fragrance reached to this heart of
mine,
With joy my being thrills.

Out of the ivory palaces into a world of woe,
Only His great eternal love made my Saviour
go.

2 His life had also its sorrow sore,
For aloes had a part;
And when I think of the Cross He
bore,
My eyes with tear-drops start.

3 His garments too were in cassia
dipped,
With healing in a touch;

Each time my feet in some sin have
slipped,
He took me from its clutch.

4 In garments glorious He will come,
To open wide the door;
And I shall enter my Heavenly home,
To dwell for evermore.

Henry Barraclough.

147 Jesus is the same for ever,
As of old, so now today;
All the hosts of hell endeavour
Vainly to obstruct His sway.
In His people's hearts He reigneth,
Finishes what He begins;
Jesus still 'all power' retaineth,
Saves His people from their sins.

2 Jesus is the same for ever;
Yes, He heals the sick today,
As of old, so now, He never
Turns one suffering child away.
He can cure the worst diseases,
For He understands our frame;
Bore our griefs, and so releases
All who dare their rights to claim.

3 Jesus is the same for ever;
Still He says 'In Me abide.'
From His love no power can sever
Those who in their Lord confide.
Sweetly from all care He frees us,
Ours the comfort—His the shame.
Blessèd Saviour; precious Jesus!
There's no music like Thy Name.

T. Price.

148 Lord of all hopefulness, Lord of all
joy,
Whose trust, ever child-like, no cares
could destroy,
Be there at our wakening, and give
us, we pray,
Your bliss in our hearts, Lord, at the
break of the day.

2 Lord of all eagerness, Lord of all faith,
Whose strong hands were skilled at
the plane and the lathe,
Be there at our labours, and give us,
we pray,
Your strength in our hearts, Lord, at
the noon of the day.

The Lord Jesus Christ

3 Lord of all kindliness, Lord of all
  grace,
  Your hands swift to welcome, your
    arms to embrace,
  Be there at our homing, and give us,
    we pray,
  Your love in our hearts, Lord, at the
    eve of the day.

4 Lord of all gentleness, Lord of all
  calm,
  Whose voice is contentment, whose
    presence is balm,
  Be there at our sleeping, and give us,
    we pray,
  Your peace in our hearts, Lord, at the
    end of the day.

Jan Struthers.

HIS CHARACTER AND TITLES

149 Join all the glorious names
    Of wisdom, love and power,
  That mortals ever knew,
  That angels ever bore:
  All are too mean to speak His worth,
  Too mean to set my Saviour forth.

2 Great Prophet of my God,
    My tongue would bless Thy name;
  By Thee the joyful news
  Of our salvation came:
  The joyful news of sins forgiven,
  Of hell subdued, and peace with
    Heaven.

3 Jesus, my great High Priest,
  Offered His blood and died;
  My guilty conscience seeks
  No sacrifice beside;
  His powerful blood did once atone—
  And now it pleads before the throne.

4 My dear Almighty Lord
  My Conqueror and my King!
  Thy matchless power and love,
  Thy saving grace, I sing:
  Thine is the power—oh, may I sit
  In willing bonds beneath Thy feet.

5 Then let my soul arise,
  And tread the tempter down;
  My Captain leads me forth
  To conquest and a crown.

The feeblest saint shall win the day,
Though death and hell obstruct the
  way.

Isaac Watts.

150 There is a Name I love to hear,
    I love to sing its worth,
  It sounds like music in mine ear,
  The sweetest name on earth.

Chorus: (1st tune only)

  Oh, how I love the Saviour's Name,
  Oh, how I love the Saviour's Name,
  Oh, how I love the Saviour's Name,
  The sweetest Name on earth.

Chorus: (2nd tune only)

  Oh, how I love Jesus,
  Oh, how I love Jesus,
  Oh, how I love Jesus,
  Because He first loved me!

2 It tells me of a Saviour's love,
  Who died to set me free,
  It tells me of His precious blood,
  The sinner's perfect plea.

3 It bids my trembling soul rejoice,
  And dries each rising tear;
  It tells me in a 'still small voice',
  To trust and never fear.

4 Jesus, the Name I love so well,
  The Name I love to hear,
  No saint on earth its worth can tell,
  No heart conceive how dear.

5 This Name shall shed its fragrance still
  Along this thorny road,
  Shall sweetly smooth the rugged hill
  That leads me up to God.

6 And there, with all the blood-bought
    throng,
  From sin and sorrow free,
  I'll sing the new eternal song
  Of Jesus' love to me.

F. Whitfield.

151 Crown Him with many crowns,
    The Lamb upon His Throne;
  Hark! how the Heavenly anthem
    drowns
  All music but its own:

Awake, my soul, and sing
Of Him who died for thee,
And hail Him as thy matchless King
Through all eternity.

2 Crown Him the Virgin's Son,
The God incarnate born,
Whose arm those crimson trophies
won
Which now His brow adorn;
Fruit of the mystic Rose,
As of that Rose the Stem;
The Root whence mercy ever flows,
The Babe of Bethlehem.

3 Crown Him the Lord of love:
Behold His hands and side,
Those wounds yet visible above
In beauty glorified:
No angel in the sky
Can fully bear that sight,
But downward bends his burning eye
At mysteries so bright.

4 Crown Him the Lord of life,
Who triumphed o'er the grave,
And rose victorious in the strife
For those He came to save;
His glories now we sing,
Who died, and rose on high,
Who died, eternal life to bring,
And lives, that death may die.

5 Crown Him the Lord of peace,
Whose power a sceptre sways
From pole to pole, that wars may
cease,
And all be prayer and praise:
His reign shall know no end,
And round His piercèd feet
Fair flowers of Paradise extend
Their fragrance ever sweet.

6 Crown Him the Lord of years,
The Potentate of time,
Creator of the rolling spheres,
Ineffably sublime:
All hail, Redeemer, hail!
For Thou hast died for me;
Thy praise shall never, never fail
Throughout eternity.
Matthew Bridges and Godfrey Thring.

152 The Name of Jesus is so sweet,
I love its music to repeat;
It makes my joys full and complete,
The precious Name of Jesus.

'Jesus!' oh, how sweet the Name!
'Jesus!' every day the same!
'Jesus!' let all saints proclaim
Its worthy praise for ever.

2 I love the Name of Him whose heart
Knows all my griefs and bears a part;
Who bids all anxious fears depart,
I love the Name of Jesus.

3 That Name I fondly love to hear,
It never fails my heart to cheer;
Its music dries the falling tear;
Exalt the Name of Jesus.

4 No word of man can ever tell
How sweet the Name I love so well;
Oh, let its praises ever swell!
Oh, praise the Name of Jesus.
W. C. Martin.

153 Thou art the Everlasting Word,
The Father's only Son;
God, manifestly seen and heard,
And Heaven's belovèd One.

Worthy, O Lamb of God, art Thou,
That every knee to Thee should bow.

2 In Thee, most perfectly expressed,
The Father's glories shine;
Of the full Deity possessed;
Eternally divine.

3 But the high mysteries of Thy Name
An angel's grasp transcend:
The Father only—glorious claim—
The Son can comprehend.

4 Yet, loving Thee, on whom His love
Ineffable doth rest,
Thy glorious worshippers above,
As one with Thee, are blest.
J. Conder.

154 The fullness of the God-head
bodily dwelleth in my Lord.
The fullness of the God-head bodily
dwelleth in my Lord.
The fullness of the God-head bodily
dwelleth in my Lord and we are
complete in Him.

The Lord Jesus Christ

Complete, complete, complete in Him
We are complete in Him.

2 It's not by works of righteousness,
but by His grace alone.
It's not by works of righteousness,
but by His grace alone.
It's not by works of righteousness,
but by His grace alone that we are
complete in Him.

3 There's nothing more that I can do,
for Jesus did it all.
There's nothing more that I can do,
for Jesus did it all.
There's nothing more that I can do,
for Jesus did it all and we are
complete in Him.

Anon.

155 Take the Name of Jesus with you,
Child of sorrow and of woe;
It will joy and comfort give you —
Take it then where'er you go.

Precious Name . . . oh, how sweet! . . .
Hope of earth and joy of Heaven;
Precious Name . . . oh, how sweet! . . .
Hope of earth and joy of Heaven.

2 Take the Name of Jesus ever,
As a shield from every snare;
If temptations round you gather,
Breathe that holy Name in prayer.

3 Oh, the precious Name of Jesus!
How it thrills our souls with joy,
When His loving arms receive us,
And His songs our tongues employ!

4 At the Name of Jesus bowing,
Falling prostrate at His feet;
King of kings in Heaven we'll crown
Him,
When our journey is complete.

Mrs. L. Baxter.

156 Never fades the Name of Jesus,
Nor is dimmed by passing time.
Jesus' Name is everlasting,
For its meaning is sublime.
Jesus' Name brings joy and gladness,
Daily sending forth new life;
In His Name there's power to gather
Souls of men from ways of strife.

How I love the Name of Jesus!
He has set my heart aflame!
I have found a great salvation
Through the merits of His Name.

2 Beautiful the Name of Jesus;
Let it echo round the earth,
For to weary, hopeless nations
Jesus' Name has matchless worth.
Hate at last must yield to Jesus,
Sinfulness before Him flee;
Through His Name shall truth and
justice
Reign again to make men free.

3 In the night His dear Name shineth
Like a lighthouse evermore,
Guiding lonely ship-wrecked seamen
Safely to salvation's shore.
When the sun's last rays are fading,
Into darkness spread His fame,
Till the ransomed hosts in Heaven
Sing the praises of His Name.

David Welander.

157 Jesus is Lord! Creation's voice
proclaims it,
For by His power each tree and flower
was planned and made.
Jesus is Lord! The universe declares it,
Sun, moon and stars in heaven cry
Jesus is Lord!

Jesus is Lord! Jesus is Lord!
Praise Him with hallelujahs for Jesus is Lord!

2 Jesus is Lord! Yet from His throne
eternal
In flesh He came to die in pain on
Calvary's tree.
Jesus is Lord! From Him all life
proceeding,
Yet gave His life a ransom thus setting
us free.

3 Jesus is Lord! O'er sin the mighty
conqueror,
From death He rose and all His foes
shall own His name.
Jesus is Lord! God sends His Holy
Spirit
To show by works of power that
Jesus is Lord.

David J. Mansell.

158 Name of Jesus! highest Name!
Name that earth and Heaven
adore!
From the heart of God it came,
Leads me to God's heart once more.

2 Name of Jesus! living tide!
Days of drought for me are past;
How much more than satisfied
Are the thirsty lips at last!

3 Name of Jesus! dearest Name!
Bread of Heaven, and balm of love:
Oil of gladness, surest claim
To the treasures stored above.

4 Jesus gives forgiveness free,
Jesus cleanses all my stains;
Jesus gives His life to me,
Jesus always He remains.

5 Only Jesus! fairest Name!
Life, and rest, and peace, and bliss,
Jesus, evermore the same,
He is mine, and I am His.

*Tersteegen
trs. Mrs. Bevan.*

159 Let earth and Heaven agree,
Angels and men be joined,
To celebrate with me
The Saviour of mankind;
To adore the all atoning Lamb,
And bless the sound of Jesu's Name.

2 Jesus, transporting sound!
The joy of earth and Heaven;
No other help is found,
No other name is given,
By which we can salvation have;
But Jesus came the world to save.

3 Jesus, harmonious Name!
It charms the hosts above;
They evermore proclaim
And wonder at His love;
'Tis all their happiness to gaze
'Tis heaven to see our Jesu's face.

4 His Name the sinner hears,
And is from sin set free;
'Tis music in his ears,

'Tis life and victory;
New songs do now His lips employ,
And dances His glad heart for joy.

5 Stung by the scorpion sin,
My poor expiring soul
The balmy sound drinks in,
And is at once made whole:
See there my Lord upon the Tree!
I hear, I feel, He died for me.

6 O unexampled love!
O all-redeeming grace!
How swiftly didst Thou move
To save a fallen race!
What shall I do to make it known
What Thou for all mankind hast done?

7 O for a trumpet voice,
On all the world to call;
To bid their hearts rejoice
In Him who died for all;
For all my Lord was crucified,
For all, for all my Saviour died!

Charles Wesley.

160 I know of a world that is sunk in
shame,
Where hearts oft faint and tire;
But I know of a Name, a precious
Name,
That can set that world on fire;
Its sound is sweet, its letters flame.

I know of a Name, a precious Name,
'Tis Jesus.

2 I know of a Book, a marvellous Book,
With a message for all who hear;
And the same dear Name, His won-
derful Name,
Illumines its pages clear;
The Book is His word, its message
I've heard.

3 I know of a home in Immanuel's
land,
Where hearts ne'er faint not tire;
And His marvellous Name, His own
dear Name,
Inspires the Heavenly choir;
Hear the melody ringing, my own
heart singing.

4 I know of a day, a glorious day,
When He will come again;
Then crown Him King, His praises
sing,
When He begins His reign;
'Tis the day of the Lord, foretold in
His word.

J. Wilbur Chapman.

161 How sweet the name of Jesus
sounds
In a believer's ear;
It soothes his sorrows, heals his
wounds
And drives away his fear.

Chorus: (2nd tune only)
Oh, how I love Jesus,
Oh, how I love Jesus,
Oh, how I love Jesus,
The sweetest name on earth.

2 It makes the wounded spirit whole,
And calms the troubled breast;
'Tis manna to the hungry soul,
And to the weary rest.

3 Dear name, the Rock on which I build
My shield and hiding-place,
My never-failing treasury, filled
With boundless stores of grace.

4 Jesus, my Shepherd, Saviour, Friend,
My Prophet, Priest and King,
My Lord, my Life, my Way, my End,
Accept the praise I bring.

5 Weak is the effort of my heart,
And cold my warmest thought;
But when I see Thee as Thou art
I'll praise Thee as I ought.

6 I would Thy boundless love proclaim
With every fleeting breath;
So shall the music of Thy Name
Refresh my soul in death.

John Newton.

HIS SUFFERINGS AND DEATH

162 Beneath the Cross of Jesus
I fain would take my stand—
The shadow of a mighty Rock,
Within a weary land;

A home within the wilderness,
A rest upon the way,
From the burning of the noontide
heat,
And the burden of the day.

2 O safe and happy shelter,
O refuge tried and sweet,
O trysting-place where Heaven's love
And Heaven's justice meet!
As to the holy patriarch
That wondrous dream was given,
So seems my Saviour's Cross to me,
A ladder up to Heaven.

3 There lies, beneath its shadow,
But on the farther side,
The darkness of an awful grave
That gapes both deep and wide;
And there between us stands the
cross,
Two arms outstretched to save;
Like a watchman set to guard the way
From that eternal grave.

4 Upon that cross of Jesus,
Mine eyes at times can see
The very dying form of One
Who suffered there for me;
And from my smitten heart, with
tears,
Two wonders I confess—
The wonders of His glorious love,
And my own worthlessness.

5 I take, O cross, thy shadow
For my abiding place;
I ask no other sunshine than
The sunshine of His face:
Content to let the world go by,
To know no gain nor loss—
My sinful self my only shame,
My glory all the cross.

Miss E. C. Clephane.

163 Alas! and did my Saviour bleed?
And did my Sovereign die?
Would He devote that sacred Head
For such a worm as I?

2 Was it for crimes that I had done
He groaned upon the Tree?
Amazing pity! grace unknown!
And love beyond degree!

3 Well might the sun in darkness hide,
And shut his glories in.
When Christ, the mighty Maker, died
For man, the creature's sin.

4 Thus might I hide my blushing face,
Whilst His dear Cross appears,
Dissolve my heart in thankfulness,
And melt mine eyes to tears.

5 But drops of grief can ne'er repay
The debt of love I owe;
Here, Lord, I give myself away;
'Tis all that I can do.

Isaac Watts.

164 I stand all amazed at the love
Jesus offers me,
Confused at the grace that so fully He
proffers me;
I tremble to know that for me He was
crucified,
That for me, a sinner, He suffered, He
bled and died.

O it is wonderful that He should care for me
Enough to die for me!
O it is wonderful, wonderful to me!

2 I marvel that He would descend from
His Throne divine
To rescue a soul so rebellious and
proud as mine;
That He should extend His great love
unto such as I,
Sufficient to own, to redeem, and to
justify.

3 I think of His hands, pierced and
bleeding to pay the debt,
Such mercy, such love and devotion
can I forget?
No, no! I will praise and adore at the
mercy seat,
Until at the glorified Throne I kneel at
His feet.

Charles H. Gabriel.

165 By the Cross of Jesus standing,
Love our straitened souls
expanding,
Taste we now the peace and grace!

Health from yonder Tree is flowing,
Heavenly light is on it glowing,
From the blessèd Sufferer's face.

2 Here is pardon's pledge and token,
Guilt's strong chain for ever broken,
Righteous peace securely made;
Brightens now the brow once shaded,
Freshens now the face once faded,
Peace with God now makes us glad.

3 All the love of God is yonder,
Love above all thought and wonder,
Perfect love that casts out fear!
Strength, like dew, is here distilling,
Glorious life our souls is filling —
Life eternal, only here!

4 Here the living water welleth;
Here the Rock, now smitten, telleth
Of salvation freely given;
This the fount of love and pity,
This the pathway to the city,
This the very gate of Heaven.

Horatius Bonar.

166 Give me a sight, O Saviour,
Of Thy wondrous love to me;
Of the love that brought Thee down
to earth,
To die on Calvary.

Oh, make me understand it,
Help me to take it in;
What it meant to Thee, the Holy One,
To bear away my sin.

2 Was it the nails, O Saviour,
That bound Thee to the Tree?
Nay, 'twas Thine everlasting love,
Thy love for me, for me.

3 Oh, wonder of all wonders,
That through Thy death for me,
My open sins, my secret sins,
Can all forgiven be.

4 Then melt my heart, O Saviour,
Bend me, yea, break me down,
Until I own Thee Conqueror,
And Lord and Sovereign crown.

Katherine A. M. Kelly.

The Lord Jesus Christ

167 I stand amazed in the presence
Of Jesus the Nazarene,
And wonder how He could love me,
A sinner, condemned, unclean.

How marvellous! how wonderful!
And my song shall ever be;
How marvellous! how wonderful!
Is my Saviour's love for me!

2 For me it was in the garden
He prayed—'Not My will, but Thine':
He had no tears for His own griefs,
But sweat drops of blood for mine.

3 In pity angels beheld Him,
And came from the world of light
To comfort Him in the sorrows
He bore for my soul that night.

4 He took my sins and my sorrows,
He made them His very own;
He bore the burden to Calvary,
And suffered, and died alone.

5 When with the ransomed in glory
His face I at last shall see,
'Twill be my joy through the ages
To sing of His love for me.

C. H. Gabriel.

168 Jesus keep me near the Cross,
There a precious fountain,
Free to all, a healing stream,
Flows from Calvary's mountain.

In the Cross, in the Cross,
Be my glory ever;
Till my raptured soul shall find
Rest beyond the river.

2 Near the Cross, a trembling soul,
Love and mercy found me;
There the bright and morning Star
Shed its beams around me.

3 Near the Cross! O Lamb of God,
Bring its scenes before me;
Help me walk from day to day,
With its shadow o'er me.

4 Near the Cross I'll watch and wait,
Hoping, trusting ever,
Till I reach the golden strand,
Just beyond the river.

Fanny J. Crosby.

169 On a hill far away stood an old
rugged Cross,
The emblem of suffering and shame;
And I love that old Cross where the
dearest and best
For a world of lost sinners was slain.

So I'll cherish the old rugged Cross . . .
Till my trophies at last I lay down;
I will cling to the old rugged Cross, . . .
And exchange it some day for a crown.

2 Oh, the old rugged Cross, so despised
by the world,
Has a wondrous attraction for me;
For the dear Lamb of God left His
glory above
To bear it to dark Calvary.

3 In the old rugged Cross, stained with
blood so divine,
A wondrous beauty I see;
For 'twas on that old Cross Jesus
suffered and died
To pardon and sanctify me.

4 To the old rugged Cross I will ever be
true,
Its shame and reproach gladly bear;
Then He'll call me some day to my
home far away,
Where His glory for ever I'll share.

George Bennard.

170 Not all the blood of beasts,
On Jewish altars slain,
Could give the guilty conscience
peace,
Or wash away the stain.

2 But Christ the Heavenly Lamb,
Takes all our sins away;
A sacrifice of nobler name
And richer blood than they.

3 My faith would lay her hand
On that dear head of Thine,
While like a penitent I stand,
And there confess my sin.

4 My soul looks back to see
The burdens Thou didst bear,
When hanging on the cursèd tree,
And knows her guilt was there.

5 Believing, we rejoice
  To see the curse remove:
  We bless the Lamb with cheerful
    voice
  And sing His bleeding love!

  Isaac Watts.

171 The blood has always precious
    been,
  'Tis precious now to me;
  Through it alone my soul has rest,
  From fear and doubt set free.

  Oh, wondrous is the crimson tide
  Which from my Saviour flowed;
  And still in Heaven my song shall be,
  The precious, precious blood.

2 I will remember now no more,
  God's faithful Word has said,
  The follies and the sins of him
  For whom My Son has bled.

3 Not all my well-remembered sins
  Can startle or dismay;
  The precious blood atones for all
  And bears my guilt away.

4 Perhaps this feeble frame of mine
  Will soon in sickness lie,
  But resting on the precious blood
  How peacefully I'll die.

  Macleod Wylie.

172 There is a green hill far away,
    Without a city wall,
  Where the dear Lord was crucified,
  Who died to save us all.

2 We may not know, we cannot tell
  What pains He had to bear;
  But we believe it was for us
  He hung and suffered there.

3 He died that we might be forgiven,
  He died to make us good,
  That we might go at last to Heaven,
  Saved by His precious blood.

4 There was no other good enough
  To pay the price of sin;
  He only could unlock the gate
  Of Heaven, and let us in.

5 O dearly, dearly has He loved,
  And we must love Him too,
  And trust in His redeeming blood,
  And try His works to do.

  Mrs. C. F. Alexander.

173 'Man of Sorrows', what a name
    For the Son of God who came
  Ruined sinners to reclaim!
  Hallelujah! what a Saviour!

2 Bearing shame and scoffing rude,
  In my place condemned He stood;
  Sealed my pardon with His blood:
  Hallelujah! what a Saviour!

3 Guilty, vile, and helpless we,
  Spotless Lamb of God was He;
  'Full atonement,' can it be?
  Hallelujah! what a Saviour!

4 Lifted up was He to die,
  'It is finished,' was His cry;
  Now in Heaven exalted high;
  Hallelujah! what a Saviour!

5 When He comes, our glorious King,
  All His ransomed home to bring;
  Then anew this song we'll sing:
  Hallelujah! what a Saviour!

  P. P. Bliss.

174 Have you read the story of the
    Cross,
  Where Jesus bled and died;
  Where your debt was paid by His
    precious blood
  That flowed from His wounded side?

  He died an atoning death for thee,
  He died an atoning death;
  Oh, wondrous love! it was for thee,
  He died an atoning death!

2 Have you read how they placed the
    crown of thorns
  Upon His lovely brow?
  When He prayed, forgive them, oh!
    forgive,
  They know not what they do.

3 Have you read how He saved the
dying thief
When hanging on the Tree?
Who looked with pitying eyes and
said,
Dear Lord, remember me.

4 Have you read that He looked to
Heaven and said,
'Tis finished—'twas for thee?
Have you ever said, I thank Thee,
Lord,
For giving Thy life for me?

Thomas Dennis.

175 They nailed my Lord upon the
Tree
And left Him, dying there:
Through love He suffered there for
me;
'Twas love beyond compare.

Crucified! crucified!
And nailed upon the Tree:
With piercèd hands and feet and side;
For you! For me!

2 Upon His head a crown of thorns,
Upon His heart my shame;
For me He prayed, for me He died,
And dying, spoke my name.

3 'Forgive him, O forgive!' He cried,
Then bowed His sacred head;
O Lamb of God! my sacrifice!
For me Thy blood was shed.

4 His voice I hear, His love I know;
I worship at His feet:
And kneeling there, at Calvary's
Cross,
Redemption is complete.

C. Austin Miles.

176 Ride on, ride on in majesty!
Hark, all the tribes Hosanna cry;
O Saviour meek, pursue Thy road
With palms and scattered garments
strowed.

2 Ride on, ride on in majesty!
In lowly pomp ride on to die;
O Christ, Thy triumphs now begin
O'er captive death and conquered sin.

3 Ride on, ride on in majesty!
The angel armies of the sky
Look down with sad and wondering
eyes
To see the approaching sacrifice.

4 Ride on, ride on in majesty!
Thy last, Thy fiercest strife is nigh;
The Father on His sapphire Throne
Awaits His own anointed Son.

5 Ride on, ride on in majesty!
In lowly pomp ride on to die;
Bow Thy meek head to mortal pain,
Then take, O God, Thy power, and
reign.

H. H. Milman.

177 My Saviour suffered on the Tree,
Glory to the bleeding Lamb;
O come and praise the Lord with me!
Glory to the bleeding Lamb.

The Lamb, the Lamb, the bleeding Lamb,
I love the sound of Jesu's name,
It sets my spirit all in a flame,
Glory to the bleeding Lamb.

2 He bore my sins and curse and
shame,
Glory to the bleeding Lamb;
And I am saved through Jesu's name,
Glory to the bleeding Lamb.

3 I know my sins are all forgiven,
Glory to the bleeding Lamb,
And I am on my way to Heaven,
Glory to the bleeding Lamb.

4 And when the storms of life are o'er,
Glory to the bleeding Lamb,
I'll sing upon a happier shore,
Glory to the bleeding Lamb.

5 And this my ceaseless song shall be,
Glory to the bleeding Lamb,
That Jesus tasted death for me,
Glory to the bleeding Lamb.

Anon.

178 What a wonderful, wonderful
Saviour,
Who would die on the Cross for me!

Freely shedding His precious life-
blood,
That the sinner might be made free.

He was nailed to the Cross for me,
He was nailed to the Cross for me,
On the Cross crucified, for me He died;
He was nailed to the Cross for me.

2 Thus He left His Heavenly glory
To accomplish His Father's plan:
He was born of the Virgin Mary,
Took upon Him the form of man.

3 He was wounded for our transgres-
sions,
And He carried our sorrows too;
He's the Healer of every sickness,
This He came to the world to do.

4 So He gave His life for others
In redeeming this world from sin,
And He's gone to prepare a mansion,
That at last we may enter in.

F. A. Graves.

179 When I survey the wondrous
Cross
On which the Prince of glory died,
My richest gain I count but loss,
And pour contempt on all my pride.

Chorus: (2nd tune only)

It was on the Cross He shed His blood,
It was there He was crucified;
But He rose again, and lives in my heart,
Where all is peace and perfect love.

2 Forbid it, Lord, that I should boast,
Save in the death of Christ, my God;
All the vain things that charm me
most,
I sacrifice them to His blood.

3 See, from His head, His hands, His
feet,
Sorrow and love flow mingled down;
Did e'er such love and sorrow meet,
Or thorns compose so rich a crown?

4 Were the whole realm of nature mine,
That were an offering far too small;
Love so amazing, so divine,
Demands my soul, my life, my all.

Isaac Watts.

180 King of my life, I crown Thee now,
Thine shall the glory be;
Lest I forget Thy thorn-crowned brow,
Lead me to Calvary.

Lest I forget Gethsemane,
Lest I forget Thine agony,
Lest I forget Thy love for me,
Lead me to Calvary.

2 Show me the tomb where Thou wast
laid,
Tenderly mourned and wept:
Angels in robes of light arrayed,
Guarded Thee whilst Thou slept.

3 Let me, like Mary, through the gloom
Come with a gift to Thee:
Show to me now the empty tomb,
Lead me to Calvary.

4 May I be willing, Lord, to bear
Daily my cross for Thee:
Even Thy cup of grief to share,
Thou hast borne all for me.

5 Fill me, O Lord, with Thy desire
For all who know not Thee;
Then touch my lips with holy fire,
To speak of Calvary.

Jenny Evelyn Hussey.

181 Extended on a cursèd tree,
Besmeared with dust, and sweat,
and blood,
See there, the King of Glory see!
Sinks and expires the Son of God.

2 Who, who, my Saviour, this hath
done?
Who could Thy sacred body wound?
No guilt Thy spotless heart hath
known,
No guile hath in Thy lips been found.

3 I, I alone, have done the deed!
'Tis I Thy sacred flesh have torn;
My sins have caused Thee, Lord, to
bleed,
Pointed the nail, and fixed the thorn.

4 The burden, for me to sustain
Too great, on Thee, my Lord, was laid;
To heal me, Thou hast borne my pain;
To bless me, Thou a curse wast made.

5 My Saviour, how shall I proclaim?
How pay the mighty debt I owe?
Let all I have and all I am,
Ceaseless to all Thy glory show.

6 Too much to Thee I cannot give;
Too much I cannot do for Thee;
Let all Thy love, and all Thy grief,
Graven on my heart for ever be!

Gerhardt.

182 There was One who was willing to
die in my stead
That a soul so unworthy might live,
And the path to the Cross He was
willing to tread,
All the sins of my life to forgive.

They are nailed to the Cross, they are nailed to
the Cross,
O how much He was willing to bear!
With what anguish and loss Jesus went to the
Cross!
And He carried my sins with Him there.

2 He is tender and loving and patient
with me,
While He cleanses my heart of its
dross,
But there's no condemnation, I know
I am free,
For my sins are all nailed to the Cross.

3 I will cling to my Saviour and never
depart,
I will joyfully journey each day,
With a song on my lips and a song in
my heart,
That my sins have been taken away.

F. A. Breck.

183 To Calvary, Lord, in spirit now
Our weary souls repair,
To dwell upon Thy dying love,
And taste its sweetness there.

2 Sweet resting-place of every heart
That feels the plague of sin.
Yet knows that deep mysterious joy,
The peace of God within.

3 There through Thine hour of deepest
woe,
Thy suffering spirit passed;

Grace there its wondrous victory
gained,
And love endured its last.

4 Dear suffering Lamb, Thy bleeding
wounds
With cords of love divine,
Have drawn our willing hearts to
Thee,
And linked our life with Thine.

5 Our longing eyes would fain behold
That bright and blessèd brow,
Once wrung with bitterest anguish,
wear
Its crown of glory now.

E. Denny.

184 Once our blessèd Christ of beauty
Was veiled off from human view;
But through suffering death and
sorrow
He has rent the veil in two.

O behold the Man of Sorrows,
O behold Him in plain view,
Lo! He is the mighty Conqueror,
Since He rent the veil in two,
Lo! He is the mighty Conqueror
Since He rent the veil in two.

2 Yes, He is with God, the Father,
Interceding there for you;
For He is the mighty Conqueror,
Since He rent the veil in two.

3 Holy angels bow before Him,
Men of earth give praises due;
For He is the well belovèd,
Since He rent the veil in two.

4 Throughout time and endless ages,
Heights and depths of love so true;
He alone can be the giver,
Since He rent the veil in two.

N. B. Herrell.

185 Jesus was slain for me,
At Calvary.
Crowned with thorns was He,
At Calvary.
There He in anguish died,

There from His opened side,
Poured forth the crimson tide,
At Calvary.

2 Pardoned is all my sin,
At Calvary.
Cleansed is my heart within,
At Calvary.
Now robes of praise I wear,
Gone are my grief and care,
Christ bore my burdens there,
At Calvary.

3 Wondrous His love for me,
At Calvary.
Glorious His victory,
At Calvary.
Vanquished are death and hell,
Oh, let His praises swell,
Ever my tongue shall tell
Of Calvary.

George Perfect.

HIS RESURRECTION

186 The strife is o'er, the battle done;
Now is the Victor's triumph won;
Now be the song of praise begun:
Alleluia!

2 The powers of death have done their
worst,
But Christ their legions hath dis-
persed:
Let shouts of holy joy outburst,
Alleluia!

3 The three sad days have quickly sped;
He rises glorious from the dead:
All glory to our risen Head!
Alleluia!

4 He closed the yawning gates of hell;
The bars from Heaven's high portals
fell:
Let hymns of praise His triumphs tell.
Alleluia!

5 Lord, by the stripes which wounded
Thee,
From death's dread sting Thy servants
free,
That we may live and sing to Thee.
Alleluia!

Hymnodia Sacra
trs. Francis Pott.

187 Low in the grave He lay—
Jesus, my Saviour!
Waiting the coming day—
Jesus, my Lord!

Up from the grave He arose, . . .
With a mighty triumph o'er His foes; . . .
He arose, a Victor from the dark domain,
And He lives for ever with His saints to reign;
He arose! . . . He arose! . . .
Hallelujah! Christ arose!

2 Vainly they watch His bed—
Jesus, my Saviour!
Vainly they seal the dead—
Jesus, my Lord!

3 Death cannot keep his prey—
Jesus, my Saviour!
He tore the bars away—
Jesus, my Lord!

Robert Lowry.

188 He dies! He dies! the lowly Man of
Sorrows,
On Whom were laid our many griefs
and woes;
Our sins He bore, beneath God's
awful billows,
And He hath triumphed over all our
foes.

'I am He that liveth, that liveth, and was dead;
I am He that liveth, that liveth, and was dead;
And behold . . . I am alive . . . for evermore . . .
Behold . . . I am alive . . . for e . . . vermore.'
I am He that liveth, that liveth and was dead;
And behold . . . I am alive . . . for evermore.

2 He lives! He lives! what glorious consolation!
Exalted at His Father's own right
hand;
He pleads for us, and by His inter-
cession,
Enables all His saints by grace to
stand.

3 He comes! He comes! Oh, blest anti-
cipation!
In keeping with His true and faithful
word;
To call us to our Heavenly consum-
mation—
Caught up, to be 'forever with the
Lord'.

C. Russell Hurditch.

189 Jesus, Prince and Saviour,
　　　Lord of life who died:
Christ, the Friend of sinners,
Sinners crucified.
For a lost world's ransom
All Himself He gave,
Lay at last death's victim
Lifeless in the grave.

　　　Lord of life triumphant,
　　　Risen now to reign!
　　　King of endless ages,
　　　Jesus lives again!

2 In His power and Godhead
Every victory won,
Pain and passion ended,
All His purpose done:
Christ the Lord is risen!
Sighs and sorrows past,
Death's dark night is over,
Morning comes at last!

3 Resurrection morning!
Sinners' bondage freed.
Christ the Lord is risen—
He is risen indeed!
Jesus, Prince and Saviour,
Lord of life who died,
Christ the King of glory
Now is glorified!

T. Dudley-Smith.

190 Christ is alive! Let Christians sing.
　　　His Cross stands empty to the
　　　sky.
Let streets and homes with praises
ring.
His love in death shall never die.

2 Christ is alive! No longer bound
To distant years in Palestine,
He comes to claim the here and now
And conquer every place and time.

3 Not throned above, remotely high,
Untouched, unmoved by human
pains,
But daily, in the midst of life,
Our Saviour with the Father reigns.

4 In every insult, rift and war,
Where colour, scorn or wealth divide,
He suffers still, yet loves the more,
And lives, though ever crucified.

5 Christ is alive! Ascendant Lord,
He rules the world His Father made,
Till in the end, His love adored
Shall be to every man displayed.

Brian Wren.

191 Thine be the glory, risen, con-
　　　quering Son,
Endless is the victory Thou o'er death
hast won;
Angels in bright raiment rolled the
stone away,
Kept the folded grave-clothes where
Thy body lay.

　　　Thine be the glory, risen, conquering Son,
　　　Endless is the victory Thou o'er death hast
　　　won.

2 Lo! Jesus meets us, risen from the
tomb;
Lovingly He greets us, scatters fear
and gloom;
Let the Church with gladness, hymns
of triumph sing,
For her Lord now liveth, death hath
lost its sting.

3 No more we doubt Thee, glorious
Prince of life;
Life is nought without Thee; aid us in
our strife:
Make us more than conquerors
through Thy deathless love:
Bring us safe through Jordan to Thy
home above.

E. L. Budry.

192 Christ the Lord is risen today!
　　　Hallelujah!
Sons of men and angels say,
　　　Hallelujah!
Raise your songs and triumphs high:
　　　Hallelujah!
Sing, ye Heavens; thou earth reply:
　　　Hallelujah!

2 Love's redeeming work is done,
Fought the fight, the battle won:
Lo! our sun's eclipse is o'er;
Lo! he sets in blood no more:

3 Vain the stone, the watch, the seal,
Christ hath burst the gates of hell;
Death in vain forbids Him rise;
Christ hath opened Paradise.

4 Lives again our glorious King:
Where, O death, is now thy sting?
Once He died our souls to save:
Where's thy victory, O grave?

5 Soar we now where Christ hath led,
Following our exalted Head:
Made like Him, like Him we rise;
Ours the Cross, the grave, the skies.

6 Hail! the Lord of earth and Heaven;
Praise to Thee by both be given,
Thee we greet triumphant now:
Hail! the Resurrection, Thou!

Charles Wesley.

HIS ASCENSION AND EXALTATION

193 Arise, my soul, arise,
Shake off thy guilty fears;
The bleeding sacrifice
In my behalf appears;
Before the Throne my surety stands,
My name is written on His hands.

2 He ever lives above,
For me to intercede;
His all redeeming love,
His precious blood to plead;
His blood atoned for all our race,
And sprinkles now the Throne of
grace.

3 Five bleeding wounds He bears,
Received on Calvary;
They pour effectual prayers,
They strongly plead for me;
'Forgive him, oh, forgive,' they cry,
'Nor let that ransomed sinner die'.

4 The Father hears Him pray,
His dear Anointed One;
He cannot turn away
The presence of His Son:
His Spirit answers to the blood,
And tells me I am born of God.

5 My God is reconciled,
His pardoning voice I hear;
He owns me for His child,
I can no longer fear;
With confidence I now draw nigh,
And 'Father, Abba, Father,' cry.

Charles Wesley.

194 Majestic sweetness sits enthroned
Upon the Saviour's brow;
His head with radiant glories crowned,
His lips with grace o'erflow.

2 No mortal can with Him compare,
Among the sons of men;
Fairer is He than all the fair
That fill the Heavenly train.

3 He saw me plunged in deep distress,
He flew to my relief;
For me He bore the shameful Cross,
And carried all my grief.

4 To Him I owe my life and breath,
And all the joys I have;
He makes me triumph over death,
He saves me from the grave.

5 To Heaven, the place of His abode,
He brings my weary feet,
Shows me the glories of my God,
And makes my joy complete.

6 Since from His bounty I receive
Such proofs of love divine;
Had I a thousand hearts to give,
Lord, they should all be Thine!

Samuel Stennett.

195 At the Name of Jesus
Every knee shall bow,
Every tongue confess Him
King of glory now:
'Tis the Father's pleasure
We should call Him Lord,
Who from the beginning
Was the Mighty Word.

The Lord Jesus Christ

2 At His voice, creation
  Sprang at once to sight,
  All the angel faces,
  All the hosts of light,
  Thrones and Dominations,
  Stars upon their way,
  All the heavenly Orders,
  In their great array.

3 Humbled for a season,
  To receive a Name
  From the lips of sinners
  Unto whom He came;
  Faithfully He bore it,
  Spotless to the last,
  Brought it back victorious,
  When from death He passed.

4 Bore it up triumphant,
  With its human light,
  Through all ranks of creatures,
  To the central height;
  To the Throne of Godhead,
  To the Father's breast,
  Filled it with the glory
  Of that perfect rest.

5 In your hearts enthrone Him;
  There let Him subdue
  All that is not holy,
  All that is not true;
  Crown Him as your Captain
  In temptation's hour;
  Let His Will enfold you
  In its light and power.

6 Brothers, this Lord Jesus
  Shall return again
  With His Father's glory,
  With His angel train;
  For all wreaths of empire
  Meet upon His brow,
  And our hearts confess Him
  King of glory now.

C. M. Noel.

196 Jesus shall reign where'er the sun
  Doth his successive journeys run;
  His Kingdom stretch from shore to
  shore,
  Till suns shall rise and set no more.

2 For Him shall endless prayer be made,
  And praises throng to crown His
  head;
  His Name like sweet perfume shall rise
  With every morning sacrifice.

3 People and realms of every tongue
  Dwell on His love with sweetest song;
  And infant voices shall proclaim
  Their young hosannas to His Name.

4 Blessings abound where'er He reigns;
  The prisoner leaps to lose his chains;
  The weary find eternal rest;
  And all the sons of want are blest.

5 Where He displays His healing power;
  Death and the curse are known no
  more;
  In Him the tribes of Adam boast
  More blessings than their father lost.

6 Let every creature rise and bring,
  Its grateful honours to our King;
  Angels descend with songs again,
  And earth prolong the joyful strain.

Isaac Watts.

197 I know that my Redeemer lives,
  What joy the blest assurance
  gives!
  He lives, He lives, who once was
  dead;
  He lives, my everlasting Head.

  I know, I know that Jesus lives and on the
  earth again shall stand;
  I know that my Redeemer lives.

2 He lives, to bless me with His love;
  He lives, to plead for me above;
  He lives, my hungry soul to feed;
  He lives, to help in time of need.

3 He lives, and grants me daily breath;
  He lives, and I shall conquer death;
  He lives, my mansion to prepare;
  He lives, to lead me safely there.

4 He lives, all glory to His name;
  He lives, my Saviour, still the same;
  What joy the blest assurance gives,
  I know that my Redeemer lives!

Samuel Medley.

198 Look, ye saints! the sight is
glorious;
See the Man of Sorrows now
From the fight return victorious,
Every knee to Him shall bow:
Crown Him! Crown Him!
Crowns become the Victor's brow.

2 Crown the Saviour! angels crown
Him,
Rich the trophies Jesus brings;
In the seat of power enthrone Him,
While the vault of Heaven rings;
Crown Him! Crown Him!
Crown the Saviour King of kings.

3 Sinners in derision crowned Him,
Mocking thus the Saviour's claim;
Saints and angels crowd around Him,
Own His title, praise His Name:
Crown Him! Crown Him!
Spread abroad the Victor's fame.

4 Hark, those bursts of acclamation!
Hark, those loud triumphant chords!
Jesus takes the highest station:
O what joy the sight affords!
Crown Him! Crown Him!
King of kings, and Lord of lords!
Thomas Kelly.

199 The head that once was crowned
with thorns,
Is crowned with glory now;
A royal diadem adorns
The mighty Victor's brow.

He lives . . . He lives . . .
I know that my Redeemer lives.

2 The highest place that Heaven affords,
Is His by sovereign right;
The King of kings, the Lord of lords,
And Heaven's eternal Light.

3 The joy of all who dwell above,
The joy of all below,
To whom He manifests His love,
And grants His Name to know.

4 To them the Cross, with all its shame,
With all its grace is given;
Their name, an everlasting name,
Their joy, the joy of Heaven.

5 The Cross He bore is life and health,
Though shame and death to Him;
His people's hope, His people's
wealth,
Their everlasting theme.
T. Kelly.

200 Jesus, when made in the likeness
of men,
Humbled Himself to the death of the
Cross;
No reputation belonged to Him then;
Emptying Himself, He esteemed it no
loss.

Far above all! . . . Far above all! . . .
God hath exalted Him far above all! . . .
Crown Him as Lord, at His feet humbly fall,
Jesus, Christ Jesus, is far above all!

2 Name that through ages to come shall
out-ring:
Jesus, the Lamb, who for sinners was
slain!
Soon to this earth He is coming as
King,
Coming in power and in glory to
reign.

3 Kingdoms of earth shall be yielded to
God;
Glorious the reign, with our Lord on
the throne!
Chained the usurper, and broken his
rod:
Jesus as King every nation shall own.

4 Jesus, my Saviour, I yield unto Thee;
Reign in my heart as Redeemer and
Lord,
Make me what Thou wouldest have
me to be,
Filled with Thy Spirit, and filled with
Thy word.
C. H. Gabriel.

201 Golden harps are sounding,
Angels voices ring,
Pearly gates are opened—
Opened for the King;
Jesus, King of glory,
Jesus, King of love,
Is gone up in triumph to
His Throne above.

The Lord Jesus Christ

All His work is ended,
Joyfully we sing,
Jesus hath ascended;
Glory to our King.

2 He who came to save us,
He who bled and died
Now is crowned with glory
At His Father's side.
Nevermore to suffer,
Nevermore to die;
Jesus, King of glory,
Is gone up on high.

3 Praying for His children
In that blessèd place;
Calling them to glory,
Sending them His grace;
His bright home preparing,
Faithful ones for you;
Jesus ever liveth,
Ever loveth too.

Frances Ridley Havergal.

202 Christ triumphant ever reigning,
Saviour, Master, King,
Lord of Heaven, our lives sustaining,
Hear us as we sing.
Yours the glory and the crown—
The high renown—
The eternal Name.

2 Word incarnate, truth revealing,
Son of Man on earth,
Power and majesty concealing
By Your humble birth.
Yours the glory and the crown—
The high renown—
The eternal Name.

3 Suffering servant, scorned, ill-treated,
Victim crucified,
Death is through the Cross defeated
Sinners justified.
Yours the glory and the crown—
The high renown—
The eternal Name.

4 Priestly King, enthroned for ever
High in Heaven above,
Sin and death and hell shall never
Stifle hymns of love.
Yours the glory and the crown—
The high renown—
The eternal Name.

5 So, our hearts and voices raising
Through the ages long,
Ceaselessly upon you gazing
This shall be our song.
Yours the glory and the crown—
The high renown—
The eternal Name.

M. Saward.

203 Rejoice, the Lord is King!
Your Lord and King adore;
Mortals, give thanks and sing,
And triumph evermore;
Lift up your heart, lift up your voice,
Rejoice, again I say, rejoice!

2 Jesus the Saviour reigns,
The God of truth and love;
When He had purged our stains,
He took His seat above;
Lift up your heart, lift up your voice,
Rejoice, again I say, rejoice!

3 His Kingdom cannot fail;
He rules o'er earth and Heaven;
The keys of death and hell
Are to our Saviour given;
Lift up your heart, lift up your voice,
Rejoice, again I say, rejoice.

4 Rejoice in glorious hope;
Jesus the Judge shall come,
And take His servants up
To their eternal home:
We soon shall hear the archangel's voice;
The trump of God shall sound, rejoice!

Charles Wesley.

204 I know that my Redeemer lives,
What joy the blest assurance gives!
He lives, He lives, who once was dead;
He lives, my everlasting Head.

2 He lives, to bless me with His love;
He lives, to plead for me above;
He lives, my hungry soul to feed;
He lives, to help in time of need.

3 He lives, and grants me daily breath;
He lives, and I shall conquer death;
He lives, my mansion to prepare;
He lives, to lead me safely there.

4 He lives, all glory to His name;
He lives, my Saviour, still the same;
What joy the blest assurance gives,
I know that my Redeemer lives!

Samuel Medley.

HIS COMING AGAIN

205 Some glorious morning sorrow
will cease,
Some glorious morning all will be
peace,
Heartaches all ended, schooldays all
done,
Heaven will open—Jesus will come.

Some golden daybreak, Jesus will come;
Some golden daybreak, battles all won;
He'll shout the victory, break through the blue,
Some golden daybreak, for me, for you.

2 Sad hearts will gladden all shall be
bright,
Goodbye for ever to earth's dark
night;
Changed in a moment, like Him to be,
Oh, glorious daybreak, Jesus I'll see.

3 Oh, what a meeting, there in the
skies,
No tears nor crying shall dim our eyes;
Loved ones united eternally,
Oh, what a daybreak that morn will be.

C. A. Blackmore.

206 Hail to the Lord's Anointed,
Great David's greater Son;
Hail in the time appointed,
His reign on earth begun!
He comes to break oppression,
To set the captive free;
To take away transgression,
And rule in equity.

2 He shall come down like showers
Upon the fruitful earth:
And love, joy, hope, like flowers,
Spring in His path to birth.

Before Him on the mountains
Shall Peace, the herald go;
And righteousness in fountains
From hill to valley flow.

3 Kings shall fall down before Him,
And gold and incense bring;
All nations shall adore Him,
His praise all people sing.
For He shall have dominion
O'er river, sea and shore,
Far as the eagle's pinion
Or dove's light wing can soar.

J. Montgomery.

207 Rejoice! rejoice! our King is
coming!
And the time will not be long,
Until we hail the radiant dawning,
And lift up the glad new song.

Oh, wondrous day! oh, glorious morning,
When the son of Man shall come!
May we with lamps all trimmed and burning
Gladly welcome His return!
Rejoice! rejoice! our King is coming!
And the time will not be long,
Until we hail the radiant dawning,
And lift up the glad new song.

2 With joy we wait our King's returning
From His Heavenly mansions fair;
And with ten thousand saints appear-
ing
We shall meet Him in the air.

3 Oh, may we never weary, watching,
Never lay our armour down,
Until He come, and with rejoicing
Give to each the promised crown.

Ira D. Sankey.

208 Sweet is the hope that is thrilling
my soul—
I know I'll see Jesus some day!
Then what if the dark clouds of sin
o'er me roll,
I know I'll see Jesus some day!

I know I'll see Jesus some day! . . .
I know I'll see Jesus some day! . . .
What a joy it will be
When His face I shall see,
I know I'll see Jesus some day!

2 Though I must travel by faith, not by
   sight,
   I know I'll see Jesus some day!
   No evil can harm me, no foe can
   affright!
   I know I'll see Jesus some day!

3 Darkness is gathering, but hope
   shines within,
   I know I'll see Jesus some day!
   What joy when He comes to wipe out
   every sin;
   I know I'll see Jesus some day!

Avis M. Christiansen.

209 Thy Kingdom come, O God!
   Thy rule, O Christ begin!
Break with Thine iron rod
The tyrannies of sin.

2 Where is Thy reign of peace,
   And purity and love?
   When shall all hatred cease,
   As in the realms above?

3 When comes the promised time
   That war shall be no more,
   And lust, oppression, crime,
   Shall flee Thy face before?

4 We pray Thee, Lord, arise,
   And come in Thy great might;
   Revive our longing eyes,
   Which languish for Thy sight.

5 Men scorn Thy sacred Name,
   And wolves devour Thy fold;
   By many deeds of shame
   We learn that love grows cold.

6 O'er lands both near and far
   Thick darkness broodeth yet:
   Arise, O morning Star,
   Arise, and never set!

Lewis Hensley.

210 Jesus is coming! sing the glad
   word,
   Coming for those He redeemed by His
   blood,
   Coming to reign as the glorified Lord;
   Jesus is coming again!

Jesus is coming, is coming again!
Jesus is coming again!
Shout the glad tidings o'er mountain and plain!
Jesus is coming again!

2 Jesus is coming! the dead shall arise,
   Loved ones shall meet in a joyful
   surprise,
   Caught up together to Him in the
   skies;
   Jesus is coming again!

3 Jesus is coming! His saints to release;
   Coming to give to the warring earth
   peace:
   Sinning and sighing and sorrow shall
   cease;
   Jesus is coming again!

4 Jesus is coming! the promise is true;
   Who are the chosen, the faithful, the
   few,
   Waiting and watching, prepared for
   review?
   Jesus is coming again!

D. W. Whittle.

211 Jesus may come today,
   Glad day, Glad day!
And I would see my Friend;
Dangers and troubles would end
If Jesus should come today.

Glad day, Glad day!
Is it the crowning day?
I'll live for today, nor anxious be;
Jesus my Lord I soon shall see.
Glad day, Glad day!
Is it the crowning day?

2 I may go home today,
   Glad day, Glad day!
   Seemeth I hear their song;
   Hail to the radiant throng!
   If I should go home today.

3 Why should I anxious be?
   Glad day, Glad day!
   Lights appear on the shore,
   Storms will affright never more,
   For He is 'at hand' today.

4 Faithful I'll be today,
   Glad day, Glad day!

And I will freely tell
Why I should love Him so well,
For He is my all today.

George Walker Whitcomb.

212 O shout aloud the tidings,
Repeat the joyful strain;
Let all the waiting nations
This message hear again:
The spotless Lamb of glory,
Who once for man was slain,
Soon o'er all the earth shall reign.

Looking for that blessèd hope, . . .
Looking for that blessèd hope; . . .
We know the hour is nearing,
The hour of His appearing:
We're looking for that blessèd hope.

2 Signs in the Heaven above us,
In sun and moon and sky,
Proclaim to all the faithful
Redemption draweth nigh;
The hearts of men are quaking,
And failing them for fear:
Jesus' coming draweth near.

3 We'll watch for His returning
With lamps well trimmed and bright;
He cometh to the careless
As thieves break through at night;
'Well done, thou good and faithful'—
O may we hear the word,
'Share the joy of Christ thy Lord.'

Thoro Harris.

213 On that bright and golden morning when the Son of Man shall
come,
And the radiance of His glory we shall
see:
When from every clime and nation
He shall call his people home—
What a gathering of the ransomed
that will be!

What a gath . . .'ring! what a gath . . .'ring
What a gathering of the ransomed in the
summer land of love!
What a gath . . .'ring! what a gath . . .'ring
Of the ransomed in that happy home above!

2 When the blest who sleep in Jesus at
His bidding shall arise
From the silence of the grave and
from the sea;

And with bodies all celestial they shall
meet Him in the skies
What a gathering and rejoicing there
will be!

3 When our eyes behold the city, with
its 'many mansions' bright,
And its river, calm and restful,
flowing free—
When the friends that death has
parted shall in bliss again unite—
What a gathering and a greeting there
will be!

4 Oh, the King is surely coming, and the
time is drawing nigh,
When the blessèd day of promise we
shall see;
Then the changing 'in a moment', 'in
the twinkling of an eye',
And for ever in His presence we shall
be!

Fanny J. Crosby.

214 It may be at morn, when the day is
awakening,
When sunlight through darkness and
shadow is breaking,
That Jesus will come in the fulness of
glory,
To receive from the world 'His own'.

O Lord Jesus, how long?
How long ere we shout the glad song?—
Christ returneth, Hallelujah!
Hallelujah! Amen!
Hallelujah! Amen!

2 It may be at midday, it may be at
twilight,
It may be, perchance, that the black-
ness of midnight
Will burst into light in the blaze of His
glory,
When Jesus receives 'His own'.

3 While hosts cry 'Hosanna!' from
Heaven descending,
With glorified saints and the angels
attending,
With grace on His brow, like a halo of
glory,
Will Jesus receive 'His own'.

4 Oh, joy! oh, delight! should we go
without dying;
No sickness, no sadness, no dread
and no crying;
Caught up through the clouds with
our Lord into glory
When Jesus receives 'His own'.

H. L. Turner.

215 Sing we the King who is coming
to reign,
Glory to Jesus, the Lamb that was
slain!
Life and salvation His empire shall
bring,
Joy to the nations when Jesus is
King.

Come let us sing . . . praise to our King: . . .
Jesus our King, . . . Jesus our King; . . .
This is our song who to Jesus belong,
Glory to Jesus, to Jesus our King.

2 All men shall dwell in His marvellous
light,
Races long severed His love shall
unite,
Justice and truth from His sceptre
shall spring,
Wrong shall be ended when Jesus is
King.

3 All shall be glad in His Kingdom of
Peace,
Freedom shall flourish and wisdom
increase,
Foe shall be friend when His triumph
we sing,
Sword shall be sickle when Jesus is
King.

4 Souls shall be saved from the burden
of sin,
Doubt shall not darken His witness
within,
Hell hath no terrors, and death hath
no sting,
Love is victorious when Jeus is King.

5 Kingdom of Christ, for Thy coming
we pray,
Hasten, O Father, the dawn of the
day,

When this new song Thy creation
shall sing,
Satan is vanquished, for Jesus is
King.

Silvester Horne.

216 When the trump of the great
archangel
Its mighty tones shall sound,
And, the end of the world proclaim-
ing,
Shall pierce the depth profound;
When the Son of Man shall come in
His glory,
With all the saints on high,
What a shouting in the skies from the
multitudes that rise,
Changed in the twinkling of an eye.

Changed in the twinkling of an eye,
Changed in the twinkling of an eye;
For the trump shall sound and the dead shall
rise,
And we shall be changed in the twinkling of an
eye.

2 When He comes in the clouds
descending,
And they who loved Him here,
From their graves shall awake and
praise Him
With joy and not with fear;
When the body and the soul are
united,
And clothed no more to die,
What a shouting there will be when
each other's face we see,
Changed in the twinkling of an eye.

3 Oh the seed that was sown in
weakness
Shall then be raised in power,
And the songs of the blood-bought
millions
Shall hail that blissful hour;
When we gather safely home in the
morning,
And night's dark shadows fly,
What a shouting on the shore when
we meet to part no more,
Changed in the twinkling of an eye.

Fanny J. Crosby.

217 When the trumpet of the Lord
shall sound, and time shall be
no more,
And the morning breaks, eternal,
bright and fair;
When the saved of earth shall gather
over on the other shore,
And the roll is called up yonder,
I'll be there.

> When the roll . . . is called up yon . . . der,
> When the roll . . . is called up yon . . . der,
> When the roll . . . is called up yonder,
> When the roll is called up yonder I'll be there.

2 On that bright and cloudless morning,
when the dead in Christ shall rise,
And the glory of His resurrection
share:
When His chosen ones shall gather to
their home beyond the skies,
And the roll is called up yonder,
I'll be there.

3 Let us labour for the Master from the
dawn till setting sun,
Let us talk of all His wondrous love
and care,
Then, when all of life is over, and our
work on earth is done,
And the roll is called up yonder,
I'll be there.

J. M. Black.

218 In these, the closing days of
time,
What joy the glorious hope affords,
That soon—O wondrous truth
sublime!
He shall reign, King of kings and Lord
of lords.

> He's coming soon, He's coming soon;
> With joy we welcome His returning;
> It may be morn, it may be night or noon—
> We know He's coming soon.

2 The signs around—in earth and air,
Or painted on the starlit sky,
God's faithful witnesses declare
That the coming of the Saviour
draweth nigh.

3 The dead in Christ who 'neath us lie,
In countless numbers, all shall rise
When through the portals of the sky
He shall come to prepare our
Paradise.

4 And we who, living, yet remain,
Caught up, shall meet our faithful
Lord;
This hope we cherish not in vain,
But we comfort one another by this
word.

Thoro Harris.

Section IV

THE HOLY SPIRIT

HIS PERSON AND WORK

219 Our blest Redeemer, ere He
breathed
His tender, last farewell,
A Guide, a Comforter, bequeathed
With us to dwell.

2 He came in tongues of living flame,
To teach, convince, subdue;
All-powerful as the wind He came,
As viewless too.

3 He came sweet influence to impart,
A gracious, willing Guest;

Where He can find one humble heart
Wherein to rest.

4 And His that gentle voice we hear,
Soft as the breath of even,
That checks each thought, and calms
each fear,
And speaks of Heaven.

5 And every virtue we possess,
And every conquest won,
And every thought of holiness
Are His alone.

6 Spirit of purity and grace,
  Our weakness pitying see:
  O make our heart Thy dwelling-place,
  And worthier Thee.

7 O praise the Father, praise the Son;
  Blest Spirit, praise to Thee;
  All praise to God, the Three in One,
  The One in Three.

Harriet Auber.

220 Spirit of God, unseen as the wind,
  Gentle as is the dove;
  Teach us the truth and help us believe,
  Show us the Saviour's love.

1 You spoke to men, long, long ago,
  Gave us the written word;
  We read it still, needing its truth,
  Through it God's voice is heard.

2 Without Your help we fail our Lord,
  We cannot live His way;
  We need Your power, we need Your
    strength,
  Following Christ each day.

Margaret Old.

221 Come, Holy Ghost, our souls
    inspire
  And lighten with celestial fire;
  Thou the anointing Spirit art,
  Who dost Thy seven-fold gifts impart.

2 Thy blessèd unction from above
  Is comfort, life, and fire of love;
  Enable with perpetual light
  The dullness of our blinded sight.

3 Anoint and cheer our soilèd face
  With the abundance of Thy grace;
  Keep far our foes; give peace at
    home:
  Where Thou art Guide no ill can
    come.

4 Teach us to know the Father, Son,
  And Thee of Both, to be but One,
  That through the ages all along
  This may be our endless song,

  Praise to Thine eternal merit,
  Father, Son, and Holy Spirit. Amen.

trs. John Cosin.

222 Spirit of faith, come down,
    Reveal the things of God;
  And make to us the Godhead known,
  And witness with the blood.
  'Tis Thine the blood to apply,
  And give us eyes to see
  Who did for every sinner die
  Hath surely died for me.

2 No man can truly say
  That Jesus is the Lord,
  Unless Thou take the veil away,
  And breathe the living word;
  Then, only then, we feel
  Our interest in His blood,
  And cry, with joy unspeakable:
  Thou art my Lord, my God!

3 O that the world might know
  The all atoning Lamb!
  Spirit of faith, descend, and show
  The virtue of His name;
  The grace which all may find,
  The saving power impart;
  And testify to all mankind,
  And speak in every heart.

4 Inspire the living faith,
  Which whosoe'er receives,
  The witness in himself he hath,
  And consciously believes;
  That faith that conquers all,
  And doth the mountain move,
  And saves whoe'er on Jesus call,
  And perfects them in love.

Charles Wesley.

223 O Breath of God, breathe on us
    now,
  And move within us while we pray;
  The spring of our new life art Thou,
  The very light of our new day.

2 O strangely art Thou with us, Lord,
  Neither in height nor depth to seek:
  In nearness shall Thy voice be heard;
  Spirit to spirit Thou dost speak.

3 Christ is our Advocate on high:
  Thou art our Advocate within.
  O plead the truth, and make reply
  To every argument of sin.

4 But ah, this faithless heart of mine!
The way I know; I know my guide:
Forgive me, O my Friend divine,
That I so often turn aside.

5 Be with me when no other friend
The mystery of my heart can share;
And be Thou known, when fears
    transcend,
By Thy best Name of Comforter.
A. H. Vine.

224 Thy Holy Spirit, Lord, alone
    Can turn our hearts from sin;
His power alone can sanctify
And keep us pure within.
O Spirit of Faith and Love!
Come in our midst, we pray,
And purify each waiting heart;
Baptize us with power today!

2 Thy Holy Spirit, Lord, alone
Can deeper love inspire;
His power alone within our souls
Can light the sacred fire.
O Spirit of Faith and Love!
Come in our midst, we pray,
And purify each waiting heart;
Baptize us with power today!

3 Thy Holy Spirit, Lord, can bring
The gifts we seek in prayer;
His voice can words of comfort speak,
And still each wave of care.
O Spirit of Faith and Love!
Come in our midst, we pray,
And purify each waiting heart;
Baptize us with power today!

4 Thy Holy Spirit, Lord, can give
The grace we need this hour;
And while we wait, O Spirit, come
In sanctifying power!
O Spirit of Love! descend,
Come in our midst, we pray,
And, like a rushing, mighty wind,
Sweep over our souls today!
Henrietta E. Blair.

225 For Your gift of God the Spirit,
    Power to make our lives anew,
Pledge of life and hope of glory,
Saviour, we would worship You.

2 He Who in creation's dawning
Brooded o'er the pathless deep,
Still across our nature's darkness
Moves to wake our souls from sleep.

3 He Himself, the living Author,
Wakes to life the sacred word;
Reads with us its holy pages,
And reveals our risen Lord.

4 He it is who works within us,
Teaching rebel hearts to pray;
He whose holy intercessions
Rise for us both night and day.

5 He, the mighty God, indwells us:
His to strengthen, help, empower;
His to overcome the tempter—
Ours to call in danger's hour.

6 In His strength we dare to battle
All the raging hosts of sin,
And by Him alone we conquer
Foes without and foes within.

7 Fill us with Your holy fullness,
God the Father, Spirit, Son;
In us, through us, then, forever,
Shall Your perfect will be done.
Margaret Clarkson.

THE PENTECOSTAL FULNESS

226 I'm rejoicing night and day,
    As I walk the pilgrim way,
For the hand of God in all my life I see,
And the reason of my bliss,
Yes, the secret all is this:
That the Comforter abides with me.

He abides, . . . He abides, . . .
Hallelujah, He abides with me!
I'm rejoicing night and day,
As I walk the narrow way,
For the Comforter abides with me.

2 Once my heart was full of sin,
Once I had no peace within,
Till I heard how Jesus died upon the
    Tree;
Then I fell down at His feet,
And there came a peace so sweet,
Now the Comforter abides with me.

3 He is with me everywhere,
And He knows my every care,
I'm as happy as a bird and just as free;
For the Spirit has control,
Jesus satisfies my soul,
Since the Comforter abides with me.

4 There's no thirsting for the things
Of the world—they've taken wings;
Long ago I gave them up, and
instantly
All my night was turned to day,
All my burdens rolled away,
Now the Comforter abides with me.

Herbert Buffum.

227 Oh, spread the tidings round,
wherever man is found,
Wherever human hearts and human
woes abound;
Let every Christian tongue proclaim
the joyful sound:
The Comforter has come!

The Comforter has come, the Comforter has
come!
The Holy Ghost from Heaven, the Father's
promise given;
Oh, spread the tidings round, wherever man
is found—
The Comforter has come!

2 Lo, the great King of kings, with
healing in His wings,
To every captive soul a full deliverance
brings;
And through the vacant cells the song
of triumph rings;
The Comforter has come!

3 O boundless Love divine! how shall
this tongue of mine
To wondering mortals tell the matchless grace divine—
That I a child of hell, should in His
image shine!
The Comforter has come!

4 Sing, till the echoes fly above the
vaulted sky,
And all the saints above to all below
reply,
In strains of endless love, the song
that ne'er will die:
The Comforter has come!

F. Bottome.

228 'The Holy Spirit's power Ye need,'
the Master said;
'So wait till comes the hour
When on you He is shed.'
So praise did all their souls employ
As tarried they with fervent joy.

2 And when ten days were passed
With one accord were they,
Heaven's windows long closed fast,
Were opened on that day;
With rushing mighty wind and flame,
The promised Holy Spirit came.

3 Their loosened tongues were filled
With strange and wondrous words;
Heaven's life their hearts had thrilled,
God's goodness they declared;
'And unto all,' th' Apostle said,
'Is the like gift, since Christ has bled'.

4 Come now, ye sons of men,
This message now receive
The Holy Spirit's given
To all who will believe;
Ye, too, may know His mighty power,
And speak with tongues this very
hour.

5 Then charity divine,
Your yearning hearts shall fill
T'wards those who now repine,
Held in sin's bondage still;
For these your zeal shall never tire
To snatch them from th' e'erlasting
fire.

E. T. Mellor.

229 Are you looking for the fulness of
the blessing of the Lord
In your heart and life today?
Claim the promise of your Father,
come according to His word,
In the blessèd old-time way.

He will fill your heart today to overflow . . .
ing,
As the Lord commandeth you, 'Bring your
vessels, not a few';
He will fill your heart today to overflow . . .
ing
With the Holy Ghost and power.

2 Bring your empty earthen vessels,
  clean through Jesus' precious blood,
Come, ye needy, one and all;
And in human consecration wait
  before the throne of God,
Till the Holy Ghost shall fall.

3 Like the cruse of oil, unfailing is His
  grace for evermore,
And His love unchanging still;
And according to His promise with
  the Holy Ghost and power,
He will every vessel fill.
                              Mrs. C. H. Morris.

230 Now I feel the sacred fire,
      Kindling, flaming, glowing,
Higher, still and rising higher,
All my soul o'erflowing;
Life immortal I receive;
Oh, the wondrous story;
I was dead, but now I live,
Glory! glory! glory!

2 Now I am from bondage freed,
  Every bond is riven,
Jesus makes me free indeed,
Just as free as Heaven;
'Tis a glorious liberty;
Oh, the wondrous story!
I was bound, but now I'm free,
Glory! glory! glory!

3 Let the testimony roll,
  Roll through every nation
Witnessing from soul to soul,
This immense salvation;
Now I know it's full and free
Oh, the wondrous story!
For I feel it saving me,
Glory! glory! glory!

4 Glory be to God on high,
  Glory be to Jesus!
He hath brought salvation nigh
From all sin He frees us;
Let the golden harps of God,
Ring the wondrous story;
Let the pilgrims shout aloud
Glory! glory! glory!

5 Let the trump of jubilee
The glad tidings thunder,
Jesus sets the captives free,
Bursts their bonds asunder;
Fetters break and dungeons fall,
Oh, the wondrous story,
This salvation's free to all,
Glory! glory! glory!

231 Ho, every one that is thirsty in
      spirit,
Ho, every one that is weary and sad;
Come to the fountain, there's fulness
  in Jesus,
All that you're longing for, come and
  be glad.

'I will pour water on him that is thirsty,
I will pour floods upon the dry ground;
Open your heart for the gift I am bringing;
While ye are seeking Me, I will be found.'

2 Child of the world, are you tired of
  your bondage?
Weary of earth-joys so false, so
  untrue?
Thirsting for God and His fulness of
  blessing?
List to the promise, a message for
  you!

3 Child of the Kingdom, be filled with
  the Spirit!
Nothing but fulness thy longing can
  meet:
'Tis the enduement for life and for
  service;
Thine is the promise, so certain, so
  sweet.
                              Lucy J. Rider.

232 O Spirit of the living God,
      In all the fullness of Thy grace,
Where'er the foot of man hath trod,
Descend on our apostate race.

2 Give tongues of fire and hearts of
  love,
To preach the reconciling word;
Give power and unction from above,
Whene'er the joyful sound is heard.

3 Be darkness, at Thy coming, light;
Confusion, order in Thy path;
Souls without strength inspire with
might;
Bid mercy triumph over wrath.

4 O Spirit of the Lord, prepare
All the round earth her God to meet;
Breathe Thou abroad like morning air
Till hearts of stone begin to beat.

5 Baptize the nations; far and nigh
The triumphs of the Cross record;
The Name of Jesus glorify,
Till every kindred call Him Lord.

James Montgomery.

HIS MANIFESTATION AND POWER

233 All around this very hour,
Falls there streams of Heavenly
power;
Falling now so full and free;
Praise the Lord, it's filling me!

Hallelujah! feel the power!
Falling like a mighty shower,
Coming now so full and free;
Praise the Lord, it's filling me!

2 Send us showers of Heavenly grace;
Let Thy presence fill this place;
Speak the word and it shall be
That Thy showers fall on me.

3 Thou alone this power canst give;
Without Thee I dare not live;
Give me power to work for Thee;
Let the stream reach even me.

Johnson Oatman.

234 God sent His mighty power
To this poor, sinful heart,
To keep me every hour,
And needful grace impart:
And since His Spirit came
To take supreme control,
The love enkindled flame
Is burning in my soul.

'Tis burning in my soul,
'Tis burning in my soul;
The fire of Heavenly love is burning in my soul;
The Holy Spirit came,
All glory to His name!
The fire of Heavenly love is burning in my soul.

2 Before the Cross I bow,
Upon the altar lay
A willing off'ring now,
My all from day to day.
My Saviour paid the price,
My name He sweetly calls;
Upon the sacrifice
The fire from Heaven falls.

3 No good that I have done,
His promise I embrace;
Accepted in the Son,
He saves me by His grace;
All glory be to God!
Let hallelujahs roll;
His love is shed abroad,
The fire is in my soul.

Delia T. White.

235 Come, Holy Ghost, our hearts
inspire,
Let us Thine influence prove;
Source of the old prophetic fire,
Fountain of light and love.

2 Come, Holy Ghost, for, moved by
Thee,
The prophets wrote and spoke;
Unlock the truth, Thyself the Key,
Unseal the sacred book.

3 Expand Thy wings, celestial Dove,
Brood o'er our nature's night;
On our disordered spirits move,
And let there now be light.

4 God, through Himself, we then shall
know,
If Thou within us shine;
And sound, with all Thy saints below,
The depths of love divine.

Charles Wesley.

236 Indwelling Power, the promise of
the Master,
Transform our lives and make our
hearts Your own,
With You as Guide, our feet may
follow faster,
Surer our step, when we are not
alone.

2 Clearer the Way, as You interpret for
   us,
   Shedding new light upon God's Holy
   Word;
   Above the noise of this world's
   clamorous chorus
   Your 'still small voice' can be dis-
   tinctly heard.

3 Voice of assurance! Voice, too, of
   conviction,
   Making us conscious of the stain of
   sin—
   We need Your cleansing, and Your
   benediction,
   Before we know a sense of peace
   within.

4 If courage fails, when called upon to
   witness,
   Bring to our minds our Master's
   words and deeds:
   We do not have to trust in human
   fitness—
   Your prompting power provides for
   all our needs.

5 When dark days come, or over-
   whelming sorrow,
   We turn to You, strong Comforter
   and Friend,
   To lead us through the stress towards
   a morrow
   Calm with a radiance that shall never
   end.

6 We celebrate Your coming, with
   thanksgiving,
   At that first Pentecost so long ago,
   And, in these days, with power for
   present living,
   Which, mighty Spirit, You on us
   bestow.
                                Eileen Abbott.

237 Come, Holy Spirit, come;
   Let Thy bright beams arise,
   Dispel the darkness from our minds
   And open all our eyes.

2 Revive our drooping faith,
   Our doubts and fears remove,
   And kindle in our hearts the flame
   Of never dying love.

3 'Tis Thine to cleanse the heart,
   To sanctify the soul,
   To pour fresh life in every part,
   And new create the whole.

4 Dwell therefore in our hearts,
   Our minds from bondage free;
   Then shall we know and praise and
   love
   The Father, Son, and Thee.
                                Joseph Hart.

238 Thy sons and daughters, Lord,
   behold,
   More precious than the finest gold,
   O guide them with Thine eye!
   Thy Holy Spirit richly pour,
   And fill their hearts this gracious hour,
   That they may prophesy.

2 May signs and wonders still be
   wrought,
   And numbers, by their preaching
   brought
   To know the truth divine:
   May all the powers of hell give way,
   And thousands, taught to sing and
   pray,
   In holy worship join.

3 Endue them, Lord, with power and
   grace,
   To preach Thy word in every place,
   To sinners born to die:
   Enlarge their power of doing good,
   That millions, sprinkled with Thy
   blood,
   May meet Thee in the sky.

4 Bring them at last to see Thy face,
   And triumph in redeeming grace,
   With all Thy saints in light;
   And, seated round Thy Throne divine,
   With angels and archangels join
   To worship in Thy sight.
                                Anon.

239 When God the Spirit came
   Upon His Church outpoured
   In sound of wind and sign of flame
   They spread His truth abroad,
   And filled with the Spirit
   Proclaimed that Christ is Lord.

2 What courage, power and grace
That youthful Church displayed!
To men of every tribe and race
They witnessed unafraid,
And filled with the Spirit
They broke their bread and prayed.

3 They saw God's Word prevail,
His Kingdom still increase,
No part of all His purpose fail,
No promised blessing cease,
And filled with the Spirit
Knew love and joy and peace.

4 Their theme was Christ alone,
The Lord who lived and died,
Who rose to His eternal Throne
At God the Father's side;
And filled with the Spirit
The Church was multiplied.

5 So to this present hour
Our task is still the same,
In Pentecostal love and power
His gospel to proclaim,
And filled with the Spirit,
Rejoice in Jesus' Name.

Timothy Dudley-Smith.

3 When the Spirit cometh,
Loosened lips shall tell,
Of the wondrous blessing
Which upon them fell;
Life of Jesus springing
Like a well within,
Hearts with loud hosannas
Constantly shall ring.

4 When with joy we follow
In Christ's triumph train,
And our lives are flooded
With the Latter Rain;
Then the world around us
Shall the impact feel,
Of a Church with vision,
Fired with holy zeal.

5 Then the Lord of glory
Shall be magnified,
He who trod the winepress,
Fully satisfied;
Walking in the Spirit,
Condemnation o'er,
Blessèd life of worship,
Now and evermore.

E. C. W. Boulton.

240 Tarry for the Spirit,
He shall come in showers,
Energizing wholly
All your ransomed powers;
Signs shall follow service
In the Holy Ghost,
Then the Church of Jesus
Prove a mighty host.

On, then, Church of Jesus,
Claim your Pentecost;
God shall now baptize thee
In the Holy Ghost.

2 'Rivers' is Thy promise,
This shall be our plea,
Less than this can never
Meet our cry for Thee;
Tired of lukewarm service,
And the loss it brings,
We would live entirely
For eternal things.

241 Born by the Holy Spirit's breath,
Loosed from the law of sin and death,
Now cleared in Christ from every claim
No judgement stands against our name.

2 In us the Spirit makes His home
That we in Him may overcome;
Christ's risen life, in all its powers,
Its all-prevailing strength, is ours.

3 Sons, then, and heirs of God most high,
We by His Spirit 'Father' cry;
That Spirit with our spirit shares
To frame and breathe our wordless prayers.

4 One is His love, His purpose one;
To form the likeness of His Son
In all who, called and justified,
Shall reign in glory at His side.

5 Nor death nor life, nor powers un-
seen,
Nor height nor depth can come
between;
We know through peril, pain and
sword,
The love of God in Christ our Lord.
Timothy Dudley-Smith.

242 Is there a mountain in your way?
Do doubts and fears abound?
Press on, oh, hear the Spirit say,
This mountain shall come down.

Not by might, not by power;
By my Spirit saith the Lord of Hosts
Not by might, not by power;
By my Spirit saith the Lord
This mountain shall be removed;
This mountain shall be removed;
This mountain shall be removed;
By my Spirit saith the Lord.

2 Is there a river in your path?
A river deep and wide?
Step in, the waters will roll back
You'll reach the other side.

3 Is there a fiery furnace trial!
Far more than you can bear?
Behold the blessèd Son of God,
Is walking with you there.

4 Then trust alone the mighty God,
He speaks the winds obey.
Take courage, then, oh fainting heart
For you He'll make a way.
Almeda Herrick.

243 Lord, as of old at Pentecost
Thou didst Thy power display,
With cleansing, purifying flame
Descend on us today.

Lord, send the old-time power, the
Pentecostal power!
Thy flood-gates of blessing on us throw
open wide!
Lord, send the old-time power, the
Pentecostal power,
That sinners be converted and Thy Name
glorified!

2 For mighty works for Thee prepare,
And strengthen every heart;
Come, take possession of Thine own,
And never more depart.

3 All self consume, all sin destroy!
With earnest zeal endue
Each waiting heart to work for Thee;
O Lord, our faith renew!

4 Speak, Lord! before Thy throne we
wait,
Thy promise we believe,
And will not let Thee go until
The blessing we receive!
Charlotte G. Homer.

244 When first the risen Lord of power
His chosen ones sent forth,
A charge He gave, that solemn hour,
To preach His saving worth.
'Go ye', said He, 'to all mankind;
Declare My Word and ye shall find:
These signs shall surely follow them
Who on My Name believe.'

2 'No demons shall before them stand,
No poison do them harm;
Nor subtle serpent in their hand
Cause pain or dread alarm.'
For Satan's kingdom He o'ercame,
To give His people right to claim:
These signs shall surely follow them
Who on My Name believe.

3 'They shall with other tongues declare
The wonders of their God:
The sick beneath their hands, by
prayer,
Shall rise to prove My Word.'
So let it be! Firm as His Throne
Stands this clear promise to His own:
These signs shall surely follow them
Who on My Name believe.

4 Crowned with the flame of Pentecost,
A faithful, fearless band
Proclaimed His Name: a ransomed
host
Arose from every land.
The Lord worked with them from on
High,
His proven Word could none deny:
These signs shall surely follow them
Who on My Name believe.

5 No word of Thine is void of power;
No promise, Lord, is vain.
Be this a Pentecostal hour—
Confirm Thy Word again!
Nor can'st Thou fail! Thou art the same
As when of old Thou did'st proclaim:
These signs shall surely follow them
Who on My Name believe.

L. F. W. Woodford.

PENTECOSTAL REVIVAL

245 Floods of revival,
Lord, let them fall;
Streams of salvation
Reaching to all.
Pour out Thy Spirit,
Great is our need;
Sweep o'er our beings
Now whilst we plead.

Spirit divine, O quicken us now,
Whilst in Thy presence, humbly we bow,
Set all our hearts ablaze with Thy love,
Teach us the secret of life from above.

2 Utterly yielded,
Longing to know
All the blest fulness
Love can bestow.
Ready and willing,
Eager to give
Perfect obedience,
Bravely to live.

3 Raise up a people
Holy and free;
Hearts with a vision
Like unto Thee;
Souls that would rather
Die than give in;
Lives with a passion
Victory to win.

4 O for a deluge—
Holy Ghost power;
Lord we are waiting,
Send it this hour.
Open the windows
Of Heaven we pray;
All on the altar
Gladly we lay.

E. C. W. Boulton.

246 There's a sound upon the waters,
There's a murmur in the air,
For a wave of coming glory moves my soul;
There's the sign of a revival—
All ye saints, prepare for war;
For the hosts of God are marching to the goal.

Hallelujah! Hallelujah! Hallelujah to the Lord;
We shall triumph, we shall triumph
Through the everlasting Word;
There's a sound upon the waters,
There's a murmur in the air;
For a sound of coming glory moves my soul.

2 Sing, the Lord has come to battle,
He's a mighty Man of war,
He is girding on the sword to smite the foe;
He will lead His people onward
In the fulness of His power—
Hark! the hosts of God are singing as they go.

3 We are coming, we are coming
To the help of Judah's King,
Every heart and hand is ready for the fray;
Lift the Banner of Salvation,
Jesus leads us—march away!
Glory, glory, we shall win the well-fought day!

J. Flanagan.

247 They were gathered in an upper chamber,
As commanded by the risen Lord,
And the promise of the Father
There they sought with one accord,
When the Holy Ghost from Heaven descended
Like a rushing wind and tongues of fire:
So, dear Lord, we seek Thy blessing,
Come with glory now our hearts inspire.

Let the fire fall, let the fire fall,
Let the fire from Heaven fall; . . .
We are waiting and expecting,
Now in faith, dear Lord, we call; . . .
Let the fire fall, let the fire fall,
On Thy promise we depend;
From the glory of Thy presence
Let the Pentecostal fire descend.

2 As Elijah we would raise the altar
For our testimony clear and true,
Christ the Saviour, loving Healer,
Coming Lord, Baptizer too,
Ever-flowing grace and full salvation
For a ruined race Thy love has planned;
For this blessèd revelation,
For Thy written Word we dare to stand.

3 'Tis the covenanted promise given
To as many as the Lord shall call,
To the fathers and their children,
To Thy people, one and all;
So rejoicing in Thy word unfailing,
We draw nigh in faith Thy power to know—
Come, O come, Thou burning Spirit,
Set our hearts with Heavenly fire aglow.

4 With a living coal from off Thy altar
Touch our lips to swell Thy wondrous praise,
To extol Thee, bless, adore Thee,
And our songs of worship raise;
Let the cloud of glory now descending
Fill our hearts with holy ecstasy,
Come in all Thy glorious fulness,
Blessèd Holy Spirit, have Thy way.

H. Tee.

248 Coming now to Thee, O Christ my Lord,
Trusting only in Thy precious word,
Let my humble prayer to Thee be heard,
And send a great revival in my soul.

Send a great revival in my soul,
Send a great revival in my soul;
Let the Holy Spirit come and take control,
And send a great revival in my soul. . . .

2 Send a great revival, Lord, in me,
Help me that I may rejoice in Thee;
Give me strength to win the victory,
And send a great revival in my soul.

3 Help me go for Thee, dear Lord, today,
To some lonely soul that's gone astray;

Help me lead them in the homeward way,
Oh, send a great revival in my soul.

B. B. McKinney.

249 There'll be showers of blessing
from our Father's hand,
On His word of promise we may firmly stand;
There'll be rains refreshing on the thirsty land
When the tithes are gathered in.

Tithes of love and willing service,
Tithes of silver and of gold;
When the tithes are gathered in,
When the tithes are gathered in
There'll be blessings more than we can contain,
When the tithes are gathered in.

2 There'll be shouts of triumph from the conquering host,
There'll be perfect freedom in the Holy Ghost;
Every one empowered as at Pentecost,
When the tithes are gathered in.

3 Then will come the dawning of the reign of peace,
When the wars and conflicts shall forever cease,
And for struggling saints shall come a sweet release,
When the tithes are gathered in.

4 We will rob no longer, then, our Lord and King,
What to Him belongeth we will gladly bring,
And we'll shout hosanna, while the glad harps ring,
When the tithes are gathered in.

Mrs. C. H. Morris.

250 For a world-wide revival,
Blessèd Master we pray,
Let the power of the Highest,
Be upon us today;
For this world dearly purchased,
By the blood of God's Son,
Back from Satan's dominion,
And from sin must be won.

Send the power, Oh Lord,
Send the power, Oh Lord,
Send the Holy Ghost power, let it now be
outpoured,
Send it surging and sweeping like the waves of
the sea,
Send a world-wide revival, and begin it in me.

2 Send the showers of blessing,
As declared in Thy Word,
Let the Spirit of promise,
On all flesh be outpoured;
Send the Latter Rain on us,
Till the land overflows,
Till the desert rejoicing,
Blossoms forth as the rose.

3 There's a sound of a going
In the mulberry trees,
News of nations awaking,
Borne upon ev'ry breeze;
For the prayers of His children,
God in mercy doth own,
The revival's beginning,
And the power's coming down.

Mrs. C. H. Morris.

251 God is here, and that to bless us
With the Spirit's quickening
power;
See the cloud already bending,
Waits to drop the grateful shower.

Let it come, O Lord, we pray Thee,
Let the shower of blessing fall:
We are waiting, we are waiting,
Oh, revive the hearts of all.

2 God is here! we feel His presence
In this consecrated place;
But we need the soul refreshing
Of His free unbounded grace.

3 God is here! oh, then, believing,
Bring to Him our one desire;
That His love may now be kindled,
Till its flame each heart inspire.

4 Saviour, grant the prayer we offer,
While in simple faith we bow,
From the windows of Thy mercy
Pour us out a blessing now.

James L. Black.

252 Here in Thy Name we are
gathered,
Come and revive us, O Lord;
'There shall be showers of blessing',
Thou hast declared in Thy Word.

Oh, graciously hear us,
Graciously hear us we pray:
Pour from Thy windows upon us
Showers of blessing today.

2 Oh! that the showers of blessing
Now on our souls may descend,
While at the footstool of mercy
Pleading Thy promise we bend!

3 'There shall be showers of blessing',
Promise that never can fail;
Thou wilt regard our petition;
Surely our faith will prevail.

4 Showers of blessing, we need them,
Showers of blessing from Thee;
Showers of blessing, oh, grant them,
Thine all the glory shall be.

Jennie Garnett.

253 In Thy name, O blessèd Saviour,
Gathered in this sacred place;
Here we seek a Father's blessing,
Plead and pray for needed grace;
From the ocean of Thy fulness,
Boundless, fathomless and free;
Let a tidal wave come sweeping,
Setting hearts at liberty.

Lift the floodgates, lift the floodgates,
Let the tide come sweeping in;
Blessèd tide of full salvation,
Washing, cleansing, from all sin.

2 Lift the floodgates, let salvation
In tremendous currents flow,
To the uttermost fulfilling
Thy blest mission here below;
Until myriads of sinners,
Borne on love's resistless tide,
Shall be swept into the Kingdom,
And believers sanctified.

3 It is coming, we believe it,
Thou dost hear and answer prayer;
It is coming, we shall see it,
Thine almighty arm made bare;

Tides of power, tides of glory,
Holy tides of perfect love,
Satisfying, overflowing,
Coming on us from above.
Mrs. C. H. Morris.

---

254 Joys are flowing like a river,
Since the Comforter has come;
He abides with us forever,
Makes the trusting heart His home.

Blessèd quietness, holy quietness,
What assurance in my soul!
On the stormy sea, He speaks peace to me,
How the billows cease to roll.

2 Bringing life, and health, and gladness,
All around this Heavenly Guest;
Banished unbelief and sadness,
Changed our weariness to rest.

3 Like the rain that falls from heaven,
Like the sunlight from the sky,
So the Holy Ghost is given,
Coming on us from on high.

4 What a wonderful salvation,
Where we always see His face;
What a perfect habitation,
What a quiet resting-place.
Mamie Payne Ferguson.

---

255 Revive Thy work, O Lord!
Thy mighty arm make bare;
Speak with the voice that wakes the dead,
And make Thy people hear!

Revive Thy work, O Lord,
While here to Thee we bow;
Descend, O gracious Lord, descend,
Oh, come and bless us now.

2 Revive Thy work, O Lord!
Disturb this sleep of death;
Quicken the smouldering embers now
By Thine Almighty breath.

3 Revive Thy work, O Lord!
Create soul-thirst for Thee;
And hung'ring for the bread of life,
Oh, may our spirits be!

4 Revive Thy work, O Lord!
Exalt Thy precious Name:
And by the Holy Ghost, our love
For Thee and Thine inflame.
Albert Midlane
arr. Fanny J. Crosby.

---

256 Search me, O God, and know my heart today;
Try me, O Lord, and know my thoughts I pray:
See if there be some wicked way in me,
Cleanse me from every sin and set me free.

2 I praise Thee, Lord, for cleansing me from sin;
Fulfil Thy Word, and make me pure within;
Fill me with fire, where once I burned with shame
Grant my desire to magnify Thy Name.

3 Lord, take my life, and make it wholly Thine;
Fill my poor heart with Thy great love divine;
Take all my will, my passion, self and pride;
I now surrender—Lord, in me abide.

4 O Holy Ghost, revival comes from Thee;
Send a revival—start the work in me:
Thy Word declares Thou wilt supply our need;
For blessing now, O Lord, I humbly plead.
Edwin Orr.

---

257 Thou Christ of burning, cleansing flame,
Send the fire!
Thy blood-bought gift today we claim,
Send the fire!
Look down and see this waiting host,
Give us the promised Holy Ghost,
We want another Pentecost,
Send the fire!

2 God of Elijah, hear our cry!
Send the fire!
Oh, make us fit to live or die!
Send the fire!
To burn up every trace of sin,
To bring the light and glory in,
The revolution now begin,
Send the fire!

3 'Tis fire we want, for fire we plead,
Send the fire!
The fire will meet our every need,
Send the fire!
For strength to ever do the right,
For grace to conquer in the fight,
For power to walk the world in white,
Send the fire!

4 To make our weak heart strong and brave,
Send the fire!
To live a dying world to save,
Send the fire!
Oh, see us on Thy altar lay
Our lives, our all, this very day;
To crown the offering now, we pray,
Send the fire!

William Booth.

258 There's a shout in the camp 'Keep the fires brightly burning
All the night long,'
That the lost may return to the fold of the shepherd
From paths of wrong.

There's a shout in the camp, Hallelujah!
Glory to God!
There's an echo in Heaven, Hallelujah!
Glory to God!

2 There's a shout in the camp for the victory is coming
O'er Satan's power;
Through the word of the Lord we the battle are gaining
This very hour.

3 There's a shout in the camp over sinners returning
Home to the fold,
From the byways of sin with its burden of sorrow
To joy untold.

4 There's a shout in the camp, 'tis a glad 'Hallelujah!
Praise ye the Lord!'
All who trust in His Name shall receive His salvation,
'Tis God's own word.

C. Austin Miles.

259 'There shall be showers of blessing':
This is the promise of love;
There shall be seasons refreshing,
Sent from the Saviour above.

Show . . .ers of blessing,
Showers of blessing we need;
Mercy drops round us are falling,
But for the showers we plead.

2 'There shall be showers of blessing' —
Precious reviving again;
Over the hills and the valleys,
Sound of abundance of rain.

3 'There shall be showers of blessing':
Send them upon us, O Lord!
Grant to us now a refreshing;
Come, and now honour Thy Word.

4 'There shall be showers of blessing',
Oh, that today they might fall,
Now, as to God, we're confessing,
Now as on Jesus we call!

5 'There shall be showers of blessing',
If we but trust and obey;
There shall be seasons refreshing,
If we let God have His way.

El Nathan.

Section V

THE HOLY SCRIPTURES

260 These are the facts as we have
    received them,
These are the truths that the Christian
    believes,
This is the basis of all our preaching,
Christ died for sinners and rose from
    the tomb.

2 These are the facts as we have
    received them,
Christ has fulfilled what the Scriptures
    foretold,
Adam's whole family in death had
    been sleeping,
Christ through His rising restores us
    to life.

3 These are the facts as we have
    received them,
We, with our Saviour, have died on
    the Cross,
Now, having risen, our Jesus lives in
    us,
Give us His Spirit and makes us His
    home.

4 These are the facts as we have
    received them,
We shall be changed in the blink of an
    eye,
Trumpets shall sound as we face life
    immortal,
This is the victory through Jesus, our
    Lord.

5 These are the facts as we have
    received them,
These are the truths that the Christian
    believes,
This is the basis of all our preaching,
Christ died for sinners and rose from
    the tomb.

Michael Saward.

261 Break Thou the bread of life,
    Dear Lord, to me,
As Thou didst break the loaves

Beside the sea,
Beyond the sacred page
I seek Thee, Lord;
My spirit pants for Thee,
O Living Word!

2 Break Thou the bread of life,
    O Lord, to me,
That hid within my heart
Thy Word may be:
Mould Thou each inward thought,
From self set free,
And let my steps be all
Controlled by Thee.

3 Open Thy Word of Truth,
    That I may see
Thy message written clear
And plain for me;
Then in sweet fellowship
Walking with Thee,
Thine image on my life
Engraved will be.

4 O send Thy Spirit, Lord,
    Now unto me,
That He may touch my eyes
And make me see:
Show me the truth concealed
Within Thy Word,
And in Thy Book revealed
I see the Lord.

5 Bless Thou the truth, dear Lord,
    To me, to me,
As Thou didst bless the bread
By Galilee:
Then shall all bondage cease,
All fetters fall;
And I shall find my peace,
My All in All!

Mary A. Lathbury
verse 4 Alexander Groves.

262 Hungry, Lord, for Thy Word of
    truth,
Sitting at my Saviour's feet;
Rising, gleaning, just like Ruth,
Feed me on the finest of the wheat.

Bread of life it is now to me,
Honey, wine and meat;
In Thy love I will ever be
Fed upon the finest of the wheat.

2 Work for the Master I will do,
Trusting in His strength so great;
Living in His pastures new,
Feed me on the finest of the wheat.

3 Then to the harvest let us go,
Reaping in His fields so sweet;
Workers for Jesus, He wants you
Fed upon the finest of the wheat.

F. A. Graves.

263 How firm a foundation, ye saints
of the Lord,
Is laid for your faith in His excellent
Word!
What more can He say than to you He
hath said,
You who unto Jesus for refuge have
fled?

2 Fear not, I am with Thee, O be not
dismayed!
I, I am thy God and will still give Thee
aid:
I'll strengthen thee, help thee, and
cause thee to stand,
Upheld by My righteous, omnipotent
hand.

3 When through the deep waters I call
thee to go,
The rivers of grief shall not thee overflow:
For I will be with thee in trouble to
bless:
And sanctify to thee thy deepest
distress.

4 The soul that on Jesus hath leaned for
repose,
I will not, I will not, desert to its foes!
That soul, though all hell should
endeavour to shake,
I'll never, no, never, no, never,
forsake!

George Keith.

264 Powerful in making us wise to
salvation,
Witness to faith in Christ Jesus the
Word;
Breathed out to men by the life-giving
Father—
These are the Scriptures, and thus
speaks the Lord.

2 Tool for employment and compass
for travel,
Map in the desert and lamp in the
dark,
Teaching, rebuking, correcting, and
training—
These are the Scriptures, and this is
their work.

3 Prophecy, history, and song, and
commandment,
Gospel and letter and dream from on
high;
Written by men borne along by the
Spirit—
These are the Scriptures; on them we
rely.

4 Gift for God's servants to fit them
completely,
Fully equipping to walk in His ways;
Guide to good work and effective
believing—
These are the Scriptures; for these we
give praise!

Christopher Idle.

265 Lord, Thy Word abideth,
And our footsteps guideth,
Who its truth believeth,
Light and joy receiveth.

2 When our foes are near us,
Then Thy Word doth cheer us,
Word of consolation,
Message of salvation.

3 When the storms are o'er us,
And dark clouds before us,
Then its light directeth,
And our way protecteth.

4 Who can tell the pleasure,
Who recount the treasure,
By Thy Word imparted
To the simple-hearted?

5 Word of mercy, giving
Succour to the living;
Word of life, supplying
Comfort to the dying!

6 O that we, discerning
Its most holy learning,
Lord, may love and fear Thee,
Evermore be near Thee!
H. W. Baker.

266 Oh, wonderful, wonderful Word
of the Lord!
True wisdom its pages unfold:
And though we may read them a
thousand times o'er,
They never, no, never grow old.
Each line hath a treasure, each
promise a pearl,
That all if they will may secure;
And we know that when time and the
world pass away,
God's Word shall for ever endure.

2 Oh, wonderful, wonderful Word of
the Lord!
The Lamp that our Father above
So kindly has lighted to teach us the
way
That leads to the arms of His love!
Its warnings, its counsels, are faithful
and just;
Its judgments are perfect and pure;
And we know that when time and the
world pass away,
God's Word shall for ever endure.

3 Oh, wonderful, wonderful Word of
the Lord!
Our only salvation is there;
It carries conviction down deep in the
heart,
And shows us ourselves as we are.
It tells of a Saviour, and points to the
Cross,
Where pardon we now may secure;
For we know that when time and the
world pass away,
God's Word shall for ever endure.

4 Oh, wonderful, wonderful Word of
the Lord!
The hope of our friends in the past;
Its truth where so firmly they
anchored their trust,
Through ages eternal shall last.
Oh, wonderful, wonderful Word of
the Lord!
Unchanging, abiding, and sure;
For we know that when time and the
world pass away,
God's Word shall for ever endure.
Julia Sterling.

267 Standing on the promises of
Christ our King,
Through eternal ages let His praises
ring:
Glory in the highest, I will shout and
sing,
Standing on the promises of God.

Stand . . . ing, stand . . . ing,
Standing on the promises of God my
Saviour,
Stand . . . ing, stand . . . ing,
I'm standing on the promises of God.

2 Standing on the promises that cannot
fail,
When the howling storms of doubt
and fear assail
By the living word of God I shall
prevail,
Standing on the promises of God.

3 Standing on the promises I now can
see
Perfect, present cleansing in the
blood for me;
Standing in the liberty where Christ
makes free,
Standing on the promises of God.

4 Standing on the promises of Christ
the Lord,
Bound to Him eternally by love's
strong cord,
Overcoming daily with the Spirit's
sword,
Standing on the promises of God.
R. Kelso Carter.

268 May words of truth inform our minds
That we may understand Your will,
And see, with open eyes, how best
Your purposes we may fulfil.

2 May words of righteousness make plain
How much our lives are spoiled by sin.
Grant open ears that we may learn
The way to conquer sin within.

3 May words of comfort, love and peace
Dispel anxiety and care.
Within open heart, filled from above,
May loving deeds replace despair.

4 May words of life, from Christ our Lord,
Give us each day a worthy aim
With ready hands, grant we may work
With zeal to glorify His name.

Peter Tongeman.

269 Thy words unto my taste are sweet,
O Lord of hosts, Thy truth I love;
The light it sheds before my feet
Streams from Thy dazzling place above.

2 O joy, within the page to find
Such wondrous treasures all my own;
To trace the mysteries of Thy mind,
And reach the splendours of Thy throne!

3 No human wisdom touched that height,
No creature tongue sang that high strain;
Thy breath breathed forth the holy light,
Thy finger scrolled the message plain.

4 Yet, Mighty Word, Thou stoopedst low
To faltering lip and feeble hand,
For humble men spake long ago
Such wisdom as Thy Spirit planned.

5 To profit him that hungereth
With rich delight and doctrine pure,
To quicken love and strengthen faith
And make His Heavenly calling sure.

6 O Truth, Who grandly traced the way,
O Love, Who trod it with delight,
Grant all Thy children grace, we pray,
To walk well-pleasing in Thy sight.

Harold Horton.

Section VI

THE GOSPEL

PROCLAMATION AND INVITATION

270 Go forth and tell! O Church of God, awake!
God's saving news to all the nations take.
Proclaim Christ Jesus, Saviour, Lord and King,
That all the world His worthy praise may sing.

2 Go forth and tell! God's love embraces all:
He will in grace respond to all who call.

How shall they call if they have never heard
The gracious invitation of His Word?

3 Go forth and tell! Men still in darkness lie:
In wealth or want, in sin they live and die.
Give us, O Lord, concern of heart and mind,
A love like yours which cares for all mankind.

4 Go forth and tell! The doors are open wide:

Share God's good gifts with men so
  long denied.
Live out your life as Christ, your Lord,
  shall choose,
Your ransomed powers for His sole
  glory use.

5 Go forth and tell! O Church of God,
  arise:
Go in the strength which Christ your
  Lord supplies.
Go, till all nations His great Name
  adore
And serve Him Lord and King for
  evermore.

J. E. Seddon.

271 Is there a heart that is willing to lay
  Burdens on Jesus' breast?
He is so loving and gentle and true,
Come unto Him and rest.

  Lord, it is I who need Thy love!
  Need Thy strength and power;
  O keep me, use me, and hold me fast!
  Each moment, each day, each hour.

2 Is there a heart that is lonely today
Needing a faithful Friend?
Jesus will always keep close by your
  side,
Loving you to the end.

3 Is there a heart that has failed to o'er-
  come
Sin with its mighty power?
Jesus is stronger than Satan and sin,
Trust Him this very hour.

4 Is there a heart that is longing to bring
Blessing to some lost soul?
Jesus is willing the weakest to use,
Let Him Thy life control.

M. R. Boyd and F. P. Wood.

272 I love to tell the story
  Of unseen things above,
Of Jesus and His glory,
Of Jesus and His love;
I love to tell the story
Because I know it's true,
It satisfies my longings,
As nothing else would do.

2 I love to tell the story,
More wonderful it seems
Than all the golden fancies
Of all the golden dreams;
I love to tell the story,
It did so much for me,
And this is just the reason
I tell it now to thee.

3 I love to tell the story,
'Tis pleasant to repeat
What seems, each time I tell it,
More wonderfully sweet:
I love to tell the story,
For some have never heard
The message of salvation
From God's own holy Word.

4 I love to tell the story,
For those who know it best
Seem hungering and thirsting
To hear it, like the rest;
And when, in scenes of glory,
I sing the new, new song,
'Twill be—the old, old story
That I have loved so long.

Kate Hankey.

273 Come every soul by sin
  oppressed,
There's mercy with the Lord,
And He will surely give you rest
By trusting in His Word.

  Only trust Him, only trust Him,
  Only trust Him now,
  He will save you, He will save you,
  He will save you now.

2 For Jesus shed His precious blood
Rich blessings to bestow,
Plunge now into the crimson flood
That washes white as snow.

3 Yes, Jesus is the truth, the way
That leads you into rest,
Believe in Him without delay
And you are fully blest.

4 Come, then, and join this holy band,
And on to glory go,
To dwell in that celestial land
Where joys immortal flow.

John H. Stockton.

The Gospel

274 A ruler once came to Jesus by night,
To ask Him the way of salvation and light;
The Master made answer in words true and plain,
'Ye must be born again!'

'Ye must be born again . . .!
Ye must be born again . . .!
I verily, verily say unto you—
Ye must be born again . . .!'

2 Ye children of men attend to the word
So solemnly uttered by Jesus, the Lord,
And let not this message to you be in vain,
'Ye must be born again!'

3 O ye who would enter the glorious rest,
And sing with the ransomed the song of the blest;
The life everlasting if ye would obtain,
'Ye must be born again!'

4 A dear one in Heaven thy heart yearns to see,
At the beautiful gates may be watching for thee;
Then list to the note of this solemn refrain,
'Ye must be born again!'

W. T. Sleeper.

275 Beautiful words of Jesus,
Spoken so long ago,
Yet, as we sing them over,
Dearer to us they grow,
Calling the heavy laden,
Calling to hearts oppressed,
'Come unto Me, ye weary,
Come, I will give you rest.'

Hear the call of His voice so sweet;
Bring your load to the Saviour's feet;
Lean your heart on His loving breast
Come, O come and He will give you rest.

2 Beautiful words of Jesus,
Cheering us, day by day;
Throwing a gleam of sunshine
Over a cloudy way:

Casting on Him the burden
We are too weak to bear,
He will give grace sufficient,
He will regard our prayer.

3 Beautiful words of Jesus,
Tokens of endless rest,
When, by and by, we enter
Into His presence blest;
There shall we see His beauty,
Meet with Him face to face;
There shall we sing His glory,
Praising His matchless grace.

E. E. Hewitt.

276 Come, let us sing of a wonderful love,
Tender and true;
Out of the heart of the Father above,
Streaming to me and to you.
Wonderful love,
Dwells in the heart of the Father above.

2 Jesus the Saviour this Gospel to tell
Joyfully came—
Came with the helpless and hopeless to dwell,
Sharing their sorrow and shame:
Seeking the lost,
Saving, redeeming at measureless cost.

3 Jesus is seeking the wanderers yet—
Why do they roam?
Love only waits to forgive and forget:
Home! weary wanderers, home!
Wonderful love,
Dwells in the heart of the Father above.

4 Come to my heart, O Thou wonderful love!
Come and abide;
Lifting my life till it rises above
Envy and falsehood and pride:
Seeking to be,
Lowly and humble, a learner of Thee.

Robert Walmsley.

277 Free from the law, oh, happy
condition,
Jesus hath bled, and there is
remission,
Cursed by the law and bruised by the
fall,
Grace hath redeemed us once for all.

Once for all, oh, sinner receive it,
Once for all, oh, brother believe it;
Cling to the Cross, the burden will fall,
Christ hath redeemed us once for all.

2 Now are we free—there's no con-
demnation,
Jesus provides a perfect salvation;
'Come unto Me,' oh, hear His sweet
call,
Come, and He saves us once for all.

3 'Children of God,' oh, glorious calling,
Surely His grace will keep us from
falling;
Passing from death to life at His call,
Blessèd salvation once for all.

Philipp Bliss.

278 Hark! the gospel news is
sounding,
Christ has suffered on the Tree;
Streams of mercy are abounding,
Grace for all is rich and free.
Now, poor sinner,
Come to Him who died for thee.

2 Oh! escape to yonder mountain,
Refuge find in Him today;
Christ invites you to the fountain,
Come and wash your sins away;
Do not tarry,
Come to Jesus while you may.

3 Grace is flowing like a river,
Millions there have been supplied;
Still it flows as fresh as ever
From the Saviour's wounded side;
None need perish,
All may live, for Christ hath died.

4 Christ alone shall be our portion;
Soon we hope to meet above;
Then we'll bathe in the full ocean
Of the great Redeemer's love;

All His fulness
We shall then forever prove.

H. Bourne and W. Sanders.

279 Hark! 'tis the Shepherd's voice I
hear,
Out in the desert dark and drear,
Calling the lambs who've gone astray,
Far from the Shepherd's fold away.

Bring them in, bring them in,
Bring them in from the fields of sin;
Bring them in, bring them in,
Bring the wandering ones to Jesus.

2 Who'll go and help this Shepherd
kind,
Help Him the wandering lambs to
find?
Who'll bring the lost ones to the fold,
Where they'll be sheltered from the
cold?

3 Out in the desert hear their cry:
Out on the mountain wild and high;
Hark! 'tis the Master speaks to thee,
'Go, find My lambs, where'er they
be!'

Alexcenah Thomas.

280 Hark! there comes a whisper,
Stealing on thine ear;
'Tis the Saviour calling,
Soft, soft and clear.

'Give thy heart to Me, to Me,
Once I died for thee, for thee';
Hark! hark! thy Saviour calls:
Come, sinner, come!

2 With that voice so gentle,
Dost thou hear Him say?
'Tell Me all thy sorrows;
Come, come away!'

3 Would'st thou find a refuge
For thy soul opprest?
Jesus kindly answers,
'I am thy rest.'

4 At the Cross of Jesus
Let thy burden fall;
While He gently whispers,
'I'll bear it all.'

Fanny J. Crosby.

The Gospel

281 Come with me, visit Calvary,
   Where our Redeemer died;
His blood, it fills the fountain,
'Tis full, 'tis deep, 'tis wide.
He died from sin so sever,
Our hearts and lives complete;
He saves and keeps for ever
Those lying at His feet.

   To the uttermost He saves,
   To the uttermost He saves,
   Dare you now believe and His love receive,
   To the uttermost Jesus saves.

2 I will surrender fully,
   And do His blessèd will;
His blood doth make me holy,
His presence me doth fill.
He's saving, I'm believing,
This blessing now I claim:
His Spirit I'm receiving,
My heart is in a flame.

3 I've wondrous peace through trusting,
   A well of joy within;
This rest is everlasting,
Each day I triumph win.
He gives me Heavenly measure
'Pressed down' and 'running o'er,'
Oh, what a priceless treasure,
Glory for evermore!

                                    J. Lawley.

282 Days are filled with sorrow and
   care,
Hearts are lonely and drear;
Burdens are lifted at Calvary,
Jesus is very near.

   Burdens are lifted at Calvary,
   Calvary, Calvary,
   Burdens are lifted at Calvary,
   Jesus is very near.

2 Cast your care on Jesus today,
   Leave your worry and fear;
Burdens are lifted at Calvary,
Jesus is very near.

3 Troubled soul, the Saviour can see
   Every heartache and tear;
Burdens are lifted at Calvary,
Jesus is very near.

                                John M. Moore.

283 Tell me the old, old story
   Of unseen things above,
Of Jesus and His glory,
Of Jesus and His love.
Tell me the story simply,
As to a little child;
For I am weak and weary,
And helpless and defiled.

2 Tell me the story slowly,
   That I may take it in,
That wonderful redemption,
God's remedy for sin.
Tell me the story often
For I forget so soon!
The 'early dew' of morning
Has passed away at noon.

3 Tell me the story softly,
   With earnest tones, and grave;
Remember! I'm the sinner,
Whom Jesus came to save.
Tell me the story always,
If you would really be,
In any time of trouble
A comforter to me.

4 Tell me the same old story,
   When you have cause to fear
That this world's empty glory
Is costing me too dear.
Yes, and when that world's glory
Is dawning on my soul,
Tell me the old, old story,
'Christ Jesus makes thee whole.'

                                Kate Hankey.

284 I've a message from the Lord,
   hallelujah!
The message unto you I'll give,
'Tis recorded in His Word, hallelujah!
It is only that you 'look and live'.

   'Look and live,' . . . my brother, live, . . .
   Look to Jesus now and live,
   'Tis recorded in His Word, hallelujah!
   It is only that you 'look and live.'

2 I've a message full of love, hallelujah!
   A message, O my friend, for you.
'Tis a message from above, hallelujah!
Jesus said it, and I know 'tis true.

3 Life is offered unto you, hallelujah!
Eternal life your soul shall have,
If you'll only look to Him, hallelujah!
Look to Jesus who alone can save.
W. A. Ogden.

285 Come sinners to the living One,
He's just the same Jesus
As when He raised the widow's son,
The very same Jesus.

The very same Jesus,
The wonder-working Jesus;
O praise His Name, He's just the same!
The very same Jesus.

2 Come, feast upon the living bread,
He's just the same Jesus
As when the multitudes He fed,
The very same Jesus.

3 Come, tell Him all your griefs and
fears,
He's just the same Jesus
As when He shed those loving tears,
The very same Jesus.

4 Still follow Him for clearer light,
He's just the same Jesus
As when He gave the blind their sight,
The very same Jesus.

5 Then calm 'midst waves of trouble be,
He's just the same Jesus
As when He hushed the raging sea,
The very same Jesus.

6 Some day our raptured eyes shall see
He's just the same Jesus,
O blessèd day for you and me!
The very same Jesus.
L. H. Edmonds.

286 There is no love like the love of
Jesus —
Never to fade or fall,
Till into the fold of the peace of God
He has gathered us all.

Jesus' love, precious love,
Boundless and pure and free;
Oh, turn to that love, weary wandering soul:
Jesus pleadeth with thee!

2 There is no eye like the eye of Jesus,
Piercing so far away;
Ne'er out of the sight of its tender
light
Can the wanderer stray.

3 There is no voice like the voice of
Jesus,
Tender and sweet its chime,
Like musical ring of a flowing spring
In the bright summer time.

4 There is no heart like the heart of
Jesus,
Filled with a tender love;
No throb nor throe that our hearts can
know,
But He feels it above.
W. E. Littlewood.

287 There is joy in the presence of the
angels in Heaven,
When a sinner returns to his God;
When in humble faith he welcomes
the forgiveness freely given
Through the shedding of the
Saviour's precious blood.

And this joy is mine, . . .
Boundless and divine, . . .
Since I hearkened to the Gospel of His grace.

2 There is joy to the Father when He
sees His erring son
Coming back from his folly and
shame;
As he weeps in deep contrition o'er
the sin that he has done,
Pleading nothing but the worth of
Jesus' Name.

3 There is joy in the bosom of the
Shepherd homeward bound,
With the sheep on His shoulders
strong;
Though so weary, faint and bleating,
yet the wandering one is found,
And the night is turned to noonday
with a song.

4 There is joy overflowing unto all who
   will believe,
Who on Jesus will wholly rely;
He will fully cleanse and pardon, He
   will comfort and relieve,
Filling all the days with glory from on
   high.

5 Come, then, turn to the Saviour, seek
   Him now with heart and voice,
And respond to the call of His love;
Dare to take Him as your choice and
   He will cause you to rejoice,
Till you hear His 'Welcome home!' to
   realms above.

   And this joy divine,
   Will be surely thine,
   If you hearken to the Gospel of His grace.
                   L. F. W. Woodford.

288 There is a cleansing fountain,
   It flows from Calvary,
'Twas opened by the Saviour,
From sin each soul to free:
And now His voice is calling
With accents, oh, so sweet—
'Come to the cleansing river,
Down at the mercy seat!'

   Oh, Calvary's stream is flowing,
   Calvary's stream is flowing,
   Flowing so free for you and for me,
   Calvary's stream is flowing.

2 Though worn and heavy laden,
And burdened with your sin,
There's virtue in the river—
O will you enter in?
There's healing in its waters,
There's cleansing in its stream;
Then look away to Calvary
Where mercy's light does beam.

3 This stream of life eternal
For you is flowing free;
O bow yourself for cleansing,
And gain your liberty.
Then Christ shall be your Saviour,
And out of you shall flow
A life of peace and heaven,
God's Paradise below.
                   J. C. Bateman.

289 The gospel bells are ringing,
   Over land, from sea to sea;
Blessèd news of free salvation
Do they offer you and me.
'For God so loved the world,
That His only Son He gave!
Whosoe'er believeth in Him
Everlasting life shall have'.

   Gospel bells! how they ring,
   Over land from sea to sea;
   Gospel bells freely bring
   Blessèd news to you and me.

2 The gospel bells invite us
To a feast prepared for all;
Do not slight the invitation,
Nor reject the gracious call.
'I am the Bread of life;
Eat of Me, thou hungry soul;
Though your sins be red as crimson,
They shall be as white as wool'.

3 The gospel bells give warning,
As they sound from day to day,
Of the fate which doth await them
Who for ever will delay.
'Escape thou for thy life!
Tarry not in all the plain:
Nor behind thee look, oh, never,
Lest thou be consumed in pain'.

4 The gospel bells are joyful
As they echo far and wide,
Bearing notes of perfect pardon,
Through a Saviour crucified:
'Good tidings of great joy
To all people do I bring;
Unto you is born a Saviour,
Which is Christ, the Lord and King'.
                   S. Wesley Martin.

290 'Tis the grandest theme through
        the ages rung;
'Tis the grandest theme for a mortal
        tongue;
'Tis the grandest theme that the world
        e'er sung,
'Our God is able to deliver thee'.

   He is able to deliver thee,
   He is able to deliver thee:
   Though by sin opprest, Go to Him for rest;
   Our God is able to deliver thee.

2 'Tis the grandest theme in the earth or
   main!
   'Tis the grandest theme for a mortal
   strain,
   'Tis the grandest theme, tell the world
   again,
   'Our God is able to deliver thee'.

3 'Tis the grandest theme, let the
   tidings roll
   To the guilty heart, to the sinful soul,
   Look to God in faith, He will make
   thee whole,
   'Our God is able to deliver thee'.
                                    W. A. Ogden.

291 The Cross it standeth fast:
        Hallelujah, hallelujah!
Defying every blast:
Hallelujah, hallelujah!
The winds of hell have blown,
The world its hate hath shown,
Yet it is not overthrown:
Hallelujah for the Cross!

   Hallelujah, hallelujah, hallelujah for the Cross!
   Hallelujah, hallelujah, it shall never suffer loss!

2 It is the old Cross still:
   Hallelujah, hallelujah!
   Its triumph let us tell:
   Hallelujah, hallelujah!
   The grace of God here shone
   Through Christ the blessèd Son,
   Who did for sin atone:
   Hallelujah for the Cross!

3 'Twas here the debt was paid:
   Hallelujah, hallelujah!
   Our sins on Jesus laid:
   Hallelujah, hallelujah!
   So round the Cross we sing
   Of Christ our offering,
   Of Christ our living King:
   Hallelujah for the Cross!
                                 arr. Horatius Bonar.

292 The Lord made man, the
        Scriptures tell,
   To bear His image and His sign;
   Yet we by nature share as well
   The ancient mark of Adam's line.

2 In Adam's fall falls every man,
   With every gift the Father gave:
   The crown of all creation's plan
   Becomes a rebel and a slave.

3 Herein all woes are brought to birth,
   All aching hearts and sunless skies:
   Brightness is gone from all the earth,
   The innocence of nature dies.

4 Yet Adam's children, born to pain,
   By self enslaved, by sin enticed,
   Still may by grace be born again,
   Children of God, beloved in Christ.

5 In Christ is Adam's ransom met;
   Earth, by His Cross, is holy ground;
   Eden indeed is with us yet!
   In Christ are life and freedom found!
                              Timothy Dudley-Smith.

293 We have a gospel to proclaim,
        Good news for men in all the
        earth;
   The Gospel of a Saviour's Name:
   We sing His glory, tell his worth.

2 Tell of His birth at Bethlehem
   Not in a royal house or hall
   But in a stable dark and dim,
   The Word made flesh, a light for all.

3 Tell of His death at Calvary,
   Hated by those He came to save,
   In lonely suffering on the Cross;
   For all He loved His life He gave.

4 Tell of that glorious Easter morn:
   Empty the tomb, for He was free.
   He broke the power of death and hell
   That we might share His victory.

5 Tell of His reign at God's right hand,
   By all creation glorified.
   He sends His Spirit on His Church
   To live for Him, the Lamb who died.

6 Now we rejoice to name Him King:
   Jesus is Lord of all the earth.
   This gospel-message we proclaim:
   We sing His glory, tell His worth.
                                  Edward J. Burns.

294 Jesus only is our Message,
　　Jesus all our theme shall be,
We will lift up Jesus ever,
Jesus only will we see.

　　Jesus only, Jesus ever,
　　Jesus all in all we sing;
　　Saviour, Sanctifier, Healer,
　　Glorious Lord and coming King.

2 Jesus only is our Saviour,
　All our guilt He bore away,
　All our righteousness He gives us,
　All our strength from day to day.

3 Jesus is our Sanctifier,
　Cleansing us from self and sin,
　And with all His Spirit's fulness,
　Filling all our hearts within.

4 Jesus only is our Healer,
　All our sicknesses He bare,
　And His risen life and fulness,
　All His members still may share.

5 Jesus only is our Power,
　His the gift of Pentecost;
　Jesus, breathe Thy power upon us,
　Fill us with the Holy Ghost.

6 And for Jesus we are waiting,
　Listening for the Advent call,
　But 'twill still be Jesus only,
　Jesus ever, all in all.
　　　　　　　　　　A. B. Simpson.

295 Wonderful story of love; tell it to
　　me again;
Wonderful story of love; wake the
　　immortal strain!
Angels with rapture announce it,
　　shepherds with wonder receive it;
Sinner, O won't you believe it?
　　Wonderful story of love.

　　Won . . . der . . . ful! Won . . . der . . . ful!
　　Won . . . der . . . ful!
　　Wonderful story of love!

2 Wonderful story of love; though you
　are far away;
Wonderful story of love; still He doth
　call today;
Calling from Calvary's mountain,
　down from the crystal bright
　fountain,
E'en from the dawn of creation,
　Wonderful story of love.

3 Wonderful story of love; Jesus
　provides a rest;
Wonderful story of love; for all the
　pure and blest;
Rest in those mansions above us,
　with those who've gone on before
　us,
Singing the rapturous chorus,
　Wonderful story of love.
　　　　　　　　　　J. M. Driver.

296 Come to the Saviour, make no
　　delay;
Here in His Word He has shown us
　the way;
Here in our midst He's standing
　today,
Tenderly saying, 'Come!'

　　Joyful, joyful will the meeting be,
　　When from sin our hearts are pure and free,
　　And we shall gather, Saviour, with Thee,
　　In our eternal home.

2 'Suffer the children!' oh, hear His
　voice!
Let every heart leap forth and rejoice!
And let us freely make Him our
　choice,
Do not delay, but come.

3 Think once again, He's with us today;
Heed now His blest command and
　obey;
Hear now His accents tenderly say,
'Will you, My children, come?'
　　　　　　　　　　George F. Root.

297 'Twas Jesus, my Saviour who
　　died on the Tree,
To open a fountain for sinners like me,

His blood is the fountain that pardon
bestows,
And cleanses the foulest wherever it
flows.

> For the conquering Saviour shall break every
> chain,
> And give us the victory again and again.
> For the conquering Saviour shall break every
> chain.
> And give us the victory again and again.

2 And when I was willing with all things
to part
He gave me my bounty, His love in my
heart,
So now I am joined with the conquering band,
Who are marching to glory at Jesus'
command.

3 Though round me the storms of
adversity roll,
And the waves of destruction encom-
pass my soul,
In vain this frail vessel the tempest
shall toss,
My hopes rest secure on the blood of
the Cross.

4 And when with the ransomed of
Jesus, my Head,
From fountain to fountain I then shall
be led,
I'll fall at His feet and His mercy adore,
And sing of the blood of the Cross
evermore.

5 Come, sinners, to Jesus! no longer
delay!
A full free salvation He offers today,
Arouse your dark spirits, awake from
your dream,
And Christ will support you in coming
to Him.

Henry Q. Wilson.

298 Sinners Jesus will receive!
Sound this word of grace to all
Who the Heavenly pathway leave,
All who linger, all who fall!

> Sing it o'er . . . and o'er again . . .
> Christ receiv . . . eth sinful men; . . .
> Make the mes . . . sage clear and plain . . .
> Christ receiveth sinful men.

2 Come: and He will give you rest;
Trust Him; for His Word is plain;
He will take the sinfulest;
Christ receiveth sinful men.

3 Now my heart condemns me not,
Pure before the law I stand;
He who cleansed me from all spot
Satisfied its last demand.

4 Christ receiveth sinful men,
Even me with all my sin;
Purged from every spot and stain,
Heaven with Him I enter in.

Neumeister
arr. D.W.W.

299 Sound the gospel of grace
abroad,
There's life in the risen Lord!
Spread the news of the gift of God,
There's life in the risen Lord.
God above desires it!
Sinful man requires it!

> Tell it around, let it abound,
> There's life in the risen Lord.
> Tell it around, let it abound,
> There's life in the risen Lord.

2 All by nature are doomed to die,
So saith the Holy Word;
Welcome therefore the joyful cry,
There's life in the risen Lord.
Welcome news of gladness—
Antidote of sadness.

3 Saints, apostles, and prophets, all
Published with one accord,
This deliverance from the fall—
This life in the risen Lord.
Glory be to Jesus,
Who from bondage frees us.

4 Pardon, power, and perfect peace
The words of this life afford,
Never then let the tidings cease,
Of life in the risen Lord.
Open wide the portal,
Unto ev'ry mortal.

P. P. Bliss.

300 'Whosoever heareth!' shout,
shout the sound!
Send the blessèd tidings all the world
around!
Spread the joyful news wherever man
is found:
'Whosoever will may come'.

'Whosoever will! whosoever will!'
Send the proclamation over vale and hill:
'Tis the loving Father calls the wanderer home;
'Whosoever will may come.'

2 Whosoever cometh need not delay;
Now the door is open, enter while you
may;
Jesus is the true and only Living Way,
'Whosoever will may come'.

3 'Whosoever will!' the promise is
secure;
'Whosoever will!' for ever shall
endure;
'Whosoever will!' — 'tis life for evermore;
'Whosoever will may come'.

P. P. Bliss.

301 Would you be free from your
burden of sin?
There's power in the blood, power in
the blood;
Would you o'er evil a victory win?
There's wonderful power in the
blood.

There is power . . . power, wonder-working
power.
In the blood . . . of the Lamb . . .
There is power . . . power, wonder-working
power
In the precious blood of the Lamb.

2 Would you be free from your passion
and pride?
There's power in the blood, power in
the blood;
Come for a cleansing to Calvary's
tide,
There's wonderful power in the
blood.

3 Would you be whiter, much whiter
than snow?
There's power in the blood, power in
the blood;

Sin stains are lost in its life-giving
flow,
There's wonderful power in the
blood.

4 Would you do service for Jesus your
King?
There's power in the blood, power in
the blood;
Would you live daily His praises to
sing?
There's wonderful power in the
blood.

L. E. Jones.

302 There is life for a look at the
Crucified One,
There is life at this moment for thee.
Then look, sinner, look unto Him and
be saved,
Unto Him who was nailed to the Tree.

Look, look, look and live,
There is life for a look at the Crucified One,
There is life at this moment for thee.

2 Oh, why was He there as a Bearer of
sin,
If on Jesus thy sins were not laid?
Oh, why from His side flowed the sin-
cleansing blood,
If His dying thy debt has not paid?

3 It is not thy tears of repentance nor
prayers,
But the blood that atones for the soul;
On Him then believe, and a pardon
receive,
For His blood can now make thee
quite whole.

4 We are healed by His stripes; wouldst
thou add to the word?
And He is our righteousness made;
The best robe of Heaven He bids thee
to wear,
Oh, couldst thou be better arrayed?

5 Then doubt not thy welcome, since
God has declared
There remaineth no more to be done;
That once in the end of the world He
appeared,
And completed the work He begun.

6 But take, with rejoicing, from Jesus at once
The life everlasting He gives;
And know with assurance thou never canst die,
Since Jesus thy righteousness lives.
Asa M. Hull.

303 There's not a friend like the lowly Jesus,
No, not one! no, not one!
None else could heal all our soul's diseases,
No, not one! no, not one!

Jesus knows all about our struggles,
He will guide till the day is done;
There's not a friend like the lowly Jesus,
No, not one! no, not one!

2 No friend like Him is so high and holy,
No, not one! no, not one!
And yet no friend is so meek and lowly,
No, not one! no, not one!

3 There's not an hour that He is not near us,
No, not one! no, not one!
No night so dark but His love can cheer us,
No, not one! no, not one!

4 Did ever saint find this Friend forsake him?
No, not one! no, not one!
Or sinner find that He would not take him?
No, not one! no, not one!

5 Was e'er a gift like the Saviour given?
No, not one! no, not one!
Will He refuse us a home in Heaven?
No, not one! no, not one!
Johnson Oatman.

304 O what a Saviour that He died for me!
From condemnation He hath made me free;

'He that believeth on the Son', saith He
'Hath everlasting life.'

'Verily, verily,' I say unto you,
'Verily, verily,' message ever new;
'He that believeth on the Son', 'tis true,
'Hath everlasting life.'

2 All my inquities on Him were laid,
All my indebtedness by Him was paid;
All who believe on Him, the Lord hath said,
'Have everlasting life.'

3 Though poor and needy I can trust my Lord,
Though weak and sinful I believe His Word
O glad message! ev'ry child of God,
'Hath everlasting life.'

4 Though all unworthy, yet I will not doubt,
For him that cometh, He will not cast out.
'He that believeth', O the good news shout,'
'Hath everlasting life.'
J. McGranahan.

305 Have you been to Jesus for the cleansing power?
Are you washed in the blood of the Lamb?
Are you fully trusting in His grace this hour?
Are you washed in the blood of the Lamb?

Are you washed . . . in the blood . . .
In the soul-cleansing blood of the Lamb?
Are your garments spotless? Are they white as snow?
Are you washed in the blood of the Lamb?

2 Are you walking daily by the Saviour's side?
Are you washed in the blood of the Lamb?
Do you rest each moment in the Crucified?
Are you washed in the blood of the Lamb?

3 When the Bridegroom cometh will
   your robes be white?
Pure and white in the blood of the
   Lamb?
Will your soul be ready for the
   mansions bright,
And be washed in the blood of the
   Lamb?

4 Lay aside the garments that are
   stained by sin,
And be washed in the blood of the
   Lamb;
There's a fountain flowing for the soul
   unclean,
Oh be washed in the blood of the
   Lamb.

Elisha A. Hoffman.

306 Under the burdens of guilt and
   care,
Many a spirit is grieving,
Who in the joy of the Lord might
   share,
Life everlasting receiving.

   Life! life! eternal life!
   Jesus alone is the Giver!
   Life! life! abundant life!
   Glory to Jesus for ever!

2 Bearing our burden of guilt, there
   came
One Who is strong to deliver,
Bringing to men, through His
   wondrous Name,
Life 'more abundant' for ever.

3 Burdened one, why will you longer
   bear
Sorrows from which He releases?
Open your heart, and rejoicing share,
Life 'more abundant' in Jesus.

4 Leaving the mountain, the streamlet
   grows,
Flooding the vale with a river;
So, from the hill of the Cross, there
   flows
Life 'more abundant' for ever.

5 Oh, for the floods on the thirsty land!
Oh, for a mighty revival!
Oh, for a sanctified, fearless band,
Ready to hail its arrival.

W. Leslie.

WARNING AND REPENTANCE

307 Today Thy mercy calls me,
   To wash away my sin;
However great my trespass,
Whate'er I may have been.
However long from mercy
I may have turned away,
Thy blood, O Christ, can cleanse me,
And make me white today.

2 Today Thy gate is open,
And all who enter in,
Shall find a Father's welcome,
And pardon for their sin;
The past shall be forgotten,
A present joy be given,
A future grace be promised—
A glorious crown in Heaven.

3 O all-embracing mercy,
Thou ever open door,
What should I do without Thee,
When heart and eyes run o'er?
When all things seem against me,
To drive me to despair,
I know one gate is open,
One ear will hear my prayer.

Oswald Allen.

308 Rock of Ages, cleft for me,
   Let me hide myself in Thee!
Let the water and the blood,
From Thy riven side which flowed,
Be of sin the double cure;
Cleanse me from its guilt and power.

2 Not the labours of my hands,
Can fulfil Thy law's demands;
Could my zeal no respite know,
Could my tears for ever flow,
All for sin could not atone;
Thou must save and Thou alone.

3 Nothing in my hand I bring,
Simply to Thy cross I cling;
Naked, come to Thee for dress;
Helpless, look to Thee for grace:
Foul, I to the fountain fly;
Wash me, Saviour, or I die.

4 While I draw this fleeting breath,
When my eyelids close in death,
When I soar to worlds unknown,
See Thee on Thy judgement throne,
Rock of Ages, cleft for me,
Let me hide myself in Thee.

A. M. Toplady.

309 Will your anchor hold in the
storms of life?
When the clouds unfold their wings of
strife;
When the strong tides lift and the
cables strain,
Will your anchor drift, or firm remain?

We have an anchor that keeps the soul
Steadfast and sure while the billows roll,
Fastened to the Rock which cannot move,
Grounded firm and deep in the Saviour's love!

2 It is safely moored, 'twill the storm
withstand,
For 'tis well secured by the Saviour's
hand;
And the cables passed from His heart
to mine
Can defy the blast, through strength
divine.

3 It will firmly hold in the straits of fear,
When the breakers have told the reef
is near,
Though the tempest rave and the wild
winds blow,
Not an angry wave shall our bark
o'erflow.

4 It will surely hold in the floods of
death,
When the waters cold chill our latest
breath,
On the rising tide it can never fail,
While our hopes abide within the veil!

5 When our eyes behold, through the
gathering night
The city of gold, our harbour bright,
We shall anchor fast by the Heavenly
shore,
With the storms all past for evermore.

Priscilla J. Owens.

310 Lord, I hear of showers of
blessing,
Thou art scattering full and free,
Showers the thirsty land refreshing,
Let some drops now fall on me.

Even me, even me,
Let some drops now fall on me.

2 Pass me not, O God, my Father,
Sinful though my heart may be,
Thou might'st leave me, but the
rather
Let Thy mercy light on me.
Even me.

3 Pass me not, O mighty Spirit,
Thou canst make the blind to see:
Witnesser of Jesus' merit,
Speak the word of power to me.
Even me.

4 Love of God, so pure and changeless,
Blood of Christ, so rich and free;
Grace of God, so rich and boundless,
Magnify it all in me.
Even me.

5 Pass me not, Thy lost one bringing;
Bind my heart, O Lord, to Thee,
Whilst the streams of life are
springing,
Blessing others, oh, bless me!
Even me!

Mrs. E. Codner.

311 O Lamb of God whose perfect
love,
In face of hate and human wrong,
Has found a way to meet my need
By patient suffering—silence strong!
I cannot pass Your outstretched arms
To face a fate forlorn and long.

The Gospel

2 Your mercy pleads for my response,
Your grace abounding claims my soul,
Your seamless robe of righteousness
Can cover me and make me whole;
How can I try in naked shame
To brave the fight with sin's control?

3 I have no right to claim Your aid,
Nor can I plead what I have done;
In Your pure presence nothing hides
My secret sins, O searching Sun;
Yet You have overcome my sin
By victory already won!

4 Your death for sin has cancelled all
The shame and guilt You saw in me,
Your risen life of joy and peace
Is mine by glorious guarantee.
Your Spirit's seal I welcome now
And yield to love so glad and free.

Ron Pavey.

312 Jesus, see me at Thy feet,
Nothing but Thy blood can save me;
Thou alone my need canst meet,
Nothing but Thy blood can save me.

No! No! Nothing do I bring,
But by faith I'm clinging
To Thy Cross, O Lamb of God!
Nothing but Thy blood can save me.

2 See my heart, Lord, torn with grief,
Nothing but Thy blood can save me;
Me unpardoned do not leave,
Nothing but Thy blood can save me.

3 Dark, indeed, the past has been,
Nothing but Thy blood can save me;
Yet in mercy take me in,
Nothing but Thy blood can save me.

4 As I am, O hear me pray!
Nothing but Thy blood can save me;
I can come no other way,
Nothing but Thy blood can save me.

5 All that I can do is vain,
Nothing but Thy blood can save me;
I can ne'er remove a stain,
Nothing but Thy blood can save me.

6 Lord, I cast myself on Thee,
Nothing but Thy blood can save me;
From my guilt, O set me free!
Nothing but Thy blood can save me.

Richard Slater.

313 Depth of mercy! can there be
Mercy still reserved for me?
Can my God His wrath forbear?
Me, the chief of sinners spare?

2 I have long withstood His grace,
Long provoked Him to His face;
Would not hearken to His calls,
Grieved Him by a thousand falls.

3 Whence to me this waste of love?
Ask my Advocate above!
See the cause in Jesus' face,
Now before the throne of grace.

4 There for me the Saviour stands,
Shows His wounds, and spreads His hands:
God is love, I know, I feel;
Jesus lives and loves me still.

5 If I rightly read Thy heart,
If Thou all compassion art,
Bow Thine ear, in mercy bow,
Pardon and accept me now!

Charles Wesley.

314 I bring Thee my cares and my sorrows,
I bring Thee my doubts and my fears.
I bring Thee the sins which have burdened my soul
And shadowed my pathway for years.

O save me, dear Lord!
O save me, dear Lord!
I plead by Thy mercy,
O save me, dear Lord!

2 O Thou who doth know human frailties,
Prepare me for gain or for loss;
Though born of the dust, Lord, our Father art Thou,
The builder of sun and the Cross.

3 Forgive all my blindness and folly,
My prodigal wanderings and shame.
O heed now the outcrying pains of my
heart!
I come as the prodigal came.

4 We thank Thee we find in life's
wilderness
Established Thy gardens of grace,
In temptation's desert a cool shading
rock,
In darkness the light of Thy face.

Evangeline Booth.

315 I've wandered far away from God,
Now I'm coming home;
The paths of sin too long I've trod,
Lord, I'm coming home!

Coming home, coming home,
Never more to roam,
Open wide Thine arms of love,
Lord I'm coming home!

2 I've wasted many precious years,
Now I'm coming home;
I now repent with bitter tears,
Lord, I'm coming home!

3 I'm tired of sin and straying, Lord,
Now I'm coming home;
I'll trust Thy love, believe Thy word,
Lord, I'm coming home!

4 My soul is sick, my heart is sore,
Now I'm coming home;
My strength renew, my hope restore,
Lord, I'm coming home!

William J. Kirkpatrick.

316 Where will you spend eternity?
This question comes to you and
me!
Tell me, what shall your answer be?
Where will you spend eternity?

Chorus: (2nd tune only)
Eternity! eternity!
Where will you spend eternity?

2 Many are choosing Christ today
Turning from all their sins away:
Heaven shall their happy portion be,
Where will you spend eternity?

Eternity! eternity!
Where will you spend eternity?

3 Leaving the strait and narrow way,
Going the downward road today,
Sad will their final ending be,
Lost through a long eternity!

Eternity! eternity!
Lost through a long eternity!

4 Repent, believe, this very hour,
Trust in the Saviour's grace and
power,
Then will your joyous answer be,
Saved through a long eternity!

Eternity! eternity!
Saved through a long eternity!

E. A. Hoffman.

317 Pass me not, O gentle Saviour,
Hear my humble cry;
While on others Thou art calling,
Do not pass me by.

Saviour, Saviour,
Hear my humble cry;
While on others Thou art calling,
Do not pass me by.

2 Let me, at Thy throne of mercy
Find a sweet relief;
Kneeling there in deep contrition,
Help my unbelief.

3 Trusting only in Thy merit
Would I seek Thy face;
Heal my wounded, broken spirit,
Save me by Thy grace.

4 Thou, the spring of all my comfort,
More than life to me—
Whom have I on earth beside Thee?
Whom in Heaven but Thee?

Fanny J. Crosby.

318 Lord through the blood of the
Lamb that was slain,
Cleansing for me, cleansing for me:
From all the guilt of my sins now I
claim
Cleansing from Thee, cleansing from
Thee:
Sinful and black though the past may
have been,
Many the crushing defeats I have
seen,
Yet on Thy promise, O Lord, now I
lean!
Cleansing for me, cleansing for me!

2 From all the doubts that have filled me
with gloom,
Cleansing for me, cleansing for me:
From all the fears that would point me
to doom,
Cleansing for me, cleansing for me:
Jesus although I may not understand,
In child-like faith now I put forth my
hand,
And through Thy Word and Thy grace
I shall stand,
Cleansèd by Thee, cleansèd by Thee.

3 From all the care of what men think or
say,
Cleansing for me, cleansing for me:
From ever fearing to speak, sing or
pray,
Cleansing for me, cleansing for me:
Lord in Thy love and Thy power make
me strong,
That all may know that to Thee I
belong,
When I am tempted let this be my
song,
Cleansing for me, cleansing for me.

H. H. Booth.

319 Lord Jesus, I long to be perfectly
whole,
I want Thee for ever to live in my soul;
Break down every idol, cast out every
foe:
Now wash me, and I shall be whiter
than snow.

Whiter than snow; yes, whiter than snow;
Now wash me and I shall be whiter than snow.

2 Lord Jesus, let nothing unholy
remain,
Apply Thine own blood and extract
every stain;
To get this blest cleansing I all things
forego:
Now wash me, and I shall be whiter
than snow.

3 Lord Jesus, look down from Thy
throne in the skies,
And help me to make a complete
sacrifice;
I give up myself and whatever I know:
Now wash me, and I shall be whiter
than snow.

4 Lord Jesus, for this I most humbly
entreat;
I wait, blessèd Lord, at Thy crucified
feet;
By faith, for my cleansing I see Thy
blood flow:
Now wash me, and I shall be whiter
than snow.

5 Lord Jesus, Thou seest I patiently
wait;
Come now, and within me a new
heart create;
To those who have sought Thee Thou
never saidst, No:
Now wash me, and I shall be whiter
than snow.

James Nicholson.

320 I hear Thy welcome voice,
That calls me, Lord, to Thee
For cleansing in Thy precious blood
That flowed on Calvary.

I am coming, Lord,
Coming now to Thee:
Trusting only in the blood
That flowed on Calvary.

2 Though coming weak and vile,
Thou dost my strength assure:
Thou dost my vileness fully cleanse,
Till spotless all and pure.

3 'Tis Jesus calls me on
To perfect faith and love,
To perfect hope, and peace, and
trust,
For earth and Heaven above.

4 'Tis Jesus who confirms
The blessèd work within,
By adding grace to welcomed grace,
Where reigned the power of sin.

5 And He the witness gives
To loyal hearts and free,
That every promise is fulfilled,
If faith but brings the plea.

6 All hail, atoning blood!
All hail, redeeming grace!
All hail, the gift of Christ, our Lord,
Our strength and righteousness!

L. Hartsough.

321 Ring the bells of Heaven! there is
joy today,
For a soul returning from the wild;
See! the Father meets him out upon
the way,
Welcoming His weary, wandering
child.

Glory! glory! how the angels sing!
Glory! glory! how the loud harps ring!
'Tis the ransomed army, like a mighty sea,
Pealing forth the anthem of the free!

2 Ring the bells of Heaven! there is joy
today,
For the wanderer now is reconciled;
Yes, a soul is rescued from his sinful
way,
And is born anew a ransomed child.

3 Ring the bells of Heaven! spread the
feast today!
Angels swell the glad triumphant
strain!
Tell the joyful tidings! bear it far away!
For a precious soul is born again.
W. O. Cushing.

322 'Almost persuaded' now to
believe;
'Almost persuaded:' Christ to receive;
Seems now some soul to say?—
'Go, Spirit, go Thy way:
Some more convenient day
On Thee I'll call'.

2 'Almost persuaded:' come, come
today!
'Almost persuaded:' turn not away!
Jesus invites you here,
Angels are lingering near,
Prayers rise from hearts so dear,
O wanderer, come!

3 'Almost persuaded:' harvest is past!
'Almost persuaded:' doom comes at
last!
'Almost' can not avail;
'Almost' is but to fail:
Sad, sad, that bitter wail—
'Almost'—*but lost!*
P. P. Bliss.

GRACE AND FORGIVENESS

323 Oh, this uttermost salvation!
'Tis a fountain full and free,
Pure, exhaustless, ever flowing,
Wondrous grace! it reaches me!

It reaches me! it reaches me!
Wondrous grace! it reaches me!
Pure, exhaustless, ever flowing,
Wondrous grace! it reaches me!

2 How amazing God's compassion,
That so vile a worm should prove
This stupendous bliss of Heaven,
This unmeasured wealth of love!

3 Jesus, Saviour, I adore Thee!
Now Thy love I will proclaim;
I will tell the blessèd story,
I will magnify Thy Name!
Mary D. James.

324 There is a fountain filled with
blood,
Drawn from Immanuel's veins,
And sinners plunged beneath that
flood
Lose all their guilty stains.

2 The dying thief rejoiced to see
That fountain in his day;
And there may I, though vile as he,
Wash all my sins away.

3 I do believe, I will believe,
That Jesus died for me!
That on the Cross He shed His blood,
From sin to set me free.

4 Dear dying Lamb! Thy precious blood
Shall never lose its power,
Till all the ransomed Church of God
Be saved to sin no more.

5 E'er since by faith I saw the stream
Thy flowing wounds supply,
Redeeming love has been my theme,
And shall be till I die.
W. Cowper.

325 Years I spent in vanity and pride,
Caring not my Lord was crucified,
Knowing not it was for me He died
On Calvary.

Mercy there was great and grace was free,
Pardon there was multiplied to me,
There my burdened sould found liberty,
At Calvary.

2 By God's Word at last my sin I
learned,
Then I trembled at the law I'd
spurned,
Till my guilty soul, imploring turned
To Calvary.

3 Now I've given to Jesus everything,
Now I gladly own Him as my King,
Now my raptured soul can only sing
Of Calvary.

4 Oh! the love that drew salvation's
plan,
Oh! the grace that brought it down to
man,
Oh! the mighty gulf that God did span
At Calvary.

William R. Newell.

326 There's nothing like the old, old
story,
Grace is free, grace is free!
Which saints and martyrs tell in glory,
Grace is free, grace is free!
It brought them through the flood and
flame,
By it they fought and overcame,
And now they cry through His dear
Name,
Grace is free, grace is free!

There's nothing like the old, old story,
Grace is free, grace is free!
Which saints and martyrs tell in glory,
Grace is free, grace is free!

2 There's only hope in trusting Jesus,
Grace is free, grace is free!
From sin that doomed He died to free
us,
Grace is free, grace is free!
Who would not tell the story sweet
Of love so wondrous, so complete,
And fall in rapture at His feet,
Grace is free, grace is free!

3 From age to age the theme is telling,
Grace is free, grace is free!
From shore to shore the strains are
swelling,

Grace is free, grace is free!
And when that time shall cease to be
And faith is crowned with victory,
'Twill sound through all eternity,
Grace is free, grace is free!

Emma M. Johnston.

327 What can wash away my stain?
Nothing but the blood of Jesus:
What can make me whole again?
Nothing but the blood of Jesus.

Oh, precious is the flow
That makes me white as snow;
No other fount I know,
Nothing but the blood of Jesus.

2 For my cleansing this I see,
Nothing but the blood of Jesus:
For my pardon this my plea,
Nothing but the blood of Jesus.

3 Nothing can for sin atone,
Nothing but the blood of Jesus:
Nought of good that I have done,
Nothing but the blood of Jesus.

4 This is all my hope and peace,
Nothing but the blood of Jesus:
He is all my righteousness,
Nothing but the blood of Jesus.

5 Now by this I overcome:
Nothing but the blood of Jesus:
Now by this I'll reach my home:
Nothing but the blood of Jesus!

R. Lowry.

328 Would Jesus have the sinner die?
Why hangs He then on yonder
tree?
What means that strange expiring
cry?
Sinners, He prays for you and me;
Forgive them, Father, O forgive!
They know not that by Me they live.

2 Thou loving, all-atoning Lamb,
Thee—by Thy painful agony,
Thy blood-like sweat, Thy grief and
shame,
Thy Cross and passion on the tree,
Thy precious death and life—I pray,
Take all, take all my sins away!

3 Oh let me kiss Thy piercèd feet,
  And bathe and wash them with my
    tears!
  The story of Thy love repeat
  In every drooping sinner's ears,
  That all may hear the quickening
    sound,
  Since I even I have mercy found.

4 O let Thy love my heart constrain!
  Thy love for every sinner free
  That every fallen soul of man
  May taste the grace that found out
    me;
  That all mankind with me may prove
  Thy sovereign everlasting love.
                        Charles Wesley.

329 Amazing grace—how sweet the
        sound
  That saved a wretch like me!
  I once was lost but now am found,
  Was blind but now I see.

2 'Twas grace that taught my heart to
    fear,
  And grace my fears relieved;
  How precious did that grace appear
  The hour I first believed!

3 Through many dangers, toils and
    snares
  I have already come,
  'Tis grace hath brought me safe thus
    far
  And grace will lead me home.

4 When we've been there ten thousand
    years,
  Bright shining as the sun,
  We've no less days to sing God's
    praise
  Than when we first begun.
                        John Newton.

330 Out of my bondage, sorrow and
        night,
  Jesus I come, Jesus, I come;
  Into Thy freedom, gladness and light,
  Jesus, I come to Thee;

Out of my sickness into Thy health,
Out of my want and into Thy wealth,
Out of my sin and into Thyself,
Jesus, I come to Thee.

2 Out of my shameful failure and loss,
  Jesus I come, Jesus, I come;
  Into the glorious gain of Thy cross,
  Jesus, I come to Thee;
  Out of earth's sorrows into Thy balm,
  Out of life's storms and into Thy calm,
  Out of distress to jubilant psalm,
  Jesus, I come to Thee.

3 Out of unrest and arrogant pride,
  Jesus I come, Jesus, I come;
  Into Thy blessèd will to abide,
  Jesus, I come to Thee;
  Out of myself to dwell in Thy love,
  Out of despair into raptures above,
  Upward for aye on wings like a dove,
  Jesus, I come to Thee.

4 Out of the fear and dread of the tomb,
  Jesus I come, Jesus, I come;
  Into the joy and light of my home,
  Jesus, I come to Thee;
  Out of the depths of ruin untold,
  Into the peace of Thy sheltering fold,
  Ever Thy glorious face to behold,
  Jesus, I come to Thee.
                        William T. Sleeper.

331 Blessed be the Fountain of blood,
        To a world of sinners revealed;
  Blessed be the dear Son of God;
  Only by His stripes are we healed.
  Though I've wandered far from His
    fold,
  Bringing to my heart pain and woe,
  Wash me in the blood of the Lamb,
  And I shall be whiter than snow.

  Whiter than the snow . . .
  Whiter than the snow, . . .
  Wash me in the blood of the Lamb, . . .
  And I shall be whiter than snow. . . .

2 Thorny was the crown that He wore,
  And the Cross His body o'ercame;
  Grievous were the sorrows He bore,
  But He suffered thus not in vain.
  May I to that Fountain be led,
  Made to cleanse my sins here below;
  Wash me in the blood that He shed,
  And I shall be whiter than snow.

3 Father, I have wandered from Thee,
Often has my heart gone astray;
Crimson do my sins seem to me:
Water cannot wash them away,
Jesus, to that Fountain of Thine,
Leaning on Thy promise I go,
Cleanse me by Thy washing divine,
And I shall be whiter than snow.

E. R. Latta.

332 God loved the world of sinners
lost
And ruined by the fall,
Salvation full, at highest cost,
He offers free to all.

Oh, 'twas love, 'twas wondrous love!
The love of God to me;
It brought my Saviour from above,
To die on Calvary.

2 Eternal praises, Lord, to Thee,
Thou blessèd Son of God;
For Thy deep love in cleansing me
In Thy most precious blood.

3 Love brings the glorious fulness in,
And to His saints makes known
The blessèd rest from inbred sin
Through faith in Christ alone.

4 Believing souls, rejoicing go;
There shall to you be given
A glorious foretaste, here below,
Of endless life in Heaven.

5 Of victory now o'er Satan's power
Let all the ransomed sing,
And triumph in the dying hour
Through Christ, the Lord, our King.

Mrs. M. M. Stockton.

333 Grace! 'tis a charming sound,
Harmonious to the ear,
Heaven with the echo shall resound,
And all the earth shall hear.

Saved by grace alone!
This is all my plea:
Jesus died for all mankind,
And Jesus died for me.

2 'Twas grace that wrote my name
In life's eternal book;
'Twas grace that gave me to the
Lamb,
Who all my sorrows took.

3 Grace taught my wandering feet
To tread the Heavenly road,
And new supplies each hour I meet,
While pressing up to God.

4 Grace taught my soul to pray,
And made mine eyes o'erflow;
'Tis grace has kept me to this day,
And will not let me go.

5 Oh, let Thy grace inspire
My soul with strength divine!
May all my powers to Thee aspire,
And all my days be Thine.

P. Doddridge.

334 Great God of wonders! all Thy
ways
Display the attributes divine;
But countless acts of pard'ning grace
Beyond Thine other wonders shine:
Who is a pard'ning God like Thee?
Or who has grace so rich and free?

2 In wonder lost, with trembling joy
We take the pardon of our God;
Pardon for crimes of deepest dye,
A pardon bought with Jesu's blood;
Who is a pard'ning God like Thee?
Or who has grace so rich and free?

3 Pardon—from an offended God!
Pardon—for sins of deepest dye!
Pardon—bestowed through Jesu's
blood!
Pardon—that brings the rebel nigh!
Who is a pard'ning God like Thee?
Or who has grace so rich and free?

4 O may this strange, this matchless
grace,
This God-like miracle of love,
Fill the wide earth with grateful praise,
As now it fills the choirs above!
Who is a pard'ning God like Thee?
Or who has grace so rich and free?

Samuel Davies.

335 I am happy today and the sun shines bright,
The clouds have been rolled away;
For the Saviour said, whosoever will
May come with Him to stay.

Whosoever, surely meaneth me,
Surely meaneth me, O surely meaneth me;
Whosoever, surely meaneth me,
Whosoever, meaneth me.

2 All my hopes have been raised, O His name be praised,
His glory has filled my soul;
I've been lifted up, and from sin set free,
His blood has made me whole.

3 O what wonderful love, O what grace divine,
That Jesus should die for me;
I was lost in sin, for the world I pined,
But now I am set free.

J. Edwin McConnell.

336 If human hearts are often tender,
And human minds can pity know,
If human love is touched with splendour,
And human hands compassion show,

Then how much more shall God our Father
In love forgive, in love forgive!
Then how much more shall God our Father
Our wants supply and none deny!

2 If sometimes men can live for others,
And sometimes give where gifts are spurned,
If sometimes treat their foes as brothers,
And love where love is not returned,

3 If men will often share their gladness,
If men respond when children cry,
If men can feel each other's sadness,
Each other's tears attempt to dry.

John Gowans.

337 In the misty days of yore, Jesus' precious blood had power;
Even the thief upon the Cross to save;
Like a bird his spirit flies to its home in Paradise,

Through the power of Calvary's crimson wave.

And the blood . . . has never lost its power, . . .
No, never; . . . no, never; . . .
Jesus' blood . . . avails for sin for ever, . . .
And will never lose its power.

2 I was lost and steeped in guilt, but the blood for sinners spilt
Washed away my sins and set me free;
Now and evermore the same, praise, O praise His holy name!
Will the cleansing stream availing be.

3 God in mercy asks you why, brother sinner, will you die,
When such full redemption He provides?
You have but to look and live, life eternal He will give,
For the power of Calvary still abides.

4 Bring your burdens, come today, turn from all your sins away,
He can fully save and sanctify;
From the wrath to come now flee, let your name recorded be
With the blood-washed and redeemed on high.

Mrs. C. H. Morris.

338 The great Physician now is near,
The sympathizing Jesus;
He speaks the drooping heart to cheer,
Oh, hear the voice of Jesus.

Sweetest note in seraph song,
Sweetest name on mortal tongue;
Sweetest carol ever sung,
Jesus, blessèd Jesus.

2 Your many sins are all forgiven,
Oh, hear the voice of Jesus;
Go on your way in peace to Heaven,
And wear a crown with Jesus.

3 All glory to the dying Lamb!
I now believe in Jesus;
I love the blessèd Saviour's Name,
I love the Name of Jesus.

4 His name dispels my guilt and fear,
  No other name but Jesus,
  Oh! how my soul delights to hear
  The precious Name of Jesus.
                            William Hunter.

339 There is a story sweet to hear,
        I love to tell it too:
  It fills my heart with hope and cheer,
  'Tis old, yet ever new.

  'Tis old, . . . yet ever new,
  'Tis old, . . . yet ever new,
  I know, . . . I feel 'tis true,
  'Tis old, yet ever new.

2 It tells me God the Son came down
  From glory's throne to die,
  That I might live and wear a crown,
  And reign with Him on high.

3 It says He bore the Cross for me,
  And suffered in my place,
  That I from sin might ransomed be,
  And praise Him for His grace.

4 Oh wondrous love, so great, so vast,
  So boundless and so free!
  Lord, at Thy feet myself I cast;
  My all I give to Thee!
                            W. A. Williams.

340 A message sweet is borne to me
        On wings of joy divine,
  A wondrous message, glad and free,
  That thrills this heart of mine.

  O glorious song, . . . That all day long, . . .
  With tuneful note is ringing!
  I'm saved by grace, . . . amazing grace, . . .
  And that is why I'm singing.

2 I'm saved by grace, by grace alone,
  Through Christ whose love I claim,
  No other could for sin atone,
  Hosanna to His Name!

3 I hear the message that I love
  When morning dawns anew,
  I read it in the sun above,
  That shines across the blue.

4 I hear it in the twilight still,
  And at the sunset hour;
  I'm saved by grace! what words can
      thrill
  With such a magic power?

5 O wondrous grace for all mankind
  That spreads from sea to sea!
  It heals the sick and leads the blind,
  And sets the prisoner free.

6 The soul that seeks it cannot fail
  To see the Saviour's face,
  And Satan's power cannot prevail
  If we are saved by grace.
                            Ida Scott Taylor.

341 O what a wonderful Saviour
        In Jesus my Lord I have found,
  Though I had sins without number,
  His grace unto me did abound.

  His grace aboundeth more . . .
  His grace aboundeth more,
  Though sin abounded in my heart,
  His grace aboundeth more.

2 When a poor sinner He found me,
  No goodness to offer had I;
  Often His law I had broken,
  And merited naught but to die.

3 Nothing of merit possessing,
  All helpless before Him I lay,
  But in the precious blood flowing
  He washed all my sin-stains away.

4 In Him my gracious Redeemer,
  My Prophet, my Priest and my King;
  Mercy I find and forgiveness,
  My all to His keeping I bring.

5 How can I keep from rejoicing?
  I'll sing of the joy in my soul;
  Praising the love of my Saviour,
  While years of eternity roll.
                            Kate Ulmer.

342 O sweet is the story of Jesus,
        The wonderful Saviour of men,
  Who suffered and died for the
      sinner—
  I'll tell it again and again!

O won . . . derful, wonderful sto . . . ry,
The dear . . . est that ever was told, . . .
I'll repeat it in glo . . . ry, the wonderful
    sto . . . ry,
Where I . . . shall His beauty behold. . . .

2 He came from the brightest of glory;
  His blood as a ransom He gave
  To purchase eternal redemption,
  And oh, He is mighty to save!

3 His mercy flows on like a river,
  His love is unmeasured and free;
  His grace is forever sufficient,
  It reaches and purifies me.
                C. H. Gabriel.

343 And can it be, that I should gain
      An interest in the Saviour's
      blood?
  Died He for me, who caused His pain?
  For me, who Him to death pursued?
  Amazing love! how can it be
  That Thou, my God, shouldst die for
  me?

2 'Tis mystery all! The Immortal dies!
  Who can explore His strange design?
  In vain the first-born seraph tries
  To sound the depth of love divine!
  'Tis mercy all! let earth adore,
  Let angel-minds inquire no more.

3 He left His Father's throne above,
  So free, so infinite His grace!
  Emptied Himself of all but love,
  And bled for Adam's helpless race:
  'Tis mercy all, immense and free,
  For, O my God, it found out me!

4 Long my imprisoned spirit lay
  Fast bound in sin and nature's night;
  Thine eye diffused a quickening ray,
  I woke, the dungeon flamed with
    light:
  My chains fell off, my heart was free,
  I rose, went forth, and followed Thee.

5 No condemnation now I dread,
  Jesus, and all in Him, is mine;
  Alive in Him, my living Head,
  And clothed in righteousness divine.

Bold I approach the eternal throne,
And claim the crown, through Christ,
  my own.
                Charles Wesley.

344 Jesus, the Name high over all,
      In hell, or earth, or sky;
  Angels and men before it fall
  And devils fear and fly.

2 He breaks the power of cancelled sin,
  And sets the prisoner free;
  His blood can make the foulest clean,
  His blood avails for me.

3 Jesus! the Name to sinners dear,
  The Name to sinners given;
  It scatters all their guilty fear;
  It turns their hell to Heaven.

4 Jesus the prisoner's fetters breaks,
  And bruises Satan's head,
  Power into strengthless souls He
    speaks,
  And life unto the dead.

5 Oh, that the world might taste and see
  The riches of His grace!
  The arms of love that compass me
  Would all mankind embrace.
                Charles Wesley.

THE APPEAL

345 Are you seeking joys that will not
      fade,
  Lasting pleasure by God's mercy
    made?
  Christ is waiting, fulness of joy He
    brings;
  Swing wide the door of your heart to
    the King of kings.

    Swing wide the door of your heart to the King
      of kings,
    Bid Him welcome, for wonderful peace He
      brings,
    He will shelter thee under His outstretched
      wings;
    Swing wide the door of your heart to the King
      of kings.

2 Are you longing perfect peace to win?
Turn to Jesus, bid Him enter in;
Peace is found but under His shelter-
ing wings;
Swing wide the door of your heart to
the King of kings.

3 Now He calls you with His wondrous
voice,
Bid Him welcome, make His will your
choice;
At His coming Heavenly music rings;
Swing wide the door of your heart to
the King of kings.

Sidney E. Cox.

346 O soul, are you weary and
troubled?
No light in the darkness you see?
There's light for a look at the Saviour,
And life more abundant and free!

Turn your eyes upon Jesus,
Look full in His wonderful face;
And the things of earth will grow strangely dim
In the light of His glory and grace.

2 Through death into life everlasting
He passed, and we follow Him there;
Over us sin no more hath dominion
For more than conquerors we are!

3 His word shall not fail you — He
promised;
Believe Him and all will be well;
Then go to a world that is dying,
His perfect salvation to tell!

Helen H. Lemmel.

347 Sinner, how thy heart is troubled,
God is coming very near;
Do not hide thy deep emotion,
Do not check that falling tear.

Oh, be saved His grace is free!
Oh, be saved, He died for thee!

2 Jesus now is bending o'er thee,
Jesus lowly, meek and mild;
To the Friend who died to save thee,
Wilt thou not be reconciled?

3 Art thou waiting till the morrow?
Thou mayest never see its light;
Come at once! accept His mercy:
He is waiting — come tonight!

4 With a lowly, contrite spirit,
Kneeling at the Saviour's feet,
Thou canst feel, this very moment,
Pardon — precious, pure, and sweet.

5 Let the angels bear the tidings
Upward to the courts of Heaven!
Let them sing with holy rapture,
O'er another soul forgiven!

Fanny J. Crosby.

348 In times like these you need a
Saviour,
In times like these you need an
anchor;
Be very sure, be very sure,
Your anchor holds and grips the Solid
Rock!

This Rock is Jesus, yes, He's the One,
This Rock is Jesus, the only One;
Be very sure, be very sure
Your anchor holds and grips the Solid Rock!

2 In times like these you need the Bible,
In times like these, oh, be not idle;
Be very sure, be very sure,
Your anchor holds and grips the Solid
Rock!

3 In times like these I have a Saviour,
In times like these I have an anchor;
I'm very sure, I'm very sure
My anchor holds and grips the Solid
Rock!

This Rock is Jesus, yes, He's the One,
This Rock is Jesus, the only One;
I'm very sure, I'm very sure
My anchor holds and grips the Solid Rock!

Ruth Caye Jones.

349 Patiently, tenderly pleading,
Jesus is standing today;
At your heart's door He knocks as
before,
Oh, turn Him no longer away.

Don't turn Him away, don't turn Him away,
He has come back to your heart again,
Although you've gone astray;
Oh, how you'll need Him to plead your cause
On that eternal day!
Don't turn the Saviour away from your heart,
Don't turn Him away.

2 Gracious, compassionate mercy
Brought Him from mansions above;
Caused Him to wait just outside your gate,
Oh, yield to His wonderful love.

3 Can you not now hear Him calling?
Do not ill-treat such a friend;
Give up your sin, oh, let Him come in,
Lo! He will be true to the end.

4 Now is the time to receive Him,
Grant Him admission today;
Grieve Him no more, but open your door,
And turn Him no longer away.

Haldor Lillenas.

350 This is God's moment, before you
Christ pleads,
His blood shed on Calvary for you intercedes;
His grace is sufficient to meet all your needs,
For this is God's moment for you.

This is God's moment, God's moment for you,
A moment so solemn, yet joyous and new;
Forgiven is all sinning, real life is beginning,
For this is God's moment for you.

2 This is God's moment, His message you've heard,
A long-silent chord in your heart has been stirred;
Within you faith rises, you trust in His Word,
For this is God's moment for you.

3 This is God's moment, a new day now breaks,
Released from sin's bondage your soul-life awakes,
And thrills to the blessing of which it partakes,
For this is God's moment for you.

Flora Larsson.

351 Behold Me standing at the door,
And hear Me pleading evermore
With gentle voice: Oh, heart of sin,
May I come in? may I come in?

Behold Me standing at the door,
And hear Me pleading evermore;
Say, weary heart, opprest with sin,
May I come in? may I come in?

2 I bore the cruel thorns for thee,
I waited long and patiently:
Say, weary heart, opprest with sin,
May I come in? may I come in?

3 I would not plead with thee in vain;
Remember all My grief and pain!
I died to ransom thee from sin,
May I come in? may I come in?

4 I bring thee joy from Heaven above,
I bring thee pardon, peace, and love:
Say, weary heart, opprest with sin,
May I come in? may I come in?

Fanny J. Crosby.

352 Precious, precious blood of Jesus,
Shed on Calvary;
Shed for rebels, shed for sinners,
Shed for thee!

Precious, precious blood of Jesus,
Ever flowing free;
Oh, believe it; Oh, receive it,
'Tis for thee.

2 Precious, precious blood of Jesus,
Let it make thee whole;
Let it flow in mighty cleansing
O'er thy soul.

3 Though thy sins are red like crimson,
Deep in scarlet glow,
Jesus' precious blood shall wash thee
White as snow.

4 Precious blood that hath redeemed us!
All the price is paid!
Perfect pardon now is offered,
Peace is made.

5 Now the holiest with boldness
We may enter in;
For the open fountain cleanseth
From all sin.

6 Precious blood! by this we conquer
In the fiercest fight,
Sin and Satan overcoming
By its might.

7 Precious blood whose full atonement
Makes us nigh to God!
Precious blood, our way of glory,
Praise and laud.

F. R. Havergal.

353 I have a Saviour, He's pleading in glory,
A dear, loving Saviour though earth-friends be few;
And now He is watching in tenderness o'er me:
And oh, that my Saviour were your Saviour too!

For you I am praying,
For you I am praying,
For you I am praying,
I'm praying for you.

2 I have a Father: to me He has given
A hope for eternity, blessèd and true;
And soon He will call me to meet Him in Heaven,
But oh, may He lead you to go with me too!

3 I have a robe: 'tis resplendent in whiteness,
Awaiting in glory my wondering view;
Oh, when I receive it all shining in brightness,
Dear friend, could I see you receiving one too!

4 I have a peace: it is calm as a river,
A peace that the friends of this world never knew;
My Saviour alone is its Author and Giver,
And oh, could I know it was given to you!

5 When Jesus has found you, tell others the story,
That my loving Saviour is your Saviour too;
Then pray that your Saviour may bring them to glory,
And prayer will be answered, t'was answered for you!

Samuel O'M. Cluff.

354 If you from sin are longing to be free,
Look to the Lamb of God;
He, to redeem you, died on Calvary,
Look to the Lamb of God.

Look to the Lamb of God,
Look to the Lamb of God,
For He alone is able to save you;
Look to the Lamb of God.

2 When Satan tempts, and doubts and fears assail,
Look to the Lamb of God;
You in His strength shall over all prevail,
Look to the Lamb of God.

3 Are you aweary, does the way seem long?
Look to the Lamb of God;
His love will cheer and fill your heart with song,
Look to the Lamb of God.

4 Fear not when shadows on your pathway fall,
Look to the Lamb of God;
In joy or sorrow Christ is all in all,
Look to the Lamb of God.

H. G. Jackson.

355 Is there a heart that is waiting,
Longing for pardon today?
Hear the glad message proclaiming,
Jesus is passing this way.

Jesus is passing this way, . . .
This way; . . . today; . . .
Jesus is passing this way, . . .
Is passing this way today.

2 Is there a heart that has wandered?
Come with thy burden today;
Mercy is tenderly pleading,
Jesus is passing this way.

3 Is there a heart that is broken?
Weary and sighing for rest?
Come to the arms of thy Saviour,
Pillow thy head on His breast.

4 Come to thy only Redeemer,
Come to His infinite love;
Come to the gate that is leading
Homeward to mansions above.

Annie L. James.

356 Jesus is tenderly calling thee
home—
Calling today, calling today!
Why from the sunshine of love wilt
thou roam,
Farther and farther away?

Call . . . ing today! call . . . ing today! . . .
Je . . . sus is call . . . ing, is tenderly calling
today!

2 Jesus is calling the weary to rest—
Calling today, calling today!
Bring Him thy burden and thou shalt
be blest:
He will not turn thee away.

3 Jesus is waiting, oh, come to Him
now—
Waiting today, waiting today!
Come with thy sins, at His feel lowly
bow;
Come, and no longer delay!

4 Jesus is pleading; oh, list to His
voice—
Hear Him today, hear Him today!
They who believe on His Name shall
rejoice;
Quickly arise and away!

Fanny J. Crosby.

357 Have you any room for Jesus,
He who bore your load of sin?
As He knocks and asks admission,
Sinner, will you let Him in?

Room for Jesus, King of glory,
Hasten now, His word obey,
Swing the heart's door widely open,
Bid Him enter while you may.

2 Room for pleasure, room for
business,
But for Christ the Crucified;
Not a place that He can enter,
In your heart for which He died?

3 Have you any time for Jesus,
As in grace He calls again?
O today is time accepted,
Tomorrow you may call in vain.

4 Room and time now give to Jesus,
Soon will pass God's day of grace;
Soon thy heart left cold and silent,
And thy Saviour's pleading cease.

D. W. Whittle.

358 Just as I am, without one plea,
But that Thy blood was shed for
me,
And that Thou bidst me come to
Thee,
O Lamb of God, I come.

2 Just as I am, and waiting not
To rid my soul of one dark blot,
To Thee, whose blood can cleanse
each spot,
O Lamb of God, I come.

3 Just as I am—though tossed about
With many a conflict, many a doubt,
Fightings and fears within, without,
O Lamb of God, I come.

4 Just as I am—poor, wretched,
blind—
Sight, riches, healing of the mind,
Yea, all I need, in Thee to find,
O Lamb of God, I come.

5 Just as I am, Thou wilt receive,
Wilt welcome, pardon, cleanse,
relieve;
Because Thy promise I believe,
O Lamb of God, I come.

The Gospel

6 Just as I am—Thy love unknown
Has broken every barrier down;
Now to be Thine, yea, Thine alone,
O Lamb of God, I come.

7 Just as I am, of that free love
The breadth, length, depth and height
to prove,
Here for a season, then above,
O Lamb of God, I come.

Charlotte Elliott.

359 Will you take Jesus to be your
Guide?
His love will brighten the way;
Safe in His keeping you may abide:
Will you take Jesus today?

Will you take Jesus today?
Will you take Jesus today?
He offers pardon and peace to all:
Will you take Jesus today?

2 For you the Saviour was crucified,
Accept His love while you may;
The door of mercy stands open wide:
Will you take Jesus today?

3 He longs to enter your heart of sin—
How can you turn Him away?
Throw wide the portal and let Him in:
Will you take Jesus today?

4 I will take Jesus, my Lord and King,
His Word I gladly obey;
My sins forgiven, His praise I'll sing:
I will take Jesus today.

I will take Jesus today!
I will take Jesus today!
He offers pardon and peace to all:
I will take Jesus today!

William W. Rock.

360 Only a step to Jesus!
Then why not take it now?
Come, and thy sin confessing,
To Him thy Saviour bow.

Only a step, only a step;
Come, He waits for thee;
Come, and thy sin confessing,
Thou shalt receive a blessing;
Do not reject the mercy
He freely offers thee.

2 Only a step to Jesus!
Believe, and thou shalt live;
Lovingly now He's waiting,
And ready to forgive.

3 Only a step to Jesus!
A step from sin to grace;
What hast thy heart decided?
The moments fly apace.

4 Only a step to Jesus!
O why not come, and say,
Gladly to Thee, my Saviour,
I give myself away.

Fanny J. Crosby.

361 Softly and tenderly Jesus is
calling,
Calling for you and for me;
See, on the portals He's waiting and
watching,
Watching for you and for me.

Come home, . . . come home, . . .
Ye who are weary, come home,
Earnestly, tenderly Jesus is calling,
Calling, O sinner, come home!

2 Why should we tarry when Jesus is
pleading,
Pleading for you and for me?
Why should we linger and heed not
His mercies,
Mercies for you and for me?

3 Time is now fleeting, the moments are
passing,
Passing from you and from me;
Shadows are gathering, deathbeds
are coming,
Coming for you and for me.

4 Oh for the wonderful love He has
promised,
Promised for you and for me;
Though we had sinned He has mercy
and pardon,
Pardon for you and for me.

Will L. Thompson.

Section VII

THE CHRISTIAN LIFE

ASSURANCE AND CONFIDENCE

362 'Fear not, I am with thee';
    Blessèd golden ray,
Like a star of glory
Lighting up my way!
Through the clouds of midnight
This bright promise shone,
'I will never leave thee,
Never will leave thee alone.'

    No . . . never alone, . . . no never alone;
    He promised never to leave me,
    Never to leave me alone.

2 Roses fade around me,
Lilies bloom and die,
Earthly sunbeams vanish,
Radiant still the sky!
Jesus, Rose of Sharon,
Blooming for His own,
Jesus, Heaven's sunshine,
Never will leave me alone.

3 Steps unseen before me,
Hidden dangers near;
Nearer still my Saviour,
Whispering, 'Be of cheer',
Joys, like birds of springtime,
To my heart have flown,
Singing all so sweetly,
'He will not leave me alone'.
E. E. Hewitt.

363 My soul is now united
    To Christ the Living Vine;
His grace I long have slighted,
But now I know He's mine;
I was to God a stranger
Till Jesus took me in;
He freed my soul from danger,
And pardoned all my sin.

2 Soon as my all I ventured
On the atoning blood,
The Holy Spirit entered,
And I was born of God;

Still Christ is my salvation—
What can I covet more?
I fear no condemnation,
My Father's wrath is o'er.

3 By floods and flames surrounded,
I now my way pursue;
Nor shall I be confounded,
With glory in my view;
I taste a Heavenly pleasure,
And need not fear a frown:
Christ is my joy and treasure,
My glory and my crown.

4 Christians be not faint-hearted,
Though least among the flock;
From Christ you'll ne'er be parted
While built upon the rock;
Let's speed our pace to glory,
We soon shall meet above,
And tell the wondrous story
Of His redeeming love.

364 From every stormy wind that
    blows,
From every swelling tide of woes,
There is a calm, a sure retreat;
'Tis found beneath the mercy-seat.

2 There is a place where Jesus sheds
The oil of gladness on our heads—
A place than all beside more sweet;
It is the blood-stained mercy-seat.

3 There is a scene where spirits blend,
And friend holds fellowship with
    friend;
Though sundered far, by faith we
    meet
Around one common mercy-seat.

4 There, there on eagle wing we soar,
And time and sense seem all no more;
And Heaven comes down our souls to
    greet,
And glory crowns the mercy-seat.
Hugh Stowell.

365 Thou hast snapped my fetters;
Thou hast made me free:
Liberty and gladness
I have found in Thee;
Liberty from bondage,
From my weary load,
Satan's slave no longer,
Now a child of God!

> I am Thine, Lord Jesus
> Ever Thine, Thine I am,
> And my heart is singing,
> 'Glory to the Lamb.'

2 Living in the sunshine,
Shining in Thy light,
Fighting as Thy soldier,
Mighty in Thy might;
Going on Thy mission,
Pointing men to Thee,
Telling of the Saviour
Who can set them free.

3 Such the life, Lord Jesus,
I would ever live,
Such the grateful tribute
I would ever give;
Witnessing for Thee, Lord,
Everywhere I go,
Of the Blood that cleanseth,
Washing white as snow.

4 And when life is ended,
When the vict'ry's won,
When I hear from Thee, Lord,
The glad words, 'Well done'.
With what joy and rapture
Shall I sing of Thee,
Who from sin's dark chains didst
Set my spirit free!

366 Jesus, lover of my soul,
Let me to Thy bosom fly,
While the nearer waters roll,
While the tempest still is high:
Hide me, O my Saviour, hide,
Till the storm of life is past;
Safe into the haven guide;
Oh, receive my soul at last.

2 Other refuge have I none;
Hangs my helpless soul on Thee;
Leave, ah! leave me not alone,
Still support and comfort me.

All my trust on Thee is stayed,
All my help from Thee I bring;
Cover my defenceless head
With the shadow of Thy wing.

3 Thou, O Christ! art all I want;
More than all in Thee I find:
Raise the fallen, cheer the faint,
Heal the sick, and lead the blind.
Just and holy is Thy Name,
I am all unrighteousness;
Vile and full of sin I am,
Thou art full of truth and grace.

4 Plenteous grace with Thee is found,
Grace to cover all my sin;
Let the healing streams abound,
Make and keep me pure within:
Thou of life the fountain art,
Freely let me take of Thee;
Spring Thou up within my heart,
Rise to all eternity.

Charles Wesley.

367 Upon life's boundless ocean
where mighty billows roll,
I've found my hope in Jesus, blest
anchor of my soul;
When trials fierce assail me as storms
are gathering o'er,
I rest upon His mercy and trust Him
more.

> I've anchored in Jesus, the storms of life I'll
> brave,
> I've anchored in Jesus, I fear no wind or wave,
> I've anchored in Jesus for He hath power to
> save,
> I've anchored to the Rock of Ages.

2 He keeps my soul from evil and gives
me blessèd peace,
His voice hath stilled the waters and
bid their tumult cease;
My Pilot and Deliverer, to Him I all
confide,
For always when I need Him He's at
my side.

3 He is my Friend and Saviour, in Him
my anchor's cast,
He drives away my sorrows and
shields me from the blast;

By faith I'm looking upward beyond life's troubled sea,
There I behold a haven prepared for me.

L. E. Jones.

368 A mind at 'perfect peace' with God;
Oh, what a word is this!
A sinner reconciled through blood;
This, this indeed is peace!

2 By nature and by practice far,
How very far from God!
Yet now by grace brought nigh to Him.
Through faith in Jesus' blood.

3 So nigh, so very nigh to God,
I cannot nearer be;
For in the person of His Son
I am as near as He.

4 So dear, so very dear to God,
More dear I cannot be;
The love wherewith He loves the Son—
Such is His love to me!

5 Why should I ever anxious be,
Since such a God is mine?
He watches o'er me night and day,
And tells me 'Mine is thine.'

Catesby Paget.

369 A wonderful Saviour is Jesus my Lord,
A wonderful Saviour to me,
He hideth my soul in the cleft of the rock,
Where rivers of pleasure I see.

He hideth my soul in the cleft of the rock,
That shadows a dry thirsty land;
He hideth my life in the depths of His love,
And covers me there with His hand,
And covers me there with His hand.

2 A wonderful Saviour is Jesus my Lord,
He taketh my burden away,

He holdeth me up, and I shall not be moved,
He giveth me strength as my day.

3 With numberless blessings each moment He crowns,
And filled with His fulness divine,
I sing in my rapture, oh, glory to God
For such a Redeemer as mine.

4 When clothed in His brightness transported I rise,
To meet Him in clouds of the sky,
His perfect salvation, His wonderful love,
I'll shout with the millions on high.

Fanny J. Crosby.

370 Through the love of God our Saviour
All will be well;
Free and changeless is His favour,
All, all is well:
Precious is the blood that healed us;
Perfect is the grace that sealed us;
Strong the hand stretched forth to shield us,
All must be well.

2 Though we pass through tribulation
All will be well;
Ours is such a full salvation,
All, all is well:
Happy still in God confiding;
Fruitful if in Christ abiding;
Holy through the Spirit's guiding;
All must be well.

3 We expect a bright tomorrow;
All will be well;
Faith can sing through days of sorrow,
All, all is well:
On our Father's love relying,
Jesus every need supplying,
Or in living or in dying
All must be well.

Mary Peters.

371 Abiding, oh, so wondrous sweet!
I'm resting at the Saviour's feet,
I trust in Him, I'm satisfied,
I'm resting in the Crucified!

Abid . . . ing, abid . . . ing,
Oh, so wondrous sweet! . . .
I'm rest . . . ing, rest . . . ing
At the Saviour's feet. . . .

2 He speaks, and by His word is given
His peace, a rich foretaste of Heaven!
Not as the world He peace doth give,
'Tis through this hope my soul shall
live.

3 I live; not I; through Him alone
By Whom the mighty work is done,
Dead to myself, alive to Him,
I count all loss His rest to gain.

4 Now rest, my heart, the work is done,
I'm saved through the Eternal Son!
Let all my powers my soul employ,
To tell the world my peace and joy.
Chas. B. J. Root.

372 Blessèd Lily of the Valley, oh,
how fair is He!
He is mine, . . . I am His; . . .
Sweeter than the angels' music is His
voice to me,
He is mine, . . . I am His! . . .
Where the lilies fair are blooming by
the waters calm,
There He leads me, and upholds me
by His strong right arm;
All the air is love around me, I can feel
no harm,
He is mine, . . . I am His. . . .

Lily of the Valley, He . . . is mine!
Lily of the Valley, I am His!
Sweeter than the angels' music is His voice to
me,
He is mine, . . . I am His! . . .

2 Let me sing of all His mercies, of His
kindness true,
He is mine, . . . I am His; . . .
Fresh at morn, and in the evening,
comes a blessing new,
He is mine, . . . I am His! . . .
With the deepening shadows comes a
whisper, 'Safely rest!
Sleep in peace, for I am near thee,
naught shall thee molest;
I will linger till the morning, Keeper,
Friend and Guest,'
He is mine, . . . I am His. . . .

3 Though He lead me through the valley
of the shade of death,
He is mine, . . . I am His; . . .
Should I fear, when oh, so tenderly,
He whispereth,
He is mine, . . . I am His! . . .
For the sunshine of His presence doth
illume the night,
And He leads me through the valley to
the mountain height:
Out of bondage into freedom, into
cloudless light,
He is mine, . . . I am His. . . .
Grace Elizabeth Cobb.

373 Come, let us all unite to sing—
God is love!
While Heaven and earth their praises
bring—
God is love!
Let every soul from sin awake,
Each in his heart sweet music make,
And sweetly sing for Jesus' sake—
God is love!

God is love, . . .
God is love! . . .
Come, let us all unite to sing:
God is love!

2 Oh, tell to earth's remotest bound,
God is love!
In Christ is full redemption found—
God is love!
His blood can cleanse our sins away;
His Spirit turns our night to day,
And leads our souls with joy to say—
God is love!

3 How happy is our portion here—
God is love!
His promises our spirits cheer—
God is love!
He is our Sun and Shield by day,
Our help, our hope, our strength, our
stay,
He will be with us all the way—
God is love!

4 What though my heart and flesh shall
fail—
God is love!
Through Christ I shall o'er death
prevail—

God is love!
E'en Jordan's swell I will not fear,
For Jesus will be with me there,
My soul above the waves to bear—
God is love!

Howard Kingsbury.

374 Dear Saviour, Thou art mine,
    How sweet the thought to me!
Let me repeat Thy Name,
And lift my heart to Thee.

  Mine! mine! mine! I know Thou art mine;
  Saviour, dear Saviour, I know Thou art mine.

2 Thou art the sinner's friend,
So I Thy friendship claim,
A sinner saved by grace,
When Thy sweet message came.

3 My hardened heart was touched;
Thy pardoning voice I heard;
And joy and peace came in
While listening to Thy word.

4 So, let me sing Thy praise,
So, let me call Thee mine.
I cannot doubt Thy word,
I know that I am Thine.

Anna Hudson.

375 My hope is built on nothing less
    Than Jesus' blood and righteous-
      ness;
I dare not trust the sweetest frame,
But wholly lean on Jesus' Name.

  On Christ, the Solid Rock, I stand;
  All other ground is sinking sand.

2 When darkness seems to veil His face
I rest on His unchanging grace;
In every high and stormy gale
My anchor holds within the veil.

3 His oath, His covenant, and blood
Support me in the 'whelming flood;
When all around my soul gives way
He then is all my hope and stay.

4 When He shall come with trumpet
    sound,
Oh, may I then in Him be found;

Dressed in His righteousness alone,
Faultless to stand before the throne.

Edward Mote.

376 Dying with Jesus, by death
    reckoned mine;
Living with Jesus a new life divine;
Looking to Jesus till glory doth shine;
Moment by moment, O Lord, I am
  Thine.

  Moment by moment I'm kept in His love,
  Moment by moment I've life from above;
  Looking to Jesus till glory doth shine;
  Moment by moment, O Lord, I am Thine.

2 Never a battle with wrong for the
    right,
Never a contest that He doth not
    fight;
Lifting above us His banner so
    white—
Moment by moment I'm kept in His
    sight.

3 Never a trial that He is not there,
Never a burden that He doth not bear,
Never a sorrow that He doth not
    share—
Moment by moment I'm under His
    care.

4 Never a heartache, and never a groan,
Never a teardrop, and never a moan;
Never a danger but there on the
    throne
Moment by moment He thinks of His
    own.

5 Never a weakness that He doth not
    feel,
Never a sickness that He cannot heal;
Moment by moment, in woe or in
    weal,
Jesus my Saviour abides with me still.

D. W. Whittle.

377 My faith has found a resting
    place,
Not in device nor creed;
I trust the Ever-living One,
His wounds for me shall plead.

I need no other argument,
I need no other plea,
It is enough that Jesus died,
And that He died for me.

2 Enough for me that Jesus saves,
This ends my fear and doubt;
A sinful soul I come to Him,
He'll never cast me out.

3 My heart is leaning on the Word,
The written Word of God,
Salvation by my Saviour's Name,
Salvation through His blood.

4 My great Physician heals the sick,
The lost He came to save;
For me His precious blood He shed,
For me His life He gave.
L. H. Edmonds.

378 'Tis the promise of God full
salvation to give
Unto him who on Jesus, His Son, will
believe.

Hallelujah! 'tis done,
I believe on the Son;
I am saved by the blood of the Crucified One.

2 Though the pathway be lonely and
dangerous too,
Surely Jesus is able to carry me
through.

3 Many loved ones have I in yon
Heavenly throng,
They are safe now in glory, and this is
their song.

4 There are prophets and kings in that
throng I behold,
And they sing while they march
through the streets of pure gold.

5 There's a part in that chorus for you
and for me,
And the theme of our praises for ever
will be:
P. P. Bliss.

379 Come, sing my soul, and praise
the Lord,
Who hath redeemed thee by His
blood;

Delivered thee from chains that
bound,
And brought thee to redemption
ground.

Redemption ground, the ground of peace!
Redemption ground, O wondrous grace!
Here let our praise to God abound,
Who saves us on redemption ground!

2 Once from my God I wandered far,
And with His holy will made war;
But now my songs to God abound;
I'm standing on redemption ground.

3 O joyous hour! when God to me
A vision gave of Calvary;
My bonds were loosed, my soul
unbound;
I sang upon redemption ground.

4 No works of merit now I plead,
But Jesus take for all my need;
No righteousness in me is found,
Except upon redemption ground.

5 Come, weary soul, and here find rest;
Accept redemption and be blest;
The Christ who died, by God is
crowned
To pardon on redemption ground.
El. Nathan.

380 I am weak but Thou art strong;
Jesu, keep me from all wrong;
I'll be satisfied as long
As I walk, let me walk, close with
Thee:

Just a closer walk with Thee,
Grant it, Jesus, this my plea,
Daily walking close with Thee,
Let it be, dear Lord, let it be.

2 Through this world of toils and
snares,
If I falter, Lord, who cares?
Who with me my burden shares?
None but Thee, dear Lord, none but
Thee:

3 When my feeble life is o'er,
Time for me will be no more,
Guide me gently, safely home,
To Thy Kingdom's shore, to Thy
shore:

381 I don't know about tomorrow,
I just live from day to day;
I don't borrow from its sunshine,
For its skies may turn to grey;
I don't worry o'er the future,
For I know what Jesus said,
And today I'll walk beside Him,
For He knows what is ahead.

> Many things about tomorrow I don't seem to understand
> But I know who holds tomorrow, and I know who holds my hand.

2 Every step is getting brighter
As the golden stairs I climb;
Every burden's getting lighter,
Every cloud is silver lined;
There the sun is always shining,
There no tear will dim the eye,
At the ending of the rainbow,
Where the mountains touch the sky.

3 I don't know about tomorrow,
It may bring me poverty;
But the One who feeds the sparrow,
Is the One who stands by me,
And the path that be my portion,
May be through the flame or flood,
But His presence goes before me,
And I'm covered with His blood.

Ira Stanphill.

382 I know my Heavenly Father knows
The storms that would my way oppose;
But he can drive the clouds away,
And turn my darkness into day.

> He knows, . . . He knows, . . .
> The storms that would my way oppose,
> He knows, . . . He knows, . . .
> And tempers every wind . . . that . . . blows.

2 I know my Heavenly Father knows
The balm I need to soothe my woes;
And with His touch of love divine
He heals this wounded soul of mine.

3 I know my Heavenly Father knows
How frail I am to meet my foes;
But He my cause will e'er defend,
Uphold and keep me to the end.

4 I know my Heavenly Father knows
The hour my journey here will close,
And may that hour, O faithful Guide,
Find me safe sheltered by Thy side.

S. M. I. Henry.

383 I know not why God's wondrous grace
To me He hath made known,
Nor why, unworthy, Christ in love
Redeemed me for His own.

> But 'I know whom I have believed,
> And am persuaded that He is able
> To keep that which I've committed
> Unto Him against that day'.

2 I know not how this saving faith
To me He did impart,
Nor how believing in His Word
Wrought peace within my heart.

3 I know not how the Spirit moves,
Convincing men of sin,
Revealing Jesus through the Word,
Creating faith in Him.

4 I know not what of good or ill
May be reserved for me,
Of weary ways or golden days
Before His face I see.

5 I know not when my Lord may come,
At night or noonday fair,
Nor if I'll walk the vale with Him,
Or 'meet Him in the air'.

El. Nathan.

384 Jesus hath died and hath risen again,
Pardon and peace to bestow;
Fully I trust Him; from sin's guilty stain
Jesus saves me now.

> Jesus saves me now!
> Jesus saves me now!
> Yes, Jesus saves me all the time,
> Jesus saves me now!

2 Sin's condemnation is over and gone,
Jesus alone knoweth how;
Life and salvation my soul hath put on;
Jesus saves me now.

3 Jesus is stronger than Satan and sin,
Satan to Jesus must bow,
Therefore I triumph without and
within;
Jesus saves me now.

4 Sorrow and pain may beset me about,
Nothing can darken my brow;
Battling in faith I can joyfully shout:
Jesus saves me now.

Anon.

385 A debtor to mercy alone,
Of covenant mercy I sing;
Nor fear, with God's righteousness on,
My person and offering to bring.
The terrors of law and of God
With me can have nothing to do;
My Saviour's obedience and blood
Hide all my transgressions from view.

2 The work which His goodness began,
The arm of His strength will complete;
His promise is Yea and Amen,
And never was forfeited yet.
Things future, nor things that are
now,
Nor all things below or above,
Can make Him His purpose forgo,
Or sever my soul from His love.

3 My name from the palms of His hands
Eternity will not erase;
Impressed on His heart it remains,
In marks of indelible grace.
Yes, I to the end shall endure,
As sure as the earnest is given;
More happy, but not more secure,
The glorified spirits in Heaven.

A. M. Toplady.

386 Jesus, Thy blood and righteous-
ness
My beauty are, my glorious dress;
'Midst flaming worlds, in these
arrayed,
With joy shall I lift up my head.

2 Bold shall I stand in that great day,
For who aught to my charge shall lay?
Fully absolved through these I am,
From sin and fear, from guilt and
shame.

3 When from the dust of death I rise,
To claim my mansion in the skies,
E'en then shall this be all my plea,
'Jesus hath lived, and died, for me.'

4 This spotless robe the same appears,
When ruined nature sinks in years;
No age can change its glorious hue,
The robe of Christ is ever new.

5 Oh, let the dead now hear Thy voice,
Bid, Lord, Thy banished ones rejoice;
Their beauty this, their glorious dress,
Jesus, the Lord our Righteousness!

Zinzendorf.

387 Jesus my Lord will love me
forever,
From Him no power of evil can sever;
He gave His life to ransom my soul.
Now I belong to Him!

Now I belong to Jesus, Jesus belongs to me,
Not for the years of time alone, but for
eternity.

2 Once I was lost in sin's degradation,
Jesus came down to bring me
salvation;
Lifted me up from sorrow and shame,
Now I belong to Him.

3 Joy floods my soul, for Jesus has
saved me,
Freed me from sin that long had
enslaved me;
His precious blood He gave to
redeem.
Now I belong to Him.

Norman J. Clayton.

388 Thou hidden source of calm
repose,
Thou all sufficient love divine;
My help and refuge from my foes,
Secure I am, if thou art mine,

From sin and grief, from guilt and
   shame:
I hide me, Jesus, in Thy Name.

2 Thy mighty Name salvation is,
And keeps my happy soul above;
Comfort it brings, and power and
   peace,
And joy and everlasting love;
To me, with Thy dear Name are given
Pardon and holiness and Heaven.

3 Jesus, my all in all Thou art,
My rest in toil, mine ease in pain;
The med'cine of my broken heart;
In war, my peace; in loss, my gain:
My smile beneath the tyrant's frown;
In shame, my glory and my crown.

4 In want, my plentiful supply;
In weakness, mine almighty power;
In bonds, my perfect liberty;
My light in Satan's darkest hour;
In grief, my joy unspeakable;
My life in death; my Heaven, my all.
Charles Wesley.

389 I'm not ashamed to own my Lord,
   Or to defend His cause;
Maintain the honour of His Word,
The glory of His Cross.

   At the Cross, at the Cross, where I first saw
   the light,
   And the burden of my heart rolled away, . . .
   It was there by faith I received my sight,
   And now I am happy all the day.

2 Jesus, my Lord! I know His Name—
His Name is all my trust,
Nor will He put my soul to shame,
Nor let my hope be lost.

3 Firm as His throne, His promise
   stands,
And He can well secure
What I've committed to His hands,
Till the decisive hour.

4 Then will He own my worthless name
Before His Father's face;
And in the new Jerusalem,
Appoint my soul a place.
Isaac Watts.

390 Loved with everlasting love,
   Led by grace that love to know,
Spirit breathing from above,
Thou hast taught me it is so.
Oh, this full and perfect peace!
Oh, this transport all divine!
In a love which cannot cease,
I am His and He is mine.

2 Heaven above is softer blue,
Earth around is sweeter green;
Something lives in every hue
Christless eyes have never seen:
Birds with gladder songs o'erflow,
Flowers with deeper beauties shine,
Since I know, as now I know,
I am His and He is mine.

3 Things that once were wild alarms
Cannot now disturb my rest;
Closed in everlasting arms,
Pillowed on the loving breast:
Oh, to lie for ever here!
Doubt and care and self resign,
While He whispers in my ear—
I am His and He is mine.

4 His for ever, only His;
Who the Lord and me shall part?
Ah, with what a rest of bliss,
Christ can fill the loving heart!
Heaven and earth may fade and flee;
Firstborn light in gloom decline;
But while God and I shall be,
I am His and He is mine.
G. Wade Robinson.

391 Blessèd assurance, Jesus is mine!
   Oh, what a foretaste of glory
   divine!
Heir of salvation, purchase of God,
Born of His Spirit, washed in His
   blood.

   This is my story, this is my song,
   Praising my Saviour all the day long.

2 Perfect submission, perfect delight,
Visions of rapture now burst on my
   sight,
Angels descending, bring from above
Echoes of mercy, whispers of love.

3 Perfect submission, all is at rest,
I in my Saviour am happy and blest,
Watching and waiting, looking above,
Filled with His goodness, lost in His
love.

Fanny J. Crosby.

392 God holds the key of all unknown,
And I am glad:
If other hands should hold the key.
Or if He trusted it to me,
I might be sad.

2 What if tomorrow's cares were here
Without its rest?
I'd rather He unlocked the day,
And, as the hours swing open, say,
'My will is best.'

3 The very dimness of my sight
Makes me secure;
For, groping in my misty way,
I feel His hand; I hear Him say,
'My help is sure.'

4 I cannot read His future plans;
But this I know:
I have the smiling of His face,
And all the refuge of His grace,
While here below.

5 Enough: this covers all my wants;
And so I rest!
For what I cannot, He can see,
And in His care I saved shall be,
For ever blest.

J. Parker.

393 What though clouds are hovering
o'er me,
And I seem to walk alone,
Longing, 'mid my cares and crosses,
For the joys that now are flown!
If I've Jesus, 'Jesus only,'
Then my sky will have a gem;
He's the Sun of brightest splendour,
And the Star of Bethlehem.

2 What though all my earthly journey
Bringeth naught but weary hours;
And, in grasping for life's roses,
Thorns I find instead of flowers!

If I've Jesus, 'Jesus only,'
I possess a cluster rare;
He's the 'Lily of the Valley',
And the 'Rose of Sharon' fair.

3 What though all my heart is yearning
For the loved of long ago—
Bitter lessons sadly learning
From the shadowy page of woe!
If I've Jesus, 'Jesus only,'
He'll be with me to the end;
And, unseen by mortal vision,
Angel bands will o'er me bend.

4 When I soar to realms of glory,
And an entrance I await,
If I whisper, 'Jesus only!'
Wide will ope the pearly gate;
When I join the Heavenly chorus,
And the angel-hosts I see,
Precious Jesus, 'Jesus only,'
Will my theme of rapture be.

Hattie M. Conrey.

394 Rejoice in the Lord! oh, let His
mercy cheer;
He sunders the bands that enthrall;
Redeemed by His blood why should
we ever fear
Since Jesus is our 'all in all'?

If God be for us, if God be for us,
If God be for us, who can be against us?
Who? who? who? who can be against us,
against us?

2 Be strong in the Lord! rejoicing in His
might,
Be loyal and true day by day;
When evils assail, be valiant for the
right,
And He will be our strength and stay.

3 Confide in His Word—His promises
so sure;
In Christ they are 'yea and amen';
Though earth pass away, they ever
shall endure,
'Tis written o'er and o'er again.

4 Abide in the Lord: secure in His
control,
'Tis life everlasting begun;

To pluck from His hand the weakest,
trembling soul—
It never, never can be done!

G. M. J.

395 Love Divine, so great and
wondrous,
Deep and mighty, pure, sublime!
Coming from the heart of Jesus,
Just the same through tests of time.

> He the pearly gates will open
> So that I may enter in;
> For He purchased my redemption
> And forgave me all my sin.

2 Like a dove when hunted, frightened
As a wounded fawn was I;
Broken-hearted, yet He healed me,
He will heed the sinner's cry.

3 Love Divine, so great and wondrous,
All my sins He then forgave!
I will sing His praise forever,
For His blood, His power to save.

4 In life's eventide, at twilight,
At His door I'll knock and wait;
By the precious love of Jesus
I shall enter Heaven's gate.

Fred Blom.
trs. Nathaniel Carson.

396 When the storms of life are
raging,
Tempests wild on sea and land,
I will seek a place of refuge
In the shadow of God's hand.

> He will hide . . . me, . . . He will hide . . .
> me, . . .
> Where no harm . . . can e'er betide me;
> He will hide . . . me, . . . safely hide . . . me
> In the shadow of His hand.

2 Though He may send some affliction
'Twill but make me long for home;
For in love, and not in anger,
All His chastenings will come.

3 Enemies may strive to injure,
Satan all His arts employ;
He will turn what seems to harm me
Into everlasting joy.

4 So, while here the cross I'm bearing,
Meeting storms and billows wild,
Jesus, for my soul is caring,
Naught can harm His Father's child.

M. E. Servoss.

397 When I fear my faith will fail
Christ Will hold me fast;
When the tempter would prevail
He can hold me fast:

> He will hold me fast,
> He will hold me fast;
> For my Saviour loves me so,
> He will hold me fast.

2 I could never keep my hold,
He must hold me fast;
For my love is often cold,
He must hold me fast:

3 I am precious in His sight,
He will hold me fast;
Those He saves are His delight
He will hold me fast:

4 He'll not let my soul be lost,
Christ will hold me fast;
Bought by Him at such a cost,
He will hold me fast:

Ada R. Habershon.

GROWTH IN GRACE

398 I'm pressing on the upward way,
New heights I'm gaining every
day;
Still praying as I onward bound,
'Lord, plant my feet on higher
ground'.

> Lord, lift me up and let me stand,
> By faith, on Heaven's table-land;
> Where love, and joy, and light abound,
> Lord, plant my feet on higher ground.

2 My heart has no desire to stay
Where doubts arise, and fears
dismay;
Though some may dwell where these
abound,
My constant aim is higher ground.

3 Beyond the mist I fain would rise,
To rest beneath unclouded skies,
Above earth's turmoil peace is found
By those who dwell on higher ground.

4 I long to scale the utmost height,
Though rough the way, and hard the
fight,
My song, while climbing, shall
resound,
Lord, lead me on to higher ground.

5 Lord, lead me up the mountain side,
I dare not climb without my Guide;
And, Heaven gained, I'll gaze around
With grateful heart from higher
ground.
Johnson Oatman, Jnr. and Ada R. Habershon.

399 We shall see the desert as the
rose,
Walking in the King's highway;
There'll be singing where salvation
goes,
Walking in the King's highway.

There's a highway there, and a way, . . .
Where sorrow shall flee away, . . .
And the light shines bright as the day . . .
Walking in the King's highway.

2 We shall see the glory of the Lord,
Walking in the King's highway;
And behold the beauty of His Word,
Walking in the King's highway.

3 There the rain shall come upon the
ground,
Walking in the King's highway;
And the springs of water will be
found,
Walking in the King's highway.

4 There no rav'nous beast shall make
afraid,
Walking in the King's highway;
For the purified the way is made,
Walking in the King's highway.

5 No unclean thing shall pass o'er here,
Walking in the King's highway;
But the ransomed ones without a
fear,
Walking in the King's highway.
Florence Horton.

400 Once far from God and dead in
sin
No light my heart could see;
But in God's Word the light I found,
Now Christ liveth in me.

Christ liveth in me, . . .
Christ liveth in me, . . .
Oh, what a salvation this,
That Christ liveth in me.

2 As rays of light from yonder sun
The flowers of earth set free,
So life and light and love came forth
From Christ living in me.

3 As lives the flower within the seed,
As in the cone the tree,
So, praise the God of truth and grace,
His Spirit dwelleth in me.

4 With longing all my heart is filled,
That like Him I may be,
As on the wondrous thought I dwell,
That Christ liveth in me.
El. Nathan.

401 More about Jesus would I know,
More of His grace to others show;
More of His saving fulness see,
More of His love who died for me.

More, more about Jesus,
More, more about Jesus;
More of His saving fulness see,
More of His love who died for me.

2 More about Jesus let me learn,
More of His holy will discern;
Spirit of God, my teacher be,
Showing the things of Christ to me.

3 More about Jesus, in His Word,
Holding communion with my Lord;
Hearing His voice in every line,
Making each faithful saying mine.

4 More about Jesus, on His throne,
Riches in glory all His own;
More of His Kingdom's sure increase;
More of His coming, Prince of Peace.
E. E. Hewitt.

402 O to be like Thee, blessèd
Redeemer,
This is my constant longing and
prayer;
Gladly I'll forfeit all of earth's
treasures,
Jesus, Thy perfect likeness to wear.

O to be like Thee, O to be like Thee,
Blessèd Redeemer, pure as Thou art;
Come in Thy sweetness, come in Thy fulness;
Stamp Thine own image deep on my heart.

2 O to be like Thee, full of compassion,
Loving, forgiving, tender and kind,
Helping the helpless, cheering the
fainting,
Seeking the wandering sinner to find.

3 O to be like Thee, lowly in spirit,
Holy and harmless, patient and brave;
Meekly enduring cruel reproaches,
Willing to suffer, others to save.

4 O to be like Thee, Lord, I am coming,
Now to receive the anointing divine,
All that I am and have I am bringing,
Lord, from this moment all shall be
Thine.

5 O to be like Thee, while I am pleading
Pour out Thy Spirit, fill with Thy love,
Make me a temple meet for Thy
dwelling,
Fit me for life and Heaven above.
T. O. Chisholm.

403 Are you trusting Jesus,
All along the way?
Does He grow more precious
To your heart each day?
Are you His disciple?
Test His word and see,
He will give the Spirit
More abundantly.

More . . . abundantly, more . . . abundantly,
'That they might have life, and more
abundantly'.

2 For His matchless favour
Magnify the Name
Of our gracious Saviour
Who from glory came;

Let the saints adore Him
For this wondrous word,
Sealing our redemption
Through the crimson flood.

3 Come to Him believing,
Harken to His call;
All from Him receiving,
Yield to Him your all;
Jesus will accept you
When to Him you flee;
He will grant His blessing
More abundantly.
Thoro Harris.

404 Deeper, deeper in the love of
Jesus
Daily let me go;
Higher, higher in the school of
wisdom,
More of grace to know.

O deep . . . er yet I pray, . . .
And high . . . er every day, . . .
And wis . . . er, blessèd Lord, . . .
In Thy precious, holy Word.

2 Deeper, deeper! blessèd Holy Spirit,
Take me deeper still,
Till my life is wholly lost in Jesus
And His perfect will.

3 Deeper, deeper! though it cost hard
trials,
Deeper let me go!
Rooted in the holy love of Jesus
Let me fruitful grow.

4 Deeper, higher every day in Jesus,
Till all conflict past
Finds me conqueror, and in His own
image
Perfected at last.
Charles Price Jones.

405 Trying to walk in the steps of the
Saviour,
Trying to follow our Saviour and
King;
Shaping our lives by His blessèd
example,
Happy, how happy, the songs that we
bring.

How beautiful to walk in the steps of the Saviour,
Stepping in the light, stepping in the light;
How beautiful to walk in the steps of the Saviour,
Led in paths of light.

2 Pressing more closely to Him who is leading
When we are tempted to turn from the way;
Trusting the arm that is strong to defend us,
Happy, how happy our praises each day.

3 Walking in footsteps of gentle forebearance,
Footsteps of faithfulness, mercy, and love,
Looking to Him for the grace freely promised,
Happy, how happy, our journey above.

4 Trying to walk in the steps of the Saviour,
Upward, still upward, we'll follow our Guide,
When we shall see Him, 'the King in His beauty',
Happy, how happy, our place at His side.

Eliza E. Hewitt.

406 Hark, my soul, it is the Lord;
'Tis thy Saviour; hear His Word;
Jesus speaks, and speaks to thee,
'Say, poor sinner, lov'st thou Me?'

2 'I delivered thee when bound,
And when bleeding, healed thy wound;
Sought thee wandering, set thee right,
Turned thy darkness into light.

3 'Can a woman's tender care
Cease towards the child she bare?
Yes, she may forgetful be,
Yet will I remember thee.

4 'Mine is an unchanging love,
Higher than the heights above,
Deeper than the depths beneath,
Free and faithful, strong as death.

5 'Thou shalt see My glory soon,
When the work of grace is done;
Partner of My throne shalt be;
Say, poor sinner, lov'st thou Me?'

6 Lord, it is my chief complaint
That my love is weak and faint;
Yet I love Thee, and adore;
O for grace to love Thee more.

W. Cowper.

407 Jesus, lead me up the mountain,
Where the whitest robes are seen,
Where the saints can see the fountain,
Where the pure are keeping clean.

Bring me high . . . er up the mountain,
Into fel . . . lowship with Thee; . . .
In Thy light . . . I see the fountain,
And the blood that cleanseth me. . . .

2 Higher up, where light increases,
Rich above all earthly good,
Where the life of sinning ceases,
Where the Spirit comes in flood.

3 Bring me higher, nothing dreading,
In the race that has no stop,
In Thy footsteps keep me treading,
Give me strength to reach the top.

4 Make me better, make me purer,
Keep me where the fire refines.
Where the breath of God is sweeter,
Where the brightest glory shines.

408 Take time to be holy, speak oft
with thy Lord;
Abide in Him always, and feed on His Word;
Make friends of God's children, help those who are weak;
Forgetting in nothing His blessing to seek.

2 Take time to be holy, the world rushes on;
Spend much time in secret with Jesus alone—
By looking to Jesus, like Him thou shalt be;
Thy friends in thy conduct His likeness shall see.

3 Take time to be holy, let Him be thy
   Guide;
   And run not before Him, whatever
   betide;
   In joy or in sorrow still follow thy
   Lord,
   And, looking to Jesus, still trust in His
   Word.

4 Take time to be holy, be calm in thy
   soul;
   Each thought and each temper
   beneath His control:
   Thus led by His Spirit to fountains of
   love,
   Thou soon shalt be fitted for service
   above.

W. D. Longstaff.

409 O tell me more of Christ, my
       Saviour;
   On this glad theme dwell o'er and
   o'er;
   His boundless grace, His saving
   favour,
   His precious Name, O tell me more!

> O tell me more! so much I need
> His power to keep, His hand to lead;
> O tell me more of Him I love,
> Until I see His face above.

2 O tell me more of love's sweet story,
   If you would cheer and comfort me;
   How Jesus wept, the King of glory,
   Those tender tears of sympathy.

3 O tell me more! and I repeating
   The happy news shall spread the joy;
   Come blessèd Lord, Thy work
   completing,
   Till songs of praise our lips employ.

E. E. Hewitt.

410 Nearer, my God to Thee,
       Nearer to Thee;
   E'en though it be a cross
   That raiseth me,
   Still all my song shall be,
   Nearer my God to Thee,
   Nearer to Thee.

2 Though, like the wanderer,
   The sun gone down,
   Darkness be over me,
   My rest a stone,
   Yet in my dreams I'd be
   Nearer, my God, to Thee,
   Nearer to Thee!

3 There let the way appear
   Steps unto Heaven;
   All that Thou send'st to me
   In mercy given;
   Angels to beckon me
   Nearer, my God, to Thee,
   Nearer to Thee!

4 Then, with my waking thoughts
   Bright with Thy praise,
   Out of my stony griefs
   Bethel I'll raise;
   So by my woes to be
   Nearer, my God, to Thee,
   Nearer to Thee!

5 Or if on joyful wing
   Cleaving the sky,
   Sun, moon, and stars forgot,
   Upwards I fly,
   Still all my song shall be,
   Nearer, my God, to Thee,
   Nearer to Thee!

Sarah F. Adams.

411 Earthly pleasures vainly call me,
       I would be like Jesus;
   Nothing worldly shall enthrall me,
   I would be like Jesus.

> Be like Jesus, this my song,
> In the home and in the throng;
> Be like Jesus, all day long!
> I would be like Jesus.

2 He has broken every fetter,
   I would be like Jesus;
   That my soul may serve Him better,
   I would be like Jesus.

3 All the way from earth to glory,
   I would be like Jesus;
   Telling o'er and o'er my story,
   I would be like Jesus.

4 That in Heaven He may meet me,
   I would be like Jesus;
   That His words 'Well done' may greet
   me,
   I would be like Jesus.

J. Rowe.

CONFLICT AND VICTORY

412 Sound the battle cry!
   See! the foe is nigh;
Raise the standard high
For the Lord;
Gird your armour on,
Stand firm every one;
Rest your cause upon
His holy Word.

   Rouse, then, soldiers! rally round the banner!
   Ready, steady, pass the word along;
   Onward, forward, shout aloud Hosannah!
   Christ is Captain of the mighty throng.

2 Strong to meet the foe,
   Marching on we go,
   While our cause we know
   Must prevail;
   Shield and banner bright
   Gleaming in the light;
   Battling for the right,
   We ne'er can fail.

3 Oh! Thou God of all,
   Hear us when we call;
   Help us one and all
   By Thy grace;
   When the battle's done,
   And the victory won,
   May we wear the crown
   Before Thy face.

W. F. Sherwin.

413 Stand up! stand up for Jesus,
   Ye soldiers of the Cross!
Lift high His royal banner;
It must not suffer loss.
From victory unto victory
His army shall He lead,
Till every foe is vanquished,
And Christ is Lord indeed.

   Stand up for Jesus,
   Ye soldiers of the Cross!
   Lift high His royal banner,
   It must not! It must not suffer loss!

2 Stand up! stand up for Jesus!
   The trumpet call obey;
   Forth to the mighty conflict
   In this His glorious day;
   Ye that are men now serve Him
   Against unnumbered foes;
   Let courage rise with danger,
   And strength to strength oppose.

3 Stand up! stand up for Jesus!
   Stand in His strength alone;
   The arm of flesh will fail you,
   Ye dare not trust your own;
   Put on the gospel armour,
   And watching unto prayer;
   Where duty calls, or danger,
   Be never wanting there.

4 Stand up! stand up for Jesus!
   The strife will not be long;
   This day the noise of battle,
   The next the victor's song;
   To him that overcometh
   A crown of life shall be;
   He with the King of glory
   Shall reign eternally.

G. Duffield.

414 The fight is on, the trumpet sound
   is ringing out,
   The cry, 'To arms!' is heard afar and
   near;
   The Lord of hosts is marching on to
   victory,
   The triumph of the right will soon
   appear.

   The fight is on, O Christian soldier,
   And face to face in stern array,
   With armour gleaming, and colours streaming,
   The right and wrong engage today!
   The fight is on, but be not weary;
   Be strong, and in His might hold fast;
   If God be for us, His banner o'er us,
   We'll sing the victor's song at last!

2 The fight is on, arouse ye soldiers
   brave and true;
   Jehovah leads, and victory will
   assure;

Go buckle on the armour God has
given you,
And in His strength unto the end
endure.

3 The Lord is leading on to certain
victory,
The bow of promise spans the eastern
sky;
His glorious Name in every land shall
honoured be,
The morn will break, the dawn of
peace is nigh.

Leila N. Morris.

415 We never need be vanquished,
We never need give in,
Though waging war with Satan,
And compassed round by sin.
Temptations will beset us,
Allurements oft assail,
But in the Name of Jesus
We shall, we must prevail.

Victory in Jesus' name,
Victory our hearts proclaim,
Victory, glorious victory.

2 He leads us on in triumph,
An overcoming band,
While victory crowns His progress,
'For none can stay His hand'.
Our eyes are on our Leader,
His presence is our might;
He arms us for the conflict,
And trains our hands to fight.

3 God wills not that His people
By sin enthralled should be,
But that their lives henceforward
Be lives of victory;
And so at our disposal
He places all His power,
That we from its resources
May draw in danger's hour.

4 Herein is hid the secret
Of an all-glorious life,
Whereby we conquer Satan
And rise above sin's strife.
Abiding in the Saviour,
Self-prostrate in the dust,
We live to do His bidding
In glad perpetual trust.

5 We in ourselves are nothing,
A small and feeble host,
Nor have we aught of prowess
Wherewith to make our boast.
Our stronghold is Christ Jesus,
His grace alone we plead,
His Name our shield and banner,
Himself just all we need.

W. A. Garrett.

416 When upon life's billows you are
tempest-tossed,
When you are discouraged, thinking
all is lost,
Count your many blessings, name
them one by one,
And it will surprise you what the Lord
hath done.

Count your blessings, name them one by one,
Count your blessings, see what God hath
done;
Count your blessings, name them one by one,
And it will surprise you what the Lord hath
done.

2 Are you ever burdened with a load of
care?
Does the cross seem heavy you are
called to bear?
Count your many blessings, every
doubt will fly,
And you will be singing as the days go
by.

3 When you look at others with their
lands and gold,
Think that Christ has promised you
His wealth untold,
Count your many blessings, money
cannot buy
Your reward in Heaven, nor your
home on high.

4 So amid the conflict, whether great or
small,
Do not be discouraged, God is over
all,
Count your many blessings, angels
will attend,
Help and comfort give you to your
journey's end.

Johnson Oatman, Jr.

417 They who know the Saviour shall in Him be strong,
Mighty in the conflict of the right 'gainst wrong.
This the blessèd promise given in God's Word,
Doing wondrous exploits, they who know the Lord.

Victory! victory! blessèd blood-bought victory,
Victory! victory! victory all the time.
As Jehovah liveth, strength divine He giveth,
Unto those who know Him victory all the time.

2 In the midst of battle be not thou dismayed,
Though the powers of darkness 'gainst thee are arrayed;
God, thy strength, is with thee, causing thee to stand,
Heaven's allied armies wait at thy command.

3 Brave to bear life's testing, strong the foe to meet,
Walking like a hero midst the furnace heat,
Doing wondrous exploits with the Spirit's sword
Winning souls for Jesus, praise, O praise the Lord.

Mrs. C. H. Morris.

418 Christ, our mighty Captain, leads against the foe;
We will never falter when He bids us go:
Though His righteous purpose we may never know
Yet we'll follow all the way.

Forward! forward! 'tis the Lord's command,
Forward! forward! to the promised land;
Forward! forward! let the chorus ring:
We are sure to win with Christ, our King!

2 Satan's fearful onslaughts cannot make us yield,
While we trust in Christ, our Buckler and our Shield;
Pressing ever on—the Spirit's sword we wield,
And we follow all the way.

3 Let our glorious banner ever be unfurled—
From its mighty stronghold evil shall be hurled;
Christ, our mighty Captain, overcomes the world,
And we follow all the way.

4 Fierce the battle rages, but 'twill not be long,
Then triumphant—shall we join the blessèd throng,
Joyfully uniting in the victor's song—
If we follow all the way.

Mrs. Frank A. Breck.

419 Conquerors and overcomers now are we,
Through the precious blood of Christ we've victory,
If the Lord be for us, we can never fail;
Nothing 'gainst His mighty power can e'er prevail.

Conquerors are we, . . . through the blood,
. . . through the blood; . . .
God will give . . . us victory, . . . through the blood, . . . through the blood; . . .
Through the Lamb for sinners slain,
Yet who lives and reigns again,
More than conquerors are we.

2 In the name of Israel's God we'll onward press,
Overcoming sin and all unrighteousness;
Not to us, but unto Him the praise shall be
For salvation and for blood-bought victory.

3 Unto him that overcometh shall be given
Here to eat of 'hidden manna' sent from Heaven;
Over yonder he the victor's palm shall bear
And a robe of white and golden crown shall wear.

Leila N. Morris.

420 Encamped along the hills of light,
Ye Christian soldiers, rise —
And press the battle ere the night
Shall veil the glowing skies;
Against the foe in vales below
Let all our strength be hurled;
Faith is the victory, we know,
That overcomes the world.

  Faith is the victory!
  Faith is the victory!
  O glorious victory
  That overcomes the world.

2 His banner over us is love.
Our sword the Word of God;
We tread the road the saints above
With shouts of triumph trod.
By faith they, like a whirlwind's
breath,
Swept on o'er every field;
The faith by which they conquered
death
Is still our shining shield.

3 On every hand the foe we find
Drawn up in dread array;
Let tents of ease be left behind,
And onward to the fray.
Salvation's helmet on each head,
With truth all girt about,
The earth shall tremble 'neath our
tread
And echo with our shout.

4 To him that overcomes the foe
White raiment shall be given;
Before the angels he shall know
His name confessed in Heaven.
Then onward from the hills of light,
Our hearts with love aflame,
We'll vanquish all the hosts of night
In Jesus' conquering Name.

John H. Yates.

421 'We rest on Thee,' our Shield and
Defender!
We go not forth alone against the foe;
Strong in Thy strength, safe in Thy
keeping tender,
'We rest on Thee, and in Thy Name
we go.'

Strong in Thy strength, safe in Thy
keeping tender,
'We rest on Thee, and in Thy Name
we go.'

2 Yes, 'in Thy name,' O Captain of
salvation!
In Thy dear Name, all other names
above;
Jesus our Righteousness, our sure
Foundation,
Our Prince of glory and our King of
love.
Jesus our Righteousness, our sure
Foundation,
Our Prince of glory and our King of
love.

3 We go in faith, our own great
weakness feeling,
And needing more each day Thy
grace to know:
Yet from our hearts a song of triumph
pealing;
'We rest on Thee, and in Thy Name
we go.'
Yet from our hearts a song of triumph
pealing;
'We rest on Thee, and in Thy Name
we go.'

4 'We rest on Thee,' our Shield and our
Defender!
Thine is the battle, Thine shall be the
praise;
When passing through the gates of
pearly splendour,
Victors — we rest *with* Thee, through
endless days.
When passing through the gates of
pearly splendour,
Victors — we rest *with* Thee, through
endless days.

Edith G. Cherry.

422 Hark to the sound of voices!
Hark to the tramp of feet!
Is it a mighty army
Treading the busy street?
Nearer it comes and nearer,
Singing a glad refrain:
List what they say as they haste away
To the sound of a martial strain:

The Christian Life

Marching beneath the banner,
Fighting beneath the Cross,
Trusting in Him who saves us,
Ne'er shall we suffer loss!
Singing the songs of homeland,
Loudly the chorus rings,
We march to the fight in our armour bright,
At the call of the King of kings.

2 Out of the mist of error,
Out of the realms of night,
Out of the pride of learning,
Seeking the home of light;
Out of the strife for power,
Out of the greed of gold,
Onward they roam to their Heavenly home,
And the treasure that grows not old.

3 Out of the bonds of evil,
Out of the chains of sin,
Ever they're pressing onward,
Fighting the fight within;
Holding the passions under,
Ruling the sense with soul,
Wielding the sword in the Name of the Lord,
As they march to their Heavenly goal.

4 On then, ye gallant soldiers,
On to your home above!
Yours is the truth and glory,
Yours is the power and love.
Here are ye trained for heroes,
Yonder ye serve the King;
March to the light 'neath the banner white,
With the song that ye love to sing:

Colin Sterne.

423 Are you heavy laden and with sorrow tried?
Look in faith to Christ, your Helper, Friend, and Guide;
Think of all your mercies, such a boundless store,
Tears will change to praises as you count them o'er.

Count . . . your mercies, such a boundless store,
Count . . . your mercies, pressed and running o'er,
All . . . your mercies, count them o'er and o'er;
Lost in love and wonder at the boundless store.

2 Think of hidden dangers He has brought you through,
Of the cares and burdens He has borne for you,
Of His words of comfort in your deepest need,
Count the times when Jesus proved a Friend indeed.

3 Does your pathway darken when the clouds draw near?
Count your many mercies, dry the flowing tear;
Trust Him in the shadows dim and have no fear;
Heaven will be the sweeter for the dark down here.

4 As He looks from Heaven down on you and me,
Know you not He chooseth what each day shall be?
Trust His loving wisdom, though the hot tears start,
Give to Him the incense of a grateful heart.

Flora Kirkland.

424 Fight the good fight with all thy might,
Christ is thy strength, and Christ thy right;
Lay hold on life, and it shall be
Thy joy and crown eternally.

2 Run the straight race through God's good grace,
Lift up thine eyes, and seek His face;
Life with its way before thee lies,
Christ is the path, and Christ thy prize.

3 Cast care aside, lean on thy Guide;
His boundless mercy will provide;
Lean, and the trusting soul shall prove
Christ is its life, and Christ its love.

4 Faint not, nor fear, His arms are near,
He changeth not, and thou art dear;
Only believe, and thou shalt see
That Christ is all in all to thee.

J. S. B. Monsell.

425 Marching on in the light of God,
Marching on, I'm marching on:
Up the path that the Master trod,
Marching, marching on.

A robe of white, a crown of gold,
A harp, a home, a mansion fair,
A victor's palm, a joy untold,
Are mine when I get there,
For Jesus is my Saviour, He's washed my sins
away,
Paid my debt on Calvary's mountain,
Happy in His dying love, singing all the day,
I'm living, yes, I'm living in the Fountain.

2 Marching on through the hosts of sin,
Marching on, I'm marching on:
Victory's mine while I've Christ within.
Marching, marching on.

3 Marching on while the worldings
sneer,
Marching on, I'm marching on:
Perfect love casteth out all fear,
Marching, marching on.

4 Marching on in the Spirit's might,
Marching on, I'm marching on:
More than conqueror in every fight,
Marching, marching on.

5 Marching on to the realms above,
Marching on, I'm marching on:
There to sing of redeeming love,
Marching, marching on.
R. Johnson.

426 Onward, Christian soldiers!
Marching as to war,
Looking unto Jesus
Who is gone before;
Christ, the Royal Master,
Leads against the foe;
Forward into battle
See His banners go.

Onward, Christian soldiers!
Marching as to war,
Looking unto Jesus
Who is gone before.

2 At the name of Jesus
Satan's host doth flee;
On then, Christian soldiers,
On to victory!

Hell's foundations quiver
At the shout of praise:
Brothers, lift your voices,
Loud your anthems raise.

3 Like a mighty army
Moves the Church of God:
Brothers, we are treading
Where the saints have trod.
We are not divided,
All one body we—
One in hope and doctrine,
One in charity.

4 Crowns and thrones may perish,
Kingdoms rise and wane;
But the Church of Jesus
Constant will remain:
Gates of hell can never
'Gainst that Church prevail;
We have Christ's own promise—
And that cannot fail.

5 Onward then, ye people,
Join our happy throng;
Blend with ours your voices
In the triumph song:
'Glory, praise and honour,
Unto Christ the King,'—
This, through countless ages,
Men and angels sing.
S. Baring-Gould.

427 Blessèd Lord, in Thee is refuge,
Safety for my trembling soul,
Power to lift my head when drooping,
'Midst the angry billows roll.
I will trust Thee,
All my life Thou shalt control.

2 In the past too unbelieving
'Midst the tempest I have been,
And my heart has slowly trusted
What my eyes have never seen.
Blessèd Jesus,
Teach me on Thine arm to lean.

3 Oh, for trust that brings me triumph,
When defeat seems strangely near!
Oh, for faith that changes fighting
Into victory's ringing cheer!
Faith triumphant!
Knowing not defeat or fear.

The Christian Life

4 Faith triumphant—blessèd victory!
  Every barrier swept away!
  Heaven descending, joy and fulness,
  Dawn of everlasting day!
  Jesus only—
  Him to love and Him obey.

H. H. Booth.

428 He lives in us, the Christ of God,
  His Spirit joins with ours;
He brings to us the Father's grace
With powers beyond our powers.

2 And if enticing sin grows strong,
  When human nature fails,
  God's Spirit in our inner self
  Fights with us, and prevails.

3 Our pangs of guilt and fears of death
  Are Satan's strategems:
  By Jesus Christ who died for us
  God pardons; who condemns?

4 And when we cannot feel our faith
  Nor bring ourselves to pray,
  The Spirit pleads with God for us
  In words we could not say.

5 God gave His Son to save us all—
  No other love like this!—
  Then shall He ever turn away
  From those He marks as His?

6 And God has raised Him from the
    grave,
  In this we stand assured;
  So none can tear us from His love
  In Jesus Christ our Lord.

Michael Perry.

429 Who is on the Lord's side?
  Who will serve the King?
Who will be His helpers
Other lives to bring?
Who will leave the world's side?
Who will face the foe?
Who is on the Lord's side?
Who for Him will go?
By Thy call of mercy,
By Thy grace divine,
We are on the Lord's side,
Saviour, we are Thine!

2 Not for weight of glory,
  Not for crown and palm,
  Enter we the army,
  Raise the warrior psalm;
  But for love that claimeth
  Lives for whom He died:
  He whom Jesus nameth
  Must be on His side!
  By Thy love constraining,
  By Thy grace divine,
  We are on the Lord's side,
  Saviour, we are Thine!

3 Jesus, Thou has bought us,
  Not with gold or gem,
  But with Thine own life-blood
  For Thy diadem
  With Thy blessing filling
  All who come to Thee,
  Thou hast made us willing,
  Thou hast made us free.
  By Thy grand redemption,
  By Thy grace divine,
  We are on the Lord's side,
  Saviour, we are Thine!

4 Fierce may be the conflict,
  Strong may be the foe;
  But the King's own army
  None can overthrow:
  Round His standard ranging,
  Victory is secure,
  For His truth unchanging
  Makes the triumph sure.
  Joyfully enlisting,
  By Thy grace divine,
  We are on the Lord's side,
  Saviour, we are Thine!

Frances Ridley Havergal.

430 Soldiers of Christ, arise—
  And put your armour on,
Strong in the strength which God
    supplies
Through His eternal Son!

2 Strong in the Lord of hosts,
  Stand in His mighty power;
  Who in the strength of Jesus trusts
  Is more than conqueror!

3 Stand then in His great might,
With all His strength endued;
And take, to arm you for the fight,
The panoply of God.

4 To keep your armour bright,
Attend with constant care;
Still marching in your Captain's sight,
And watching unto prayer.

5 From strength to strength go on,
Wrestle and fight and pray,
Tread all the powers of darkness
down
And win the well-fought day.

6 Then, having all things done,
And every conflict past—
Accepted each through Christ alone,
You shall be crowned at last.

Charles Wesley.

431 He who would valiant be
'Gainst all disaster,
Let him in constancy
Follow the Master,
There's no discouragement
Shall make him once relent
His first avowed intent
To be a pilgrim.

2 Who so beset him round
With dismal stories,
Do but themselves confound—
His strength the more is.
No foes shall stay his might,
Though he with giants fight:
He will make good his right
To be a pilgrim.

3 Since, Lord, Thou dost defend
Us with Thy Spirit,
We know we at the end
Shall life inherit.
Then fancies flee away!
I'll fear not what men say,
I'll labour night and day
To be a pilgrim.

John Bunyan and others.

GUIDANCE AND SECURITY

432 Eternal Father, strong to save,
Whose arm hath bound the
restless wave,
Who bidd'st the mighty ocean deep
Its own appointed limits keep;
O hear us when we cry to Thee
For those in peril on the sea.

2 O Christ, Whose voice the waters
heard,
And hushed their raging at Thy Word,
Who walkedst on the foaming deep,
And calm amid the storm didst sleep;
O hear us when we cry to Thee
For those in peril on the sea.

3 O Holy Spirit, Who did'st brood
Upon the waters dark and rude,
And bid their angry tumult cease,
And give, for wild confusion, peace;
O hear us when we cry to Thee
For those in peril on the sea.

4 O Trinity of love and power,
Our brethren shield in danger's hour;
From rock and tempest, fire and foe,
Protect them; wheresoe'er they go;
Thus evermore shall rise to Thee
Glad hymns of praise from land and
sea.

William Whiting.

433 Jesus will walk with me down
through the valley,
Jesus will walk with me over the plain;
When in the shadow or when in the
sunshine,
If He goes with me I shall not
complain.

Jesus will walk with me, He will talk with me,
He will walk with me, in joy or in sorrow,
Today and tomorrow I know He will walk with
me.

2 Jesus will walk with me when I am
tempted,
Giving me strength as my need may
demand;
When in affliction His presence is near
me,
I am upheld by His almighty hand.

3 Jesus will walk with me, guarding me
ever,
Giving me victory through storm and
through strife,
He is my Comforter, Counsellor,
Leader,
Over the uneven journey of life.

4 Jesus will walk with me in life's fair
morning,
And when the shadows of evening
must come,
Living or dying He will not forsake me,
Jesus will walk with me all the way
home.

Haldor Lillenas.

434 Who shall dare to separate us
From the love of Christ, our Lord?
Neither pain nor tribulation,
Persecution, want nor sword.

2 Nay, in all things that may hurt us
We shall more than conquerors be,
Through the Christ who proved He
loved us
By His dying on the Tree.

3 Neither death, nor life, nor angels,
Principalities nor powers,
Nor things present, nor things future
Can disturb this faith of ours.

4 Height, nor depth, nor any creature—
'Tis the promise of His Word—
Shall have power to separate us
From the love of Christ, our Lord.

A. R. Wiggins.

435 Travelling on the sea of life we're
homeward bound,
Drifting wrecks and struggling souls
are all around;
But we do not fear the voyage, for we
know
That the Saviour steers us as we
onward go.

We're homeward bound for glory, . . .
homeward bound for glory; . . .
There we'll meet with loved ones gone before,
We're homeward bound for glory, . . .
homeward bound for glory, . . .
All the storms of life will soon be o'er.

2 Jesus guides our storm-tossed barque
across the seas,
He will bring us safely to the port of
peace;
He's the Pilot; He is standing at the
helm,
And no angry winds or waves can
overwhelm.

3 Come on board the Gospel vessel, do
not stay,
And we'll help you as we journey on
the way;
Soon to harbour at our Father's blest
abode,
We will worship in the city of our
God.

R. F. Beveridge.

436 Oh, safe to the Rock that is higher
than I
My soul in its conflicts and sorrows
would fly.
So sinful, so weary, Thine, Thine
would I be;
Thou blest 'Rock of Ages', I'm hiding
in Thee.

Hiding in Thee, hiding in Thee,
Thou blest 'Rock of Ages', I'm hiding in Thee.

2 In the calm of the noontide, in
sorrow's lone hour,
In times when temptation casts o'er
me its power;
In the tempests of life, on its wide
heaving sea,
Thou blest 'Rock of Ages', I'm hiding
in Thee.

3 How oft in the conflict, when pressed
by the foe
I have fled to my Refuge and breathed
out my woe;
How often when trials like sea billows
roll
Have I hidden in Thee, O Thou Rock
of my soul.

W. O. Cushing.

437 Teach me Thy way, O Lord,
Teach me Thy way!
Thy gracious aid afford,
Teach me Thy way!

Help me to walk aright,
More by faith, less by sight;
Lead me with Heavenly light:
Teach me Thy way!

2 When doubts and fears arise,
Teach me Thy way!
When storms o'erspread the skies,
Teach me Thy way!
Shine through the cloud and rain,
Through sorrow, toil, and pain;
Make Thou my pathway plain:
Teach me Thy way!

3 Long as my life shall last,
Teach me Thy way!
Where'er my lot be cast,
Teach me Thy way!
Until the race is run,
Until the journey's done,
Until the crown is won,
Teach me Thy way!

B. Mansell Ramsey.

438 As I journey through the land
singing as I go,
Pointing souls to Calvary—to the
crimson flow,
Many arrows pierce my soul from
without, within;
But my Lord leads me on, through
Him I must win.

Oh, I want to see Him, look upon His face,
There to sing forever of His saving grace; . . .
On the streets of Glory let me lift my voice;
Cares all past, home at last, ever to rejoice.

2 When in service for my Lord dark may
be the night,
But I'll cling more close to Him, He
will give me light;
Satan's snares may vex my soul, turn
my thoughts aside;
But my Lord goes ahead, leads
whate'er betide.

3 When in valleys low I look toward the
mountain height,
And behold my Saviour there, leading
in the fight,
With a tender hand outstretched
toward the valley low,
Guiding me, I can see, as I onward go.

4 When before me billows rise from the
mighty deep,
Then my Lord directs my barque; He
doth safely keep,
And He leads me gently on through
this world below,
He's a real Friend to me, Oh, I love
Him so.

R. H. Cornelius.

439 Be not dismayed whate'er betide,
God will take care of you!
Beneath His wings of love abide,
God will take care of you!

God will take care of you,
Through every day, o'er all the way;
He will take care of you:
God will take care of you!

2 Through days of toil when heart doth
fail,
God will take care of you!
When dangers fierce your path assail,
God will take care of you!

3 All you may need He will provide,
God will take care of you!
Trust Him, and you will be satisfied,
God will take care of you!

4 Lonely or sad, from friends apart,
God will take care of you!
He will give peace to your aching
heart,
God will take care of you!

5 No matter what may be the test,
God will take care of you!
Lean, weary one, upon His breast,
God will take care of you!

C. D. Martin and H. C. A. D.

440 In Heavenly love abiding,
No change my heart shall fear;
And safe is such confiding,
For nothing changes here:
The storm may roar without me,
My heart may low be laid;
But God is round about me,
And can I be dismayed?

The Christian Life

2 Wherever He may guide me,
No want shall turn me back;
My Shepherd is beside me,
And nothing can I lack:
His wisdom ever waketh,
His sight is never dim;
He knows the way He taketh,
And I will walk with Him.

3 Green pastures are before me
Which yet I have not seen;
Bright skies will soon be o'er me,
Where the dark clouds have been:
My hope I cannot measure,
My path to life is free;
My Saviour has my treasure,
And He will walk with me.

Anna L. Waring.

441 It may be in the valley, where
countless dangers hide;
It may be in the sunshine, that I in
peace abide;
But this one thing I know—if it be
dark or fair,
If Jesus is with me, I'll go anywhere!

If Jesus goes with me, I'll go . . . anywhere!
'Tis Heaven to me, where'er I may be, if He is
there!
I count it a privilege here . . . His Cross to bear;
If Jesus goes with me, I'll go anywhere.

2 It may be I must carry the blessèd
Word of life
Across the burning deserts to those in
sinful strife;
And though it be my lot to bear my
colours there,
If Jesus goes with me, I'll go
anywhere!

3 But if it be my portion to bear my
cross at home,
While others bear their burdens
beyond the billow's foam,
I'll prove my faith in Him—confess His
judgments fair,
And if He stays with me, I'll stay
anywhere!

4 It is not mine to question the
judgments of my Lord,
It is but mine to follow the leadings of
His Word;

But if I go or stay, or whether here or
there,
I'll be with my Saviour, content
anywhere!

C. Austin Miles.

442 Guide me, O Thou Great
Jehovah!
Pilgrim through this barren land;
I am weak, but Thou art mighty,
Hold me with Thy powerful hand:
Bread of Heaven!
Feed me now and evermore.

2 Open Thou the crystal fountain
Whence the healing stream doth flow:
Let the fiery, cloudy pillar
Lead me all my journey through:
Strong Deliverer!
Be Thou still my strength and shield.

3 If I tread the verge of Jordan,
Bid my anxious fears subside:
Bear me through the swelling torrent,
Land me safe on Canaan's side:
Songs of praises
I will ever give to Thee.

4 Saviour, come! we long to see Thee,
Long to dwell with Thee above;
And to know in full communion,
All the sweetness of Thy love.
Come, Lord Jesus!
Take Thy waiting people home.

W. Williams.

443 I have a Shepherd, One I love so
well;
How He has blessed me tongue can
never tell;
On the Cross He suffered, shed His
blood and died
That I might ever in His love confide.

Following Jesus, ever day by day,
Nothing can harm me when He leads the way;
Darkness or sunshine, whate'er befall,
Jesus, the Shepherd, is my All in all.

2 Pastures abundant doth His hand
provide,
Still waters flowing ever at my side,

Goodness and mercy follow on my
track,
With such a Shepherd nothing can I
lack.

3 When I would wander from the path
astray
Then He will draw me back into the
way;
In the darkest valley I need fear no ill
For He, my Shepherd, will be with me
still.

4 When labour's ended and the journey
done,
Then He will lead me safely to my
home;
There I shall dwell in rapture sure and
sweet
With all the loved ones gathered
round His feet.

Leonard Weaver.

444 I must have the Saviour with me
For I dare not walk alone,
I must feel His presence near me,
And His arm around me thrown.

Then my soul . . . shall fear no ill, . . .
Let Him lead . . . me where He will, . . .
I will go without a murmur,
And His footsteps follow still.

2 I must have the Saviour with me
For my faith at best is weak;
He can whisper words of comfort
That no other voice can speak.

3 I must have the Saviour with me
In the onward march of life,
Through the tempest and the sun-
shine,
Through the battle and the strife.

4 I must have the Saviour with me,
And His eye the way must guide
Till I reach the vale of Jordan,
Till I cross the rolling tide.

Lizzie Edwards.

445 Once upon the tide I drifted
With no guide to yonder shore;
But I've found a side once rifted,
Where I'm safe for evermore.

I am anchored, safely anchored,
Anchored, never more to roam,
Anchored by the side of Jesus,
Anchored in the soul's bright home.

2 Let the storms sweep o'er life's
ocean,
They can do me no more harm;
Anchored far from their commotion
I am resting 'neath His arm.

3 Here my peace flows like a river,
Here my soul o'erflows with song;
Prayer and praises to the Giver
Fill my glad heart all day long.

4 When this life below is ended
I shall anchor on that shore;
Where my praises will be blended
With ten thousand thousand more.

Johnson Oatman.

446 Precious promise God hath given
To the weary passer by,
'On the way from earth to Heaven,
I will guide thee with Mine eye.'

'I will guide thee, I will guide thee,
I will guide thee with Mine eye;
On the way from earth to Heaven,
I will guide thee with Mine eye.'

2 When temptations almost win thee,
And thy trusted watchers fly,
Let this promise ring within thee:
'I will guide thee with Mine eye.'

3 When thy secret hopes have perished
In the grave of years gone by,
Let this promise still be cherished,
'I will guide thee with Mine eye.'

4 When the shades of life are falling,
And the hour has come to die,
Hear thy trusty Leader calling,
'I will guide thee with Mine eye.'

N. Niles.

447 All the way my Saviour leads me:
What have I to ask beside?
Can I doubt His tender mercy,
Who through life has been my Guide?
Heavenly peace, divinest comfort,
Here by faith in Him to dwell!
For I know whate'er befall me,
Jesus doeth all things well.

2 All the way my Saviour leads me,
  Cheers each winding path I tread,
  Gives me grace for every trial,
  Feeds me with the Living Bread.
  Though my weary steps may falter,
  And my soul athirst may be,
  Gushing from the Rock before me,
  Lo! a spring of joy I see.

3 All the way my Saviour leads me;
  Oh, the fulness of His love!
  Perfect rest to me is promised
  In my Father's house above.
  When my spirit, clothed, immortal,
  Wings its flight to realms of day,
  This my song through endless ages,
  Jesus led me all the way.
                              Fanny J. Crosby.

448 Give me, dear Lord, the power I
    need
  To live this day aright;
  May every thought and word and
    deed
  Be pleasing in Your sight.

2 Give me Your sympathy today
  For those whom I shall meet,
  Who walk a hard and lonely way
  With sad and weary feet.

3 Give me Your wisdom too for those
  With charm and humour too,
  And yet whose every action shows
  They have no place for You.

4 Your patience too for those, I plead,
  Who can't believe it's true
  That all their great exceeding need
  Can still be met by You.

5 But richer than Your gifts in this:
  The fact of Who You are;
  Compared with them Your presence is
  More wonderful by far.
                              John Eddison.

449 Only in Thee, O Saviour mine,
    Dwelleth my soul in peace divine —
  Peace that the world, though all
    combine,
  Never can take from me!

Pleasures of earth, so seemingly
    sweet,
  Fail at the last my longings to meet;
  Only in Thee my bliss is complete,
  Only, dear Lord, in Thee!

2 Only in Thee a radiance bright
  Shines like a beacon in the night,
  Guiding my pilgrim barque aright
  Over life's trackless sea!
  Only in Thee, when troubles molest,
  When with temptation I am
    oppressed,
  There is a sweet pavilion of rest,
  Only, dear Lord, in Thee!

3 Only in Thee, when days are drear,
  When neither sun nor stars appear —
  Still I can trust and feel no fear,
  Sing when I cannot see!
  Only in Thee, whatever betide,
  All of my need is freely supplied:
  There is no hope or helper beside,
  Only, dear Lord, in Thee!

4 Only in Thee, dear Saviour slain,
  Losing Thy life my own to gain;
  Trusting, I'm cleansed from every
    stain —
  Thou art my only plea!
  Only in Thee my heart will delight,
  Till in that land where cometh no
    night,
  Faith will be lost in Heavenly sight —
  Only, dear Lord, in Thee!
                              T. O. Chisholm.

450 O God of Bethel, by whose hand
    Thy people still are fed,
  Who through this weary pilgrimage
  Hast all our fathers led.

2 Our vows, our prayers we now
    present
  Before Thy throne of grace;
  God of our fathers, be the God
  Of their succeeding race.

3 Through each perplexing path of life
  Our wandering footsteps guide:
  Give us, each day, our daily bread,
  And raiment fit provide.

4 O spread Thy covering wings around,
Till all our wanderings cease,
And at our Father's loved abode
Our souls arrive in peace.

5 Such blessings from Thy gracious
hand
Our humble prayers implore;
And Thou shalt be our chosen God
And portion evermore.

Doddridge and Logan.

451 Sweet is the promise 'I will not
forget thee';
Nothing can molest or turn my soul
away;
E'en though the night be dark within
the valley,
Just beyond is shining an eternal day.

> I . . . will not forget thee or leave thee,
> In My hands I'll hold thee, in My arms I'll fold
> thee;
> I . . . will not forget thee or leave thee—
> I am thy Redeemer, I will care for thee.

2 How can I show my gratitude to
Jesus,
For His love unfailing and His tender
care?
I will proclaim to others His salvation,
That they may accept Him and His
promise share.

3 Trusting the promise 'I will not forget
thee',
Onward will I go with songs of joy and
praise;
Though earth despise me, though my
friends forsake me,
Jesus will be near me, gladdening my
days.

4 When at the golden portals I am
standing,
All my tribulations, all my sorrows
past,
How sweet to hear the blessèd
proclamation:
'Enter faithful servant, welcome home
at last.'

arr. Charles H. Gabriel.

452 Who the child of God shall sever
From the faith in which he stands?
Who shall wound or who shall pluck
him
From the careful Shepherd's hands?
Not distress or persecution,
Neither peril nor the sword;
For in days of tribulation
Shines the glory of the Lord.

2 His abundant grace is given
To the heart resigned and meek,
Mercy moves the King of Heaven
To the penitent and weak;
Lowly paths our Lord has taken,
And He proved by word and deed,
For the lonely and forsaken
There is grace beyond all need.

3 Faith is not afraid of darkness,
Hope will triumph over loss,
Love is not afraid of hardness,
Patience helps to bear the cross;
These are all the gifts of Heaven,
Beautiful are they and free,
Graces that the Lord has given;
O that they may shine in me!

4 Works or wealth can never buy them,
Nor a single grace impart;
God Himself has sanctified them
In the meek and lowly heart;
All besides is vain endeavour,
Failure every work of mine;
Saviour, let Thy grace for ever
Cleanse and blend my will with Thine.

Albert Orsborn.

453 I must needs go home by the way
of the Cross,
There's no other way but this;
I shall ne'er get sight of the Gates of
Light
If the way of the Cross I miss.

> The way of the Cross leads home, . . .
> The way of the Cross leads home; . . .
> It is sweet to know, as I onward go,
> The way of the Cross leads home.

2 I must needs go on in the blood-
sprinkled way,
The path that the Saviour trod,
If I ever climb to the heights sublime,
Where the soul is at home with God.

3 Then I bid farewell to the way of the
world,
To walk in it never more;
For my Lord says 'Come,' and I seek
my home
Where He waits at the open door.

J. B. Pounds.

454 The Lord's our Rock, in Him we
hide:
A shelter in the time of storm!
Secure whatever ill betide:
A shelter in the time of storm!

Oh, Jesus is a Rock in a weary land!
A weary land, a weary land;
Oh, Jesus is a Rock in a weary land,
A shelter in the time of storm!

2 A shade by day, defence by night:
A shelter in the time of storm!
No fears alarm, no foes affright:
A shelter in the time of storm!

3 The raging storms may round us beat:
A shelter in the time of storm!
We'll never leave our safe retreat,
A shelter in the time of storm!

4 O Rock Divine, O Refuge dear:
A shelter in the time of storm!
Be Thou our helper ever near,
A shelter in the time of storm!

V. J. C.

455 Where He may lead me I will go,
For I have learned to trust Him so,
And I remember 'twas for me
That He was slain on Calvary.

Jesus shall lead me night and day,
Jesus shall lead me all the way:
He is the truest Friend to me,
For I remember Calvary.

2 O I delight in His command,
Love to be led by His dear hand,
His divine will is sweet to me,
Hallowed by blood-stained Calvary.

3 Onward I go, nor doubt nor fear,
Happy with Christ, my Saviour near,
Trusting some day that I shall see
Jesus, my Friend of Calvary.

W. C. Martin.

TRUST AND OBEDIENCE

456 All things are possible to him
That can in Jesu's Name believe;
Lord, I no more Thy Name blaspheme,
Thy truth I lovingly receive.
I can, I do believe in Thee;
All things are possible to me.

2 'Twas most impossible of all
That here sin's reign in me should
cease;
Yet shall it be, I know it shall;
Jesus I trust Thy faithfulness!
If nothing is too hard for Thee,
All things are possible to me.

3 Though earth and hell the Word
gainsay,
The Word of God shall never fail;
The Lord can break sin's iron sway;
'Tis certain, though impossible.
The thing impossible shall be,
All things are possible to me.

4 All things are possible to God;
To Christ, the power of God in man;
To me when I am all renewed
In Christ am fully formed again.
And from the reign of sin set free,
All things are possible to me.

5 All things are possible to God;
To Christ, the power of God in me;
Now shed Thy mighty Self abroad,
Let me no longer live, but Thee;
Give me this hour in Thee to prove
The sweet omnipotence of love.

Charles Wesley.

457 When we walk with the Lord
In the light of His Word,
What a glory He sheds on our way!
While we do His good will
He abides with us still,
And with all who will trust and obey.

Trust and obey; for there's no other way
To be happy in Jesus, but to trust and obey.

2 Not a shadow can rise,
Not a cloud in the skies,
But His smile quickly drives it away;
Not a doubt nor a fear,
Not a sigh nor a tear
Can abide while we trust and obey.

3 Not a burden we bear,
Not a sorrow we share,
But our toil He doth richly repay;
Not a grief nor a loss,
Not a frown nor a cross,
But is blest if we trust and obey.

4 But we never can prove
The delights of His love,
Until all on the altar we lay;
For the favour He shows
And the joy He bestows
Are for them who will trust and obey.

5 Then in fellowship sweet
We will sit at His feet,
Or we'll walk by His side in the way;
What He says we will do,
Where He sends we will go,
Never fear, only trust and obey.
J. H. Sammis.

458 What a fellowship, what a joy divine,
Leaning on the everlasting arms;
What a blessèdness, what a peace is mine,
Leaning on the everlasting arms.

Lean . . . ing, lean . . . ing,
Safe and secure from all alarms;
Lean . . . ing, lean . . . ing,
Leaning on the everlasting arms.

2 Oh, how sweet to walk in this pilgrim way,
Leaning on the everlasting arms;
Oh, how bright the path grows from day to day,
Leaning on the everlasting arms.

3 What have I to dread, what have I to fear,
Leaning on the everlasting arms?;
I have blessèd peace with my Lord so near,
Leaning on the everlasting arms.
E. A. Hoffman.

459 Master, speak! Thy servant heareth,
Waiting for Thy gracious Word,
Longing for Thy voice that cheereth,
Master, let it now be heard.
I am listening, Lord, for Thee:
What hast Thou to say to me?

2 Speak to me by name, O Master,
Let me know it is to me;
Speak, that I may follow faster,
With a step more firm and free,
Where the Shepherd leads the flock
In the shadow of the Rock.

3 Master, speak! though least and lowest,
Let me not unheard depart;
Master, speak! for oh, Thou knowest
All the yearning of my heart,
Knowest all its truest need;
Speak! and make me blest indeed.

4 Master, speak! and make me ready,
When Thy voice is truly heard,
With obedience glad and steady
Still to follow every word.
I am listening, Lord, for Thee:
Master, speak, oh, speak to me!
Frances Ridley Havergal.

460 Days are filled with gladness,
nights are filled with song,
Walking in the King's highway;
And the world grows brighter as we pass along,
Walking in the King's highway.

Walking, walking in the King's highway,
Walking in the King's highway,
To the place of many mansions
I shall come at last,
Walking in the King's highway.

2 Music from the homeland fills me with delight,
Walking in the King's highway;
Visions of the glory break upon my sight,
Walking in the King's highway.

3 Crowned with tender mercies,
guarded by His love,
Walking in the King's highway;
Jesus gives a foretaste of the joys above,
Walking in the King's highway.
A. H. Ackley.

461 I am trusting Thee, Lord Jesus,
Trusting only Thee!
Trusting Thee for full salvation,
Great and free.

2 I am trusting Thee for pardon,
At Thy feet I bow;
For Thy grace and tender mercy,
Trusting now.

3 I am trusting Thee for cleansing
In the crimson flood;
Trusting Thee to make me holy
By Thy blood.

4 I am trusting Thee to guide me,
Thou alone shalt lead,
Every day and hour supplying
All my need.

5 I am trusting Thee for power,
Thine can never fail;
Words which Thou Thyself shalt give
me
Must prevail.

6 I am trusting Thee, Lord Jesus,
Never let me fall!
I am trusting Thee for ever,
And for all.

Frances Ridley Havergal.

462 My heart is fixed, eternal God,
Fixed on Thee,
And my immortal choice is made:
Christ for me.
He is my Prophet, Priest and King
Who did for me salvation bring;
And while I've breath I mean to sing:
Christ for me.

2 In Him I see the Godhead shine,
Christ for me.
He is the Majesty Divine;
Christ for me.
The Father's well-belovèd Son,
Co-partner of His royal throne,
Who did for human guilt atone;
Christ for me.

3 In pining sickness or in health,
Christ for me.
In deepest poverty or wealth,
Christ for me.

And in that all-important day,
When I the summons must obey,
And pass from this dark world away,
Christ for me.

4 Let others boast of heaps of gold,
Christ for me,
His riches never can be told,
Christ for me!
Your gold will waste and wear away,
Your honours perish in a day,
My portion never can decay:
Christ for me!

Richard Jukes.

463 Father of Jesus Christ, my Lord,
My Saviour, and my Head,
I trust in Thee, whose powerful Word
Hath raised Him from the dead.

2 Eternal life to all mankind
Thou hast in Jesus given;
And all who seek, in Him shall find
The happiness of Heaven.

3 Faith in Thy power Thou seest I have
For Thou this faith hast wrought;
Dead souls Thou callest from their
grave,
And seekest worlds from nought.

4 In hope, against all human hope,
Self-desperate, I believe;
Thy quickening Word shall raise me
up,
Thou shalt Thy Spirit give.

5 The thing surpasses all my thought,
But faithful is my Lord;
Through unbelief I stagger not
For God hath spoke the Word.

6 Faith, mighty faith, the promise sees,
And looks to that alone;
Laughs at impossibilities,
And cries: It shall be done!

Charles Wesley.

464 The Lord hath declared and the
Lord will perform:
'Behold! I am near to deliver,
A refuge and fortress, a covert in
storm';
He keepeth His promise for ever.

For ever! for ever! O not for a day!
He keepeth His promise for ever!
To all who believe, to all who obey,
He keepeth His promise for ever!

2 Who seek Him shall find Him, shall
find Him today,
The word is to all, 'whosoever!'
No soul that entreateth He turneth
away;
He keepeth His promise for ever.

3 Though often my toil seems but
labour in vain,
I leave with the Lord my endeavour!
I patiently wait for the sunshine and
rain,
He keepeth His promise for ever.

4 The bonds that unite us in earth's
dearest ties
The rude hand of Time will dis-sever;
But we shall renew them again in the
skies;
He keepeth His promise for ever.

S. C. Kirk.

465 Firm are the promises standing,
Nor can they ever fail,
Sealed with the blood of our Jesus,
They must, they shall avail!

Heaven and earth may perish,
Mountain and hill may vanish;
Yet stands the Word we cherish,
Ever to faith made sure.

2 Follow in Abraham's footsteps,
Turn to the heavens your eyes;
Counting the stars without number,
Your faith, your hope will rise.

3 Trust, though the darkness be
falling—
Soon will the sun arise,
Shedding bright beams in the morning
O'er earth and sea and skies.

4 Trust, though the world may beset
you;
Faith has no dread or fear:
Lo, in the fiery furnace
The Son of God draws near!

5 Trust, though your friends disappoint
you,
Leaving you one by one;
Jesus, true Friend, will stand by you
Till pilgrim days are done.

6 Trust Him, whatever betide you;
Soon in the mansions bright
All will be clear as the noonday:
Faith turned to glorious sight!

Lewi Pethrus.

466 Down in the valley with my
Saviour I would go,
Where the flowers are blooming and
the sweet waters flow;
Everywhere He leads me I would
follow, follow on;
Walking in His footsteps till the crown
be won.

Follow! follow! I would follow Jesus;
Anywhere, everywhere, I would follow on!
Follow! follow! I would follow Jesus!
Everywhere He leads me I would follow on!

2 Down in the valley with my Saviour I
would go,
Where the storms are sweeping and
the dark waters flow;
With His hand to lead me I will never,
never fear;
Danger cannot harm me if my Lord is
near.

3 Down in the valley or upon the
mountain steep,
Close beside my Saviour would my
soul ever keep;
He will lead me safely in the path that
He has trod,
Up to where they gather on the hills of
God.

W. O. Cushing.

467 I believe that God the Father
Can be seen in God the Son,
In the gentleness of Jesus
Love for all the world is shown.
Though men crucify their Saviour,
And His tenderness rebuff,
God is love, the Cross is saying,
Calvary is proof enough.

2 I believe in transformation
   God can change the hearts of men,
   And refine the evil nature
   Till it glows with grace again.
   Others may reject the weakling,
   I believe he can be changed,
   To the family of Jesus
   All God's children may belong.

3 In a world of shifting values,
   There are standards that remain,
   I believe that holy living
   By God's grace we may attain.
   All would hear the Holy Spirit
   If they listen to His voice,
   Every Christian may be Christlike
   And in liberty rejoice.

4 All the promises of Jesus
   Are unchanged in every way,
   In my yesterdays I proved them,
   I believe them for today.
   Still God gives His willing servant
   Full equipment for the task;
   Power is found by those who seek it,
   Grace is given to those who ask.

John Gowans.

468 Simply trusting every day,
        Trusting through a stormy way;
   Even when my faith is small,
   Trusting Jesus, that is all.

   Trusting as the moments fly,
   Trusting as the days go by;
   Trusting Him whate'er befall,
   Trusting Jesus, that is all.

2 Brightly doth His Spirit shine
   Into this poor heart of mine;
   While He leads I cannot fall;
   Trusting Jesus, that is all.

3 Singing if my way be clear:
   Praying if the path be drear;
   If in danger, for Him call;
   Trusting Jesus, that is all.

4 Trusting Him while life shall last,
   Trusting Him till earth be past;
   Till within the jasper wall;
   Trusting Jesus, that is all.

E. Page.

469 'Tis so sweet to trust in Jesus,
        Just to take Him at His Word,
   Just to rest upon His promise;
   Just to know 'Thus saith the Lord'.

   Jesus, Jesus, how I trust Him!
   How I've proved Him o'er and o'er!
   Jesus, Jesus, precious Jesus!
   Oh, for grace to trust Him more.

2 Oh, how sweet to trust in Jesus,
   Just to trust His cleansing blood;
   Just in simple faith to plunge me
   'Neath the healing, cleansing flood.

3 Yes, 'tis sweet to trust in Jesus,
   Just from sin and self to cease;
   Just from Jesus simply taking
   Life and rest, and joy and peace.

4 I'm so glad I learned to trust Thee,
   Precious Jesus, Saviour, Friend;
   And I know that Thou art with me,
   Wilt be with me to the end.

Louisa M. R. Stead.

470 Why should I charge my soul with
        care?
   The wealth in every mine
   Belongs to Christ, God's Son and
   Heir,
   And He's a Friend of mine.

   Yes, He's a Friend of mine,
   And He with me doth all things share;
   Since all is Christ's and Christ is mine,
   Why should I have a care?
   For Jesus is a Friend of mine.

2 The silver moon, the golden sun,
   And all the stars that shine
   Are His alone, yes every one,
   And He's a Friend of mine.

3 He daily spreads a glorious feast,
   And at His table dine
   The whole creation, man and beast,
   And He's a Friend of mine.

4 And when He comes in bright array,
   And leads the conquering line,
   It will be glory then to say
   That He's a Friend of mine.

J. H. Sammis.

471 I clasp the hand of Love divine,
I claim the gracious promise mine,
And add to His my countersign,
'I take—He undertakes'.

I take Thee, blessèd Lord,
I give myself to Thee,
And Thou, according to Thy Word,
Dost undertake for me.

2 I take salvation full and free
Through Him who gave His life for
me,
He undertakes my All to be,
'I take—He undertakes'.

3 I take Him as my holiness,
My spirit's spotless Heavenly dress,
I take the Lord, my Righteousness,
'I take—He undertakes'.

4 I take the promised Holy Ghost,
I take the power of Pentecost,
To fill me to the uttermost,
'I take—He undertakes'.

5 I take Him for this mortal frame,
I take my healing through His Name,
And all His risen life I claim,
'I take—He undertakes'.

A. B. Simpson.

LOVE, JOY AND PEACE

472 I have a song that Jesus gave me,
It was sent from Heaven above;
There never was a sweeter melody,
'Tis a melody of love.

In my heart there rings a melody,
There rings a melody with Heaven's harmony;
In my heart there rings a melody,
There rings a melody of love.

2 I love the Christ that died on Calvary,
For He washed my sins away;
He put within my heart a melody,
And I know it's there to stay.

3 'Twill be my endless theme in glory,
With the angels I will sing;
'Twill be a song with glorious
harmony,
When the courts of Heaven ring.

Elton M. Roth.

473 Peace like a river is flooding my
soul
Since Christ, my Saviour, maketh me
whole;
Sweet peace abiding my portion shall
be—
Jesus, my Saviour, is precious to me.

Pre . . . cious to me, . . .
Pre . . . cious is He: . . .
Je . . . sus shall ever . . . be pre . . . cious to
me. . . .

2 Joy is abounding—my heart gaily
sings,
Cleave I the heavens, mount up on
wings;
Christ hath exalted, my soul He set
free—
Jesus, my Saviour, is precious to me.

3 Oh precious Jesus, how lovely Thou
art!
Come and abiding rule in my heart;
Break every fetter, Thy face let me
see,
Then Thou shalt ever be precious
to me.

G. C. Tullar.

474 I feel like singing all the time,
My tears are wiped away;
For Jesus is a Friend of mine,
I'll serve Him every day.

I'll praise Him! praise Him! praise him all the
time!
Praise Him! praise Him! I'll praise Him all the
time!

2 When on the Cross my Lord I saw,
Nailed there by sins of mine,
Fast fell the burning tears; but now
I'm singing all the time.

3 When fierce temptations try my heart,
I'll sing, 'Jesus is mine!'
And so, though tears at times may
start,
I'm singing all the time.

4 The wondrous story of the Lamb
Tell with that voice of thine,
Till others, with the glad new song,
Go singing all the time.

E. P. Hammond.

The Christian Life

475 When peace, like a river attendeth my way,
When sorrows, like sea billows roll;
Whatever my lot, Thou hast taught me to know,
'It is well, it is well with my soul.'

> It is well, . . . with my soul, . . .
> It is well, it is well with my soul.

2 Though Satan should buffet, if trials should come,
Let this blest assurance control,
That Christ hath regarded my helpless estate,
And hath shed His own blood for my soul.

3 My sin—oh, the bliss of this glorious thought—
My sin-not in part-but the whole
Is nailed to His Cross: and I bear it no more:
Praise the Lord, praise the Lord, O my soul.

4 For me, be it Christ, be it Christ hence to live!
If Jordan above me shall roll.
No pang shall be mine, for in death as in life
Thou wilt whisper Thy peace to my soul.

5 But Lord, 'tis for Thee, for Thy coming we wait,
The sky, not the grave, is our goal:
Oh, trump of the angel! oh, voice of the Lord!
Blessèd hope! blessèd rest of my soul.

H. G. Spafford.

476 Home to Zion we are bound,
Happy in the love of Jesus;
Peace abiding we have found,
Happy in the love of Jesus.

> Happy, happy,
> Singing all the way, happy all the day;
> Happy, happy,
> Happy in the love of Jesus.

2 Trusting, we will foward go,
Happy in the love of Jesus,
Treading changeful paths below,
Happy in the love of Jesus.

3 Soon we'll reach the homeland fair,
Happy in the love of Jesus,
And shall dwell for ever there,
Happy in the love of Jesus.

Jennie Wilson.

477 The love of God is greater far
Than tongue or pen can ever tell;
It goes beyond the highest star,
And reaches to the lowest hell:
The guilty pair, bowed down with care,
God gave His Son to win;
His erring child He reconciled,
And pardoned from his sin.

> Oh, love of God, how rich and pure!
> How measureless and strong!
> It shall for evermore endure—
> The saints, and angels' song.

2 When hoary time shall pass away,
And earthly thrones and kingdoms fall;
When men who here refuse to pray,
On rocks and hills and mountains call;
God's love, so sure, shall still endure,
All measureless and strong;
Redeeming grace to Adam's race—
The saints' and angels' song.

3 Could we with ink the ocean fill,
And were the skies of parchment made;
Were every stalk on earth a quill,
And every man a scribe by trade;
To write the love of God above
Would drain the ocean dry;
Nor could the scroll contain the whole,
Though stretched from sky to sky.

F. M. Lehman.

478 Far away in the depths of my spirit tonight
Rolls a melody sweeter than psalm;
In celestial-like strains it unceasingly falls
O'er my soul like an infinite calm.

> Peace! peace! wonderful peace,
> Coming down from the Father above,
> Sweep over my spirit for ever, I pray,
> In fathomless billows of love!

2 What a treasure I have in this
   wonderful peace,
   Buried deep in the heart of my soul,
   So secure that no power can mine it
   away,
   While the years of eternity roll!

3 I am resting tonight in this wonderful
   peace,
   Resting sweetly in Jesus' control;
   For I'm kept from all danger by night
   and by day,
   And His glory is flooding my soul.

4 And methinks when I rise to that city
   of peace,
   Where the Author of peace I shall see,
   That one strain of the song which the
   ransomed will sing
   In that Heavenly Kingdom will be.

5 Ah, soul! are you here without
   comfort and rest
   Marching down the rough pathway of
   time?
   Make Jesus your Friend ere the
   shadows grow dark;
   O accept of this peace so sublime.
                                    W. D. Cornell.

479 The dear loving Saviour hath
      found me,
      And shattered the fetters that bound
      me,
      Though all was confusion around me
      He came and spake peace to my soul;
      The blessèd Redeemer that bought
      me,
      In tenderness constantly sought me;
      The way of salvation He taught me
      And made my heart perfectly whole.

      He saves me, He saves me,
      His love fills my soul, hallelujah,
      Oh glory, oh glory, His Spirit abideth within;
      He saves me, He saves me,
      His love fills my soul, hallelujah,
      Oh glory, oh glory,
      His blood cleanseth me from all sin.

2 He sought me so long ere I knew Him,
   But finally winning me to Him,
   I yielded my all to pursue Him,
   And asked to be filled with His grace;

Although a vile sinner before Him,
   Through faith I was led to implore
   Him,
   And now I rejoice and adore Him,
   Restored to His loving embrace.

3 I never, no never will leave Him,
   Grow weary of service and grieve
   Him,
   I'll constantly trust and believe Him,
   Remain in His presence divine;
   Abiding in love ever flowing,
   In knowledge and grace ever growing,
   Confiding implicitly, knowing
   That Jesus the Saviour is mine.
                             J. W. Van De Venter.

480 God's abiding peace is in my soul
      today,
      Yes, I feel it now, yes, I feel it now;
      He has taken all my doubts and fears
      away,
      Though I cannot tell you how.

      It is mine, . . . mine, . . . blessèd be His name!
      He has given peace, perfect peace to me;
      It is mine, . . . mine, . . . blessèd be His name!
      Mine for all eternity!

2 He has wrought in me a sweet and
   perfect rest,
   In my raptured heart I can feel it now;
   He each passing moment keeps me
   saved and blest,
   Floods with light my heart and brow.

3 He has given me a never-failing joy,
   Oh, I have it now! oh, I have it now!
   To His praise I will my ransomed
   powers employ,
   And renew my grateful vow.

4 Oh, the love of God is comforting my
   soul,
   For His love is mine, yes, His love is
   mine!
   Waves of joy and gladness o'er my
   spirit roll,
   Thrilling me with life divine.
                              Elisha A. Hoffman.

481 There is a song in my heart today,
      Something I never had;
      Jesus has taken my sins away,
      Oh say, but I'm glad!

Oh say, but I'm glad, I'm glad,
Oh say, but I'm glad!
Jesus has come and my cup's overrun,
Oh say, but I'm glad!

2 Wonderful, marvellous love He brings
Into a heart that's sad;
Through darkest tunnels the soul just
sings,
Oh say, but I'm glad!

3 We have a fellowship rich and sweet,
Tongues can never relate;
Abiding in Him is a real treat,
Oh say, but I'm glad!

4 Won't you come to Him with all your
care,
Weary and worn and sad?
You, too, will sing as His love you
share,
Oh say, but I'm glad!

James P. Sullivan.

482 O Christ, in Thee my soul hath
found,
And found in Thee alone,
The peace, the joy I sought so long,
The bliss till now unknown.

Now none but Christ can satisfy,
None other name for me;
There's love and life and lasting joy,
Lord Jesus found in Thee.

2 I sighed for rest and happiness,
I yearned for them, not Thee;
But while I passed my Saviour by
His love laid hold on me.

3 I tried the broken cisterns, Lord,
But, ah! the waters failed!
E'en as I stooped to drink they fled,
And mocked me as I wailed.

4 The pleasures lost I sadly mourned,
But never wept for Thee;
Till grace my sightless eyes received,
Thy loveliness to see.

arr. B. E.

483 There will never be a sweeter
story,
Story of the Saviour's love divine;
Love that brought Him from the
realms of glory
Just to save a sinful soul like mine.

Isn't the love of Jesus something wonderful!
Wonderful! wonderful!
Oh, isn't the love of Jesus something
wonderful!
Wonderful it is to me!

2 Boundless as the universe around me,
Reaching to the farthest soul away;
Saving, keeping love it was that found
me,
That is why my heart can truly say:

3 Love beyond our human compre-
hending,
Love of God in Christ how can it be!
This will be my theme and never
ending,
Great redeeming love of Calvary.

John W. Peterson.

484 I have found a wondrous Saviour,
Jesus Christ, the soul's delight;
Every blessing of His favour
Fills my heart with hope so bright.

Jesus is the Joy of Living,
He's the King of Life to me;
Unto Him my all I'm giving,
His for evermore to be.
I will do what He commands me,
Anywhere He leads I'll go;
Jesus is the Joy of Living,
He's the dearest Friend I know.

2 Life is growing rich with beauty,
Toil has lost its weary strain,
Now a halo crowns each duty,
And I sing a glad refrain.

3 Heavenly wisdom He provides me,
Grace to keep my spirit free;
In His own sweet way He guides me
When the path I cannot see.

4 O what splendour, O what glory,
O what matchless power divine
Is the Christ of Gospel story,
Christ the Saviour, who is mine.
A. H. Ackley.

485 I have found His grace is all
complete,
He supplieth every need;
While I sit and learn at Jesus' feet,
I am free, yes free indeed.

It is joy unspeakable and full of glory,
Full of glory, full of glory:
It is joy unspeakable and full of glory,
Oh, the half has never yet been told.

2 I have found the pleasure I once
craved,
It is joy and peace within;
What a wondrous blessing! I am
saved
From the awful gulf of sin.

3 I have found that hope so bright and
clear,
Living in the realm of grace;
Oh, the Saviour's presence is so near,
I can see His smiling face.

4 I have found the joy no tongue can
tell,
How its waves of glory roll!
It is like a great o'erflowing well,
Springing up within my soul.
B. E. Warren.

486 A friend of Jesus, oh, what bliss
That one so weak as I
Should ever have a friend like this
To lead me to the sky.

Friendship with Jesus,
Fellowship divine;
Oh, what blessèd sweet communion,
Jesus is a friend of mine.

2 A friend when other friendships
cease,
A friend when others fail;
A friend who gives me joy and peace,
A friend who will prevail.

3 A friend to lead me in the dark,
A friend who knows the way;
A friend to steer my weak, frail, bark,
A friend my debts to pay.

4 A friend when sickness lays me low,
A friend when death draws near;
A friend as through the vale I go,
A friend to help and cheer.

5 A friend when life's rough voyage is
o'er,
A friend when death is past;
A friend to greet on Heaven's shore,
A friend when home at last.
J. C. Ludgate.

487 O what a wonderful, wonderful
day,
Day I will never forget!
After I'd wandered in darkness away,
Jesus my Saviour I met!
O what a tender, compassionate
friend,
He met the need of my heart!
Shadows dispelling, with joy I am
telling,
He made all the darkness depart.

Heaven came down and glory filled my soul,
When at the Cross the Saviour made me
whole;
My sins were washed away,
And my night was turned to day,
Heaven came down and glory filled my soul.

2 Born of the Spirit with life from above
Into God's family divine,
Justified fully through Calvary's love,
O what a standing is mine!
And the transaction so quickly was
made
When as a sinner I came,
Took of the offer of grace He did
proffer,
He saved me, O praise His dear Name!

3 Now I've a hope that will surely
endure
After the passing of time,
I have a future in Heaven for sure,
There in those mansions sublime.
And it's because of that wonderful
day,
When at the Cross I believed;
Riches eternal and blessing supernal
From His precious hand I received.
John W. Peterson.

488 Jesus comes with power to gladden,
When loves shines in,
Every life that woe can sadden,
When love shines in.
Love will teach us how to pray,
Love will drive the gloom away,
Turn our darkness into day,
When love shines in.

> When love shines in, . . . when love shines in,
> How the heart is tuned to singing when love
> shines in; . . .
> When love shines in, . . . when love shines in,
> Joy and peace to others bringing, when love
> shines in.

2 How the world will glow with beauty,
When love shines in,
And the heart rejoice in duty,
When love shines in.
Trials may be sanctified,
And the soul in peace abide,
Life will all be glorified,
When love shines in.

3 Darkest sorrows will grow brighter,
When love shines in,
And the heaviest burden lighter,
When love shines in.
'Tis the glory that will throw
Light to show us where to go;
O the heart shall blessing know
When love shines in.

4 We may have unfading splendour,
When love shines in,
And a friendship true and tender,
When love shines in.
When earth-victories shall be won,
And our life in Heaven begun,
There will be no need of sun,
For love shines in.

Mrs. Frank A. Breck.

489 Jesus my King, my wonderful Saviour,
All of my life is given to Thee;
I am rejoicing in Thy salvation,
Thy precious blood now maketh me free.

> Wonderful Saviour, wonderful Saviour,
> Thou art so near, so precious to me;
> Wonderful Saviour, wonderful Saviour,
> My heart is filled with praises to Thee.

2 Freedom from sin, oh, wonderful story!
All of its stains washed whiter than snow,
Jesus has come to live in His temple,
And with His love my heart is aglow.

3 Jesus my Lord, I'll ever adore Thee,
Lay at Thy feet my treasures of love;
Lead me in ways to show forth Thy glory,
Ways that will end in Heaven above.

4 When in that bright and beautiful city
I shall behold Thy glories untold,
I shall be like Thee, wonderful Saviour,
And I will sing while ages unfold.

J. M. Harris.

490 Like a river, glorious,
Is God's perfect peace,
Over all victorious
In its bright increase;
Perfect, yet it floweth
Fuller every day,
Perfect, yet it groweth
Deeper all the way.

> Stayed upon Jehovah,
> Hearts are fully blest;
> Finding, as He promised,
> Perfect peace and rest.

2 Hidden in the hollow
Of His blessèd hand,
Never foe can follow,
Never traitor stand;
Not a surge of worry,
Not a shade of care,
Not a blast of hurry
Touch the spirit there.

3 Every joy or trial
Falleth from above,
Traced upon our dial
By the Sun of Love,
We may trust Him fully
All for us to do,
They who trust Him wholly
Find Him wholly true.

Frances Ridley Havergal.

491 Love, wonderful love of God,
 So boundless and so free,
To think that Christ His only Son
Should die on Calvary.
Oh, love so great so vast, so high,
That He should for the sinner die.

> Love, wonderful love, the love of God to me,
> Love, wonderful love, so great, so rich, so
> free;
> Wide, as wide as the ocean, deep, as deep as
> the sea,
> High, as high as the heavens above, His love
> to me.

2 Love, wonderful love of God,
 To me has been made known,
To me the Spirit freely gives,
And claims me for His own.
Oh, love so wondrous, so divine,
That I am His and He is mine.

3 Love, wonderful love of God,
 With joy I now proclaim
To sinners lost, that they may have
Salvation through His Name.
That they may now with others prove,
'Christ's dying, and undying love.'
> *Seth Sykes.*

492 Master, the tempest is raging!
 The billows are tossing high!
The sky is o'ershadowed with black-
 ness,
No shelter or help is nigh:
'Carest Thou not that we perish?'
How canst Thou lie asleep,
When each moment so madly is
 threatening
A grave in the angry deep?

> 'The winds and the waves shall obey My will,
> Peace, . . . be still! . . .
> Whether the wrath of the storm-tossed sea,
> Or demons, or men, or whatever it be,
> No waters can swallow the ship where lies
> The Master of ocean, and earth, and skies;
> They all shall sweetly obey My will:
> Peace, be still! Peace, be still!
> They all shall sweetly obey My will:
> Peace, peace, be still!'

2 Master, with anguish of spirit
 I bow in my grief today;
The depths of my sad heart are
 troubled;
Oh, waken and save, I pray!

Torrents of sin and of anguish
Sweep o'er my sinking soul;
And I perish! I perish! dear Master:
Oh hasten, and take control.

3 Master, the terror is over,
 The elements sweetly rest;
Earth's sun in the calm lake is
 mirrored,
And Heaven's within my breast;
Linger, O blessèd Redeemer,
Leave me alone no more;
And with joy I shall make the blest
 harbour,
And rest on the blissful shore.
> *Mary A. Baker.*

493 I sing the love of God, my Father,
 Whose Spirit abides within;
Who changes all my grief to gladness,
And pardons me all my sin.
Though clouds may lower, dark and
 dreary,
Yet He has promised to be near;
He gives me sunshine for my shadow,
And 'beauty for ashes,' here.

> He gives me joy . . . in place of sor . . . row,
> He gives me love . . . that casts out fear; . . .
> He gives me sunshine for my shadow,
> And 'beauty for ashes,' here.

2 I sing the love of Christ, my Saviour,
 Who suffered upon the Tree;
That, in the secret of His presence,
My bondage might freedom be,
He comes 'to bind the broken-
 hearted;'
He comes the fainting soul to cheer;
He gives me 'oil of joy' for mourning,
And 'beauty for ashes,' here.

3 I sing the beauty of the Gospel
 That scatters not thorns, but flowers;
That bids me scatter smiles and
 sunbeams
Wherever are lonely hours.
The 'garment of His praise' it offers
For 'heaviness of spirit,' drear;
It gives me sunshine for my shadow,
And 'beauty for ashes,' here.
> *J. G. Crabbe.*

494 New! every morning it's new!
The love of God to me is wonderfully new!
New! every morning it's new!
The mercy of the Lord is wonderfully new!
Great is His faithfulness,
Constant is His love,
Great is His saving power
Coming from above!

2 New! every morning it's new!
The love of Calvary is wonderfully new!
New! every morning it's new!
The mercy fresh outpoured is wonderfully new!
He is our daily strength,
He's our daily guide
If we will wait on Him
And in Him abide!

3 New! every morning it's new!
The love of God to me is wonderfully new!
New! every morning it's new!
The mercy of the Lord is wonderfully new!

M. A. Baughen.

495 I've seen the face of Jesus,
He smiled in love on me;
It filled my heart with rapture,
My soul with ecstasy.
The scars of deepest anguish
Were lost in glory bright;
I've seen the face of Jesus,
It was a wondrous sight!

Oh! glorious face of beauty,
Oh! gentle touch of care;
If here it is so blessèd,
What will it be up there?

2 And since I've seen His beauty
All else I count but loss;
The world, its fame and pleasure,
Is now to me but dross.
His light dispelled my darkness,
His smile was, oh! so sweet;
I've seen the face of Jesus,
I can but kiss His feet.

3 I've heard the voice of Jesus,
He told me of His love,
And called me His own treasure,
His undefiled, His dove.
It came like softest music
Across an ocean calm,
And seemed to play so sweetly
Some wondrous holy psalm.

4 I felt the hand of Jesus—
My brow it throbbed with care;
He placed it there so softly,
And whispered, 'Do not fear.'
Like clouds before the sunshine
My cares have rolled away;
I'm sitting in His presence—
It is a cloudless day.

5 I know He's coming shortly
To take us all above;
We'll sing redemption's story,
The story of His love;
We'll hear His voice of music,
We'll feel His hand of care;
He'll never rest—He says so—
Until He has us there.

W. Spencer Walton.

496 Once I thought I walked with Jesus,
Yet such changeful moods I had;
Sometimes trusting, sometimes doubting,
Sometimes joyful, sometimes sad.

Oh, the peace my Saviour gives,
Peace I never knew before;
For my way has brighter grown,
Since I learned to trust Him more.

2 For He called me closer to Him,
Bade my doubting tremors cease;
And when I had fully trusted—
Filled my soul with perfect peace.

3 Now I'm trusting every moment,
Less than this is not enough;
And my Saviour bears me gently
O'er the places once so rough.

4 Blessèd Saviour, Thou dost keep me
By Thy power from day to day,
And my heart is full of gladness
For Thou'lt keep me all the way.

F. A. Blackmer.

497 My Jesus, I love Thee, I know
Thou art mine,
For Thee all the pleasures of sin I
resign;
My gracious Redeemer, my Saviour
art Thou,
If ever I loved Thee, my Jesus, 'tis
now!

2 I love Thee because Thou has first
lovèd me,
And purchased my pardon when
nailed to the Tree;
I love Thee for wearing the thorns on
Thy brow,
If ever I loved Thee, my Jesus, 'tis
now!

3 I'll love Thee in life, I will love Thee in
death,
And praise Thee as long as Thou
lendest me breath,
And say, should the death-dew lie
cold on my brow,
If ever I loved Thee, my Jesus, 'tis
now!

4 In mansions of glory and endless
delight,
I'll ever adore Thee in Heaven so
bright;
I'll sing with the glittering crown on
my brow,
If ever I loved Thee, my Jesus, 'tis
now!

W. R. Featherstone.

498 Rich are the moments of blessing
Jesus my Saviour bestows;
Pure is the well of salvation
Fresh from His mercy that flows.

Ever He walketh beside me,
Brightly His sunshine appears,
Spreading a beautiful rainbow
Over the valley of tears.

2 Rich are the moments of blessing,
Lovely and hallowed and sweet,
When from my labour at noontide
Calmly I rest at His feet.

3 Why should I ever grow weary?
Why should I faint by the way?
Has He not promised to give me
Strength for the toils of the day?

4 Though by the mist and the shadow
Sometimes my sky may be dim,
Rich are the moments of blessing
Spent in communion with Him.

Fanny J. Crosby.

499 Give me joy in my heart, keep me
praising,
Give me joy in my heart, I pray;
Give me joy in my heart, keep me
praising,
Keep me praising till the break of day.

Sing hosanna! sing hosanna!
Sing hosanna to the King of kings!
Sing hosanna! sing hosanna!
Sing hosanna to the King.

2 Give me peace in my heart, keep me
loving,
Give me peace in my heart, I pray;
Give me peace in my heart, keep me
loving,
Keep me loving till the break of day.

3 Give me love in my heart, keep me
serving,
Give me love in my heart, I pray;
Give me love in my heart, keep me
serving,
Keep me serving till the break of day.

Traditional.

500 There comes to my heart one
sweet strain.
A glad and a joyous refrain,
I sing it again and again,
Sweet peace, the gift of God's love.

Peace, peace, sweet peace,
Wonderful gift from above;
O wonderful, wonderful peace!
Sweet peace, the gift of God's love.

2 By Christ on the Cross peace was
made,
My debt by His death was all paid,
No other foundation is laid
For peace, the gift of God's love.

3 When Jesus, as Lord I had crowned,
My heart with this peace did abound,
In Him the rich blessing I found,
Sweet peace, the gift of God's love.

4 In Jesus for peace I abide,
And as I keep close to His side
There's nothing but peace doth
betide,
Sweet peace, the gift of God's love.

P. P. Bilhorn.

501 Since Christ my soul from sin set
free,
This world has been a heaven to me;
And 'mid earth's sorrows and its woe
'Tis heaven my Jesus here to know.

O hallelujah, yes, 'tis heaven.
'Tis heaven to know my sins forgiven;
On land or sea, what matters where,
Where Jesus is, 'tis heaven there.

2 Once Heaven seemed a far-off place
Till Jesus showed His smiling face;
Now it's begun within my soul,
'Twill last while endless ages roll.

3 What matters where on earth we
dwell?
On mountain top, or in the dell?
In cottage, or in mansion fair,
Where Jesus is, 'tis heaven there.

C. F. Butler.

502 The dear old story of a Saviour's
love
Is sweeter as the days go by;
The glad assurance of a home above
Is sweeter as the days go by.

We'll fill . . . the days with joy . . . ful praise,
We'll sing as the happy moments fly; . . .
The song of love to Him above
Grows sweeter as the days go by.

2 The sunbeams shining from the living
Light
Are brighter as the days go by;
The stars of promise cheering
sorrow's night
Are brighter as the days go by.

3 Hope's anchor, holding in the stormy
strife,
Is stronger as the days go by;
We feel the throbbings of immortal
life
Grow stronger as the days go by.

4 The peace that Jesus gives to us
anew
Is deeper as the days go by;
The prospects opening to the
Christian's view
Are grander as the days go by.

Emily E. Hewitt.

503 There's within my heart a melody,
Jesus whispers sweet and low,
'Fear not, I am with thee, peace be
still,'
In all of life's ebb and flow.

Jesus, Jesus, Jesus,
Sweetest Name I know,
Fills my every longing,
Keeps me singing as I go.

2 All my life was wrecked by sin and
strife,
Discord filled my heart with pain,
Jesus swept across the broken
strings,
Stirred the slumbering chords again.

3 Feasting on the riches of His grace,
Resting 'neath His sheltering wing,
Always looking on His smiling face,
That is why I shout and sing.

4 Though sometimes He leads through
waters deep,
Trials fall across the way,
Though sometimes the path seems
rough and steep,
See His footprints all the way.

5 Soon He's coming back to welcome
me
Far beyond the starry sky:
I shall wing my flight to worlds
unknown,
I shall reign with Him on high.

L. B. Bridgers.

504 Who can cheer the heart like
Jesus,
By His presence all divine?
True and tender, pure and precious,
O how blest to call Him mine!

All that thrills my soul is Jesus;
He is more than life to me;
And the fairest of ten thousand,
In my blessèd Lord I see.

2 Love of Christ so freely given,
Grace of God beyond degree,
Mercy higher than the heaven,
Deeper than the deepest sea.

3 What a wonderful redemption!
Never can a mortal know
How my sin, though red like crimson,
Can be whiter than the snow.

4 Every need His hand supplying,
Every good in Him I see;
On His strength divine relying,
He is all in all to me.

5 By the crystal-flowing river
With the ransomed I will sing,
And for ever and for ever
Praise and glorify the King.

Thoro Harris.

505 There is sunshine in my soul
today,
More glorious and bright
Than glows in any earthly sky,
For Jesus is my light.

Oh, there's sunshine, blessèd sunshine,
While the peaceful, happy moments roll;
When Jesus shows His smiling face
There is sunshine in my soul.

2 There is music in my soul today,
A carol to my King,
And Jesus, listening, can hear
The song I cannot sing.

3 There is springtime in my soul today,
For when the Lord is near
The dove of peace sings in my heart,
The flowers of grace appear.

4 There is gladness in my soul today,
And hope, and praise, and love,
For blessings which He gives me now,
For joys 'laid up' above.

E. E. Hewitt.

PRAYER

506 We seek, dear Lord, Your
presence,
In Jesus' precious Name,
Our needs to lay before You,
Your promises to claim.
Take from us all distractions,
Our wandering thoughts remove,
That we in faith and meekness
Your love and power may prove.

2 First, to ourselves as sinners,
Your cleansing, Lord, impart,
Remove the secret shadows
Of sin from every heart.
Then for ourselves as servants
Your fullness, Lord, we seek,
Your grace to heal the broken,
Your power to fill the meek.

3 Then lead us out, dear Master,
In interceding prayer,
For those who do not know You,
For those who do not care.
In Satan's power and bondage,
Asleep in sin they lie,
Oh show them Your salvation
In answer to our cry.

4 With humble expectation
We wait upon You now,
In fuller, richer measure
Your saving power to know;
Then send us out, Lord Jesus,
To labour on for You,
Content to see Your glory
In hearts and lives made new.

John Eddison.

507 'Tis the blessèd hour of prayer,
when our hearts lowly bend,
And we gather to Jesus, our
Saviour and Friend;
If we come to Him in faith, His
protection to share;
What a balm for the weary! O how
sweet to be there!

Blessèd hour of prayer,
Blessèd hour of prayer;
What a balm for the weary!
O how sweet to be there.

2 'Tis the blessèd hour of prayer, when
the Saviour draws near
With a tender compassion His children
to hear;
When He tells us we may cast at His
feet every care;
What a balm for the weary! O how
sweet to be there!

3 'Tis the blessèd hour of prayer, when
the tempted and tried
To the Saviour who loves them their
sorrow confide;
With a sympathizing heart He removes
every care;
What a balm for the weary! O how
sweet to be there!

4 At the blessèd hour of prayer, trusting
Him we believe
That the blessings we're needing we'll
surely receive,
In the fulness of this trust we shall
lose every care;
What a balm for the weary! O how
sweet to be there!

Fanny J. Crosby.

508 We come before Thy throne
today,
Thy promised presence claim;
O come and enter now our hearts,
And set our souls aflame.

Lord, send Thy blessing, Lord, send Thy
blessing,
Lord, send Thy blessing on our waiting souls!

2 We know that Thou art present here,
Thy grace to us reveal;
We fain would know Thy blessèd will,
Thy holy presence feel.

3 O send to us Thy quickening power,
All guilt and dross remove;
O let our waiting hearts be filled,
Dear Saviour, with Thy love.

4 Accept the homage that we bring,
O Lord, we humbly pray;
Bestow Thy richest blessings now,
And meet with us today.

Irvin H. Mack.

509 What a Friend we have in Jesus,
All our sins and griefs to bear;
What a privilege to carry
Everything to God in prayer.
Oh, what peace we often forfeit,
Oh, what needless pain we bear—
All because we do not carry
Everything to God in prayer.

2 Have we trials and temptations?
Is there trouble anywhere?
We should never be discouraged,
Take it to the Lord in prayer.
Can we find a Friend so faithful
Who will all our sorrows share?
Jesus knows our every weakness,
Take it to the Lord in prayer.

3 Are we weak and heavy laden,
Cumbered with a load of care?
Precious Saviour, still our refuge,
Take it to the Lord in prayer.
Do thy friends despise, forsake thee?
Take it to the Lord in prayer;
In His arms He'll take and shield thee,
Thou wilt find a solace there.

Joseph Scriven.

510 Sweet hour of prayer, sweet hour
of prayer,
That calls me from a world of care,
And bids me at my Father's throne
Make all my wants and wishes
known:
In seasons of distress and grief
My soul has often found relief,
And oft escaped the tempter's snare
By thy return, sweet hour of prayer.

2 Sweet hour of prayer, sweet hour of
prayer,
The joy I feel, the bliss I share
Of those whose anxious spirits burn
With strong desires for thy return!
With such I hasten to the place

Where God, my Saviour, shows His
  face,
And gladly take my station there
And wait for thee, sweet hour of
  prayer.

3 Sweet hour of prayer, sweet hour of
    prayer,
Thy wings shall my petition bear
To Him whose truth and faithfulness
Engage the waiting soul to bless;
And since He bids me seek His face,
Believe His Word, and trust His grace,
I'll cast on Him my every care
And wait for thee, sweet hour of
  prayer.

W. W. Walford.

511 Are you weary, are you heavy-
    hearted?
Tell it to Jesus, tell it to Jesus;
Are you grieving over joys departed?
Tell it to Jesus alone.

Tell it to Jesus, tell it to Jesus,
He is a Friend that's well known,
You have no other such a friend or brother,
Tell it to Jesus alone.

2 Do the tears flow down your cheeks
    unbidden?
Tell it to Jesus, tell it to Jesus;
Have you sins that to man's eyes are
  hidden?
Tell it to Jesus alone.

3 Do you fear the gathering clouds of
    sorrow?
Tell it to Jesus, tell it to Jesus;
Are you anxious what shall be
  tomorrow?
Tell it to Jesus alone.

4 Are you troubled with the thought of
    dying?
Tell it to Jesus, tell it to Jesus;
For Christ's coming Kingdom are you
  sighing?
Tell it to Jesus alone.

J. E. Rankin.

512 I must tell Jesus all of my trials,
  I cannot bear these burdens alone;
In my distress He kindly will help me;
He ever loves and cares for His own.

I must tell Jesus! I must tell Jesus!
I cannot bear my burdens alone;
I must tell Jesus! I must tell Jesus!
Jesus can help me, Jesus alone.

2 I must tell Jesus all of my troubles;
He is a kind, compassionate Friend;
If I but ask Him, He will deliver,
Make of my troubles quickly an end.

3 Tempted and tried, I need a great
    Saviour,
One who can help my burdens to
  bear;
I must tell Jesus, I must tell Jesus,
He all my cares and sorrows will
  share.

4 O how the world to evil allures me!
O how my heart is tempted to sin!
I must tell Jesus and He will help me
Over the world the victory to win.

Elisha Hoffman.

513 I need Thee every hour,
    Most gracious Lord;
No tender voice like Thine
Can peace afford.

I need Thee, oh, I need Thee,
Every hour I need Thee;
Oh, bless me now, my Saviour,
I come to Thee!

2 I need Thee every hour,
Stay Thou near by;
Temptations lose their power
When Thou art nigh.

3 I need Thee every hour
In joy or pain;
Come quickly and abide
Or life is vain.

4 I need Thee every hour,
Teach me Thy will;
And Thy rich promises
In me fulfil.

5 I need Thee ever hour,
Most Holy One;
Oh, make me Thine indeed,
Thou blessèd Son!

Annie Hawkes.

The Christian Life

514 Our Father, which art in Heaven,
Hallowed be Thy name.
Thy Kingdom come.
Thy will be done, in earth as it is in
Heaven.
Give us this day our daily bread.
And forgive us our trespasses,
As we forgive them that trespass
against us.
And lead us not into temptation;
But deliver us from evil:
For thine is the Kingdom,
The power, and the glory,
For ever and ever.
Amen.

515 Speak to my soul, Lord Jesus,
Speak now in tend'rest tone;
Whisper in loving kindness:
'Thou art not left alone.'
Open my heart to hear Thee,
Quickly to hear Thy voice,
Fill Thou my soul with praises,
Let me in Thee rejoice.

Speak Thou in softest whispers,
Whispers of love to me;
'Thou shalt be always conqueror,
Thou shalt be always free.'
Speak Thou to me each day, Lord,
Always in tend'rest tone;
Let me now hear Thy whisper,
'Thou art not left alone.'

2 Speak to Thy children ever,
Lead in the holy way;
Fill them with joy and gladness,
Teach them to watch and pray,
May they in consecration
Yield their whole lives to Thee,
Hasten Thy coming Kingdom,
Till our dear Lord we see.

3 Speak now as in the old time
Thou didst reveal Thy will;
Let me know all my duty,
Let me Thy law fulfil.
Lead me to glorify Thee,
Help me to show Thy praise,
Gladly to do Thy bidding,
Honour Thee all my days.
L. L. Pickett.

516 If the world from you withhold of
its silver and its gold,
And you have to get along with
meagre fare,
Just remember, in His Word, how He
feeds the little bird;
Take your burden to the Lord and
leave it there.

Leave it there, . . . leave it there, . . .
Take your burden to the Lord and leave it
there; . . .
If you trust and never doubt
He will surely bring you out;
Take your burden to the Lord and leave it
there. . . .

2 If your body suffers pain and your
health you can't regain,
And your soul is almost sinking in
despair,
Jesus knows the pain you feel, He can
save and He can heal;
Take your burden to the Lord and
leave it there.

3 When your enemies assail and your
heart begins to fail
Don't forget that God in Heaven
answers prayer;
He will make a way for you and will
lead you safely through;
Take your burden to the Lord and
leave it there.

4 When your youthful days are gone
and old age is stealing on,
And your body bends beneath the
weight of care;
He will never leave you then, He'll go
with you to the end;
Take your burden to the Lord and
leave it there.
C. Albert Tindley.

517 My faith looks up to Thee, Thou
Lamb of Calvary,
Saviour divine;
Now hear me while I pray,
Take all my guilt away,
Oh let me from this day be wholly
Thine!

2 May Thy rich grace impart strength to
my fainting heart,
My zeal inspire!
As Thou hast died for me,
Oh may my love to Thee, pure, warm
and changeless be
A living fire!

3 While life's dark maze I tread,
And griefs around me spread
Be Thou my Guide;
Bid darkness turn to day,
Wipe sorrow's tears away,
Nor let me ever stray from Thee aside.

4 When ends life's transient dream,
When death's cold sullen stream
Shall o'er me roll;
Blest Saviour, then, in love,
Fear and distrust remove,
Oh, bear me safe above,
A ransomed soul.

Ray Palmer.

518 Pray, always pray; the Holy Spirit
pleads
Within thee all thy daily, hourly needs.

2 Pray, always pray; beneath sin's
heaviest load
Prayer sees the blood from Jesus' side
that flowed.

3 Pray, always pray; though weary,
faint, and lone,
Prayer nestles by the Father's
sheltering throne.

4 Pray, always pray; amid the world's
turmoil
Prayer keeps the heart at rest, and
nerves for toil.

5 Pray, always pray; if joys thy pathway
throng,
Prayer strikes the harp, and sings the
angels' song.

6 Pray, always pray; if loved ones pass
the veil,
Prayer drinks with them of springs
that cannot fail.

7 All earthly things with earth shall pass
away;
Prayer grasps eternity; pray, always
pray.

E. H. Bickersteth.

519 Jesus, Lord, we look to Thee,
Let us in Thy Name agree:
Show Thyself the Prince of Peace;
Bid all strife for ever cease.

2 Make us of one heart and mind,
Courteous, full of pity, kind,
Lowly, meek, in thought and word,
Altogether like the Lord.

3 Let us for each other care,
Each the other's burden bear,
To Thy Church the pattern give,
Show how true believers live.

4 Free from anger and from pride,
Let us thus in God abide;
All the depths of love express,
All the heights of holiness.

5 Closer knit to Thee, our Head,
Nourish us, O Christ, and feed!
Let us daily grace receive,
More and more in Jesus live.

6 Fill us with the Father's love,
Never from our souls remove;
Dwell in us, and we shall be
Thine through all eternity.

Charles Wesley.

520 I am praying, blessèd Saviour,
To be more and more like Thee;
I am praying that Thy Spirit
Like a dove may rest on me.

Thou who knowest all my weakness,
Thou who knowest all my care,
While I plead each precious promise,
Hear, oh, hear and answer prayer!

2 I am praying, blessèd Saviour,
For a faith so clear and bright
That its eye will see Thy glory
Through the deepest, darkest night.

The Christian Life

3 I am praying to be humbled
By the power of grace divine,
To be clothed upon with meekness,
And to have no will but Thine.

4 I am praying, blessèd Saviour,
And my constant prayer shall be,
For a perfect consecration,
That shall make me more like Thee.

Fanny J. Crosby.

521 Prayer is the soul's sincere desire,
Uttered or unexpressed!
The motion of a hidden fire
That trembles in the breast.

2 Prayer is the burden of a sigh,
The falling of a tear,
The upward glancing of an eye,
When none but God is near.

3 Prayer is the simplest form of speech
That infant lips can try;
Prayer, the sublimest strains that reach
The Majesty on high.

4 Prayer is the Christian's vital breath,
The Christian's native air:
His watchword at the gates of death,
He enters Heaven with prayer.

5 The saints in prayer appear as one,
In word, and deed, and mind:
While with the Father and the Son
Sweet fellowship they find.

6 O Thou by whom we come to God,
The Life, the Truth, the Way!
The path of prayer Thyself hast trod,
Lord, teach us how to pray!

Jas. Montgomery.

SERVICE

522 Blessèd is the service of our Lord and King,
Precious are the jewels we may help to bring;
Down the passing ages words of counsel ring,
He that winneth souls is wise.

He that winneth souls is wise; . . .
In the home beyond the skies, . . .
There's a crown of glory, oh, the wondrous prize
He that winneth souls is wise.

2 In the quiet home-life, showing love's bright ray,
More and more like Jesus living every day,
We may guide a dear one to the Heaven-ward way,
He that winneth souls is wise.

3 Out upon the highway, going forth with prayer
For the lost and straying, seeking everywhere,
Close beside the Shepherd, we His joy may share,
He that winneth souls is wise.

4 Sow beside all waters, sow the gospel seed,
Here a word in season, there a loving deed,
Sinners to the Saviour be it ours to lead,
He that winneth souls is wise.

E. E. Hewitt.

523 Once it was the blessing,
Now it is the Lord;
Once it was the feeling,
Now it is His Word;
Once His gifts I wanted,
Now the Giver own;
Once I sought for healing,
Now Himself alone.

All in all for ever,
Jesus will I sing;
Everything in Jesus,
And Jesus everything.

2 Once 'twas painful trying,
Now 'tis perfect trust;
Once a half salvation,
Now the uttermost;
Once 'twas ceaseless holding,
Now He holds me fast;
Once 'twas constant drifting,
Now my anchor's cast.

3 Once 'twas busy planning,
Now 'tis trustful prayer;
Once 'twas anxious caring,
Now He has the care;
Once 'twas what I wanted,
Now what Jesus says;
Once 'twas constant asking,
Now 'tis ceaseless praise.

4 Once it was my working,
His it hence shall be;
Once I tried to use Him,
Now He uses me;
Once the power I wanted,
Now the Mighty One;
Once for self I laboured,
Now for Him alone.

5 Once I hoped in Jesus,
Now I know He's mine;
Once my lamps were dying,
Now they brightly shine;
Once for death I waited,
Now His coming hail;
And my hopes are anchored
Safe within the veil.

A. B. Simpson.

524 There is joy in serving Jesus,
As I journey on my way,
Joy that fills the heart with praises,
Every hour and every day.

There is joy, joy,
Joy in serving Jesus,
Joy that throbs within my heart;
Every moment, every hour,
As I draw upon His power,
There is joy, joy,
Joy that never shall depart.

2 There is joy in serving Jesus,
Joy that triumphs over pain;
Fills my soul with Heaven's music,
Till I join the glad refrain.

3 There is joy in serving Jesus,
As I walk alone with God;
'Tis the joy of Christ, my Saviour,
Who the path of suffering trod.

4 There is joy in serving Jesus,
Joy amid the darkest night,
For I've learned the wondrous secret,
And I'm walking in the light.

Oswald J. Smith.

525 The Master hath come, and He
calls us to follow
The track of the footprints He leaves
on our way;
Far over the mountain, and through
the deep hollow,
The path leads us on to the mansions
of day.
The Master hath called us, the
children who fear Him,
Who march 'neath Christ's banner,
His own little band;
We love Him, and seek Him, we long
to be near Him,
And rest in the light of His beautiful
land.

2 The Master hath called us; the road
may be dreary,
And dangers and sorrows are strewn
on the track;
But God's Holy Spirit shall comfort
the weary—
We follow the Saviour, and cannot
turn back.
The Master hath called us: though
doubt and temptation
May compass our journey, we cheer-
fully sing,
'Press onward, look upward,' through
much tribulation
The children of Zion must follow their
King.

3 The Master hath called us: in life's
early morning
With spirits as fresh as the dew on the
sod:
We turn from the world, with its
smiles and its scorning,
To cast in our lot with the people of
God.
The Master hath called us, His sons
and His daughters,
We plead for His blessing, and trust in
His love;
And through the green pastures,
beside the still waters,
He'll lead us at last to His Kingdom
above.

Sarah Doudney.

526 There's a work for Jesus
　　Ready at your hand,
'Tis a task the Master
Just for you has planned.
Haste to do His bidding,
Yield Him service true;
There's a work for Jesus
None but you can do.

　　Work for Jesus, day by day,
　　Serve Him ever, falter never, Christ obey.
　　Yield Him service, loyal, true:
　　There's a work for Jesus none but you can do.

2 There's a work for Jesus,
Humble though it be,
'Tis the very service
He would ask of thee.
Go where fields are whitened,
And the labourers few;
There's a work for Jesus
None but you can do.

3 There's a work for Jesus,
Precious souls to bring,
Tell them of His mercies,
Tell them of your King.
Faint not, grow not weary,
He will strength renew;
There's a work for Jesus
None but you can do.

　　　　　　　　　　　　　　Elsie Yale.

527 To the work! to the work! we are
　　servants of God,
Let us follow the path that our Master
has trod;
With the balm of His counsel our
strength to renew,
Let us do with our might what our
hands find to do.

　　Toiling on, . . . toiling on, . . .
　　Toiling on, . . . toiling on; . . .
　　Let us hope, . . . let us watch, . . .
　　And labour till the Master comes.

2 To the work! to the work! let the
hungry be fed,
To the fountain of life let the weary be
led!
In the Cross and its banner our glory
shall be
While we herald the tidings,
'Salvation is free!'

3 To the work! to the work! there is
labour for all,
For the kingdom of darkness and error
shall fall:
And the Name of Jehovah exalted
shall be
In the loud-swelling chorus,
'Salvation is free!'

4 To the work! to the work! in the
strength of the Lord,
And a robe and a crown shall our
labour reward
When the home of the faithful our
dwelling shall be
And we shout with the ransomed,
'Salvation is free!'

　　　　　　　　　　　　　　Fanny J. Crosby.

528 Sowing in the morning, sowing
　　seeds of kindness,
Sowing in the noontide and the dewy
eve;
Waiting for the harvest and the time
of reaping,
We shall come rejoicing, bringing in
the sheaves.

　　Bringing in the sheaves, bringing in the
　　sheaves,
　　We shall come rejoicing, bringing in the
　　sheaves.

2 Sowing in the sunshine, sowing in the
shadows,
Fearing neither clouds nor winter's
chilling breeze;
By and by the harvest and the labour
ended,
We shall come rejoicing, bringing in
the sheaves.

3 Going forth with weeping, sowing for
the Master,
Though the loss sustained our spirit
often grieves;
When our weeping's over He will bid
us welcome,
We shall come rejoicing, bringing in
the sheaves.

　　　　　　　　　　　　　　Knowles Shaw.

529 Take the world, but give me
Jesus,
All its joys are but a name;
But His love abideth ever,
Through eternal years the same.

Oh, the height and depth of mercy!
Oh, the length and breadth of love!
Oh, the fulness of redemption,
Pledge of endless life above.

2 Take the world, but give me Jesus,
Sweetest comfort of my soul;
With my Saviour watching o'er me
I can sing, though billows roll.

3 Take the world, but give me Jesus,
Let me view His constant smile;
Then throughout my pilgrim journey
Light will cheer me all the while.

4 Take the world, but give me Jesus,
In His Cross my trust shall be,
Till, with clearer, brighter vision,
Face to face my Lord I see.

Fanny J. Crosby.

530 We are marching on with shield
and banner bright;
We will work for God and battle for
the right;
We will praise His Name, rejoicing in
His might,
And we'll work till Jesus calls.
From the youthful ranks our army we
prepare,
As we rally round our blessèd
standard here;
And the Saviour's Cross we early
learn to bear
While we work till Jesus calls.

Then awake, . . . then awake, . . .
Happy song, . . . happy song, . . .
Shout for joy, . . . shout for joy, . . .
As we gladly march along.
We are marching onward, singing as we go,
To the promised land where living waters flow;
Come and join our ranks as pilgrims here
below,
Come and work till Jesus calls.

2 We are marching on: our Captain,
ever near,
Will protect us still, His gentle voice
we hear:

Let the foe advance, we'll never,
never fear,
For we'll work till Jesus calls.
Then awake, awake, our happy,
happy song,
We will shout for joy, and gladly
march along;
In the Lord of hosts let every heart be
strong
While we work till Jesus calls.

3 We are marching on the strait and
narrow way
That will lead to life and everlasting
day,
To the smiling fields, that never will
decay:
But we'll work till Jesus calls.
We are marching on, and pressing
t'wards the prize,
To a glorious crown beyond the
glowing skies,
To the radiant fields where pleasure
never dies,
And we'll work till Jesus calls.

Fanny J. Crosby.

531 Hear the Lord of harvest sweetly
calling,
'Who will go and work for Me today?
Who will bring to Me the lost and
dying?
Who will point them to the narrow
way?'

Speak, my Lord, . . . speak to me, . . .
Speak, and I'll be quick to answer Thee; . . .
Speak, my Lord, . . . speak to me,
Speak, and I will answer, 'Lord, send me.'. . .

2 When the coal of fire touched the
prophet,
Making him as pure, as pure can be,
When the voice of God said, 'Who'll
go for us?'
Then he answered, 'Here I am, send
me.'

3 Millions now in sin and shame are
dying;
Listen to their sad and bitter cry;
Hasten, brother, hasten to the rescue;
Quickly answer, 'Master, here am I.'

4 Soon the time for reaping will be over;
Soon we'll gather for the harvest-
home;
May the Lord of harvest smile upon us,
May we hear His blessèd, 'Child, well
done!'

Geo. Bennard.

532 Is your life a channel of blessing?
Is the love of God flowing through
you?
Are you telling the lost of the Saviour?
Are you ready His service to do?

Make me a channel of blessing today,
Make me a channel of blessing, I pray:
My life possessing, my service blessing,
Make me a channel of blessing today.

2 Is your life a channel of blessing?
Are you burdened for those that are
lost?
Have you urged upon those who are
straying
The Saviour who died on the Cross?

3 Is your life a channel of blessing?
Is it daily telling for Him?
Have you spoken the word of
salvation
To those who are dying in sin?

4 We cannot be channels of blessing
If our lives are not free from all sin;
We will barriers be and a hindrance
To those we are trying to win.

H. G. Smyth.

533 Jesus calls us; o'er the tumult
Of our life's wild, restless sea,
Day by day His sweet voice soundeth,
Saying, "Christian, follow Me".

2 As of old apostles heard it
By the Galilean lake,
Turned from home and toil and
kindred,
Leaving all for His dear sake.

3 Jesus calls us from the worship
Of the vain world's golden store,
From each idol that would keep us,
Saying, "Christian, love Me more".

4 In our joys and in our sorrows,
Days of toil and hours of ease,
Still He calls, in cares and pleasures,
That we love Him more than these.

5 Jesus calls us; by Thy mercies,
Saviour, may we hear Thy call,
Give our hearts to Thy obedience,
Serve and love Thee best of all.

C. F. Alexander.

534 How I praise Thee, precious
Saviour,
That Thy love laid hold of me;
Thou hast saved and cleansed and
filled me,
That I might Thy channel be.

Channels only, blessèd Master,
But with all Thy wondrous power
Flowing through us Thou canst use us,
Every day and every hour.

2 Just a channel, full of blessing,
To the thirsty hearts around;
To tell out Thy full salvation,
All Thy loving message sound.

3 Emptied that Thou shouldest fill me,
A clean vessel in Thy hand;
With no power but as Thou givest,
Graciously with each command.

4 Witnessing Thy power to save me,
Setting free from self and sin;
Thou hast bought me to possess me,
In Thy fulness, Lord, come in.

5 Jesus, fill now with Thy Spirit
Hearts that full surrender know;
That the streams of living water
From our inner man may flow.

Mary E. Maxwell.

535 I love, I love my Master,
I will not go out free!
For He is my Redeemer;
He paid the price for me.
I would not leave His service,
It is so sweet and blest;
And in the weariest moments
He gives the truest rest.

2 My Master shed His life-blood
My vassal life to win,
And save me from the bondage
Of tyrant self and sin.
He chose me for His service,
And gave me power to choose
That blessèd, perfect freedom,
Which I shall never lose.

3 I would not halve my service,
His only it must be!
His *only*—Who so loved me,
And gave Himself for me.
Rejoicing and adoring,
Henceforth my song shall be—
'I love, I love my Master,
I will not go out free!'

Frances Ridley Havergal.

536 Give me the faith which can
remove
And sink the mountain to a plain;
Give me the child-like praying love
Which longs to build Thy house again;
Thy love let it my heart o'erpower,
And all my simple soul devour.

2 I want an even strong desire,
I want a calmly fervent zeal
To save poor souls out of the fire,
To snatch them from the verge of hell,
And turn them to a pardoning God,
And quench the brands in Jesu's
blood.

3 I would the precious time redeem,
And longer live for this alone,
To spend, and to be spent, for them
Who have not yet my Saviour known;
Fully on these my mission prove,
And only breathe, to breathe Thy
love.

4 My talents, gifts, and graces, Lord,
Into Thy blessèd hands receive;
And let me live to preach Thy Word,
And let me to Thy glory live;
My every sacred moment spend
In publishing the sinner's Friend.

5 Enlarge, inflame, and fill my heart
With boundless charity divine!
So shall I all my strength exert,
And love them with a zeal like Thine;
And lead them to Thy open side,
The sheep for whom their Shepherd
died.

Charles Wesley.

537 Jesus, and shall it ever be,
A mortal man ashamed of Thee?
Ashamed of Thee, whom angels
praise,
Whose glories shine through endless
days!

2 Ashamed of Jesus? sooner far
Let evening blush to own a star;
He shed the beams of light divine
O'er this benighted soul of mine.

3 Ashamed of Jesus? just as soon
Let midnight be ashamed of noon:
'Twas midnight with my soul till He,
Bright morning star, bade darkness
flee.

4 Ashamed of Jesus? that dear Friend
On whom my hopes of Heaven
depend!
No! when I blush be this my shame
That I no more revere His Name.

5 Ashamed of Jesus? yes, I may
When I've no guilt to wash away;
No tear to wipe, no good to crave,
No fears to quell, no soul to save.

6 Till then—nor is my boasting vain—
Till then I boast a Saviour slain;
And oh! may this my glory be
That Christ is not ashamed of me.

J. Grigg.

538 O Thou who camest from above
The pure celestial fire to impart,
Kindle a flame of sacred love
On the mean altar of my heart!

2 There let it for Thy glory burn
With inextinguishable blaze;
And trembling to its source return,
In humble prayer and fervent praise.

3 Jesus, confirm my heart's desire
   To work, and speak, and think for
     Thee;
   Still let me guard the holy fire,
   And still stir up Thy gift in me.

4 Ready for all Thy perfect will,
   My acts of faith and love repeat,
   Till death Thy endless mercies seal,
   And make the sacrifice complete.

Charles Wesley.

539 Anywhere with Jesus I can safely
     go,
   Anywhere He leads me in this world
     below.
   Anywhere without Him, dearest joys
     would fade,
   Anywhere with Jesus I am not afraid.

   Anywhere! anywhere!
   Fear I cannot know.
   Anywhere with Jesus
   I can safely go.

2 Anywhere with Jesus I am not alone,
   Other friends may fail me, He is still
     my own.
   Though His hand may lead me over
     drearest ways,
   Anywhere with Jesus is a house of
     praise.

3 Anywhere with Jesus I can go to
     sleep
   When the darkening shadows round
     about me creep;
   Knowing I shall waken, never more to
     roam,
   Anywhere with Jesus will be home,
     sweet home.

Jessie H. Brown.

540 Saviour! Thy dying love
     Thou gavest me,
   Nor should I aught withold,
   My Lord, from Thee;
   In love my soul would bow,
   My heart fulfil its vow,
   Some offering bring Thee now,
   Something for Thee.

2 At the blest mercy seat,
   Pleading for me,
   My feeble faith looks up,
   Jesus, to Thee:
   Help me the cross to bear,
   Thy wondrous love declare,
   Some song to raise, or prayer,
   Something for Thee.

3 Give me a faithful heart—
   Likeness to Thee—
   That each departing day
   Henceforth may see
   Some work of love begun,
   Some deed of kindness done,
   Some wanderer sought and won,
   Something for Thee.

4 All that I am and have—
   Thy gifts so free—
   In joy, in grief, through life,
   O Lord, for Thee!
   And when Thy face I see,
   My ransomed soul shall be,
   Through all eternity,
   Something for Thee.

S. D. Phelps.

541 Living for Jesus a life that is true,
     Striving to please Him in all that
       I do,
   Yielding allegiance, glad-hearted and
     free,
   This is the pathway of blessing for me.

   O Jesus, Lord and Saviour,
   I give myself to Thee;
   For Thou, in Thine atonement,
   Didst give Thyself for me;
   I own no other Master,
   My heart shall be Thy throne,
   My life I give, henceforth to live,
   O Christ, for Thee alone.

2 Living for Jesus who died in my place,
   Bearing on Calvary my sin and
     disgrace,
   Such love constrains me to answer
     His call,
   Follow His leading and give Him my
     all.

3 Living for Jesus wherever I am,
   Doing each duty in His Holy Name,
   Willing to suffer affliction or loss,
   Deeming each trial a part of my cross.

4 Living for Jesus through earth's little
while,
My dearest treasure, the light of His
smile,
Seeking the lost ones He died to
redeem,
Bringing the weary to find rest in Him.

T. O. Chisholm.

CONSECRATION & HOLINESS

542 'Called unto holiness,' Church of
our God,
Purchase of Jesus, redeemed by His
blood;
Called from the world and its idols to
flee,
Called from the bondage of sin to be
free.

'Holiness unto the Lord,' is our watchword
and song,
'Holiness unto the Lord,' as we're marching
along:
Sing . . . it, shout it, loud . . . and long,
'Holiness unto the Lord,' now and for ever.

2 'Called unto holiness,' children of
light,
Walking with Jesus in garments of
white;
Raiment unsullied, nor tarnished with
sin,
God's Holy Spirit abiding within.

3 'Called unto holiness,' praise His dear
Name,
This blessèd secret to faith now made
plain.
Not our own righteousness, but Christ
within,
Living and reigning, and saving from
sin.

4 'Called unto holiness,' glorious
thought!
Up from the wilderness wanderings
brought
Out from the shadows and darkness
of night
Into the Canaan of perfect delight.

5 'Called unto holiness,' Bride of the
Lamb,
Waiting the Bridegroom's returning
again;

Lift up your heads, for the day
draweth near
When in His beauty the King shall
appear.

Mrs. C. H. Morris.

543 Though days are long, oft filled
with care,
Though burdens seem so hard to
bear,
No matter what my lot may be,
I'll live for Him who died for me.

I'll live for Jesus day after day,
I'll live for Jesus let come what may,
The Holy Spirit I will obey,
And live for Jesus day after day.

2 Through every day new joy I find,
He gives to me real peace of mind,
Until the day when Christ I'll see,
I'll live for Him who died for me.

P. J. Schultz.

544 Father of love, of justice and of
mercy,
Thou art the dawn, the star at
eventide;
Show Thou Thy face, and light my
way to Calvary,
There all my sins in Thee to hide.
I bring Thee all my sins,
None can forgive but Thee.

I bring Thee all,
I bring Thee all;
Oh, give Thyself to me,
I bring Thee all.

2 O Thou, of whom the heavens are but
a symbol,
Be Thou the sun that draws my heart
to Thee;
Be Thou the light the stars at night do
kindle;
Thy love is more than all to me.
I bring Thee all my heart,
None do I love like Thee.

3 O Man of Sorrows, praying in the garden,
Thy sweat as blood falls down upon the ground.
In that dark agony my sins are pardoned;
My solace in Thy grief is found.
I bring Thee all my tears,
None can console like Thee.

Evangeline Booth.

545 O Lamb of God! Thou wonderful sin-bearer;
Hard after Thee my soul doth follow on:
As pants the hart for streams in desert dreary,
So pants my soul for Thee, O Thou life-giving One.

At Thy feet I fall, yield Thee up my all,
To suffer, live, or die for my Lord crucified.

2 I mourn, I mourn, the sin that drove Thee from me,
And blackest darkness brought into my soul;
Now, I renounce the accursèd thing that hindered,
And come once more to Thee, to be made fully whole.

3 Descend the Heavens, Thou Whom my soul adoreth!
Exchange Thy throne for my poor longing heart.
For Thee, for Thee, I watch as for the morning;
No rest or peace is mine from my Saviour apart.

4 Come, Holy Ghost, Thy mighty aid bestowing,
Destroy the works of sin, the self, the pride;
Burn, burn in me, my idols over-throwing,
Prepare my heart for Him—for my Lord crucified.

C. Booth-Clibborn.

546 My stubborn will at last hath yielded;
I would be Thine and Thine alone;
And this the prayer my lips are bringing,
Lord, let in me Thy will be done.

Sweet will of God, still fold me closer,
Till I am wholly lost in Thee;
Sweet will of God, still fold me closer,
Till I am wholly lost in Thee.

2 I'm tired of sin, footsore and weary,
The darksome path hath dreary grown,
But now a light has risen to cheer me!
I find in Thee my Star, my Sun.

3 Thy precious will, O conquering Saviour.
Doth now embrace and compass me;
All discords hushed, my peace a river,
My soul, a prisoned bird set free.

4 Shut in with Thee, O Lord, for ever,
My wayward feet no more to roam;
What power from Thee my soul can sever?
The centre of God's will my home.

Mrs. C. H. Morris.

547 O Love that wilt not let me go,
I rest my weary soul in Thee;
I give Thee back the life I owe,
That in Thine ocean depths its flow
May richer, fuller be.

2 O Light that followest all my way,
I yield my flickering torch to Thee:
My heart restores its borrowed ray,
That in Thy sunshine's blaze its day
May brighter, fairer be.

3 O Joy that seekest me through pain,
I cannot close my heart to Thee:
I trace the rainbow through the rain
And feel the promise is not vain,
That morn shall tearless be.

4 O Cross that liftest up my head,
I dare not ask to fly from Thee;
I lay in dust life's glory dead,
And from the ground there blossoms red
Life that shall endless be.

George Matheson.

548 I want my life to be all filled with praise to Thee,
My precious Lord divine Who died for me,
Let all my will be Thine, controlled by love divine,
Live out in me Thy life, O mighty Saviour.

> Thy blessèd will divine, with joy I make it mine,
> My heart shall be Thy throne, and Thine alone.
> Choose Thou the path I tread and whither I am led,
> Help me to follow on, O mighty Saviour.

2 A pilgrim born anew, a stranger going through,
Not of this world am I, since I am Thine.
Weaned from its passing show, transformed Thy love to know,
Hold Thou my hand in Thine, O mighty Saviour.

3 When evil foes assail and almost would prevail,
In that dark hour be Thou my strength and shield.
Lend then Thy strong embrace, uphold me by Thy grace,
In weakness be my strength, O mighty Saviour.

4 Yea, choose the path for me, although I may not see
The reason Thou dost will to lead me so.
I know the toilsome way will lead to realms of day
Where I shall dwell with Thee, O mighty Saviour.

H. Tee.

549 Breathe on me, Breath of God,
Fill me with life anew,
That I may love what Thou dost love,
And do what Thou wouldst do.

2 Breathe on me, Breath of God,
Until my heart is pure,
Until with Thee I will one will,
To do and to endure.

3 Breathe on me, Breath of God,
Till I am wholly Thine,
Till all this earthly part of me
Glows with Thy fire divine.

4 Breathe on me, Breath of God,
So shall I never die,
But live with Thee the perfect life
Of Thine eternity.

Edwin Hatch.

550 Burn, fire of God! my ransomed soul possessing;
Pure fire Thou art, and I would dwell in Thee.
Light of my life, true source of every blessing,
Grant all my days one holy flame to be.

2 Burn, fire of God! Thy grace and glory knowing,
My cleansèd heart shall be all fire within:
Love all-constraining, tenderness o'erflowing,
One kindling passion other lives to win.

3 Burn, fire of God! Thy cloven tongue bestowing,
Baptizing me with Heavenly energy.
Touched with live coals from off Thine altar glowing
My purgèd lips shall speak alone of Thee.

4 Burn, fire of God! with sevenfold refining,
Till, mirrored from my deeps Thine eyes shall see
In purest gold Thy perfect image shining:
Thy Christ revealed in clear irradiancy.

5 Burn, fire of God! by Thine own love transcending,
Let all I hold be Thine, and Thine alone!
Heart, mind and will, a sacrifice ascending,
Consumed by fire from out Thy fiery Throne.

L. F. W. Woodford.

The Christian Life

551 Called to separation
With the Crucified,
Temples of the Spirit,
Saved and sanctified,
Set apart for service,
By God's hand ordained,
We the Cross have taken,
By His love constrained.

Step by step with Jesus,
All along life's way,
Now the Cross and conflict,
Then the perfect day.

2 Christ the veil has entered
With the blood He shed,
Sin's great debt is cancelled,
Love's own feast is spread;
Now in Christ we're chosen
Kings and priests to be,
Living offerings bringing,
His own blood our plea.

3 Like a boundless ocean
Ever rolling in,
Comes this flood of blessing,
Seeking lives to win;
Who such love can fathom,
From God's heart which flows,
Or such grace e'er measure,
Which His hand bestows?

4 Pressing onward, upward,
Life grows pure and strong,
'Tis the vision splendid
Saves from all that's wrong;
In the steps of Jesus
We would plant our own,
Blessèd path of triumph
Leading to the Throne.

E. C. W. Boulton.

552 Wash me, O Lamb of God,
Wash me from sin!
By Thine atoning blood,
Oh, make me clean!
Purge me from every stain,
Let me Thine image gain,
In love and mercy reign
O'er all within.

2 Wash me, O Lamb of God,
Wash me from sin!
I long to be like Thee—
All pure within.

Now let the crimson tide
Shed from Thy wounded side
Be to my heart applied,
And make me clean.

3 Wash me, O Lamb of God,
Wash me from sin!
I will not, cannot, rest
Till pure within.
All human skill is vain,
But Thou canst cleanse each stain
Till not a spot remain—
Made wholly clean.

4 Wash me, O Lamb of God,
Wash me from sin!
By faith Thy cleansing blood
Now makes me clean.
So near art Thou to me,
So sweet my rest in Thee—
Oh, blessèd purity,
Saved, saved from sin!

5 Wash me, O Lamb of God,
Wash me from sin!
Thou, while I trust in Thee,
Wilt keep me clean.
Each day to Thee I bring
Heart, life—yea, everything;
Saved, while to Thee I cling,
Saved from all sin!

H. B. Beagle.

553 Come, Jesus, Lord, with holy fire!
Come, and my quickened heart
inspire,
Cleansed in Thy precious blood.
Now to my soul Thyself reveal,
Thy mighty working let me feel,
Since I am born of God.

2 Let nothing now my heart divide;
Since with Thee I am crucified,
And live to God in Thee.
Dead to the world and all its toys,
Its idle pomp, and fading joys,
Jesus, my glory be!

3 Me with a quenchless thirst inspire,
A longing, infinite desire,
And fill my craving heart.
Less than Thyself, oh, do not give;
In might Thyself within me live,
Come, all Thou hast and art!

4 My will be swallowed up in Thee,
Light in Thy light still may I see
In Thine unclouded face;
Called the full strength of trust to
prove,
Let all my quickened heart be love,
My spotless life be praise.

Charles Wesley.

554 Have Thine own way, Lord!
Have Thine own way!
Thou art the Potter;
I am the clay.
Mould me and make me
After Thy will,
While I am waiting
Yielded and still.

2 Have Thine own way, Lord!
Have Thine own way!
Search me and try me,
Master, today!
Whiter than snow, Lord,
Wash me just now,
As in Thy presence
Humbly I bow.

3 Have Thine own way, Lord!
Have Thine own way!
Wounded and weary
Help me, I pray!
Power—all power—
Surely is Thine!
Touch me and heal me,
Saviour Divine!

4 Have Thine own way, Lord!
Have Thine own way!
Hold o'er my being
Absolute sway!
Fill with Thy Spirit
Till all shall see
Christ only, always,
Living in me!

A. A. Pollard.

555 More holiness give me,
More strivings within;
More patience in suffering,
More sorrow for sin;

More faith in my Saviour,
More sense of His care;
More joy in His service,
More purpose in prayer.

2 More gratitude give me,
More trust in the Lord;
More pride in His glory,
More hope in His Word;
More tears for His sorrows,
More pain at His grief;
More meekness in trial,
More praise for relief.

3 More purity give me,
More strength to o'ercome;
More freedom from earth-stains,
More longings for home;
More fit for the Kingdom,
More used would I be;
More blessèd and holy,
More, Saviour, like Thee.

Philip P. Bliss.

556 O Jesus, I have promised
To serve Thee to the end;
Be Thou for ever near me,
My Master and my Friend:
I shall not fear the battle
If Thou art by my side,
Nor wander from the pathway
If Thou wilt be my Guide.

2 O let me feel Thee near me;
The world is ever near;
I see the sights that dazzle,
The tempting sounds I hear;
My foes are ever near me,
Around me and within;
But, Jesus, draw Thou nearer,
And shield my soul from sin.

3 O let me hear Thee speaking
In accents clear and still,
Above the storms of passion,
The murmurs of self-will;
O speak to reassure me,
To hasten or control;
O speak and make me listen,
Thou Guardian of my soul.

4 O Jesus, Thou hast promised
To all who follow Thee,
That where Thou art in glory
There shall Thy servant be;
And, Jesus, I have promised
To serve Thee to the end;
O give me grace to follow
My Master and my Friend.

John Ernest Bode.

557 Make me a captive, Lord,
And then I shall be free;
Force me to render up my sword,
And I shall conqueror be.
I sink in life's alarms
When by myself I stand;
Imprison me within Thine arms,
And strong shall be my hand.

2 My heart is weak and poor
Until it master find;
It has no spring of action sure—
It varies with the wind.
It cannot freely move
Till Thou hast wrought its chain;
Enslave it with Thy matchless love,
And deathless it shall reign.

3 My power is faint and low
Till I have learned to serve:
It wants the needed fire to glow,
It wants the breeze to nerve;
It cannot drive the world
Until itself be driven;
Its flag can only be unfurled
When Thou shalt breathe from
Heaven.

4 My will is not my own
Till Thou hast made it Thine;
If it would reach a monarch's throne
It must its crown resign;
It only stands unbent,
Amid the clashing strife,
When on Thy bosom it has leant
And found in Thee its life.

George Matheson.

558 Oh, for a heart to praise my God,
A heart from sin set free,
A heart that always feels the blood
So freely shed for me.

2 A heart resigned, submissive, meek,
My great Redeemer's throne,
Where only Christ is heard to speak,
Where Jesus reigns alone.

3 A humble, holy, contrite heart,
Believing, true, and clean,
Which neither life nor death can part
From Him that dwells within.

4 A heart in every thought renewed,
And full of love divine,
Perfect, and right, and pure, and
good,
A copy, Lord, of Thine!

5 Thy nature, gracious Lord, impart;
Come quickly from above,
Write Thy new name upon my heart,
Thy new, best name of Love.

Charles Wesley.

559 I have found a deep peace that I
never had known
And a joy this world could not afford,
Since I yielded control of my body and
soul
To my wonderful, wonderful Lord.

My wonderful Lord, my wonderful Lord,
By angels and seraphs in Heaven adored;
I know Thou art mine, my Saviour divine,
My wonderful, wonderful Lord.

2 I desire that my life shall be ordered by
Thee,
That my will be in perfect accord
With Thine own sovereign will, Thy
desires to fulfill,
My wonderful, wonderful Lord.

3 All the talents I have I have laid at Thy
feet,
Thy approval shall be my reward;
Be my store great or small I surrender
it all
To my wonderful, wonderful Lord.

4 Thou art fairer to me than the fairest
of earth,
Thou omnipotent, life-giving Word;
O Thou Ancient of Days Thou art
worthy all praise,
My wonderful, wonderful Lord.

Haldor Lillenas.

560 Take my life, and let it be
Consecrated, Lord, to Thee;
Take my moments and my days,
Let them flow in ceaseless praise.

2 Take my hands, and let them move
At the impulse of Thy love;
Take my feet, and let them be
Swift and beautiful for Thee.

3 Take my voice and let me sing
Always, only, for my King;
Take my lips and let them be
Filled with messages from Thee.

4 Take my silver and my gold;
Not a mite would I withhold;
Take my intellect, and use
Every power as Thou shalt choose.

5 Take my will and make it Thine,
It shall be no longer mine:
Take my heart, it is Thine own;
It shall be Thy royal throne.

6 Take my love; my Lord, I pour
At Thy feet its treasure-store;
Take myself, and I will be
Ever, only, all for Thee.
Frances Ridley Havergal.

561 I am Thine, O Lord, I have heard
Thy voice
And it told Thy love to me,
But I long to rise in the arms of faith
And be closer drawn to Thee.

Draw me near . . . er, . . . nearer, blessèd Lord,
To the Cross where Thou hast died;
Draw me nearer, nearer, nearer, blessèd Lord,
To Thy precious, bleeding side.

2 Consecrate me now to Thy service,
Lord,
By the power of grace divine;
Let my soul look up with a steadfast
hope,
And my will be lost in Thine.

3 O the pure delight of a single hour
That before Thy throne I spend,
When I kneel in prayer, and with Thee
my God,
I commune as friend with friend.

4 There are depths of love that I cannot
know
Till I cross the narrow sea.
There are heights of joy that I may not
reach
Till I rest in peace with Thee.
Fanny J. Crosby.

562 Come, Thou Fount of every
blessing,
Tune my heart to sing Thy grace;
Streams of mercy, never ceasing,
Call for songs of loudest praise.
Teach me some melodious measure
Sung by flaming tongues above;
O the vast, the boundless treasure
Of my Lord's unchanging love!

2 Here I raise my Ebenezer;
Hither by Thy help I'm come;
And I hope, by Thy good pleasure,
Safely to arrive at home.
Jesus sought me when a stranger
Wandering from the fold of God;
He, to rescue me from danger,
Interposed His precious blood.

3 O to grace how great a debtor
Daily I'm constrained to be!
Let that grace, Lord, like a fetter,
Bind my wandering heart to Thee:
Prone to wander, Lord, I feel it,
Prone to leave the God I love;
Take my heart, O take and seal it,
Seal it from Thy courts above!
R. Robinson.

563 If thou would'st have the dear
Saviour from Heaven
Walk by thy side from the morn till the
even,
There is a rule that each day you must
follow,
Humble thyself to walk with God.

Humble thyself and the Lord will draw near
thee,
Humble thyself and His presence shall cheer
thee;
He will not walk with the proud or the scornful,
Humble thyself to walk with God.

2 Just as the Lord in the world's early
   ages
   Walked and communed with the
   prophets and sages,
   He will come now if you meet the
   conditions,
   Humble thyself to walk with God.

3 Just as the stream finds a bed that is
   lowly,
   So Jesus walks with the pure and the
   holy;
   Cast out thy pride, and in heartfelt
   contrition,
   Humble thyself to walk with God.
                                        J. Oatman.

564 I want, dear Lord, a heart that's
       true and clean;
   A sunlit heart with not a cloud
   between.
   A heart like Thine, a heart divine,
   A heart as white as snow;
   On me, dear Lord, a heart like this
   bestow.

2 I want, dear Lord, a love that feels for
   all;
   A deep strong love that answers every
   call.
   A love like Thine, a love divine,
   A love for high and low;
   On me, dear Lord, a love like this
   bestow.

3 I want, dear Lord, a soul on fire for
   Thee;
   A soul baptized with Heavenly energy.
   A willing mind, a ready hand
   To do whate'er I know
   To spread Thy light wherever I may
   go.
                                    George Jackson.

565 Jesus, we've prayed and we've
       read from Your Word,
   We've looked for Your guidance,
   proclaimed You the Lord,
   And often we've praised for Your life
   and Your deeds,
   But when have we followed to help
   those in need?

2 You had no fear of being seen in the
   home
   Of someone whose job made him
   scorned and alone;
   You broke social bounds to be near
   the despised
   Who knew best of all of their need of
   Your life.

3 We are afraid to break free from old
   ways,
   Fearful of all that the others will say;
   We have not learned what it means to
   step out
   And live in Your world as the children
   of light.

4 Great is our guilt, Lord, and weak are
   our hearts,
   But teach us to give, Lord, to love till
   it hurts,
   Teach us to be to each person we
   meet
   Your heart, Your involvement, Your
   hands and Your feet.
                                      Angela Reith.

566 I thirst, Thou wounded Lamb of
       God,
   To wash me in Thy cleansing blood,
   To dwell within Thy wounds; then
   pain
   Is sweet, and life or death is gain.

2 Take my poor heart, and let it be
   For ever closed to all but Thee!
   Seal Thou my breast, and let me wear
   That pledge of love for ever there.

3 How can it be, Thou Heavenly King,
   That Thou shouldst us to glory bring?
   Make slaves the partners of Thy
   Throne,
   Decked with a never-fading crown?

4 Hence our hearts melt, our eyes o'er-
   flow,
   Our words are lost: nor will we know,
   Nor will we think of aught beside,
   'My Lord, my love is crucified!'
                                    trs. J. Wesley.

567 Lord, we have come, our need
and guilt confessing:
Our souls are fed but others
hunger still.
We all, in selfish ease Your love
possessing,
Have tried, but failed, Your
purpose to fulfil.

2 Help us to break the chains of our
own making;
Open our eyes new paths ahead to
see,
Sure of the changeless message we
are taking,
Proud to proclaim its power to set
men free.

3 Give us, O Lord, a love that is
unbounded,
That reaches out to every class and
race.
Forgive us when, by prejudice
surrounded,
We set a limit to Your sovereign grace.

4 Show us the need for sacrificial living,
The Cross our pattern, inspiration, all:
For those in need our service gladly
giving,
Ready for swift obedience to Your
call.

5 Revive us, Lord, Your Spirit's power
impelling
Our lives to demonstrate Your truth
revealed:
Your Word upon our lips the Good
News telling;
Your peace within our hearts our
strength and shield.

6 So send us forth, still Your great love
possessing,
But with new vision of Your saving
power.
Your Church a channel for a mighty
blessing;
This is Your purpose, this the time,
the hour.

J. H. Cansdale.

568 All to Jesus I surrender,
All to Him I freely give;
I will ever love and trust Him,
In His presence daily live.

I surrender all, . . .
I surrender all; . . .
All to Thee, my blessèd Saviour,
I surrender all.

2 All to Jesus I surrender,
Humbly at His feet I bow;
Worldly pleasures all forsaken,
Take me, Jesus, take me now.

3 All to Jesus I surrender,
Lord, I give myself to Thee;
Fill me with Thy love and power,
Let Thy blessing fall on me.

4 All to Jesus I surrender,
Now I feel the sacred flame;
O the joy of full salvation!
Glory, glory to His Name!

J. Van de Venter.

569 Jesus, see me at Thy feet,
With my sacrifice complete;
I am bringing all to Thee,
Thine alone I'll be.

Have Thy way, Lord, have Thy way,
This with all my heart I say;
I'll obey Thee, come what may;
Dear Lord, have Thy way.

2 O how patient Thou hast been,
With my pride and inbred sin!
O what mercy Thou hast shown,
Grace and love unknown!

3 Lord, I loathe myself and sin,
Enter now and make me clean;
Make my heart just like Thine own;
Come, Lord, take Thy throne.

4 Lord, Thy love has won my all,
Let Thy Spirit on me fall;
Burn up every trace of sin;
Make me pure within.

5 Praise the Lord, the work is done!
Praise the Lord, the victory's won!
Now the blood is cleansing me,
From all sin I'm free.

George Bennard.

The Christian Life

570 Let Me have My way among you,
Do not strive, do not strive.
For Mine is the power and the glory
For ever and ever the same.
Let Me have My way among you,
Do not strive, do not strive.

2 We'll let You have Your way among us.
We'll not strive, we'll not strive.
For Yours is the power and the glory
For ever and ever the same.
We'll let You have Your way among us.
We'll not strive, we'll not strive.

3 Let My peace rule within your hearts,
Do not strive, do not strive.
For Mine is the power and the glory
For ever and ever the same.
Let My peace rule within your hearts,
Do not strive, do not strive.

4 We'll let Your peace rule within our
hearts,
We'll not strive, we'll not strive.
For Yours is the power and the glory
For ever and ever the same.
We'll let Your peace rule within our
hearts,
We'll not strive, we'll not strive.

G. Kendrick.

THE FUTURE LIFE

571 I hope to meet you all in glory
When the storms of life are o'er;
I hope to tell the dear old story
On the blessèd shining shore.

On the shining shore,
On the golden strand,
In our Father's home,
In the happy land:
I hope to meet you there,
I hope to meet you there—
A crown of victory wear—
In glory.

2 I hope to meet you all in glory
By the Tree of life so fair;
I hope to praise our dear Redeemer
For the grace that brought me there.

3 I hope to meet you all in glory
Round the Saviour's throne above;
I hope to join the ransomed army
Singing now redeeming love.

4 I hope to meet you all in glory
When my work on earth is o'er;
I hope to clasp your hands rejoicing
On the bright eternal shore.

Emma Pitt.

572 When all my labours and trials are
o'er,
And I am safe on that beautiful shore,
Just to be near the dear Lord I adore
Will through the ages be glory for me.

Oh, that will be . . . glory for me, . . .
Glory for me, . . . glory for me, . . .
When by His grace I shall look on His face,
That will be glory, be glory for me.

2 When by the gift of His infinite grace
I am accorded in Heaven a place,
Just to be there and to look on His
face
Will through the ages be glory for me.

3 Friends will be there I have loved long
ago;
Joy like a river around me will flow;
Yet, just a smile from my Saviour, I
know,
Will through the ages be glory for me.

Charles H. Gabriel.

573 I'm satisfied with just a cottage
below,
A little silver and a little gold.
But in that city, where the ransomed
will shine
I want a gold one that's silver lined.

I've got a mansion just over the hilltop
In that bright land where we'll never grow old,
And some day yonder we will never more
wander
But walk on streets that are purest gold.

2 Though often tempted, tormented
and tested,
And like the prophet, my pillow a
stone.
And though I find here no permanent
dwelling,
I know He'll give me a mansion my
own.

3 Don't think me poor or deserted or
    lonely,
  I'm not discouraged, I'm Heaven
    bound.
  I'm just a pilgrim in search of that city,
  I want a mansion, a harp and a crown.
                                    Ira Stanphill.

574 We shall see His lovely face
        Some bright, golden morning,
  When the clouds have rifted
  And the shades have flown;
  Sorrow will be turned to joy,
  Heartaches gone forever,
  No more night, only light,
  When we see His face.

2 God shall wipe away all tears
  Some bright, golden morning,
  When the journey's ended,
  And the course is run;
  No more crying, pain or death
  In that home of gladness,
  Trials cease, all is peace,
  When we see His face.

3 We shall meet to part no more,
  Some bright, golden morning,
  At the gates of glory
  Where our loved ones stand;
  Songs of victory fill the skies
  In that hour of greeting,
  Endless days, endless praise,
  When we see His face.
                              Norman J. Clayton.

575 Sing the wondrous love of Jesus,
        Sing His mercy and His grace;
  In the mansions, bright and blessèd,
  He'll prepare for us a place.

    When we all . . . get to Heaven,
    What a day of rejoicing that will be! . . .
    When we all . . . see Jesus,
    We'll sing and shout the victory. . . .

2 While we walk the pilgrim pathway
  Clouds will overspread the sky;
  But when travelling days are over
  Not a shadow, not a sigh.

3 Let us, then, be true and faithful,
  Trusting, serving every day;
  Just one glimpse of Him in glory
  Will the toils of life repay.

4 Onward to the prize before us!
  Soon His beauty we'll behold;
  Soon the pearly gates will open,
  We shall tread the streets of gold.
                                E. E. Hewitt.

576 There's a land that is fairer than
        day,
  And by faith we can see it afar:
  For the Father waits over the way
  To prepare us a dwelling-place there.

    In the sweet by and by
    We shall meet on that beautiful shore,
    In the sweet by and by
    We shall meet on that beautiful shore.

2 We shall sing on the beautiful shore
  The melodious songs of the blest,
  And our spirits shall sorrow no more,
  Not a sigh for the blessing of rest.

3 To our bountiful Father above
  We will offer our tribute of praise,
  For the glorious gift of His love,
  And the blessings that hallow our
    days.
                                S. Bennett.

577 We are never, never weary of the
        grand old song;
  Glory to God, hallelujah!
  We can sing it loud as ever with our
    faith more strong;
  Glory to God, hallelujah!

    O the children of the Lord have a right to shout
      and sing
    For the way is growing bright, and our souls
      are on the wing
    We are going by-and-by to the palace of a
      King;
    Glory to God, hallelujah!

2 We are lost amid the rapture of
    redeeming love;
  Glory to God, hallelujah!
  We are rising on its pinions to the hills
    above;
  Glory to God, hallelujah!

3 We are going to a palace that is built
   of gold;
   Glory to God, hallelujah!
   Where the King in all His splendour
   we shall soon behold;
   Glory to God, hallelujah!

4 There we'll shout redeeming mercy in
   a glad new song;
   Glory to God, hallelujah!
   There we'll sing the praise of Jesus
   with the blood-washed throng;
   Glory to God, hallelujah!

Fanny J. Crosby.

578 On the happy golden shore
   Where the faithful part no more,
   When the storms of life are o'er,
   Meet me there!
   Where the night dissolves away
   Into pure and perfect day
   I am going home to stay;
   Meet me there!

   Meet me there! . . . meet me there! . . .
   Where the Tree of life is blooming,
   Meet me there! . . .
   When the storms of life are o'er,
   On the happy golden shore
   Where the faithful part no more;
   Meet me there!

2 Here our fondest hopes are vain,
   Dearest links are rent in twain,
   But in Heaven no throb of pain,
   Meet me there!
   By the river sparkling bright,
   In the city of delight,
   Where our faith is lost in sight;
   Meet me there!

3 Where the harps of angels ring,
   And the blest for ever sing,
   In the palace of the King,
   Meet me there!
   Where in sweet communion blend
   Heart with heart, and friend with
   friend,
   In a world that ne'er shall end;
   Meet me there!

Anon.

579 For all the saints who from their
   labours rest,
   Who Thee by faith before the
   world confessed,
   Thy Name, O Jesu, be for ever
   blest,
   Alleluia!

2 Thou wast their Rock, their Fortress,
   and their Might;
   Thou, Lord, their Captain in the well-
   fought fight;
   Thou in the darkness drear their one
   true Light.
   Alleluia!

3 Oh, may Thy soldiers, faithful, true
   and bold,
   Fight as the saints who nobly fought
   of old,
   And win, with them, the victor's
   crown of gold.
   Alleluia!

4 O blest communion! fellowship
   Divine!
   We feebly struggle, they in glory
   shine;
   Yet all are one in Thee, for all are
   Thine.
   Alleluia!

5 And when the strife is fierce, the
   warfare long,
   Steals on the ear the distant triumph-
   song,
   And hearts are brave again, and arms
   are strong.
   Alleluia!

6 The golden evening brightens in the
   west;
   Soon, soon to faithful warriors comes
   their rest;
   Sweet is the calm of Paradise the
   blest.
   Alleluia!

7 But lo! there breaks a yet more
   glorious day;
   The saints triumphant rise in bright
   array:
   The King of glory passes on His way.
   Alleluia!

8 From earth's wide bounds, from ocean's farthest coast,
Through gates of pearl streams in the countless host,
Singing to Father, Son, and Holy Ghost.
Alleluia!
                              W. W. How.

580 Who, who are these beside the chilly wave,
Just on the borders of the silent grave,
Shouting Jesus' power to save,
'Washed in the blood of the Lamb'?

   'Sweeping through the gates' of the New Jerusalem,
   'Washed in the blood of the Lamb.'

2 These, these are they who, in their youthful days,
Found Jesus early, and in wisdom's ways
Proved the fulness of His grace,
'Washed in the blood of the Lamb.'

3 These, these are they who, in affliction's woes,
Ever have found in Jesus calm repose,
Such as from a pure heart flows,
'Washed in the blood of the Lamb.'

4 These, these are they who, in the conflict dire,
Boldly have stood amid the hottest fire;
Jesus now says: 'Come up higher.'
'Washed in the blood of the Lamb.'

5 Safe, safe upon the ever-shining shore,
Sin, pain, and death, and sorrow, all are o'er;
Happy now and evermore,
'Washed in the blood of the Lamb.'
                              T. C. O'Kane.

581 For ever with the Lord!
Amen, so let it be!
Life from the dead is in that word;
'Tis immortality.

Here in the body pent,
Absent from Him I roam;
Yet nightly pitch my moving tent
A day's march nearer home.

2 My Father's house on high,
Home of my soul, how near
At times to faith's foreseeing eye
Thy golden gates appear!
My thirsty spirit faints
To reach the land I love,
The bright inheritance of saints—
Jerusalem above.

3 For ever with the Lord!
Father, if 'tis Thy will,
The promise of that faithful word
E'en here to me fulfil.
Be Thou at my right hand,
Then can I never fail;
Uphold Thou me, so I shall stand,
Fight, and I must prevail.

4 So when my latest breath
Shall rend the veil in twain,
By death I shall escape from death,
And life eternal gain.
Knowing as I am known,
How shall I love that word!
And oft repeat before the throne,
For ever with the Lord!
                              James Montgomery.

582 O golden day, when light shall break
And dawn's bright glories shall unfold,
When He who knows the path I take
Shall ope for me the gates of gold.
Earth's little while will soon be past,
My pilgrim song will soon be o'er,
The grace that saves shall time outlast,
And be my theme on yonder shore.

   Then I shall know, as I am known,
   And stand complete before the throne;
   Then I shall see my Saviour's face,
   And all my song be, 'Saving grace.'

The Christian Life

2 Life's upward way, a narrow path,
Leads on to that fair dwelling-place
Where, safe from sin, and storm, and
    wrath,
They live who trust redeeming grace.
Sing, sing, my heart along the way,
The grace that saves will keep and
    guide
Till breaks the glorious crowning day,
And I shall cross to yonder side.

3 I dimly see my journey's end
But well I know who guideth me.
I follow Him, that wondrous Friend
Whose matchless love is full and free.
And when with Him I enter in,
And all the way look back to trace,
The conqueror's palm I then shall win
Through Christ, and His redeeming
    grace.

Julia H. Johnston.

583 I know that my Redeemer liveth,
    And on the earth again shall
    stand!
I know eternal life He giveth,
That grace and power are in His hand.

I know, I know . . . that Jesus liveth,
And on the earth . . . again shall stand;
I know, I know . . . that life He giveth,
That grace and power . . . are in His hand.

2 I know His promise never faileth,
The word He speaks, it cannot die;
Though cruel death my flesh assail-
eth,
Yet I shall see Him by and by.

3 I know my mansion He prepareth,
That where He is there I may be;
O wondrous thought, for me He
careth
And He at last will come for me.

Jessie H. Brown.

584 I shall wear a golden crown,
    When I get home;
I shall lay my burdens down,
When I get home;
Clad in robes of glory,
I shall sing the story
Of the Lord who bought me,
When I get home.

When I get home, when I get home,
All sorrow will be over when I get home;
When I get home, when I get home,
All sorrow will be over when I get home.

2 All the darkness will be past,
When I get home;
I shall see the light at last,
When I get home;
Light from Heaven streaming,
O'er my pathway beaming,
Ever guides me onward
Till I get home.

3 I shall see my Saviour's face,
When I get home;
Sing again of saving grace,
When I get home;
I shall stand before Him,
Gladly I'll adore Him;
Ever to be with Him,
When I get home.

C. Austin Miles.

585 I'm just a weary pilgrim
    Plodding through this world of
    sin;
Getting ready for that city
When the saints go marching in.

When the saints go marching in;
When the saints go marching in;
Lord, I want to be in that number
When the saints go marching in.

2 My father loved the Saviour,
What a soldier he had been!
But his steps will be more steady
When the saints go marching in.

3 And mother, may God bless her,
I can see her now, as then;
With a robe of white around her
When the saints go marching in.

4 Up there I'll see the Saviour
Who redeemed my soul from sin,
With extended hands He'll greet me
When the saints go marching in.

Luther G. Presley.

586 Hark 'tis the final trumpet pealing
    through the skies!
See, from their slumbers how the
    dead in Christ arise!

Far through the nations ring the resurrection cries,
Worthy is the Lamb.

Glory, glory be to Jesus,
Glory, glory be to Jesus,
Glory, glory be to Jesus
Who saves us from our sin.

2 Now it has come at last, our glorious jubilee.
Earth's ransomed multitudes are shouting 'We are free,'
Heaven and earth are joining in the melody,
Worthy is the Lamb.

3 Sorrow and anguished wailing are forever o'er;
Martyrs for Jesus' Name will suffer now no more,
We, too, are following the host gone on before,
Worthy is the Lamb.

4 Parents and children now with joy together meet;
Gather to worship round the Saviour's piercèd feet,
Walking in spotless garments on the golden street,
Worthy is the Lamb.

5 They all have washed their robes in Jesus' precious blood.
They all have made their everlasting peace with God,
They all have fought their way through storm, and fire and flood,
Worthy is the Lamb.
                                    Arthur S. Booth-Clibborn.

587 Jerusalem the golden,
  With milk and honey blest,
Beneath thy contemplation
Sink heart and voice oppressed;
I know not, oh! I know not,
What joys await us there,
What radiancy of glory,
What bliss beyond compare.

2 They stand, those halls of Zion,
All jubilant with song;
And bright with many an angel,
And all the martyr throng:

The Prince is ever in them,
The daylight is serene,
The pastures of the blessèd
Are decked in glorious sheen.

3 There is the throne of David,
And there from care released,
The shout of them that triumph,
The song of them that feast:
And they who, with their Leader,
Have conquered in the fight,
For ever and for ever
Are clothed in robes of white.

4 Oh, sweet and blessèd country,
The home of God's elect!
Oh, sweet and blessèd country
That eager hearts expect!
Jesus in mercy bring us
To that dear land of rest,
Who art, with God the Father,
And Spirit, ever blest.
                                    Bernard of Cluny
                                    trs. J. M. Neale.

588 Let us sing a song that will cheer us by the way,
In a little while we're going home;
For the night will end in the ever-lasting day,
In a little while we're going home.

In a little while, . . . in a little while . . .
We shall cross the billow's foam;
We shall meet at last
When the stormy winds are past,
In a little while we're going home.

2 We will do the work that our hands may find to do,
In a little while we're going home;
And the grace of God will our daily strength renew,
In a little while we're going home.

3 We will smooth the path for some weary, way-worn feet,
In a little while we're going home;
O may loving hearts spread around an influence sweet,
In a little while we're going home.

4 There's a rest beyond, there's relief
from every care,
In a little while we're going home;
And no tears shall fall in that city
bright and fair,
In a little while we're going home.

E. E. Hewitt.

589 Let us sing of His love once
again—
Of the love that can never decay,
Of the blood of the Lamb who was
slain,
Till we praise Him again in that day.

In the sweet by and by
We shall meet on that beautiful shore;
In the sweet by and by
We shall meet on that beautiful shore.

2 There are cleansing and healing for all
Who will wash in the life-giving flood;
There is life everlasting and joy
At the right hand of God through the
blood.

3 Even now while we taste of His love
We are filled with delight at His Name;
But what will it be when above
We shall join in the song of the Lamb!

F. Bottome.

590 My Heavenly home is bright and
fair,
I feel like travelling on,
Nor pain, nor death can enter there,
I feel like travelling on.

Yes I feel like travelling on,
I feel like travelling on,
My Heavenly home is bright and fair,
I feel like travelling on.

2 Its glittering towers the sun outshine,
I feel like travelling on,
That Heavenly mansion shall be mine,
I feel like travelling on.

3 Let others seek a home below,
I feel like travelling on,
Which flames devour, or waves o'er-
flow
I feel like travelling on.

4 The Lord has been so good to me,
I feel like travelling on,
Until that blessèd home I see,
I feel like travelling on.

William Hunter.

591 Not only, Lord, on that great day
When man before Thy throne
shall stand
I ask that Thou my Judge shalt be,
With every thought and motive
scanned;
But in the midst of common days,
O let me know that Thou art nigh,
And teach me, Lord, to meet Thy
gaze
With frank and unaverted eye!

O Saviour, search my heart today
And tell me all Thou findest there!
I must more closely dwell with Thee;
O grant me this, my earnest prayer!

2 I would not meet at life's far end
Thy final judgment with dismay;
I need Thy keen appraisal now
That I may live, from day to day,
A life that only seeks Thy ways,
A life more closely linked with Thee
Who art the Christ of working days,
The Man who walked by Galilee.

3 And if Thy judgments make me quail
And give me cause for grief and pain,
Yet shall Thy love uphold me still
And bid my spirit rise again;
And so, with eyes that see anew
The task that Thou to me hast given,
Let me my covenant renew
And bring a worthier gift to Heaven.

Miriam M. Richards.

592 There is a land of pure delight
Where saints immortal reign,
Infinite day excludes the night,
And pleasures banish pain.

We're feeding on the Living Bread,
We're drinking at the Fountain-Head;
And whoso drinketh, Jesus said,
Shall never, never thirst again.
What! never thirst again?
No, never thirst again!
What! never thirst again?
No, never thirst again!
And whoso drinketh, Jesus said,
Shall never, never thirst again!

2 There everlasting spring abides,
And never-withering flowers:
Death, like a narrow sea, divides
This Heavenly land from ours.

3 O could we make our doubts remove
Those gloomy thoughts that rise,
And see the Canaan that we love
With unbeclouded eyes.

4 Could we but climb where Moses
stood
And view the landscape o'er,
Not Jordan's stream, nor death's cold
flood,
Should fright us from the shore.

Alternative chorus:
We're marching through Immanuel's ground,
And soon shall hear the trumpet sound,
And then we shall with Jesus reign,
And never, never part again.
What, never part again?
No, never part again!
What, never part again?
No, never part again!
And then we shall with Jesus reign,
And never, never part again!

Isaac Watts.

593 Face to face with Christ my
Saviour,
Face to face—what will it be?
When with rapture I behold Him,
Jesus Christ who died for me.

Face to face shall I behold Him,
Far beyond the starry sky;
Face to face in all His glory,
I shall see Him by and by!

2 Only faintly now I see Him,
With the darkling veil between,
But a blessèd day is coming
When His glory shall be seen.

3 What rejoicing in His presence,
When are banished grief and pain;
When the crooked ways are straight-
ened
And the dark things shall be plain.

4 Face to face! O blissful moment!
Face to face—to see and know!
Face to face with my Redeemer,
Jesus Christ who loves me so.

Mrs. Frank A. Breck.

Section VIII

WITNESS AND TESTIMONY

594 It was down at the feet of Jesus,
O the happy, happy day!
That my soul found peace in
believing,
And my sins were washed away.

Let me tell the old, old story
Of His grace so full and free,
For I feel like giving Him the glory
For His wondrous love to me.

2 It was down at the feet of Jesus
Where I found such perfect rest,
Where the light first dawned on my
spirit,
And my soul was truly blest.

3 It was down at the feet of Jesus,
Where I brought my guilt and sin
That He cancelled all my trans-
gressions,
And salvation entered in.

Elisha A. Hoffman.

595 I've found a Friend; oh, such a
Friend!
He loved me ere I knew Him;
He drew me with the cords of love,
And thus He bound me to Him;
And round my heart still closely twine
Those ties which naught can sever;
For I am His, and He is mine,
For ever and for ever.

2 I've found a Friend; oh, such a
Friend!
He bled, He died to save me;
And not alone the gift of life,
But His own self He gave me.
Naught that I have my own I call,
I hold it for the Giver:
My heart, my strength, my life, my all
Are His, and His for ever.

3 I've found a Friend; oh, such a
    Friend!
All power to Him is given
To guard me on my onward course
And bring me safe to Heaven.
Eternal glories gleam afar
To nerve my faint endeavour;
So now to watch, to work, to war,
And then to rest for ever.

4 I've found a Friend; oh, such a
    Friend!
So kind, and true, and tender!
So wise a Counsellor and Guide,
So mighty a Defender!
From Him who loves me now so well
What power my soul shall sever?
Shall life, or death, or earth, or hell?
No! I am His for ever.

J. G. Small.

596 I serve a risen Saviour, He's in the
    world today;
I know that He is living, whatever men
    may say;
I see His hand of mercy, I hear His
    voice of cheer,
And just the time I need Him He's
    always near.

He lives, . . . He lives, . . . Christ Jesus lives
  today!
He walks with me and talks with me along life's
  narrow way,
He lives, . . . He lives, . . . salvation to impart!
You ask me how I know He lives? He lives
  within my heart.

2 In all the world around me I see His
    loving care,
And though my heart grows weary I
    never will despair;
I know that He is leading, through all
    the stormy blast,
The day of His appearing will come at
    last.

3 Rejoice, rejoice, O Christian, lift up
    your voice and sing
Eternal hallelujahs to Jesus Christ the
    King!
The Hope of all who seek Him, the
    Help of all who find,
None other is so loving, so good and
    kind.

A. H. Ackley.

597 I wandered in the shades of night,
    Till Jesus came to me,
And with the sunshine of His love
Bade all my darkness flee.

Sunshine, sunshine in my soul today, . . .
Sunshine, sunshine all along the way, . . .
Since the Saviour found me, took away my
  sin, . . .
I have had the sunshine of His love within.

2 Though clouds may gather in the sky,
And billows round me roll,
However dark the world may be
I've sunshine in my soul.

3 While walking in the light of God,
I, sweet communion find;
I press with holy vigour on
And leave the world behind.

4 I cross the wide extended fields,
I journey o'er the plain,
And in the sunshine of His love
I reap the golden grain.

5 Soon I shall see Him as He is,
The Light that came to me;
Behold the brightness of His face,
Throughout eternity.

J. W. Van De Venter.

598 I have a song I love to sing,
    Since I have been redeemed,
Of my Redeemer, Saviour, King,
Since I have been redeemed.

Since I . . . have been redeemed, . . .
Since I . . . have been redeemed, . . .
Since I . . . have been redeemed, . . .
I will glory in His Name
Since I . . . have been redeemed, . . .
Since I . . . have been redeemed, . . .
I will glory in the Saviour's Name.

2 I have a Christ that satisfies,
Since I have been redeemed,
To do His will my highest prize,
Since I have been redeemed.

3 I have a witness bright and clear,
Since I have been redeemed,
Dispelling every doubt and fear,
Since I have been redeemed.

4 I have a joy I can't express,
Since I have been redeemed,

All through His blood and righteousness,
Since I have been redeemed.

5 I have a home prepared for me,
Since I have been redeemed,
Where I shall dwell eternally,
Since I have been redeemed.

E. O. Excell.

599 He is not a disappointment!
Jesus is far more to me
Than in all my glowing day-dreams
I had fancied He could be;
And the more I get to know Him,
So the more I find Him true,
And the more I long that others
Should be led to know Him too.

2 He is not a disappointment!
He has saved my soul from sin:
All the guilt and all the anguish,
Which oppressed my heart within,
He has banished by His presence,
And His blessèd kiss of peace
Has assured my heart for ever
That His love will never cease.

3 He is not a disappointment!
He has healed my body too:
What a tender, mighty Saviour,
There is naught He cannot do!
When on earth He healed diseases
As they touched Him in the throng;
Has He lost His heart of pity?
Is the Risen Christ less strong?

4 He is not a disappointment!
He is coming by and by,
In my heart I have the witness
That His coming draweth nigh.
All the scoffers may despise me,
And no change around may see,
But He tells me He is coming,
And that's quite enough for me.

5 He is not a disappointment!
He is all in all to me —
Saviour, Sanctifier, Healer;
The unchanging Christ is He!
He has won my heart's affections,
And He meets my every need;
He is not a disappointment,
For He satisfies indeed.

Mary Warburton Booth.

600 Far away the noise of strife upon
my ear is falling,
Then I know the sins of earth beset on
every hand;
Doubt and fear and things of earth in
vain to me are calling,
None of these shall move me from
Beulah Land.

I'm living on the mountain, underneath a
cloudless sky, . . .
I'm drinking at the fountain that never shall run
dry,
Oh, yes! I'm feasting on the manna from a
bountiful supply,
For I am dwelling in Beulah Land.

2 Far below the storm of doubt upon
the world is beating,
Sons of men in battle long the enemy
withstand;
Safe am I within the castle of God's
Word retreating,
Nothing then can reach me, 'tis
Beulah Land.

3 Let the stormy breezes blow, their cry
cannot alarm me,
I am safely sheltered here protected
by God's hand;
Here the sun is always shining, here
there's naught can harm me,
I am safe for ever in Beulah Land.

4 Viewing here the works of God, I sink
in contemplation,
Hearing now His blessèd voice, I see
the way is planned;
Dwelling in the Spirit, here I learn of
full salvation,
Gladly will I tarry in Beulah Land.

C. Austin Miles.

601 All the darkness of the night has
passed away,
It is morning in my heart;
I am living in the sunlight of the day,
It is morning in my heart.

It is morning, it is morning in my heart, . . .
Jesus made the gloomy shadows all depart; . . .
Songs of gladness now I sing
For since Jesus is my King
It is morning, it is morning in my heart.

2 I can hear the songbirds singing their
refrain,
It is morning in my heart;
And I know that life for me begins
again,
It is morning in my heart.

3 Christ has made the world a paradise
to me,
It is morning in my heart;
Every duty in the light of love I see,
It is morning in my heart.

4 Joy has come to dwell with me for
evermore,
It is morning in my heart;
I shall sing it when I reach the other
shore,
It is morning in my heart.

A. H. Ackley.

602 A Friend I have called Jesus
Whose love is strong and true,
And never fails howe'er 'tis tried,
No matter what I do:
I've sinned against this love of His,
But when I knelt to pray,
Confessing all my guilt to Him,
The sin-clouds rolled away.

It's just like Jesus to roll the clouds away,
It's just like Jesus to keep me day by day;
It's just like Jesus all along the way,
It's just like His great love.

2 Sometimes the clouds of trouble
O'erspread the sky above,
I cannot see my Saviour's face,
I doubt His wondrous love:
But He, from Heaven's mercy seat
Beholding my despair,
In pity bursts the clouds between,
And shows me He is there.

3 O, I could sing forever
Of Jesus' love divine!
Of all His care and tenderness
For this poor life of mine:
His love is in and over all,
And wind and waves obey
When Jesus whispers, 'Peace, be
still!'
And rolls the clouds away.

Edna R. Worrell.

603 I thirsted in the barren land of sin
and shame,
And nothing satisfying there I found,
But to the blessèd Cross of Christ one
day I came,
Where springs of living water did
abound.

Drinking at the springs of living water,
Happy now am I, my soul they satisfy,
Drinking at the springs of living water,
O wonderful and bountiful supply.

2 How sweet the living water from the
hills of God,
It makes me glad and happy all the
way,
Now glory, grace and blessing mark
the path I've trod,
I'm shouting 'Hallelujah' every day.

3 O sinner, won't you come today to
Calvary?
A fountain there is flowing deep and
wide;
The Saviour now invites you to the
water free,
Where thirsting spirits can be
satisfied.

John W. Peterson.

604 I have tried to count His blessings,
and I fail to understand
Why the Lord should so richly reward;
Could I count the stars of heaven, add
to them earth's grains of sand,
Still His blessings are more, praise the
Lord!

And the end is not yet, praise the Lord, . . .
And the end is not yet, praise the Lord; . . .
Blessings new He's still bestowing,
And my cup is overflowing,
And the end is not yet, praise the Lord! . . .

2 Like an army I behold them pass
before me in review,
Oh, what joy doth the sight now
afford!
Though they may be long in passing,
still they come, battalions new,
And the end is not yet, praise the
Lord!

3 Surely goodness, love and mercy
    have been mine along life's way,
And my weak heart to strength is
    restored;
And my cup of joy and gladness keeps
    o'erflowing, day by day,
And the end is not yet, praise the
    Lord!

E. D. Elliott.

605 I had heard the gospel call,
    offering pardon free for all,
And I hearkened to the blessèd
    invitation;
Laid my sins at Jesus' feet, tasted
    there redemption sweet,
And He saved me with an uttermost
    salvation.

    Jesus saves, . . . fully saves, . . .
    Jesus saves me with an uttermost salvation;
    Though I cannot tell you how,
        Jesus fully saves me now,
    With a full and free, an uttermost salvation.

2 Now the load of sin is gone, and by
    faith I travel on,
And I rest no longer under condem-
    nation;
For the blood has been applied, and
    my soul is satisfied
With this full and free, this uttermost,
    salvation.

3 From the mire and from the clay
    Jesus took my feet away,
And He placed them on the Rock, the
    sure Foundation;
Whether now I live or die this shall be
    my constant cry,
Jesus saves me with an uttermost
    salvation.

Mrs. C. H. Morris.

606 I am so happy in Christ today
    That I go singing along my way;
Yes, I'm so happy to know and say,
    'Jesus included me too.'

    Jesus included me, yes, He included me,
    When the Lord said, 'Whosoever', He
        included me,
    Jesus included me, yes, He included me,
    When the Lord said, 'Whosoever', He
        included me.

2 Gladly I read, 'Whosoever may
    Come to the fountain of life today,'
But when I read it I always say,
    'Jesus included me too.'

3 Ever God's Spirit is saying, 'Come!'
    Hear the Bride saying, 'No longer
        roam,'
But I am sure while they're calling
    home,
Jesus included me too.

4 'Freely come drink,' words the soul to
    thrill!
O with what joy they my heart do fill
For when He said, 'Whosoever will,'
Jesus included me too.

Rev. J. Oatman, Jr.

607 A pilgrim was I, and a-wandering,
    In the cold night of sin I did roam,
When Jesus the kind Shepherd found
    me,
And now I am on my way home.

    Surely goodness and mercy shall follow me
    All the days, all the days of my life;
    Surely goodness and mercy shall follow me
    All the days, all the days of my life,
    And I shall dwell in the house of the Lord
        forever,
    And I shall feast at the table spread for me.
    Surely goodness and mercy shall follow me
    All the days, all the days of my life;

2 He restoreth my soul when I'm weary,
    He giveth me strength day by day,
He leads me beside the still waters,
    He guards me each step of the way.

3 When I walk through the dark lone-
    some valley
My Saviour will walk with me there,
And safely His great hand will lead me
To the mansions He's gone to
    prepare.

John W. Peterson and Alfred B. Smith.

608 You ask why I am happy, so I'll
    just tell you why,
Because my sins are gone;
And when I meet the scoffers who ask
    me where they are,
I say my "sins are gone".

Witness and Testimony

They're underneath the blood, on the Cross of Calvary,
As far removed as darkness is from dawn;
In the sea of God's forgetfulness, that's good enough for me,
Praise God, my sins are gone.

2 'Twas at the old-time altar where God came in my heart
And now, my sins are gone;
The Lord took full possession, the devil did depart,
I'm glad my sins are gone.

3 When Satan comes to tempt me and tries to make me doubt,
I say, "my sins are gone";
You got me into trouble, but Jesus got me out,
I'm glad my sins are gone.

4 I'm living now for Jesus, I'm happy night and day,
Because my sins are gone;
My soul is filled with music, with all my heart I say,
"I know my sins are gone."

N. B. Vandall.

609 You ask what makes me happy, my heart so free from care,
It is because my Saviour in mercy heard my prayer;
He brought me out of darkness and now the light I see,
Oh, blessèd, loving Saviour! to Him the praise shall be.

I will shout His praise in glory, . . .
And we'll all sing hallelujah in Heaven by and by,
I will shout His praise in glory, . . .
And we'll all sing hallelujah in Heaven by and by.

2 I was a friendless wanderer till Jesus took me in,
My life was full of sorrow, my heart was full of sin,
But when the blood so precious spoke pardon to my soul,
Oh, blissful, blissful moment! 'twas joy beyond control.

3 I wish that every sinner before His throne would bow;
He waits to bid them welcome, He longs to bless them now;
If they but knew the rapture that in His love I see,
They'd come and shout salvation, and sing His praise with me.

4 I mean to live for Jesus while here on earth I stay;
And when His voice shall call me to realms of endless day,
As one by one we gather, rejoicing on the shore,
We'll shout His praise in glory, and sing for evermore.

P. H. Dingman.

610 Would you know why Christ, my Saviour,
Is my constant theme and song?
Why to seek His loving favour
Is my joy the whole day long?

He redeemed me, . . . He redeemed me, . . .
How the ransomed choir repeats it o'er and o'er; . . .
He redeemed me, . . . He redeemed me, . . .
Glory, glory be to Him for evermore. . . .

2 Oh, the days are full of gladness
That I spend in His employ!
I can banish care and sadness
In that song of Heavenly joy.

3 Come, belovèd, bow before Him,
Seek the pardon of your King,
That on earth you may adore Him,
And with saints in glory sing.

George F. Root.

611 Wonderful love that rescued me,
Sunk deep in sin,
Guilty and vile as I could be—
No hope within:
When every ray of light had fled,
O glorious day,
Raising my soul from out the dead,
Love found a way.

Love found a way to redeem my soul,
Love found a way that could make me whole;
Love sent my Lord to the cross of shame,
Love found a way, O praise His holy Name!

2 Love brought my Saviour here to die
On Calvary,
For such a sinful wretch as I,
How can it be?
Love bridged the gulf 'twixt me and
Heaven,
Taught me to pray;
I am redeemed, set free, forgiven,
Love found a way.

3 Love opened wide the gates of light
To Heaven's domain,
Where in eternal power and might
Jesus shall reign;
Love lifted me from depths of woe
To endless day,
There was no help in earth below,
Love found a way.

Constance B. Ried.

612 When in His beauty my Saviour I
see,
When I shall look on His face,
Tongue cannot tell of the joy it will be,
Saved by His wonderful grace. . . .

Saved, . . . saved, . . . saved by His wonderful
grace! . . .
Saved, . . . saved, . . . granted in Heaven a
place; . . .
Saved, . . . saved, . . . saved by His wonderful
grace! . . .
Glory to Jesus, I know I am saved,
Saved by His wonderful grace! . . .

2 Long I had wandered in pathways of
sin,
Often His grace had I spurned;
Often resisted His striving within
Ere to the Saviour I turned.

3 How I rejoice that salvation is free,
That I was not turned away:
How I rejoice that my Saviour I'll see,
Where I may praise Him for aye.

G. O. Webster.

613 What a wonderful change in my
life has been wrought
Since Jesus came into my heart!

I have light in my soul which so long I
had sought
Since Jesus came into my heart!

Since Jesus came into my heart, . . .
Since Jesus came into my heart, . . .
Floods of joy o'er my soul like the sea billows
roll
Since Jesus came into my heart.

2 I have ceased from my wandering and
going astray,
Since Jesus came into my heart!
And my sins which were many are all
washed away
Since Jesus came into my heart!

3 I'm possessed of a hope that is
steadfast and sure
Since Jesus came into my heart!
And no dark clouds of doubt now my
pathway obscure,
Since Jesus came into my heart!

4 There's a light in the valley of death
now for me,
Since Jesus came into my heart!
And the gates of the City beyond I can
see,
Since Jesus came into my heart!

5 I shall go there to dwell in that City I
know,
Since Jesus came into my heart!
And I'm happy, so happy as onward I
go,
Since Jesus came into my heart!

R. H. McDaniel.

614 To Jesus every day I find my heart
is closer drawn;
He's fairer than the glory of the gold
and purple dawn;
He's all my fancy pictured in its fairest
dreams and more;
Each day He grows still sweeter than
He was the day before.

The half . . . cannot be fancied . . . this
side . . . the golden shore; . . .
O there . . . He'll be still sweeter than He ever
was before.

2 His glory broke upon me when I saw
   Him from afar;
He's fairer than the lily, brighter than
   the morning star;
He fills and satisfies my longing spirit
   o'er and o'er;
Each day He grows still sweeter than
   He was the day before.

3 My heart is sometimes heavy, but He
   comes with sweet relief;
He folds me to His bosom when I
   droop with blighting grief;
I love the Christ who all my burdens in
   His body bore;
Each day He grows still sweeter than
   He was the day before.

W. C. Martin.

615 Though life's changing values
   may vanish away,
And things that were real become
   dreams;
How blessèd to walk with the Lord
   day by day,
And know He is real as He seems.

Jesus is real to me,
Yes, Jesus is real to me;
I never will doubt Him, nor journey without
   Him,
For He is so real to me.

2 I never have seen Him with these eyes
   of mine,
But though He be hid from my sight
I know He is with me in Spirit divine,
I live in the strength of His might.

3 My Saviour and Leader each moment
   is He,
My Helper in all that I do;
Companionship with Him is blessèd
   to me,
His friendship is faithful and true.

4 My reason the unseen can never
   discern,
Nor fully explain the unknown;
But precious the truths of the Spirit I
   learn
When His Spirit speaks to my own.

Geo. H. Carr.

616 There's no one like my Saviour;
   No friend can be like Him;
My never failing sunshine
When earthly lights grow dim;
When summer flowers are blooming,
The brightness of my joy,
O, may His happy service
My heart and life employ.

No one, no one like my precious Saviour,
No one, no one such a friend can be;
No one, no one like my precious Saviour,
Glory, glory, Jesus cares for me.

2 There's no one like my Saviour;
In seasons of distress
He draws me closer to Him,
To comfort and to bless;
He gives me in temptation
The strength of His right arm;
His angels camp around me
To keep me from all harm.

3 There's no one like my Saviour,
He pardons all my sin,
And gives His Holy Spirit,
A springing well within;
He leads me out to service
With gentle touch and mild;
O, wonder of all wonders
That I should be His child.

4 There's no one like my Saviour,
Come now, and find it true!
He gave His life a ransom,
His blood was shed for you;
Then when we reach the City
Of everlasting light,
We'll sing with saints and angels,
All honour, power and might.

E. E. Hewitt.

617 There's a peace in my heart that
   the world never gave,
A peace it can not take away;
Though the trials of life may surround
   like a cloud
I've a peace that has come there to
   stay!

Con . . . stantly abid . . . ing, . . . Je . . . sus is
   mine; . . .
Con . . . stantly abid . . . ing, . . . rap . . . ture
   divine; . . .
He . . . never leaves me lone . . . ly, . . .
   whispers, O so kind: . . .
'I will never leave thee,' Jesus is mine.

2 All the world seemed to sing of a
   Saviour and King
When peace sweetly came to my
   heart;
Troubles all fled away and my night
   turned to day,
Blessèd Jesus, how glorious Thou
   art!

3 This treasure I have in a temple of
   clay,
While here on His footstool I roam;
But He's coming to take me some
   glorious day
Over there to my Heavenly home!
Mrs. Will L. Murphy.

618 There's a sweet and blessèd story
   Of the Christ who came from
   glory
Just to rescue me from sin and
   misery;
He in loving kindness sought me,
And from sin and shame hath brought
   me,
Hallelujah! Jesus ransomed me.

Hallelujah! what a Saviour!
Who can take a poor lost sinner,
Lift him from the miry clay and set him free;
I will ever tell the story,
Shouting glory, glory, glory,
Hallelujah! Jesus ransomed me.

2 From the depth of sin and sadness
To the heights of joy and gladness
Jesus lifted me, in mercy full and free;
With His precious blood He bought
   me,
When I knew Him not He sought me,
And in love divine He ransomed me.

3 From the throne of Heavenly glory—
Oh, the sweet and blessèd story!
Jesus came to lift the lost in sin and
   woe
Into liberty all glorious,
Trophies of His grace victorious,
Evermore rejoicing here below.

4 By and by with joy increasing,
And with gratitude unceasing,
Lifted up with Christ for evermore to
   be;

I will join the host there singing,
In the anthem ever ringing,
To the King of love who ransomed me.
Julia H. Johnston.

619 There's a psalm of praise filling all
   my days
Since to Jesus my heart did bow;
O what melody! Glorious harmony!
Life is wonderful now:

Life is wonderful, yes, it's wonderful!
Life is wonderful now to me!
I let Jesus in, He changed everything,
Life is wonderful now!
Since His blessings came into my heart
Joy unspeakable fills every part,
And I want to live for my Lord;
Life is wonderful now!

2 All is happiness, gone is my distress,
Peace and victory He does endow;
Since my Saviour came I can't be the
   same;
Life is wonderful now:

3 All my life is praise for His wondrous
   grace,
I will serve the Lord, this my vow;
Jesus came to me and He set me
   free;
Life is wonderful now:
I. Sutherland.

620 There is never a day so dreary,
   There is never a night so long
But the soul that is trusting Jesus
Will somewhere find a song.

Wonderful, wonderful Jesus,
In the heart He implanteth a song: . . .
A song of deliverance, of courage, of strength,
In the heart He implanteth a song. . . .

2 There is never a cross so heavy,
There is never a weight of woe
But that Jesus will help to carry,
Because He loveth so.

3 There is never a care or burden,
There is never a grief or loss
But that Jesus in love will lighten
When carried to the Cross.

4 There is never a guilty sinner,
   There is never a wandering one
   But that God can in mercy pardon
   Through Jesus Christ, His Son.

Annie B. Russell.

621 There are songs of joy that I loved
   to sing
   When my heart was blithe as a bird in
   spring,
   But the song I have learned is so full
   of cheer
   That the dawn shines out in the
   darkness drear.

   O, the new, . . . new song! . . . O, the new, . . .
   new song! . . .
   I can sing . . . it now . . . with the ran . . . somed
   throng;
   Power and dominion to Him that shall
   reign, . . .
   Glory and praise to the Lamb that was slain.

2 There are strains of home that are
   dear as life,
   And I list to them oft 'mid the din of
   strife;
   But I know of a home that is
   wondrous fair,
   And I sing the psalm they are singing
   there.

3 Can my lips be mute, or my heart be
   sad,
   When the gracious Master hath made
   me glad?
   When He points where the many
   mansions be,
   And sweetly says 'There is one for
   thee'?

4 I shall catch the gleam of its jasper
   wall
   When I come to the gloom of the
   evenfall,
   For I know that the shadows, dreary
   and dim,
   Have a path of light that will lead to
   Him.

Flora L. Best.

622 Once my way was dark and
   dreary,
   For my heart was full of sin;

But the sky is bright and cheery
Since the fulness of His love came in.

   I can never tell how much I love Him,
   I can never tell His love for me;
   For it passeth human measure
   Like a deep unfathomed sea; . . .
   'Tis redeeming love in Christ my Saviour,
   In my soul the Heavenly joys begin;
   And I live for Jesus only
   Since the fulness of His love came in.

2 There is grace for all the lowly,
   Grace to keep the trusting soul;
   Power to cleanse and make me holy,
   Jesus shall my yielded life control.

3 Let me spread abroad the story
   Other souls to Jesus win;
   For the Cross is now my glory
   Since the fulness of His love came in.

E. E. Hewitt.

623 O the grace of God is boundless,
   It is like a mighty sea,
   And it rolls on through the ages,
   Bearing love to you and me;
   But the Lord's so great in goodness
   That He opens Heaven to view,
   And not only gives us mercy
   But He gives us glory too.

   There's grace . . . and glory too, . . .
   There's grace . . . and glory too; . . .
   There's grace below for weal or woe,
   And then there's glory too.

2 There is grace for each temptation,
   There is strength for every day,
   There's a lift for every burden
   That we carry on the way;
   There's a refuge from the tempest,
   There is help for all we do,
   And when we shall end the journey
   We will find there's glory too.

3 For the grace that God has given
   I will praise Him in my song,
   I will love Him and will serve Him
   While my days of life prolong;
   And when I shall get to Heaven,
   And my journey I review,
   Then I'll bless His name for ever
   That there's grace and glory too.

T. M. Eastwood.

624 Oh, how well I remember in the old-fashioned days
When some old-fashioned people had some old-fashioned ways;
In the old-fashioned meetings, as they tarried there,
In the old-fashioned manner, God answered their prayer.

'Twas an old-fashioned meeting, in an old-fashioned place,
Where some old-fashioned people had some old-fashioned grace;
As an old-fashioned sinner I began to pray,
And God heard me, and saved me in the old-fashioned way.

2 There was singing, such singing, of those old-fashioned airs!
There was power, such power in those old-fashioned prayers,
An old-fashioned conviction made the sinner pray,
And the Lord heard and saved Him, in the old-fashioned way.

3 Well, they say it is better, 'Things have changed, don't you know,'
And the people in general, seem to think it is so;
And they call me old-fashioned when I dare to say
That I like it far better in the old-fashioned way.

4 If the Lord never changes, as the fashions of men,
If He's always the same, why, He is old-fashioned then!
As an old-fashioned sinner saved through old-time grace,
Oh, I'm sure He will take me to an old-fashioned place.

Herbert Buffum.

625 O how well do I remember how I doubted day by day,
For I did not know for certain that my sins were washed away;
When the Spirit tried to tell me I would not the truth receive,
I endeavoured to be happy, and to make myself believe.

But it's real, . . . it's real,
O I know . . . it's real;
Praise God, the doubts are settled,
For I know, I know it's real.

2 When the truth came close and searching all my joy would disappear,
For I did not have the witness of the Spirit bright and clear;
If at times the coming judgment would appear before my mind
O it made me so uneasy, for God's smile I could not find.

3 But at last I tired of living such a life of fear and doubt,
For I wanted God to give me something I would know about;
So the truth would make me happy, and the light would clearly shine,
And the Spirit gave assurance that I'm His and He is mine.

4 So I prayed to God in earnest and not caring what folks said;
I was hungry for the blessing; my poor soul it must be fed;
When at last by faith I touched Him, and, like sparks from smitten steel,
Just so quick salvation reached me; O bless God, I know it's real!

H. L. Cox.

626 Nor silver nor gold hath obtained my redemption,
No riches of earth could have saved my poor soul;
The blood of the Cross is my only foundation,
The death of my Saviour now maketh me whole.

I am redeemed, . . . but not with silver, . . .
I am bought, . . . but not with gold; . . .
Bought with a price, . . . the blood of Jesus, . . .
Precious price of love untold.

2 Nor silver nor gold hath obtained my redemption,
The guilt on my conscience too heavy had grown;
The blood of the Cross is my only foundation,
The death of my Saviour could only atone.

3 Nor silver nor gold hath obtained my
   redemption,
   The holy commandment forbade me
   draw near;
   The blood of the Cross is my only
   foundation,
   The death of my Saviour removeth
   my fear.

4 Nor silver nor gold hath obtained my
   redemption,
   The way into Heaven could not thus
   be bought;
   The blood of the Cross is my only
   foundation,
   The death of my Saviour redemption
   hath wrought.

James M. Gray.

627 Naught have I gotten but what I
   received,
   Grace hath bestowed it since I have
   believed;
   Boasting excluded, pride I abase;
   I'm only a sinner saved by grace!

   Only a sinner saved by grace!
   Only a sinner saved by grace!
   This is my story, to God be the glory,
   I'm only a sinner saved by grace!

2 Once I was foolish, and sin ruled my
   heart,
   Causing my footsteps from God to
   depart;
   Jesus hath found me, happy my case;
   I now am a sinner saved by grace!

3 Tears unavailing, no merit had I,
   Mercy had saved me, or else I must
   die;
   Sin had alarmed me, fearing God's
   face;
   But now I'm a sinner saved by grace!

4 Suffer a sinner whose heart
   overflows,
   Loving his Saviour to tell what he
   knows;
   Once more to tell it, would I embrace;
   I'm only a sinner saved by grace!

James M. Gray.

628 My path was always rough and
   drear,
   My soul was always sad;
   But now my path is smooth and
   bright,
   My soul for ever glad.

   It was Je . . . sus, my Saviour, who wrought
   this change in me;
   It was Je . . . sus my Saviour, blest Lamb of
   Calvary.
   I came to Him just as I was, from sin He set me
   free;
   It was Je . . . sus, my Saviour, who wrought
   this change in me.

2 My soul was stained with many sins,
   I lived in fear and dread;
   But now my soul is free from stain,
   And all my tears have fled.

3 O wand'ring one in paths of sin,
   The Saviour calls to thee;
   He longs to give you peace and rest,
   From sin to set you free.

James Rowe.

629 Jesus is my loving Saviour, He is
   so precious to me;
   O, how I love and adore Him, for all
   His mercies so free;
   When I was lost on the mountains,
   barren and dark and cold,
   He sought the sheep that was straying,
   He brought me back to the fold.

   Jesus, Jesus, dearer than all to me,
   Jesus, Jesus, Thine, only Thine I'll be;
   Where Thou dost lead I will follow, where'er
   the path may be;
   Then when life's journey is ended Thy face in
   glory I'll see.

2 Jesus the sweet Rose of Sharon,
   Jesus the Lily so fair;
   Jesus my rock and salvation, Jesus
   the bright morning star;
   He is my portion forever, my all in all is
   He;
   With Him I cannot be lonely, He fully
   satisfies me.

3 Jesus was born in a manger, wept in
   the garden alone;
   Poured out His life's blood on Calvary,
   died for our sin to atone;

Rose from the grave more than conqueror, went to His home on high;
Soon He is coming in glory, coming in clouds of the sky.

Geo. Bennard.

630 I've something in my heart that Jesus gave to me,
It makes me feel like singing glory all the day:
He found my captive soul and gave me liberty,
And now I feel like singing glory!

He makes the path grow brighter every passing day;
He makes the burden lighter, all along the way;
His Word is my delight, His will I now obey,
And all the time I'm singing glory!

2 My Saviour loosed my tongue that I might speak His praise;
Since then I have been singing glory all the day;
I love to tell the lost of Jesus and His ways,
And oh, it keeps me singing glory!

3 My Saviour took my feet from out the miry clay;
Since then I have been singing glory all the day:
He placed them on the Rock that shall not pass away—
I cannot keep from singing glory!

4 O weary heart and sad, O heavy-laden soul,
If you would feel like singing glory all the day
Just let the Saviour in, and let Him take control:
Then you will feel like singing glory!

L. R. Minor.

631 I've found a Friend who is all to me,
His love is ever true;
I love to tell how He lifted me,
And what His grace can do for you.

Saved . . . by His power divine!
Saved . . . to new life sublime!
Life now is sweet and my joy is complete,
For I'm saved, saved, saved!

2 He saves me from every sin and harm,
Secures my soul each day;
I'm leaning strong on His mighty arm;
I know He'll guide me all the way.

3 When poor and needy and all alone,
In love He said to me,
'Come unto Me, I will lead you home,
To live with Me eternally.'

J. P. Schofield.

632 I've found a Friend in Jesus, He's everything to me,
He's the Fairest of Ten Thousand to my soul;
The Lily of the Valley, in Him alone I see
All I need to cleanse and make me fully whole;
In sorrow He's my comfort, in trouble He's my stay,
He tells me every care on Him to roll.
He's the Lily of the Valley, the Bright and Morning Star,
He's the Fairest of Ten Thousand to my soul.

In sorrow He's my comfort, in trouble He's my stay,
He tells me every care on Him to roll.
He's the Lily of the Valley, the Bright and Morning Star,
He's the Fairest of Ten Thousand to my soul.

2 He all my griefs has taken, and all my sorrows borne;
In temptation He's my strong and mighty Tower;
I've all for Him forsaken, I've all my idols torn
From my heart, and now He keeps me by His power,
Though all the world forsake me, and Satan tempt me sore,
Through Jesus I shall safely reach the goal.
He's the Lily of the Valley, the Bright and Morning Star,
He's the Fairest of Ten Thousand to my soul.

3 He'll never, never leave me, nor yet
  forsake me here
While I live by faith and do His blessèd
  will;
A wall of fire about me, I've nothing
  now to fear,
With His manna He my hungry soul
  shall fill;
Then sweeping up to glory I'll see His
  blessèd face,
Where rivers of delight shall ever flow.
He's the Lily of the Valley, the Bright
  and Morning Star,
He's the Fairest of Ten Thousand to
  my soul.

C. W. Fry.

633 I've cast my heavy burdens down
    on Canaan's happy shore,
I'm living where the healing waters
  flow;
I'll wander in the wilderness of doubt
  and sin no more;
I'm living where the healing waters
  flow.

  Living on the shore, I'm living on the shore,
  I'm living where the healing waters flow;
  Living on the shore, I'm living on the shore,
  I'm living where the healing waters flow.

2 With Israel's trusting children I'm
    rejoicing on my way,
I'm living where the healing waters
  flow;
The cloudy, fiery pillar is my guiding
  light today;
I'm living where the healing waters
  flow.

3 My hungering soul is satisfied with
    manna from above,
I'm living where the healing waters
  flow;
No more I thirst, the Rock I've found,
  that fount of endless love;
I'm living where the healing waters
  flow.

4 I'm singing 'Hallelujah', safely
    anchored is my soul,
I'm living where the healing waters
  flow;

I'm resting on His promises; the blood
  has made me whole;
I'm living where the healing waters
  flow.

Ina Duley Ogdon.

634 In sorrow I wandered, my spirit
    opprest,
But now I am happy—securely I rest;
From morning till evening glad carols I
  sing,
And this is the reason—I walk with
  the King.

  I walk with the King, hallelujah!
  I walk with the King, praise His Name!
  No longer I roam, my soul faces home,
  I walk and I talk with the King.

2 For years in the fetters of sin I was
    bound,
The world could not help me—no
  comfort I found;
But now like the birds and the
  sunbeams of spring
I'm free and rejoicing—I walk with the
  King.

3 O soul near despair in the lowlands of
    strife,
Look up and let Jesus come into your
  life;
The joy of salvation to you He would
  bring—
Come into the sunlight and walk with
  the King.

James Rowe.

635 I will sing the wondrous story
    Of the Christ who died for me;
How He left His home in glory
For the Cross on Calvary.

  Yes, I'll sing the wondrous story
  Of the Christ who died for me;
  Sing it with the saints in glory,
  Gathered by the crystal sea.

2 I was lost; but Jesus found me—
  Found the sheep that went astray;
Threw His loving arms around me,
Drew me back into His way.

3 I was bruised but Jesus healed me—
Faint was I from many a fall;
Sight was gone and fears possessed
me
But He freed me from them all.

4 He will keep me till the river
Rolls its waters at my feet;
Then He'll bear me safely over,
Where the loved ones I shall meet.
F. H. Rawley.

636 I will sing of my Redeemer
And His wondrous love to me;
On the cruel Cross He suffered,
From the curse to set me free.

Sing, oh sing of my Redeemer,
With His blood He purchased me,
On the Cross He sealed my pardon,
Paid the debt and made me free.

2 I will tell the wondrous story,
How my lost estate to save,
In His boundless love and mercy,
He the ransom freely gave.

3 I will praise my dear Redeemer,
His triumphant power I'll tell;
How the victory He giveth
Over sin, and death, and hell.

4 I will sing of my Redeemer
And His Heavenly love to me;
He from death to life hath brought me,
Son of God, with Him to be.
Philip Bliss.

637 I was sinking deep in sin,
Sinking to rise no more,
Overwhelmed by guilt within
Mercy I did implore.
Then the Master of the sea
Heard my despairing cry,
Christ my Saviour lifted me,
Now safe am I.

Love lifted me! . . . love lifted me! . . .
When no one but Christ could help,
Love lifted me.

2 Souls in danger, look above,
Jesus completely saves;
He will lift you by His love
Out of the angry waves.
He's the Master of the sea,
Billows His will obey;
He your Saviour wants to be,
Be saved today!

3 When the waves of sorrow roll,
When I am in distress,
Jesus takes my hand in His,
Ever He loves to bless.
He will every fear dispel,
Satisfy every need;
All who heed His loving call
Find rest indeed.
arr. James Rowe.

638 I was once a sinner, but I came
Pardon to receive from my Lord:
This was freely given, and I found
That He always kept His word.

There's a new name written down in glory,
And it's mine, . . . O yes, it's mine! . . .
And the white-robed angels sing the story,
A sinner has come home. . . .
For there's a new name written down in glory,
And it's mine, . . . O yes, it's mine! . . .
With my sins forgiven I am bound for Heaven,
Never more to roam.

2 I was humbly kneeling at the Cross,
Fearing naught but God's angry
frown;
When the heavens opened and I saw
That my name was written down.

3 In the Book 'tis written 'Saved by
grace',
O the joy that came to my soul!
Now I am forgiven and I know
By the blood I am made whole.
C. Austin Miles.

639 I was lost in sin, but Jesus
rescued me,
He's a wonderful Saviour to me;
I was bound by fear, but Jesus set me
free,
He's a wonderful Saviour to me.

For He's a wonderful Saviour to me, . . .
He's a wonderful Saviour to me. . . .
I was lost in sin, but Jesus took me in:
He's a wonderful Saviour to me.

2 He's a Friend so true, so patient and
   so kind,
   He's a wonderful Saviour to me;
   Everything I need in Him I always find,
   He's a wonderful Saviour to me.

3 He is always near to comfort and to
   cheer,
   He's a wonderful Saviour to me;
   He forgives my sins, He dries my
   every tear,
   He's a wonderful Saviour to me.

4 Dearer grows the love of Jesus day by
   day,
   He's a wonderful Saviour to me;
   Sweeter is His grace while pressing on
   my way,
   He's a wonderful Saviour to me.
                                    Virgil P. Brock.

640 I've heard the glad news of the
       gospel,
It makes me so happy and free:
So I trust in my Father in Heaven,
For I know that He cares for me.

   I know He cares for me, for me,
   I know He cares for me, for me;
   I'll trust in my Father in Heaven,
   For I know that He cares for me.

2 Sometimes I walk in the darkness,
   My path then I scarcely can see;
   But I trust in my Father in Heaven,
   For I know that He cares for me.

3 Sometimes I wish I could see Him,
   And wonder how long it will be;
   But He's gone to prepare me a
   mansion,
   For I know that He cares for me.
                                    Anon.

641 I've been redeemed, all glory to
       the Lamb,
Jesus has loved me, I'm saved, I
know I am;

O wondrous love that caused my Lord
to die,
Now will I serve Him, then reign with
Him on high.

   I've been redeemed, yes, I have been
   redeemed,
   Glory to Jesus! 'tis sweet for me to know;
   I've been redeemed, yes, I have been
   redeemed,
   O hallelujah! my soul is white as snow.

2 O sinner, listen, I once was lost like
   you
   But Jesus found me, and saved me
   through and through;
   Now He is waiting for you to make a
   start,
   Come to Him quickly and choose the
   better part.

3 I am so glad I've found the way of life,
   Free from all sorrow, from sin and
   from strife;
   I am so glad I'm in this holy way,
   O hallelujah! I'm happy night and day.

4 I'm going home, all glory to the Lamb,
   Jesus will take me now just as I am;
   Soon I'll be there with friends who've
   gone before,
   O happy meeting! we'll meet to part
   no more.

642 I've reached the land of corn and
       wine,
And all its riches freely mine;
Here shines undimmed one blissful
day,
For all my night has passed away.

   Oh Beulah Land, sweet Beulah Land,
   As on thy highest mount I stand
   I look away across the sea, where mansions
   are prepared for me,
   And view the shining glory shore,
   My Heaven, my home, for evermore.

2 My Saviour comes and walks with me,
   And sweet communion here have we;
   He gently leads me by His hand,
   For this is Heaven's border-land.

3 A sweet perfume upon the breeze
   Is borne from ever vernal trees,
   And flowers that never fading grow
   Where streams of life forever flow.

4 The zephyrs seem to float to me
Sweet sounds of Heaven's melody;
As angels with the white-robed throng
Join in the sweet redemption song.
Edgar Page Stites.

643 Full Salvation! Full Salvation!
Lo! the fountain opened wide
Streams through ev'ry land and nation
From the Saviour's wounded side.
Full Salvation!
Streams an endless crimson tide.

2 Oh! the glorious revelation!
See the cleansing current flow;
Washing stains of condemnation
Whiter than the driven snow;
Full Salvation!
Oh! the rapturous bliss to know!

3 Love's resistless current sweeping
All the regions deep within;
Thought and wish and senses keeping
Now, and every instant, clean;
Full Salvation!
From the guilt and power of sin.

4 Life immortal, Heaven descending,
Lo! my heart the Spirit's shrine!
God and man in oneness blending—
Oh, what fellowship is mine!
Full Salvation!
Raised in Christ to life divine!

5 Care and doubting, gloom and sorrow,
Fear and grief are mine no more;
Faith knows nought of dark tomorrow
For my Saviour goes before.
Full Salvation!
Full and free for evermore.
F. Bottome.

644 I have a Friend whose faithful love
Is more than all the world to me,
'Tis higher than the heights above,
And deeper than the soundless sea:
So old, so new, so strong, so true;
Before the earth received its frame,
He loved me—Blessèd be His name!

2 He held the highest place above,
Adored by all the sons of flame,
Yet, such His self-denying love,
He laid aside His crown and came
To seek the lost, and, at the cost
Of Heavenly rank and earthly fame,
He sought me—Blessèd be His name!

3 It was a lonely path He trod,
From every human soul apart,
Known only to Himself and God
Was all the grief that filled His heart:
Yet from the track He turned not back
Till where I lay in want and shame
He found me—Blessèd be His name!

4 Then dawned at last that day of dread
When, desolate but undismayed,
With wearied frame and thorn-crowned head
He, now forsaken and betrayed,
Went up for me, to Calvary,
And dying there in grief and shame
He saved me—Blessèd be His name!

5 Long as I live my song shall tell
The wonders of His matchless love:
And when at last I rise to dwell
In the bright home prepared above,
My joy shall be His face to see,
And bowing then with loud acclaim,
I'll praise Him—Blessèd be His name!
C. A. Tydeman.

645 I hear the Saviour say,
"Thy strength indeed is small;
Come to Me—I'll be thy stay,
Find in Me thine all in all."

Jesus paid it all,
All to Him I owe;
Sin had left a crimson stain;
He washed it white as snow.

2 For nothing good have I
Whereby Thy grace to claim;
Jesus died my soul to save,
And blessèd be His name.

3 When from my dying bed
My ransomed soul shall rise,
"Jesus died my soul to save"
Shall rend the vaulted skies.

4 And when before the Throne
I stand in Him complete,
"Jesus died my soul to save"
My lips shall still repeat.

Elvina M. Hall.

646 O, brother, have you told how the
Lord forgave?
Let us hear you tell it over once again;
Thy coming to the Cross, where He
died to save,
Let us hear you tell it over once again.
Are you walking now in His blessèd
light?
Are you cleansed from every guilty
stain?
Is He your joy by day and your song
by night?
Let us hear you tell it over once again.

Let us hear . . . you tell it over, . . .
Tell it o . . . ver once again, . . .
Tell the sweet and blessèd story,
It will help you on to glory,
Let us hear you tell it over once again.

2 When toiling up the way was the
Saviour there?
Let us hear you tell it over once again;
Did Jesus bear you up in His tender
care?
Let us hear you tell it over once again.
Never have you found such a friend
as He
Who can help you 'midst the toil and
pain;
O all the world should hear what He's
done for thee,
Let us hear you tell it over once again.

3 Was ever on your tongue such a
blessèd theme?
Let us hear you tell it over once again;
'Tis ever sweeter far than the
sweetest dream,
Let us hear you tell it over once again.
There are aching hearts in the world's
great throng
Who have sought for rest, and all in
vain;
Hold Jesus up to them by your word
and song;
Let us hear you tell it over once again.

4 The battles you have fought, and the
victories won,
Let us hear you tell it over once again;
'Twill help them on the way who have
just begun,
Let us hear you tell it over once again.
We are striving now with the hosts of
sin,
Soon with Christ our Saviour we shall
reign;
Ye ransomed of the Lord try a soul to
win;
Let us hear you tell it over once again.

J. M. White.

647 In shady green pastures, so rich
and so sweet,
God leads His dear children along;
Where the water's cool flow bathes
the weary one's feet,
God leads His dear children along.

Some through the waters, some through the
flood,
Some through the fire, but all through the
blood;
Some through great sorrow, but God gives a
song;
In the night season and all the day long.

2 Sometimes on the mount where the
sun shines so bright
God leads His dear children along;
Sometimes in the valley in the darkest
night
God leads His dear children along.

3 Though sorrows befall us, and Satan
oppose,
God leads His dear children along;
Through grace we can conquer,
defeat all our foes:
God leads His dear children along.

4 Away from the mire, and away from
the clay,
God leads His dear children along;
Away up in glory, eternity's day
God leads His dear children along.

G. A. Young.

648 O happy day that fixed my choice
On Thee, my Saviour and my God!
Well may this glowing heart rejoice,
And tell its raptures all abroad.

O happy day, O happy day,
When Jesus washed my sins away!
He taught me how to watch and pray,
And live rejoicing every day.
O happy day, O happy day,
When Jesus washed my sins away!

2 'Tis done, the great transaction's done!
I am my Lord's and He is mine:
He drew me and I followed on,
Charmed to confess the voice divine.

3 Now rest, my long-divided heart,
Fixed on this blissful centre, rest:
Nor ever from thy Lord depart,
With Him of every good possessed.

4 High Heaven, that heard the solemn vow,
That vow renewed shall daily hear,
Till in life's latest hour I bow,
And bless in death a bond so dear.
Philip Doddridge.

649 I have such a wonderful Saviour
Who helps me wherever I go;
That I must be telling His goodness,
That everybody should know!

Everybody should know, . . .
Everbody should know, . . .
I have such a wonderful Saviour,
That everybody should know.

2 His mercy and love are unbounded,
He makes me with gladness o'erflow;
Oh, He is 'the Chief of ten thousand':
That everybody should know.

3 He helps me when trials surround me,
His grace and His goodness to show:
Oh, how can I help but adore Him!
That everybody should know.

4 My life and my love I will give Him,
And faithfully serve Him below,
Who brought me His wondrous salvation
That everybody should know.
Mrs. Frank A. Breck.

650 In tenderness He sought me,
Weary and sick with sin,
And on His shoulders brought me
Back to His fold again.
While angels in His presence sang
Until the courts of Heaven rang.

Oh, the love that sought me!
Oh, the blood that bought me!
Oh, the grace that brought me to the fold,
Wondrous grace that brought me to the fold!

2 He washed the bleeding sin-wounds,
And poured in oil and wine;
He whispered to assure me,
'I've found thee, thou art Mine';
I never heard a sweeter voice,
It made my aching heart rejoice!

3 He pointed to the nail-prints,
For me His blood was shed,
A mocking crown so thorny
Was placed upon His head:
I wondered what He saw in me
To suffer such deep agony.

4 I'm sitting in His presence,
The sunshine of His face,
While with adoring wonder
His blessings I retrace.
It seems as if eternal days
Are far too short to sound His praise.

5 So while the hours are passing,
All now is perfect rest;
I'm waiting for the morning,
The brightest and the best,
When He will call us to His side,
To be with Him, His spotless bride.
W. Spencer Walton.

651 I remember when my burdens rolled away,
I had carried them for years, night and day;
When I sought the blessèd Lord, and I took Him at His Word,
Then at once all my burdens rolled away.

Rolled away . . . rolled away . . .
I am happy since my burdens rolled away.

Witness and Testimony

2 I remember when my burdens rolled
    away,
    That I feared would never leave night
    or day;
    Jesus showed to me the loss, so I left
    them at the Cross;
    I was glad when my burdens rolled
    away.

3 I remember when my burdens rolled
    away,
    That had hindered me for years, night
    and day;
    As I sought the throne of grace, just a
    glimpse of Jesu's face,
    And I knew that my burdens could not
    stay.

4 I am singing since my burdens rolled
    away,
    There's a song within my heart night
    and day;
    I am living for my King, and with joy I
    shout and sing,
    Hallelujah, all my burdens rolled
    away.

Mrs. M. A. Steele.

652 I'm singing for my Lord every-
    where I go,
    Singing of His wondrous love that the
    world may know
    How He saved a wretch like me by His
    death on Calvary:
    I'm singing for my Lord everywhere
    I go.

2 I'm singing, but sometimes heavy is
    the rod,
    For this world is not a friend to the
    grace of God;
    Yet I sing the whole day long for He
    fills my heart with song,
    I'm singing for my Lord everywhere
    I go.

3 I'm singing for the lost just because I
    know
    Jesus Christ, whose precious blood
    washes white as snow;
    If my songs to Him can bring some
    lost soul I'll gladly sing:
    I'm singing for my Lord everywhere
    I go.

4 I'm singing for the saints as they
    journey home;
    Soon they'll reach that happy land
    where they'll never roam,
    And with me they'll join and sing
    praises to our Lord and King:
    I'm singing for my Lord everywhere
    I go.

J. Smith.

653 I am redeemed, oh, praise the
    Lord!
    My soul from bondage free
    Has found at last a resting place
    In Him who died for me!

I am redeemed! . . . I am redeemed! . . .
I'll sing it o'er and o'er;
I am redeemed! . . . oh, praise the Lord!
Redeemed for evermore!

2 I looked, and lo, from Calvary's Cross
    A healing fountain streamed;
    It cleansed my heart, and now I sing,
    Praise God, I am redeemed!

3 The debt is paid, my soul is free;
    And by His mighty power,
    The blood that washed my sins away
    Still cleanseth every hour.

4 All glory be to Jesu's Name
    I know that He is mine!
    For on my heart the Spirit seals
    His pledge of love Divine.

5 And when I reach that world more
    bright
    Than mortal ever dreamed,
    I'll cast my crown at Jesu's feet
    And cry, 'Redeemed, redeemed!'

Julia Sterling.

654 I am saved! I am saved!
    Jesus bids me go free!
    He has bought with a price
    Even me, even me!

Hallelujah! Hallelujah! Hallelujah to my
    Saviour!
Hallelujah! Hallelujah! Hallelujah! Amen.

2 I am cleansed! I am cleansed!
I am whiter than snow;
He is mighty to save,
This I know, this I know!

3 Wondrous love! wondrous love!
Now the gift I receive;
I have rest in His Word —
I believe, I believe!

4 I was weak, I am strong
In the power of His might,
And my darkness He turns
Into light, into light!

5 Praise the Lord! Praise the Lord!
Ye His saints everywhere;
I shall join in the throng
Over there, over there!

655 Jesus has promised my Shepherd
to be,
That's why I love Him so;
And to the children He said, 'Come
to Me,'
That's why I love Him so.

That's why I love Him,
That's why I love Him,
Because He first loved me; . . .
When I'm tempted and tried,
He is close by my side,
That's why I love Him so.

2 He the weak lambs to His bosom will
take,
That's why I love Him so;
Never will He for a moment forsake,
That's why I love Him so.

3 He has in Heaven prepared me a
place,
That's why I love Him so;
Where I may dwell, by His wonderful
grace,
That's why I love Him so.
Scott Lawrence.

656 My happy soul rejoices,
The sky is bright above;
I'll join the Heavenly voices,
And sing redeeming love.

For there's power in Jesus' blood,
Power in Jesus' blood;
There's power in Jesus' blood
To wash me white as snow.

2 I heard the blessèd story
Of Him who died to save;
The love of Christ swept o'er me,
My all to Him I gave.

3 His gracious words of pardon
Were music to my heart;
He took away my burden,
And bade my fears depart.

4 I plunge beneath this fountain
That cleanseth white as snow;
It pours from Calvary's mountain
With blessings in its flow.

5 O crown Him King for ever!
My Saviour and my Friend!
By Zion's crystal river
His praise shall never end.
Hope Tryaway.

657 I came to Jesus weary, worn, and
sad,
He took my sins away,
He took my sins away;
His wondrous love has made my heart
so glad,
He took my sins away.

He took my sins away, He took my sins away,
And keeps my footsteps day by day;
I'm so glad He saved my guilty soul,
And took my sins away.

2 The load of sin was more than I could
bear,
He took it all away,
He took it all away;
And now on Him I roll my every care,
He took my sins away.

3 No condemnation have I in my heart,
He took my sins away,
And keeps me day by day;
His perfect peace He did to me impart,
He took my sins away.

4 If you will come to Jesus Christ today,
He'll take your sins away,
He'll take your sins away;
And keep you happy in the narrow
way,
He'll take your sins away.

Mrs. M. J. Harris.

4 Christ is my meat, Christ is my drink,
My medicine, and my health;
My portion, mine inheritance,
Yea, all my boundless Wealth.

J. Mason.

658 I have a Friend, a precious Friend,
O how He loves me!
He says His love will never end,
O how He loves me!

O how He loves me! O how He loves me!
I know not why, I only cry, "O how He loves
me!"

2 Why He should come, I cannot tell,
O how He loves me!
In my poor broken heart to dwell,
O how He loves me!

3 He died to save my soul from death,
O how He loves me!
I'll praise Him while He gives me
breath,
O how He loves me!

4 He walks with me along life's road,
O how He loves me!
He carries every heavy load,
O how He loves me!

5 He has a home prepared for me,
O how He loves me!
With Him I'll spend eternity,
O how He loves me!

Johnson Oatman.

659 I've found the 'Pearl of greatest
price',
My heart doth sing for joy,
And sing I must, for Christ I have—
Oh, what a Christ have I!

2 My Christ, He is 'the Lord of lords',
The Sovereign 'King of kings',
The risen 'Sun of Righteousness,
With healing in His wings'.

3 My Christ, He is 'the Tree of Life'.
That in God's Eden grows;
The living 'clear as crystal' stream
Whence life for ever flows.

660 In loving kindness Jesus came
My soul in mercy to re-claim,
And from the depths of sin and
shame
Through grace He lifted me.

From sinking sand He lifted me;
With tender hand He lifted me;
From shades of night to plains of light,
Oh, praise His Name, He lifted me!

2 He called me long before I heard,
Before my sinful heart was stirred;
But when I took Him at His word,
Forgiven, He lifted me.

3 His brow was pierced with many a
thorn,
His hands by cruel nails were torn,
When from my guilt and grief, forlorn,
In love He lifted me.

4 Now on a higher plane I dwell,
And with my soul I know 'tis well;
Yet how or why, I cannot tell
He should have lifted me.

Charlotte G. Homer.

661 Down at the Cross where my
Saviour died,
Down where for cleansing from sin I
cried;
There to my heart was the blood
applied;
Glory to His Name!

Glory to His Name!
Glory to His Name!
There to my heart was the blood applied;
Glory to His Name!

2 I am so wondrously saved from sin!
Jesus so sweetly abides within;
There at the Cross where He took me
in;
Glory to His Name!

3 O precious fountain that saves from sin!
I am so glad I have entered in;
There Jesus saves me, and keeps me clean;
Glory to His Name!

4 Come to this fountain, so rich and sweet;
Cast thy poor soul at the Saviour's feet;
Plunge in today, and be made complete;
Glory to His Name!

E. A. Hoffman.

662 The trusting heart to Jesus clings,
Nor any ill forebodes,
But at the Cross of Calvary sings,
Praise God for lifted loads!

Singing I go along life's road,
Praising the Lord, praising the Lord,
Singing I go along life's road,
For Jesus has lifted my load.

2 The passing days bring many cares,
'Fear not,' I hear Him say,
And when my fears are turned to prayers
The burdens slip away.

3 He tells me of my Father's love,
And never slumbering eye;
My everlasting King above
Will all my needs supply.

4 When to the throne of grace I flee
I find the promise true,
The mighty arms upholding me
Will bear my burdens too.

E. E. Hewitt.

663 My song shall be of Jesus;
His mercy crowns my days,
He fills my cup with blessings,
And tunes my heart to praise;
My song shall be of Jesus,
The precious Lamb of God,
Who gave Himself my ransom,
And bought me with His blood.

2 My song shall be of Jesus;
When sitting at His feet
I call to mind His goodness,
In meditation sweet:
My song shall be of Jesus
Whatever ill betide;
I'll sing the grace that saves me,
And keeps me at His side.

3 My song shall be of Jesus;
While pressing on my way
To reach the blissful region
Of pure and perfect day;
And when my soul shall enter
The gate of Eden fair,
A song of praise to Jesus
I'll sing for ever there.

Fanny J. Crosby.

664 O bless the Lord! He cleansed my soul
And filled my lips with singing;
He came in my poor, sinful heart,
And set the joybells ringing.

O praise the Lord, He first loved me!
I feel new life upspringing;
He came in my poor, sinful heart,
And set the joybells ringing.

2 He placed my feet upon the Rock,
The only sure foundation;
He shows me wonders of His grace,
The blessings of salvation.

3 His promise is for all the days,
His love for me is caring;
While in the Father's House above
A mansion He's preparing.

4 His love is calling, seeking still,
Come, every burden bringing;
The touch of Christ within your heart
Will set the joybells ringing.

Eliza E. Hewitt.

665 Would you know why I love Jesus?
Why He is so dear to me?
'Tis because my blessèd Saviour
From my sins has ransomed me.

This is why . . . I love my Je . . . sus,
This is why . . . I love Him so; . . .
He has par . . . doned my transgres . . . sions,
He has washed . . . me white as snow.

2 Would you know why I love Jesus?
Why He is so dear to me?
'Tis because the blood of Jesus
Fully saves and cleanses me.

3 Would you know why I love Jesus?
Why He is so dear to me?
'Tis because, amid temptation,
He supports and strengthens me.

4 Would you know why I love Jesus?
Why He is so dear to me?
'Tis because, in every conflict,
Jesus gives me victory.

5 Would you know why I love Jesus?
Why He is so dear to me?
'Tis because my Friend and Saviour
He will ever, ever be.

E. A. Hoffman.

666 I was a sinner till the Lord sought
me out,
Till the Lord sought me out,
Till the Lord sought me out;
I was a sinner till the Lord sought me
out;
Glory to His Name!

Glory, glory, glory, glory, praise ye the Lord!
Glory, praise ye the Lord! glory, praise ye the
Lord!
Glory, glory, glory, glory, praise ye the Lord!
All glory to His name!

2 The Lord sought me out and He called
me by name,
Yes, He called me by name,
Yes, He called me by name;
The Lord sought me out and He called
me by name;
Glory to His Name!

3 The Lord called my name and He
showed me the way,
Yes, He showed me the way,
Yes, He showed me the way;
The Lord called my name and He
showed me the way;
Glory to His Name!

4 The Lord shows the way and He helps
me to walk,
Yes, He helps me to walk,
Yes, He helps me to walk;
The Lord shows the way and He helps
me to walk;
Glory to His Name!

Brian Anker.

667 Redeemed, how I love to proclaim
it,
Redeemed by the blood of the Lamb;
Redeemed through His infinite mercy,
His child and forever I am.

Redeemed, . . . Redeemed, . . .
Redeemed by the blood of the Lamb,
Redeemed, . . . Redeemed, . . .
His child and forever I am.

2 Redeemed and so happy in Jesus,
No language my rapture can tell;
I know that the light of His presence
With me doth continually dwell.

3 I think of my blessèd Redeemer,
I think of Him all the day long,
I sing, for I cannot be silent,
His love is the theme of my song.

4 I know I shall see in His beauty
The King in whose law I delight;
Who lovingly guardeth my footsteps,
And giveth me songs in the night.

5 I know there's a crown that is waiting
In yonder bright mansion for me;
And soon, with the spirits made
perfect,
At home with the Lord I shall be.

Fanny J. Crosby.

668 Christ has for sin atonement
made,
What a wonderful Saviour!
We are redeemed! the price is paid!
What a wonderful Saviour!

What a wonderful Saviour is Jesus, my Jesus!
What a wonderful Saviour is Jesus, my Lord!

2 He dwells within me day by day,
What a wonderful Saviour!
And keeps me faithful all the way,
What a wonderful Saviour!

3 He gives me overcoming power,
   What a wonderful Saviour!
   And triumph in each conflict hour,
   What a wonderful Saviour!

4 To Him I've given all my heart,
   What a wonderful Saviour!
   The world shall never share a part,
   What a wonderful Saviour!
                              E. A. Hoffman.

669 Do you know Jesus, our Lord, our
   Saviour,
   Jesus the Son of God?
   Have you ever seen Him, or shared of
   His favour?
   Jesus the Son of God.

   O sweet Wonder! O sweet Wonder!
   Jesus the Son of God;
   How I adore Thee! O how I love Thee!
   Jesus the Son of God.

2 God gave Him a ransom, our souls to
   recover,
   Jesus the Son of God.
   His blood made us worthy, His Spirit
   to hover,
   Jesus the Son of God.

3 O who would reject Him, despise or
   forsake Him,
   Jesus the Son of God?
   O who ever sought Him, and He
   would not take him?
   Jesus the Son of God.

4 Then some day from Heaven, on
   clouds of bright glory,
   Jesus the Son of God
   Will come for His jewels, most
   precious and holy,
   Jesus the Son of God.
                              G. T. Hayward.

Section XI

THE CHURCH OF GOD

THE BODY OF CHRIST

670 Lord of the Church, we pray for
   our renewing:
   Christ over all, our undivided aim.
   Fire of the Spirit, burn for our
   enduing,
   Wind of the Spirit, fan the living
   flame!
   We turn to Christ amid our fear and
   failing,
   The will that lacks the courage to be
   free,
   The weary labours, all but unavailing,
   To bring us nearer what a Church
   should be.

2 Lord of the Church, we seek a Father's
   blessing,
   A true repentance and a faith
   restored,
   A swift obedience and a new
   possessing,
   Filled with the Holy Spirit of the Lord!

We turn to Christ from all our restless
   striving,
   Unnumbered voices with a single
   prayer —
   The living water for our souls'
   reviving,
   In Christ to live, and love and serve
   and care.

3 Lord of the Church, we long for our
   uniting,
   True to one calling, by one vision
   stirred;
   One Cross proclaiming and one creed
   reciting,
   One in the truth of Jesus and His
   Word!
   So lead us on; till toil and trouble
   ended,
   One Church triumphant one new song
   shall sing,
   To praise His glory, risen and
   ascended,
   Christ over all, the everlasting King!
                              Timothy Dudley-Smith.

671 The Church's one foundation
Is Jesus Christ her Lord:
She is His new creation
By water and the Word;
From Heaven He came and sought her
To be His holy bride;
With His own blood He bought her,
And for her life He died.

2 Elect from every nation,
Yet one o'er all the earth,
Her charter of salvation
One Lord, one faith, one birth,
One holy Name she blesses,
Partakes one holy food,
And to one hope she presses
With every grace endued.

3 Though with a scornful wonder
Men see her sore oppressed,
By schisms rent asunder,
By heresies distressed,
Yet saints their watch are keeping,
Their cry goes up, 'How long?'
And soon the night of weeping
Shall be the morn of song.

4 'Mid toil and tribulation,
And tumult of her war,
She waits the consummation
Of peace for evermore.
Till with the vision glorious
Her longing eyes are blest,
And the great Church victorious
Shall be the Church at rest.

5 Yet she on earth hath union
With God the Three in One,
And mystic sweet communion
With those whose rest is won.
O happy ones and holy!
Lord, give us grace that we
Like them, the meek and lowly,
On high may dwell with Thee.
Samuel John Stone.

672 We love the place, O God,
Wherein Thine honour dwells;
The joy of Thine abode
All earthly joy excels.

2 It is the house of prayer,
Wherein Thy servants meet;
And Thou, O Lord, art there
Thy chosen flock to greet.

3 We love the Word of life,
The Word that tells of peace,
Of comfort in the strife
And joys that never cease.

4 We love to sing below
Of mercies freely given;
But O we long to know
The triumph song of Heaven!

5 Lord Jesus, give us grace
On earth to love Thee more,
In Heaven to see Thy face,
And with Thy saints adore.
William Bullock.

673 'Tis the Church triumphant singing
Worthy the Lamb;
Heaven throughout with praises
ringing,
Worthy the Lamb.
Thrones and powers before Him
bending,
Odours sweet with voice ascending,
Swell the chorus never ending,
Worthy the Lamb!

2 Every kindred, tongue and nation,
Worthy the Lamb;
Join to sing the great salvation,
Worthy the Lamb.
Loud as mighty thunders roaring,
Floods of mighty waters pouring,
Prostrate at His feet adoring,
Worthy the Lamb!

3 Harps and songs for ever sounding
Worthy the Lamb;
Mighty grace o'er sin abounding,
Worthy the Lamb.
By His blood He dearly bought us;
Wandering from the fold He sought
us,
And to glory safely brought us:
Worthy the Lamb!

4 Sing with blest anticipation
  Worthy the Lamb;
  Through the vale of tribulation,
  Worthy the Lamb.
  Sweetest notes, all notes excelling,
  On the theme for ever dwelling,
  Still untold, though ever telling,
  Worthy the Lamb!
                              J. Kent.

674 Glorious things of Thee are
       spoken,
  Zion, city of our God;
  He whose Word cannot be broken
  Formed thee for His own abode.
  On the Rock of Ages founded,
  What can shake thy sure repose?
  With salvation's walls surrounded,
  Thou may'st smile at all thy foes.

2 See! the streams of living waters
  Springing from eternal love,
  Well supply Thy sons and daughters,
  And all fear of want remove.
  Who can faint while such a river
  Ever flows their thirst to assuage?
  Grace which, like the Lord, the Giver,
  Never fails from age to age.

3 Saviour, if of Zion's city
  I, through grace, a member am,
  Let the world deride or pity,
  I will glory in Thy Name.
  Fading is the worldling's pleasure,
  All his boasted pomp and show;
  Solid joys and lasting treasure
  None but Zion's children know.
                              John Newton.

675 Christ is made the sure founda-
       tion,
  Christ the head and corner-stone,
  Chosen of the Lord, and precious,
  Binding all the Church in one,
  Holy Sion's help for ever,
  And her confidence alone.

2 All that dedicated city
  Dearly loved of God on high,
  In exultant jubilation
  Pours perpetual melody,
  God the One in Three adoring
  In glad hymns eternally.

3 To this temple, where we call Thee,
  Come, O Lord of hosts, today;
  With Thy wonted loving kindness
  Hear Thy servants as they pray;
  And Thy fullest benediction
  Shed within its walls alway.

4 Here vouchsafe to all Thy servants
  What they ask of Thee to gain,
  What they gain from Thee for ever
  With the blessèd to retain,
  And hereafter in Thy glory
  Evermore with Thee to reign.

5 Laud and honour to the Father,
  Laud and honour to the Son,
  Laud and honour to the Spirit,
  Ever Three and ever One;
  One in might, and One in glory,
  While unending ages run.
                              trs. John M. Neale.

676 God in Heaven hath a treasure,
       Riches none may count or tell;
  Hath a deep eternal pleasure,
  Christ, the Son, He loveth well.
  God hath here on earth a treasure,
  None but He its price may know,—
  Deep, unfathomable pleasure,
  Christ revealed in saints below.

2 God in tongues of fire descending,
  Chosen vessels thus to fill
  With the treasure never ending,
  Ever spent, unfailing still.
  God's own hand the vessel filling
  From the glory far above,
  Longing hearts for ever stilling
  With the riches of His love.

3 Thus though worn, and tried, and
       tempted,
  Glorious calling, saint, is thine;
  Let the Lord but find thee emptied,
  Living branch in Christ the vine!
  Vessels of the world's despising,
  Vessels weak, and poor, and base,
  Bearing wealth God's heart is prizing,
  Glory from Christ's blessèd face.

4 Oh, to be but emptier, lowlier,
Mean, unnoticed and unknown,
And to God a vessel holier,
Filled with Christ and Christ alone!
Naught of earth to cloud the glory,
Naught of self the light to dim,
Telling forth His wondrous story,
Emptied—to be filled with Him.

Frances Bevan.

THE MINISTRY

677 Move me, dear Lord, and others I
shall move
To do Thy will;
Mould Thou this life into a vessel fair
Thyself to fill;
No charm with which to draw do I
possess,
In Thee I find the secret of success.

2 O touch these yielded lips and
through them pour
Thy living thought;
I would not give to hungry souls the
words
That man hath taught;
Shall they who seek for bread a stone
receive?
It is God's Word alone that can
relieve.

3 How wonderful a channel thus to be
To those forlorn,
A messenger of peace and joy and
hope
To them that mourn;
O grant that I Thy risen life may share,
The virtue of Thy Name to others
bear.

4 Under the anointing daily let me live,
A priest and king;
Relying not on fleshly energy
Thy smile to win;
A simple soul in contact with my
Lord,
In Whom all fulness is forever stored.

5 O teach me, Lord, henceforth with
Thee to walk
In union deep;
Whilst tending other souls not to
neglect

My own to keep;
A separated soul unto the One
Whose grace and love for me so much
have done.

E. C. Boulton.

678 Go, labour on, spend, and be
spent,
Thy joy to do the Father's will;
It is the way the Master went,
Should not the servant tread it still?

2 Go, labour on; 'tis not for nought,
Thy earthly loss is Heavenly gain;
Men heed thee, love thee, praise thee
not,
The Master praises, what are men?

3 Men die in darkness at your side
Without a hope to cheer the tomb:
Take up the torch, and wave it wide,
The torch that lights time's thickest
gloom.

4 Toil on, and in thy toil rejoice,
For toil comes rest, for exile home;
Soon shalt thou hear the Bride-
groom's voice,
The midnight peal, 'Behold, I come!'

Horatius Bonar.

BELIEVERS' BAPTISM

679 Master, we Thy footsteps follow,
We Thy Word obey,
Hear us, Thy dear Name confessing,
While we pray.

2 Now into Thy death baptizèd,
We ourselves would be
Dead to all the sin that made
Thy Calvary.

3 Rising with Thee, make us like Thee,
In Thy love and care,
In Thy zeal, and in Thy labour,
And Thy prayer.

4 Let the love that knows no failing
Cast out all our fears,
Let Thy pure and faithful Spirit
Fill our years.

5 Till we hear the trumpets sounding
  On the other side,
  And for ever in Thy Heaven
  We abide.

  F. A. Jackson.

680 Witness, ye men and angels,
      now,
  Before the Lord we speak;
  To Him we make our solemn vow,
  A vow we dare not break;

2 That, long as life itself shall last,
  Ourselves to Christ we yield;
  Nor from His cause will we depart,
  Or ever quit the field.

3 We trust not in our native strength,
  But on His grace rely
  That, with returning wants, the Lord
  Will all our need supply.

4 O guide our doubtful feet aright,
  And keep us in Thy ways;
  And while we turn our vows to
      prayers,
  Turn Thou our prayers to praise.

  Benjamin Beddome.

681 Lord Jesus, in Thy footsteps
      We come to take our stand,
  And pledge Thee loyal service
  In keeping Thy command.
  As Thou in Jordan's river
  In faith and hope didst bow,
  We would go through these waters
  To make our solemn vow.

2 We know we are unworthy;
  Our hearts are soiled within.
  Lord, help us now to bury
  And wash away our sin.
  Lord, help us in the newness
  Of risen life with Thee
  Henceforth by Thine enabling
  True witnesses to be.

3 As then at Thy baptizing
  Thy Father blessed Thy Name,
  And from the opened Heaven
  The Spirit's favour came,

So, gracious Lord and Master,
  Do Thou Thy gift bestow,
  That cleansed, inspired and guided,
  We in Thy likeness grow.

4 Upon Thy grace relying
  To meet temptation's hour,
  We'd face life's tests with courage
  And conquer in Thy power.
  Thy Kingdom's sway extending,
  Thy will our vital breath,
  O Lord, may we Thy servants
  Prove faithful unto death.

  Hugh Martin.

682 Glory to God, whose Spirit draws
      Fresh soldiers to the Saviour's
      cause.
  Who thus, baptized into His Name,
  His goodness and their faith proclaim.

2 For these now added to the host
  Who in their Lord and Saviour boast,
  And consecrate to Him their days,
  Accept, O God, our grateful praise.

3 Thus may Thy mighty Spirit draw
  All here to love and keep His law;
  Themselves His subjects to declare,
  And place themselves beneath His
  care.

4 Lead them at once their Lord to own,
  To glory in His Cross alone;
  And then baptized, His truth to teach,
  His love to share, His Heaven to
  reach.

  Baptist W. Noel.

683 To Thee, O God, our hearts we
      raise
  In humble supplication
  For those who seek in early days
  A life-long consecration.
  To Thee they come with vows
      renewed,
  The right from wrong discerning;
  O send them forth with power
      endued,
  With zeal and courage burning.

2 O Saviour Christ, to Thee we pray,
With Heavenly manna feed them;
Thyself the life, the truth, the way,
Through all life's changes lead them.
When fails the heart in warfare long,
When faith and love are dying,
O make them in their weakness
strong,
While on Thy might relying.

3 O Holy Spirit, fount of life,
Through all their days protect them;
Their help in need, their shield in
strife,
With sevenfold gifts direct them.
Inspired with love and holy fear,
And pledged to high endeavour,
O grant them grace to persevere,
And seal them Thine for ever.

H. D. Dixon-Wright.

BREAKING OF BREAD

684 Wounded for me, wounded for
me,
There on the Cross He was wounded
for me;
Gone my transgressions and now I am
free,
All because Jesus was wounded for
me.

2 Risen for me, risen for me,
Up from the grave He has risen for
me;
Now evermore from death's sting I am
free,
All because Jesus has risen for me.

3 Living for me, living for me,
There on the Throne He is living for
me;
Saved to the uttermost now I shall be,
All because Jesus is living for me.

4 Coming for me, coming for me,
One day to earth He is coming for me;
Then with what joy His dear face I
shall see,
Oh, how I praise Him—He's coming
for me.

G. W. R.

685 When I saw the cleansing
fountain
Open wide for all my sin,
I obeyed the Spirit's wooing
When He said, 'Wilt thou be clean?'

I will praise Him, I will praise Him, praise Him,
Praise the Lamb for sinners slain: . . .
Give Him glory all ye people,
For His blood has washed away my stain.

2 Though the way seemed straight and
narrow,
All I claimed was swept away;
My ambition, plans and wishes,
At my feet in ashes lay.

3 Then God's fire upon the altar
Of my heart was set aflame;
I shall never cease to praise Him,
Glory! glory! to His Name.

4 Blessèd be the name of Jesus,
I'm so glad He took me in;
He has pardoned my transgressions,
He has cleansed my heart from sin.

Mrs. M. J. Harris.

686 We come as guests invited
When Jesus bids us dine,
His friends on earth united
To share the bread and wine;
The bread of life is broken,
The wine is freely poured
For us, in solemn token
Of Christ our dying Lord.

2 We eat and drink, receiving
From Christ the grace we need,
And in our hearts believing
On Him by faith we feed;
With wonder and thanksgiving
For love that knows no end,
We find in Jesus living
Our ever-present Friend.

3 One Bread is ours for sharing,
One single fruitful Vine,
Our fellowship declaring
Renewed in bread and wine—
Renewed, sustained, and given
By token, sign and word,
The pledge and seal of Heaven,
The love of Christ our Lord.

Timothy Dudley-Smith.

687 Sweet feast of love divine!
'Tis grace that makes us free
To feed upon this bread and wine
In memory, Lord, of Thee.

2 Here every welcome guest
Waits, Lord, from Thee to learn
The secrets of Thy Father's breast,
And all Thy grace discern.

3 Here conscience ends its strife,
And faith delights to prove
The sweetness of the bread of life,
The fulness of Thy love.

4 Thy blood that flowed for sin
In symbol here we see,
And feel the blessèd pledge within
That we are loved of Thee.

5 But if this glimpse of love
Is so divinely sweet,
What will it be, O Lord, above,
Thy gladdening smile to meet?

6 To see Thee face to face,
Thy perfect likeness wear,
And all Thy ways of wondrous grace
Through endless years declare!
Edward Denny.

688 Saviour, we remember Thee!
Thy deep woe and agony,
All Thy suffering on the Tree:
Saviour, we adore Thee!

2 Calvary! O Calvary!
Mercy's vast unfathomed sea,
Love, eternal love to me:
Saviour, we adore Thee!

3 Darkness hung around Thy head,
When for sin Thy blood was shed,
Victim in the sinner's stead;
Saviour, we adore Thee!

4 Jesus, Lord, Thou now art risen!
Thou hast all our sins forgiven;
Haste we to our home in Heaven:
Saviour, we adore Thee!

5 Soon, with joyful, glad surprise,
We shall hear Thy Word—"Arise!"
Mounting upward to the skies:
Glory, glory, glory!

6 Saviour, we Thy love adore;
We will praise Thee more and more;
Spread Thy Name from shore to
shore:
Saviour, we adore Thee!

689 Sweet the moments, rich in
blessing,
Which before the Cross I spend,
Life and health and peace possessing
From the sinner's dying Friend!

2 Here I rest, for ever viewing
Mercy poured in streams of blood:
Precious drops, my soul bedewing,
Plead, and claim my peace with God.

3 Truly blessèd in this station,
Low before His Cross to lie,
While I see divine compassion
Beaming in His languid eye.

4 Here it is I find my Heaven
While upon the Lamb I gaze;
Love I much?—I've much forgiven—
I'm a miracle of grace.

5 Love and grief my heart dividing,
With my tears His feet I'll bathe;
Constant still in faith abiding,
Life deriving from His death.
W. Shirley.

690 Let us for ever praise Him
Who heard us when we cried,
O come and praise our Saviour
It was for us He died.

2 He found us when we sought Him,
He gave our souls release,
He bore away our sorrows,
He is His people's peace.

3 Upon the Cross in torment
He set His people free,
From fear and condemnation
For all eternity.

4 He knows the secret sadness
    Which seems too great to bear,
    The doubts and the resentments
    Which we are loath to share.

5 He died that we might lose them,
    It was His gift of love;
    O praise our dear Redeemer
    All other Names above!

6 O praise Him for His goodness!
    He understands our need;
    He is the Lord who made us;
    His peace is peace indeed.

David Porter.

691 Lord Jesus Christ,
    You have come to us,
    You are one with us,
    Mary's son.
    Cleansing our souls from all their sin,
    Pouring Your love and goodness in,
    Jesus our love for You we sing,
    Living Lord.

2 Lord Jesus Christ,
    Now and every day
    Teach us how to pray,
    Son of God.
    You have commanded us to do
    This in remembrance, Lord, of You;
    Into our lives Your power breaks
      through,
    Living Lord.

3 Lord Jesus Christ,
    You have come to us,
    Born as one of us,
    Mary's Son.
    Led out to die on Calvary,
    Risen from death to set us free,
    Living Lord Jesus, help us see
    You are Lord.

4 Lord Jesus Christ,
    I would come to You,
    Live my life for You,
    Son of God.
    All Your commands I know are true,
    Your many gifts will make me new,
    Into my life Your power breaks
      through,
    Living Lord.

Patrick Appleford.

692 Be known to us in breaking bread,
    But do not then depart;
    Saviour, abide with us, and spread
    Thy table in our heart.

2 There sup with us in love divine;
    Thy body and Thy blood,
    That living bread, that Heavenly wine,
    Be our immortal food.

3 We would not live by bread alone,
    But by Thy Word of grace,
    In strength of which we travel on
    To our abiding place.

James Montgomery.

693 According to Thy gracious Word,
    In meek humility,
    This will I do, my dying Lord:
    I will remember Thee.

2 Thy body, broken for my sake,
    My bread from Heaven shall be;
    Thy testamental cup I take,
    And thus remember Thee.

3 Gethsemane can I forget?
    Or there Thy conflict see,
    Thine agony and bloody sweat,
    And not remember Thee?

4 When to the Cross I turn mine eyes,
    And rest on Calvary,
    O Lamb of God, my sacrifice,
    I must remember Thee.

5 Remember Thee, and all Thy pains,
    And all Thy love to me;
    Yea, while a breath, a pulse remains,
    Will I remember Thee.

6 And when these failing lips grow
      dumb,
    And mind and memory flee,
    When Thou shalt in Thy kingdom
      come
    Then, Lord, remember me.

James Montgomery.

694 I hear the words of love,
    I gaze upon the blood,
    I see the mighty Sacrifice,
    And I have peace with God.

2 'Tis everlasting peace!
   Sure as Jehovah's Name;
   'Tis stable as His steadfast throne,
   For evermore the same.

3 The clouds may go and come,
   And storms may sweep my sky—
   This blood-sealed friendship changes
      not;
   The Cross is ever nigh.

4 My love is oft-times low,
   My joy still ebbs and flows;
   But peace with Him remains the
      same,
   No change Jehovah knows.

5 I change, He changes not,
   The Christ can never die;
   His love, not mine, the resting place,
   His truth, not mine, the tie.

Horatius Bonar.

695 Fairest of all the earth beside,
   Chiefest of all unto Thy bride,
   Fulness divine in Thee I see,
   Wonderful Man of Calvary.

   That Man of Calvary
   Has won my heart from me,
   And died to set me free,
   Blest Man of Calvary!

2 Granting the sinner life and peace,
   Granting the captive sweet release,
   Shedding His blood to make us free,
   Merciful Man of Calvary!

3 Giving the gifts obtained for men,
   Pouring out love beyond our ken,
   Giving us spotless purity,
   Bountiful Man of Calvary!

4 Comfort of all my earthly way,
   Jesus, I'll meet Thee some sweet day;
   Centre of glory Thee I'll see,
   Wonderful Man of Calvary!

M. P. Ferguson.

696 Father of all, with praise
   And thanks to You we come,
   For though our sins had driven us far
   Your love has brought us home.

2 Your Son has given us grace
   And changed our sorry state;
   His death and life provide the key
   To open glory's gate.

3 This bread and wine we share:
   Christ's body we receive,
   We drink His cup and humbly seek
   His risen life to live.

4 May Christ's own Spirit flood
   The darkened world with light,
   And keep us strong in Christian hope,
   And make our witness bright.

5 So shall the earth be free—
   The earth to which Christ came—
   And all Your children join to bless
   Your great and holy Name.

David Mowbray.

697 Here, O my Lord, I see Thee face
      to face;
   Here would I touch and handle things
      unseen;
   Here grasp with firmer hand th'eternal
      grace,
   And all my weariness upon Thee lean.

2 Here would I feed upon the Bread of
      God;
   Here drink with Thee the royal Wine
      of Heaven;
   Here would I lay aside each earthly
      load,
   Here taste afresh the calm of sin
      forgiven.

3 This is the hour of banquet and of
      song,
   This is the Heavenly table spread for
      me:
   Here let me feast and, feasting still
      prolong
   The brief, bright hour of fellowship
      with Thee.

4 Too soon we rise; the symbols
      disappear;
   The feast, though not the love, is past
      and gone;
   The bread and wine remove; but Thou
      art here
   Nearer than ever; still my Shield and
      Sun.

5 Mine is the sin, but Thine the
　righteousness;
Mine is the guilt, but Thine the
　cleansing blood:
Here is my robe, my refuge, and my
　peace—
Thy blood, Thy righteousness, O
　Lord, my God.

6 Feast after feast thus comes, and
　passes by;
Yet, passing, points to the glad Feast
　above,
Giving sweet foretaste of the festal
　joy,
The Lamb's great Bridal Feast of bliss
　and love.

H. Bonar.

698 'Till He come!' Oh, let the words
　　　Linger on the trembling chords;
Let the 'little while' between
In their golden light be seen;
Let us think how Heaven and home
Lie beyond that 'Till He come!'

2 When the weary ones we love
Enter on their rest above—
Seems the earth so poor and vast?—
All our life-joy overcast?
Hush! be every murmur dumb;
It is only 'Till He come!'

3 Clouds and conflicts round us press;
Would we have one sorrow less?
All the sharpness of the Cross,
All that tells the world is loss—
Death, and darkness, and the tomb—
Only whisper 'Till He come!'

4 See, the feast of love is spread,
Drink the wine and break the bread—
Sweet memorials—till the Lord
Call us round His Heavenly board;
Some from earth, from glory some,
Severed only 'Till He come!'

E. H. Bickersteth.

699 O Christ, what burdens bowed
　　　Thy head!
Our load was laid on Thee;

Thou stoodest in the sinner's stead,
Didst bear all ill for me.
A Victim led, Thy blood was shed,
Now there's no load for me.

2 Death and the curse were in our cup,
O Christ, 'twas full for Thee!
But Thou hast drained the last dark
　drop,
'Tis empty now for me.
That bitter cup, love drank it up,
Now blessing's draught for me.

3 The tempest's awful voice was heard,
O Christ, it broke on Thee!
Thy open bosom was my ward,
It braved the storm for me:
Thy form was scarred, Thy visage
　marred;
Now cloudless peace for me.

4 For me, Lord Jesus, Thou hast died,
And I have died in Thee:
Thou'rt risen—my bands are all
　untied;
And now Thou liv'st in me;
When purified, made white and tried,
Thy glory then for me!

Anne Ross Cousin.

700 Jesus, Thou joy of loving hearts,
　　　Thou fount of life, Thou light of
　　　men!
From the best bliss that earth imparts
We turn unfilled to Thee again.

2 Thy truth unchanged hath ever stood,
Thou savest those that on Thee call;
To them that seek Thee, Thou art
　good,
To them that find Thee, All in all!

3 We taste Thee, O Thou living bread,
And long to feast upon Thee still;
We drink of Thee, the fountain-head,
And thirst our souls from Thee to fill.

4 Our restless spirits yearn for Thee,
Where'er our changeful lot is cast;
Glad when Thy gracious smile we see,
Blest when our faith can hold Thee
　fast.

5 O Jesus, ever with us stay!
Make all our moments calm and
bright;
Chase the dark night of sin away;
Shed o'er the world Thy holy light.

Bernard of Clairvaux.

701 I am amazed when I think of God's
love,
So wonderful, matchless and free;
The love that could see, from eternity,
Something worth saving in sinners
like me.

I am amazed that the Saviour should die
For sinners like me and like you;
That we may be saved by the work He has
done
And not by the works that we do.
But it's true, it's true,
This wonderful story so old, but so new.
I am amazed that the Saviour should die
For sinners like me and like you.

2 I am amazed when I think of God's
grace,
O word with Heavenly sound!
For sinners condemned, what way
could be found?
More than sufficient God's grace did
abound.

3 I am amazed when I think of God's
Son,
From glory to Calvary He came
To bear in my place sin's darkness and
shame;
O what a Saviour, and Jesus His
Name!

Sidney E. Cox.

702 By Christ redeemed, in Christ
restored,
We keep the memory adored,
And show the death of our dear Lord
Until He come.

2 His body broken in our stead
Is seen in this memorial bread,
And so our feeble love is fed
Until He come.

3 The drops of His dread agony,
His life-blood shed for us, we see,
The wine shall tell the mystery
Until He come.

4 And thus that dark betrayal-night
With the last advent we unite,
By one blest chain of loving rite,
Until He come.

5 Until the trump of God be heard,
Until the ancient graves be stirred,
And with the great commanding word
The Lord shall come.

6 O blessèd hope! with this elate,
Let not our hearts be desolate,
But, strong in faith, in patience wait
Until He come.

George Rawson.

FELLOWSHIP OF SAINTS

703 Lord, in this blest and hallowed
hour
Reveal Thy presence and Thy power;
Show to my faith Thy hands and side,
My Lord and God, the Crucified.

2 Fain would I find a calm retreat
From vain distractions near Thy feet;
And, borne above all earthly care,
Be joyful in Thy house of prayer.

3 Or let me through the opening skies
Catch one bright glimpse of Paradise
And realize, with raptured awe,
The vision dying Stephen saw.

4 But if unworthy of such joy,
Still shall Thy love my heart employ:
For of Thy favoured children's fare
'Twere bliss the very crumbs to share.

5 Yet never can my soul be fed
With less than Thee, the living Bread;
Thyself unto my soul impart,
And with Thy presence fill my heart.

Josiah Conder.

704 Abba, Father! we approach Thee
In our Saviour's precious Name;
We, Thy children, here assembling,
Access to Thy presence claim,
From our sin His blood hath washed
us;
'Tis through Him our souls draw near;
And Thy Spirit, too, hath taught us,
'Abba, Father!' name so dear.

2 Once as prodigals we wandered
In our folly far from Thee!
But Thy grace, o'er sin abounding,
Rescued us from misery.
Thou Thy prodigals hast pardoned,
Loved us with a Father's love;
Welcomed us with joy o'erflowing,
E'en to dwell with Thee above.

3 Clothed in garments of salvation,
At Thy table is our place;
We rejoice, and Thou rejoicest,
In the riches of Thy grace.
'It is meet,' we hear Thee saying,
'We should merry be and glad;
I have found My once lost children,
Now they live who once were dead.'

4 Abba, Father! all adore Thee,
All rejoice in Heaven above;
While in us they learn the wonders
Of Thy wisdom, power, and love.
Soon, before Thy throne assembled,
All Thy children shall proclaim,
'Glory, everlasting glory,
Be to God and to the Lamb!'

705 Blest be the tie that binds
Our hearts in Christian love;
The fellowship of kindred minds
Is like to that above.

2 Before our Father's throne,
We pour our ardent prayers;
Our fears, our hopes, our aims are
one,
Our comforts and our cares.

3 We share our mutual woes;
Our mutual burdens bear;
And often for each other flows
The sympathizing tear.

4 When we asunder part,
It gives us inward pain:
But we shall still be joined in heart
And hope to meet again.

5 This glorious hope revives
Our courage by the way,
While each in expectation lives,
And longs to see the day.

6 From sorrow, toil and pain,
And sin we shall be free;
And perfect love and friendship reign
Through all eternity.

John Fawcett.

706 Come, ye that love the Lord,
And let your joys be known;
Join in a song with sweet accord,
And thus surround the throne.

We're marching to Zion,
Beautiful, beautiful Zion:
We're marching upward to Zion,
The beautiful city of God.

2 Let those refuse to sing
Who never knew our God:
But children of the Heavenly King
Shall speak their joys abroad.

3 The hill of Zion yields
A thousand sacred sweets;
Before we reach the Heavenly fields
Or walk the golden streets.

4 Then let our songs abound,
And every tear be dry;
We're marching through Immanuel's
ground
To fairer worlds on high.

Isaac Watts.

707 Behold, what love, what bound-
less love,
The Father hath bestowed
On sinners lost, that we should be
Now called the sons of God!

Behold, what manner of love! . . .
What manner of love the Father hath
  bestowed upon us,
That we, that we should be called, . . .
Should be called the sons of God.

2 No longer far from Him, but now
By 'precious blood' made nigh;
Accepted in the 'Well-beloved'
Near to God's heart we lie.

3 What we in glory soon shall be,
It doth not yet appear;
But when our precious Lord we see,
We shall His image bear.

4 With such a blessèd hope in view,
We would more holy be,
More like our risen, glorious Lord,
Whose face we soon shall see.

M. S. Sullivan.

708 Come, brethren dear, that know
  the Lord,
Who taste the sweets of Jesus' Word,
In Jesus' ways go on;
Our poverty and trials here
Will only make us richer there,
When we arrive at home.

2 We feel that Heaven is now begun,
It issues from the eternal throne,
From Jesus' throne on high;
It comes in floods we can't contain,
We drink, and drink, and drink again,
And yet we still are dry.

3 But when to that bright world we
  come
And all surround the glorious throne,
We'll drink a full supply;
Jesus will lead the ransomed forth
To living streams of richest worth
That never will run dry.

4 O then we'll shine, and shout, and
  sing,
And make the Heavenly arches ring,
When all the saints get home;
Come on, come on, my brethren dear,
We soon shall meet together there,
For Jesus bids you come.

5 Amen! Amen! my soul replies,
I'm bound to meet Him in the skies,
And claim a mansion there;
Now here's my heart, and here's my
  hand,
To meet you in the Heavenly land,
Where we shall part no more.

MARRIAGE

709 O happy home where Thou art
  loved the dearest,
Thou loving Friend, and Saviour of
  our race,
And where among the guests there
  never cometh
One who can hold such high and
  honoured place!

2 O happy home where two in heart
  united
In holy faith and blessèd hope are
  one,
Whom death a little while alone
  divideth,
And cannot end the happiness begun!

3 O happy home whose little ones are
  given
Early to Thee, in humble faith and
  prayer,
To Thee, their Friend, Who from the
  heights of Heaven
Guides them, and guards with more
  than mother's care!

4 O happy home where each one serves
  Thee, lowly,
Whatever his appointed work may be,
Till every common task seems great
  and holy
When it is done, O Lord, as unto
  Thee!

5 O happy home where Thou art not
  forgotten
When joy is overflowing, full and free;
O happy home where every wounded
  spirit
Is brought, Physician, Comforter, to
  Thee.

6 Until at last, when earth's day's work
   is ended,
  All meet Thee in the blessèd home
   above
  From whence Thou camest, where
   Thou hast ascended,
  Thy everlasting home of peace and
   love!

Carl Johann Philipp Spitta.
trs. Sarah Laurie Findlater.

710   The voice that breathed o'er Eden,
    That earliest wedding-day,
  The primal marriage blessing,
  It hath not passed away.

2 Still in the pure espousal
  Of Christian man and maid,
  The Holy Three are with us,
  The threefold grace is said,

3 For dower of blessèd children,
  For love and faith's sweet sake,
  For high mysterious union
  Which nought on earth may break.

4 Be present, Heavenly Father,
  To give away this bride,
  As Eve Thou gav'st to Adam
  Out of his own pierced side.

5 Be present, gracious Saviour,
  To join their loving hands,
  As Thou didst bind two natures
  In Thine eternal bands.

6 Be present, Holy Spirit,
  To bless them as they kneel,
  As Thou for Christ the Bridegroom
  The Heavenly spouse dost seal.

7 O spread Thy pure wings o'er them!
  Let no ill power find place,
  When onward through life's journey
  The hallowed path they trace,

8 To cast their crowns before Thee,
  In perfect sacrifice,
  Till to the home of gladness
  With Christ's own bride they rise.

John Keble.

711   O Father, all-creating,
    Whose wisdom and whose power
  First bound two lives together
  In Eden's primal hour;
  Today to these Thy children
  Thine earliest gift renew;
  A home by Thee made blessèd,
  A love by Thee kept true.

2 O Saviour, Guest most bounteous
  Of old in Galilee,
  Vouchsafe today Thy presence
  With these who wait on Thee;
  Their store of earthly gladness
  Transform to Heavenly wine,
  And teach them, in the tasting,
  To know the gift is Thine.

3 O Spirit of the Father
  Breathe on them from above,
  So searching in Thy pureness,
  So tender in Thy love;
  That guarded by Thy presence,
  From sin and strife kept free,
  Their lives may own Thy guidance,
  Their hearts be ruled by Thee.

4 Except Thou built it, Father,
  The house is built in vain;
  Except Thou, Lord, sustain it,
  The joy will turn to pain:
  But nought can break the union
  Of hearts in Thee made one,
  And love which Thou hast hallowed
  Is endless love begun.

John Ellerton.

712   O perfect Love, all human thought
    transcending,
  Lowly we kneel in prayer before Thy
   throne,
  That theirs may be the love which
   knows no ending
  Whom Thou for evermore dost join in
   one.

2 O perfect Life, be Thou their full
   assurance
  Of tender charity and steadfast faith,
  Of patient hope, and quiet brave
   endurance,
  With childlike trust that fears nor pain
   nor death.

3 Grant them the joy which brightens
  earthly sorrow;
  Grant them the peace which calms all
  earthly strife,
  And to life's day the glorious
  unknown morrow
  That dawns upon eternal love and life.
  Dorothy F. Gurney.

INFANT DEDICATION AND CHILDREN

713 When mothers of Salem
  Their children brought to Jesus,
  The stern disciples drove them back
  And bade them depart:
  But Jesus saw them ere they fled,
  And sweetly smiled and kindly said,
  'Suffer little children to come unto
  Me.'

2 For I will receive them,
  And fold them in My bosom;
  I'll be a Shepherd to those lambs,
  Oh, drive them not away!
  For if their hearts to Me they give,
  They shall with Me in glory live,
  'Suffer little children to come unto
  Me.'

3 How kind was our Saviour
  To bid those children welcome!
  But there are many thousands
  Who have never heard His Name;
  The Bible they have never read;
  They know not that the Saviour said,
  'Suffer little children to come unto
  Me.'

4 Oh! soon may the heathen
  Of every tribe and nation
  Fulfil Thy blessèd Word,
  And cast their idols all away;
  Oh! shine upon them from above,
  And show Thyself a God of love,
  Teach the little children to come unto
  Thee.
  W. M. Hutchings.

714 See Israel's gentle Shepherd
  stand
  With all-engaging charms;
  Hark! how He calls the tender lambs,
  And folds them in His arms.

2 Permit them to approach, He cries,
  Nor scorn their humble name!
  For 'twas to bless such souls as these
  The Lord of angels came.

3 We bring them, Lord, in thankful
  hands,
  And yield them up to Thee;
  Joyful that we ourselves are Thine,
  Thine let our children be.
  Philip Doddridge.

715 Saviour, like a shepherd lead us;
  Much we need Thy tender care;
  In Thy pleasant pastures feed us,
  For our use Thy folds prepare:
  Blessèd Jesus,
  Thou hast bought us, Thine we are.

2 We are Thine, do Thou befriend us;
  Be the Guardian of our way;
  Keep Thy flock, from sin defend us,
  Seek us when we go astray:
  Blessèd Jesus,
  Hear us when we praise and pray.

3 Thou hast promised to receive us,
  Poor and sinful though we be;
  Thou hast mercy to relieve us,
  Grace to cleanse, and make us free:
  Blessèd Jesus,
  Early let us turn to Thee.

4 Early let us seek Thy favour;
  Early let us do Thy will;
  Gracious Lord, our only Saviour,
  With Thyself our bosoms fill:
  Blessèd Jesus,
  Thou hast loved us—love us still.
  Dorothy A. Thrupp.

716 Thy Name, O Lord, we bless,
  Our thankful hearts adore;
  Thy lavish gifts confess,
  Of rich and bounteous store.

2 To us Thou hast made known
Heaven's pure felicity;
A gracious gift we own
Of sweet simplicity.

3 What shall we render Thee,
Or how Thy love repay?
This very gift shall be
Our glad response today.

4 O Shepherd heart and kind,
Thy tender lamb now bless;
Safe kept by Thee to find
The path of righteousness.

5 Thy grace we seek, O Lord,
This life to guard and teach
According to Thy Word,
By prayerful act and speech.

6 Our charge we undertake,
Humbly Thine aid implore;
Vow Thee, for Thy dear sake,
Our all for evermore.

L. F. W. Woodford.

717 I am so glad that our Father in
Heaven
Tells of His love in the Book He has
given;
Wonderful things in the Bible I see;
This is the dearest, that Jesus loves
me.

I am so glad that Jesus loves me,
Jesus loves me, Jesus loves me,
I am so glad that Jesus loves me,
Jesus loves even me.

2 Jesus loves me and I know I love Him;
Love brought Him down my lost soul
to redeem;
Yes, it was love made Him die on the
Tree:
Oh, I am certain that Jesus loves me.

3 In this assurance I find sweetest rest,
Trusting in Jesus I know I am blest;
Satan dismayed from my soul doth
now flee
When I just tell him that Jesus loves
me.

4 Oh, if there's only one song I can sing,
When in His beauty I see the great
King,
This shall my song in eternity be,
'Oh, what a wonder that Jesus loves
me!'

5 If one should ask of me, how can I
tell?
Glory to Jesus, I know very well!
God's Holy Spirit with mine doth
agree,
Constantly witnessing—Jesus loves
me.

P. P. Bliss.

718 Jesus bids us shine
With a clear, pure light,
Like a little candle
Burning in the night:
In this world is darkness,
So we must shine,
You in your small corner
And I in mine.

2 Jesus bids us shine
First of all for Him;
Well He sees and knows it
If our light is dim;
He looks down from Heaven
To see us shine,
You in your small corner
And I in mine.

3 Jesus bids us shine,
Then for all around
Many kinds of darkness
In this world abound—
Sin and want and sorrow—
So we must shine,
You in your small corner
And I in mine.

Susan Warner.

719 Yield not to temptation,
For yielding is sin,
Each victory will help you
Some other to win;
Fight manfully onward,
Dark passions subdue,
Look ever to Jesus,
He'll carry you through.

Ask the Saviour to help you,
Comfort, strengthen and keep you,
He is willing to aid you,
He will carry you through.

2 Shun evil companions,
Bad language disdain,
God's Name hold in reverence,
Nor take it in vain;
Be thoughtful and earnest,
Kind hearted and true,
Look ever to Jesus,
He'll carry you through.

3 To him that o'ercometh
God giveth a crown;
Through faith we shall conquer,
Though often cast down;
He Who is our Saviour
Our strength will renew,
Look ever to Jesus,
He'll carry you through.

H. R. Palmer.

720 God make my life a little light
Within the world to glow;
A little flame that burneth bright
Wherever I may go.

2 God make my life a little flower
That giveth joy to all;
Content to bloom in native bower
Although the place be small.

3 God make my life a little song
That comforteth the sad;
That helpeth others to be strong,
And makes the singer glad.

4 God make my life a little staff
Whereon the weak may rest;
That so what health and strength I
have,
May serve my neighbours best.

5 God make my life a little hymn
Of tenderness and praise,
Of faith that never waxeth dim,
In all His wondrous ways.

M. Betham-Edwards.

721 Mighty army of the young
Lift the voice of cheerful song,
Send the welcome word along,
Jesus lives!
Once He died for you and me,
Bore our sins upon the Tree,
Now He lives to make us free,
Jesus lives!

Wait not till the shadows lengthen till you
older grow,
Rally now and sing for Jesus everywhere you
go;
Lift your joyful voices high, ringing clear
through earth and sky,
Let the blessèd tidings fly, Jesus lives!

2 Tongues of children light and free,
Tongues of youth all full of glee,
Sing to all on land and sea,
Jesus lives!
Light for you and all mankind,
Sight for all by sin made blind,
Life in Jesus all may find,
Jesus lives!

3 Jesus lives, O blessèd words!
King of kings, and Lord of lords!
Lift the Cross and sheathe the
swords,
Jesus lives!
See, He breaks the prison wall,
Throws aside the dreadful pall,
Conquers death at once for all,
Jesus lives!

John R. Colgan.

722 Jesus loves the little children,
Once He took them on His knee,
Gently put His arms around them,
Saying, 'Let them come to Me!'

2 Oh! He loves to see them kneeling,
And with hands together pray;
Loves to hear them call Him Jesus,
If they mean the words they say.

3 If they trust Him as their Saviour
He will wash their sins away;
He will take their hand and lead them
All along the narrow way.

4 He would have them love each other,
And be truthful, meek, and mild,
Doing as their parents bid them,
As He did when once a Child.

The Church of God

723 Children of Jerusalem
Sang the praise of Jesu's name:
Children, too, of modern days,
Join to sing the Saviour's praise.

Hark, hark, hark! while infant voices sing,
Hark, hark, hark! while infant voices sing
Loud hosannas, loud hosannas,
Loud hosannas to our King.

2 We are taught to love the Lord,
We are taught to read His Word,
We are taught the way to Heaven:
Praise for all to God be given.

3 Parents, teachers, old and young,
All unite to swell the song;
Higher and yet higher rise,
Till hosannas reach the skies.

John Henley.

724 There's a Friend for little children
Above the bright blue sky,
A Friend that never changes,
Whose love will never die:
Unlike our friends by nature,
Who change with changing years,
This Friend is always worthy
The precious Name He bears.

2 There's a rest for little children
Above the bright blue sky
Who love the blessèd Saviour,
And to His Father cry:
A rest from every trouble,
From sin and danger free;
There every little pilgrim
Shall rest eternally.

3 There's a home for little children
Above the bright blue sky,
Where Jesus reigns in glory,
A home of peace and joy:
No home on earth is like it,
Nor can with it compare,
For every one is happy,
Nor can be happier there.

4 There's a crown for little children
Above the bright blue sky,
And all who look to Jesus
Shall wear it by and by;

A crown of brightest glory,
Which He shall sure bestow
On all who love the Saviour,
And walk with Him below.

5 There's a song for little children
Above the bright blue sky,
And a harp of sweetest music
For their hymn of victory:
And all above is pleasure,
And found in Christ alone;
O come, dear little children,
That all may be your own!

Albert Midlane

725 The world looks very beautiful
And full of joy to me;
The sun shines out in glory
On everything I see:
I know I shall be happy
While in the world I stay,
For I will follow Jesus
All the way.

For I will follow Jesus,
For I will follow Jesus,
For I will follow Jesus
All the way.

2 I'm but a youthful pilgrim,
My journey's just begun;
They say I'll meet with sorrow
Before my journey's done:
The world is full of trouble,
And trials, too, they say;
But I will follow Jesus
All the way.

3 Then, like a little pilgrim,
Whatever I may meet,
I'll take it, joy or sorrow,
And lay at Jesus' feet:
He'll comfort me in trouble,
He'll wipe my tears away;
With joy I'll follow Jesus
All the way.

4 Then trials cannot vex me,
And pain I need not fear,
For when I'm close by Jesus
Grief cannot come too near:

Not even death can harm me,
When death I meet one day;
To Heaven I'll follow Jesus
All the way.

Anna B. Warner.

726 I love to hear the story
    Which angel voices tell,
How once the King of Glory
Came down on earth to dwell:
I am both weak and sinful,
But this I surely know,
The Lord came down to save me
Because He loved me so.

2 I'm glad my blessèd Saviour
Was once a child like me,
To show how pure and holy
His little ones might be;
And if I try to follow
His footsteps here below,
He never will forget me
Because He loved me so.

3 To sing His love and mercy
My sweetest songs I'll raise,
And though I cannot see Him,
I know He hears my praise;
For He has kindly promised
That I shall surely go
To sing among His angels,
Because He loved me so.

Emily H. Miller.

727 All things bright and beautiful,
    All creatures great and small,
All things wise and wonderful,
The Lord God made them all.

2 Each little flower that opens,
Each little bird that sings,
He made their glowing colours,
He made their tiny wings.

All things bright and beautiful,
All creatures great and small,
All things wise and wonderful,
The Lord God made them all.

The purple-headed mountain,
The river running by,
The sunset, and the morning
That brightens up the sky.

4 The cold wind in the winter,
The pleasant summer sun,
The ripe fruits in the garden,
He made them every one.

5 He gave us eyes to see them,
And lips that we might tell
How great is God Almighty,
Who has done all things well.

Mrs. C. F. Alexander.

728 It is a thing most wonderful,
    Almost too wonderful to be,
That God's own Son should come
    from Heaven
And die to save a child like me.

2 And yet I know that it is true:
He came to this poor world below,
And wept and toiled and mourned
    and died,
Only because He loved us so.

3 I cannot tell how He could love
A child so weak and full of sin;
His love must be most wonderful
If He could die my love to win.

4 It is most wonderful to know
His love for me so free and sure;
But 'tis more wonderful to see
My love for Him so faint and poor.

5 And yet I want to love Thee, Lord:
Oh, light the flame within my heart,
And I will love Thee more and more
Until I see Thee as Thou art.

W. W. How.

729 Safe in the arms of Jesus,
    Safe on His gentle breast,
There, by His love o'ershaded,
Sweetly my soul shall rest.
Hark! 'tis the voice of angels
Borne in a song to me
Over the fields of glory,
Over the jasper sea.

Safe in the arms of Jesus,
Safe on His gentle breast,
There, by His love o'ershaded,
Sweetly my soul shall rest.

2 Safe in the arms of Jesus,
Safe from corroding care,
Safe from the world's temptations,
Sin cannot harm me there.
Free from the blight of sorrow,
Free from my doubts and fears;
Only a few more trials,
Only a few more tears.

3 Jesus, my heart's dear refuge,
Jesus has died for me;
Firm on the Rock of Ages
Ever my trust shall be.
Here let me wait with patience,
Wait till the night is o'er;
Wait till I see the morning
Break on the golden shore.

Fanny J. Crosby.

730 Lord Jesus, bless this baby dear
Whom we present before Thee
here,
Do Thou Thy grace to him/her impart
And write Thy Name upon his/her
heart,
And write Thy Name upon his/her
heart.

William M. Page.

731 When He cometh, when He
cometh
To make up His jewels,
All His jewels, precious jewels,
His loved and His own.

Like the stars of the morning
His bright crown adorning,
They shall shine in their beauty,
Bright gems for His crown.

2 He will gather, He will gather
Bright gems for His Kingdom;
All the blood-bought, all the holy,
His loved and His own.

3 Ransomed sinners, ransomed sinners
Who have trusted in Jesus
Are the jewels, precious jewels,
His loved and His own.

William O. Cushing.

DIVINE HEALING

732 She only touched the hem of His
garment
As to His side she stole,
Amid the crowd that gathered around
Him,
And straightway she was whole.

Oh, touch the hem of His garment
And thou, too, shalt be free;
His saving power this very hour
Shall give new life to thee.

2 She came in fear and trembling before
Him,
She knew her Lord had come;
She felt that from Him virtue had
healed her;
The mighty deed was done.

3 He turned with, 'Daughter, be of
good comfort,
Thy faith hath made thee whole.'
And peace that passeth all under-
standing
With gladness filled her soul.

George F. Root.

733 Almighty Father, great must be
Your power from all eternity;
How great your love in Christ made
known
To those by suffering weighed down.

2 Christ healed the sick, the deaf, the
blind,
Brought reason to the splintered
mind.
He gave the peace of Heaven to men
And set them on their feet again.

3 Yet may these things for us be so,
With Galilee those years ago?
Is life and all its fullness still
For us the Heavenly Father's will?

4 Indeed! the Christ who wrought such
things
Is Lord of lords and King of kings:
Today as yesterday the same
To those who gather in His Name.

5 Through laying on of hands and prayer
The sick may in Christ's wholeness share,
And others, nursed to health again,
Renew their strength and lose their pain.

6 Almighty Father, let us see
In Christ man has the victory!
Help us to find, in life and death,
Your everlasting arms beneath.

David Mowbray.

734 Thine arm, O Lord, in days of old
Was strong to heal and save;
It triumphed o'er disease and death,
O'er darkness and the grave.
To Thee they went, the blind, the dumb,
The palsied and the lame,
The leper with his tainted life,
The sick with fevered frame.

2 And lo! Thy touch brought life and health,
Gave speech, and strength, and sight;
And youth renewed, and frenzy calmed,
Owned Thee, the Lord of light.
And now, O Lord, be near to bless,
Almighty as of yore,
In crowded street, by restless couch,
As by Gennesaret's shore.

3 Be Thou our great Deliverer still,
Thou Lord of life and death;
Restore and quicken, soothe and bless,
With Thine Almighty breath.
To hands that work, and eyes that see,
Give wisdom's Heavenly lore,
That whole and sick and weak and strong
May praise Thee evermore.

E. H. Plumptre.

735 He healeth me, O blessèd truth,
His mighty Word renews my youth,

By His own power from sickness free,
My precious Saviour healeth me.

He healeth me, He healeth me,
By His own Word He healeth me;
His faithful witness I would be
For by His Word He healeth me.

2 Sometimes through testing times I go,
Dark seems the way, and full of woe;
But in the furnace though I be
My great Physician healeth me.

3 Lord, I would spread this truth abroad,
The mighty power of Thy Word;
It's just the same, the blind now see,
And demons at Thy presence flee.

4 For sin and sickness doth depart
When Thou dost reign within the heart;
And I from all the curse am free
Since Christ, my Saviour, healeth me.

736 Fear not, little flock—from the Cross to the Throne,
From death into life He went for His own;
All power in earth, all power above
Is given to Him for the flock of His love.

Only believe, only believe,
All things are possible, only believe.

2 Fear not, little flock, He goeth ahead,
Your Shepherd selecteth the path you must tread;
The waters of Marah He'll sweeten for thee,
He drank all the bitter in Gethsemane.

3 Fear not, little flock, whatever your lot,
He enters all rooms, 'the doors being shut',
He never forsakes, He never is gone,
So count on His presence in darkness and dawn.

Paul Rader.

737 Shackled by a heavy burden,
'Neath a load of guilt and shame,
Then the hand of Jesus touched me
And now I am no longer the same.

> He touched me, Oh, He touched me,
> And oh, the joy that floods my soul;
> Something happened and now I know
> He touched me and made me whole.

2 Since I met this blessèd Saviour;
Since He cleansed and made me
whole
I will never cease to praise Him,
I'll shout it while eternity rolls.

William J. Gaither.

738 At even, ere the sun was set,
The sick, O Lord, around Thee
lay;
O in what divers pains they met!
O with what joy they went away!

2 Once more 'tis eventide and we,
Oppressed with various ills, draw
near;
What if Thy form we cannot see,
We know and feel that Thou art here.

3 O Saviour Christ, our woes dispel:
For some are sick, and some are sad,
And some have never loved Thee
well,
And some have lost the love they had.

4 And some are pressed with worldly
care,
And some are tried with sinful doubt,
And some such grievous passions
tear
That only Thou canst cast them out.

5 And some have found the world is
vain,
Yet from the world they break not
free;
And some have friends who give them
pain,
Yet have not sought a friend in Thee.

6 O Saviour Christ, Thou too art Man;
Thou hast been troubled, tempted
tried;

Thy kind but searching glance can
scan
The very wounds that shame would
hide!

7 Thy touch has still its ancient power;
No word from Thee can fruitless fall;
Hear in this solemn evening hour,
And in Thy mercy heal us all.

H. Twells.

739 When to our world the Saviour
came
The sick and helpless heard his Name,
And in their weakness longed to see
The healing Christ of Galilee.

2 That good Physician! Night and day
The people thronged about His way;
And wonder ran from soul to soul—
'The touch of Christ has made us
whole.'

3 His praises then were heard and sung
By opened ears and loosened tongue,
While lightened eyes could see and
know
The healing Christ of long ago.

4 Of long ago—yet living still,
Who died for us on Calvary's hill;
Who triumphed over Cross and grave,
His healing hands stretched forth to
save.

5 Those wounded hands are still the
same,
And all who serve that saving Name
May share today in Jesus' plan—
The healing Christ of everyman.

6 Then grant us, Lord, in this our day
To hear the prayers the helpless pray;
Give to us hearts their pain to share,
Make of us hands to tend and care.

7 Make us Your hands! For Christ to
live,
In prayer and service, swift to give;
Till all the world rejoice to find
The healing Christ of all mankind.

Timothy Dudley-Smith.

WORLD MISSIONS

740 The whole wide world for Jesus—
This shall our watchword be
Upon the highest mountain,
Down by the widest sea—
The whole wide world for Jesus!
To Him all men shall bow
In city or in prairie—
The world for Jesus now!

> The whole wide world, the whole wide
> world—
> Proclaim the Gospel tidings through the whole
> wide world;
> Lift up the Cross for Jesus, His banner be
> unfurled—
> Till every tongue confess Him through the
> whole wide world.

2 The whole wide world for Jesus
Inspires us with the thought
That every son of Adam
Should by His blood be bought;
The whole wide world for Jesus!
O faint not by the way!
The Cross shall surely conquer
In this our glorious day.

3 The whole wide world for Jesus—
The marching order sound—
Go ye and preach the Gospel
Wherever man is found,
The whole wide world for Jesus!
Our banner is unfurled—
We battle now for Jesus,
And faith demands the world!

Catherine Johnson.

741 We have heard a joyful sound,
Jesus saves;
Spread the gladness all around,
Jesus saves;
Bear the news to every land,
Climb the steeps and cross the waves,
Onward, 'tis our Lord's command,
Jesus saves.

2 Waft it on the rolling tide,
Jesus saves;
Tell to sinners far and wide,
Jesus saves;
Sing, ye islands of the sea,
Echo back, ye ocean caves,
Earth shall keep her jubilee,
Jesus saves.

3 Sing above the battle's strife,
Jesus saves;
By His death and endless life,
Jesus saves;
Sing it softly through the gloom,
When the heart for mercy craves,
Sing in triumph o'er the tomb,
Jesus saves.

4 Give the winds a mighty voice,
Jesus saves;
Let the nations now rejoice,
Jesus saves;
Shout salvation full and free,
Highest hills and deepest caves,
This our song of victory,
Jesus saves.

Priscilla J. Owens.

742 From Greenland's icy mountains,
From India's coral strand,
Where Afric's sunny fountains
Roll down their golden sand,
From many an ancient river,
From many a palmy plain,
They call us to deliver
Their land from error's chain.

2 What though the spicy breezes
Blow o'er Sri Lanka's isle,
Though every prospect pleases
And only man is vile;
In vain with lavish kindness
The gifts of God are strown,
The heathen in his blindness
Bows down to wood and stone.

3 Can we, whose souls are lighted
With wisdom from on high,
Can we to men benighted
The lamp of life deny?
Salvation! O Salvation!
The joyful sound proclaim
Till each remotest nation
Has learnt Messiah's name.

4 Waft, waft, ye winds, His story,
And you, ye waters, roll,
Till, like a sea of glory,
It spreads from pole to pole;
Till o'er our ransomed nature
The Lamb for sinners slain,
Redeemer, King, Creator,
In bliss returns to reign.

Reginald Heber.

743 From the brightness of the glory,
    'Go ye forth,' He said;
'Heal the sick, and cleanse the lepers,
    Raise the dead.'

2 'Freely give I thee the treasure,
    Freely give the same;
Take no store of gold and silver—
    Take My Name.'

3 'Thou art fitted for the journey,
    How so long it be;
Thou shalt come, unworn, unwearied,
    Back to Me.'

4 'Thou shalt tell Me in the glory
    All that thou hast done,
Setting forth alone; returning
    Not alone.'

5 'Thou shalt bring the ransomed with
    thee,
They with songs shall come
As the golden sheaves of harvest,
    Gathered home.'

trs. Frances Bevan.

744 There's a call comes ringing o'er
    the restless wave,
Send the light! Send the light!
There are souls to rescue, there are
    souls to save,
Send the light! Send the light!

    Send the light . . . the blessèd Gospel light,
    Let it shine . . . from shore to shore! . . .
    Send the light! . . . and let its radiant beams
    Light the world . . . for evermore. . . .

2 We have heard the Macedonian call
    today,
Send the light! Send the light!
And the golden offering at the Cross
    we lay,
Send the light! Send the light!

3 Let us pray that grace may every-
    where abound,
Send the light! Send the light!
And a Christlike spirit everywhere be
    found,
Send the light! Send the light!

4 Let us not grow weary in the work of
    love,
Send the light! Send the light!
Let us gather jewels for a crown
    above,
Send the light! Send the light!

Charles H. Gabriel.

745 Far, far away, in heathen darkness
    dwelling,
Millions of souls for ever may be lost;
Who, who will go, salvation's story
    telling,
Looking to Jesus, minding not the
    cost?

    'All power is given unto Me,
    All power is given unto Me.
    Go ye into all the world and preach the gospel,
    And lo, I am with you alway.'

2 See o'er the world wide-open doors
    inviting,
Soldiers of Christ arise and enter in!
Christians awake! your forces all
    uniting,
Send forth the gospel, break the
    chains of sin.

3 'Why will ye die?' the voice of God is
    calling,
'Why will ye die?' re-echo in His
    Name!
Jesus hath died to save from death
    appalling,
Life and salvation therefore go
    proclaim.

4 God speed the day, when those of
    every nation
'Glory to God!' triumphantly shall
    sing;
Ransomed, redeemed, rejoicing in
    salvation,
Shout 'Hallelujah, for the Lord is
    King!'

J. McGranahan.

746 We've a story to tell to the nations
    That shall turn their hearts to the
    right;
A story of truth and sweetness,
A story of peace and light.

For the darkness shall turn to dawning,
And the dawning to noonday bright,
And Christ's great Kingdom shall come on earth,
The Kingdom of Love and Light.

2 We've a song to be sung to the nations
That shall lift their hearts to the Lord;
A song that shall conquer evil,
And shatter the spear and sword.

3 We've a message to give to the nations
That the Lord who reigneth above
Hath sent us His Son to save us,
And show us that God is love.

4 We've a Saviour to show to the nations
Who the path of sorrow has trod,
That all of the world's great peoples
Might come to the truth of God.

Colin Sterne.

747 'For My sake and the Gospel's go
And tell Redemption's story';
His heralds answer, 'Be it so,
And Thine, Lord, all the glory!'
They preach His birth, His life, His Cross,
The love of His atonement,
For whom they count the world but loss,
His Easter, His enthronement.

2 Hark, hark, the trump of Jubilee
Proclaims to every nation,
From pole to pole, by land and sea,
Glad tidings of salvation:
As nearer draws the day of doom,
While still the battle rages,
The Heavenly Dayspring, through the gloom
Breaks on the night of ages.

3 Still on and on the anthems spread
Of Hallelujah voices,
In concert with the holy dead
The warrior-Church rejoices;
Their snow-white robes are washed in blood,
Their golden harps are ringing;
Earth, and the Paradise of God,
One triumph-song are singing.

4 He comes, whose Advent Trumpet drowns
The last of Time's evangels—
Emmanuel crowned with many crowns,
The Lord of saints and angels:
O Life, Light, Love, the great I AM,
Triune, who changest never;
The throne of God and of the Lamb
Is Thine, and Thine for ever!

E. H. Bickersteth.

748 Let the song go round the earth,
Jesus Christ is Lord,
Sound His praises, tell His worth,
Be His name adored;
Every clime and every tongue
Join the grand, the glorious song.

2 Let the song go round the earth!
From the eastern sea,
Where the daylight has its birth,
Glad and bright and free;
China's millions join the strains,
Waft them on to India's plains.

3 Let the song go round the earth!
Lands where Islam's sway
Darkly broods o'er home and hearth,
Cast their bonds away!
Let His praise from Afric's shore
Rise and swell her wide lands o'er.

4 Let the song go round the earth!
Where the summer smiles:
Let the notes of holy mirth
Break from distant isles!
Inland forests dark and dim,
Snowbound coasts give back the hymn.

5 Let the song go round the earth!
Jesus Christ is King!
With the story of His worth
Let the whole world ring!
Him creation all adore,
Evermore and evermore!

Sarah G. Stock.

749 See how great a flame aspires,
　　Kindled by a spark of grace!
Jesu's love the nations fires,
　　Sets the kingdoms on a blaze.
To bring fire on earth He came;
Kindled in some hearts it is;
O that all might catch the flame,
All partake the glorious bliss!

2 When He first the work begun,
　　Small and feeble was His day;
Now the Word doth swiftly run,
　　Now it wins its widening way;
More and more it spreads and grows
Ever mighty to prevail;
Sin's strongholds it now o'erthrows,
Shakes the trembling gates of hell.

3 Sons of God, your Saviour praise!
　　He the door hath opened wide;
He hath given the Word of grace,
　　Jesu's Word is glorified;
Jesus, mighty to redeem,
He alone the work hath wrought;
Worthy is the work of Him,
Him who spake a world from nought.

4 Saw ye not the cloud arise,
　　Little as a human hand?
Now it spreads along the skies,
　　Hangs o'er all the thirsty land:
Lo! the promise of a shower
Drops already from above;
But the Lord will shortly pour
All the Spirit of His love!

Charles Wesley.

Section X

CLOSING HYMNS

750 God be with you till we meet
　　again!
By His counsels guide, uphold you,
With His sheep securely fold you;
God be with you till we meet again!

　　Till we meet! . . . till we meet! . . .
　　Till we meet at Jesus' feet; . . .
　　Till we meet! . . . till we meet! . . .
　　God be with you till we meet again!

2 God be with you till we meet again!
'Neath His wings protecting hide you,
Daily manna still provide you:
God be with you till we meet again!

3 God be with you till we meet again!
When life's perils thick confound you,
Put His arms unfailing round you;
God be with you till we meet again!

4 God be with you till we meet again!
Keep love's banner floating o'er you,
Smite death's threatening wave
　　before you;
God be with you till we meet again!

Jeremiah E. Rankin.

751 Lord, keep us safe this night,
　　Secure from all our fears;
May angels guard us while we sleep
Till morning light appears.

John Leland.

752 Saviour, again to Thy dear Name
　　we raise
With one accord our parting hymn of
　　praise;
We stand to bless Thee ere our
　　worship cease,
Then, lowly kneeling, wait Thy Word
　　of peace.

2 Grant us Thy peace upon our
　　homeward way;
With Thee began, with Thee shall end
　　the day;
Guard Thou the lips from sin, the
　　hearts from shame,
That in this house have called upon
　　Thy Name.

3 Grant us Thy peace, Lord, through
　　the coming night,
Turn Thou for us its darkness into
　　light;

From harm and danger keep Thy
   children free,
For dark and light are both alike to
   Thee.

4 Grant us Thy peace throughout our
     earthly life,
   Our balm in sorrow and our stay in
     strife;
   Then, when Thy voice shall bid our
     conflict cease,
   Call us, O Lord, to Thine eternal
     peace.

J. Ellerton.

753 Sun of my soul, Thou Saviour
         dear,
   It is not night if Thou be near;
   Oh, may no earth-born cloud arise
   To hide Thee from Thy servant's eyes!

2 When the soft dews of kindly sleep
   My wearied eyelids gently steep,
   Be my last thought, how sweet to rest
   For ever on my Saviour's breast.

3 Abide with me from morn till eve,
   For without Thee I cannot live:
   Abide with me when night is nigh,
   For without Thee I dare not die.

4 If some poor wandering child of Thine
   Have spurned today the voice divine,
   Now, Lord, the gracious work begin,
   Let him no more lie down in sin.

5 Watch by the sick, enrich the poor
   With blessings from Thy boundless
     store:
   Be every mourner's sleep tonight,
   Like infants' slumbers, pure and light.

6 Come near and bless us when we
     wake,
   Ere through the world our way we
     take;
   Till, in the ocean of Thy love
   We lose ourselves in Heaven above.

John Keble.

754 The day Thou gavest, Lord, is
         ended;
   The darkness falls at Thy behest;
   To Thee our morning hymns
     ascended,
   Thy praise shall sanctify our rest.

2 We thank Thee that Thy church
     unsleeping,
   While earth rolls onward into light,
   Through all the world her watch is
     keeping,
   And rests not now by day or night.

3 As o'er each continent and island
   The dawn leads on another day,
   The voice of prayer is never silent,
   Nor dies the strain of praise away.

4 The sun that bids us rest is waking
   Our brethren 'neath the western sky,
   And hour by hour fresh lips are
     making
   Thy wondrous doings heard on high.

5 So be it, Lord! Thy throne shall never,
   Like earth's proud empires, pass
     away;
   Thy Kingdom stands and grows for
     ever,
   Till all Thy creatures own Thy sway.

John Ellerton.

755 Abide with me; fast falls the
         eventide;
   The darkness deepens; Lord, with me
     abide;
   When other helpers fail, and comforts
     flee,
   Help of the helpless, O abide with me.

2 Swift to its close ebbs out life's little
     day;
   Earth's joys grow dim, its glories pass
     away;
   Change and decay in all around I see:
   O Thou who changest not, abide with
     me!

Closing Hymns

3 I need Thy presence every passing hour;
What but Thy grace can foil the tempter's power?
Who like Thyself my guide and stay can be?
Through cloud and sunshine, O abide with me.

4 I fear no foe, with Thee at hand to bless;
Ills have no weight, and tears no bitterness;
Where is death's sting? where, grave, thy victory?
I triumph still if Thou abide with me.

5 Keep Thou Thy Cross before my closing eyes,
Shine through the gloom, and point me to the skies;
Heaven's morning breaks, and earth's vain shadows flee:
In life, in death, O Lord, abide with me!

H. F. Lyte.

756 Lord, dismiss us with Thy blessing,
Fill our hearts with joy and peace;
Let us each, Thy love possessing,
Triumph in redeeming grace;
Oh, refresh us, oh, refresh us,
Travelling through this wilderness!

2 Thanks we give, and adoration,
For Thy Gospel's joyful sound;
May the fruits of Thy salvation
In our hearts and lives abound;

May Thy presence, may Thy presence,
With us evermore be found!

3 So whene'er the signal's given
Us from earth to call away,
Borne on angels' wings to Heaven,
Glad the summons to obey,
We shall surely, we shall surely,
Reign with Christ in endless day.

J. Fawcett.

757 Praise God, from whom all blessings flow;
Praise Him, all creatures here below;
Praise Him above, ye Heavenly host,
Praise Father, Son, and Holy Ghost!

Thomas Ken.

758 God save our gracious Queen,
Long live our noble Queen,
God save the Queen!
Send her victorious,
Happy and glorious,
Long to reign over us;
God save the Queen!

2 Thy choicest gifts in store
On her be pleased to pour,
Long may she reign;
May she defend our laws,
And ever give us cause
To sing with heart and voice
God save the Queen!

INDEX OF FIRST LINES

INDEX OF FIRST LINES

INDEX OF FIRST LINES

INDEX OF FIRST LINES

INDEX OF FIRST LINES

INDEX OF CHORUSES

INDEX OF CHORUSES

INDEX OF CHORUSES